Beliefs and Rituals in Archaic Eastern North America

Beliefs and Rituals in Archaic Eastern North America

An Interpretive Guide

CHERYL CLAASSEN

THE UNIVERSITY OF ALABAMA PRESS
Tuscaloosa

The University of Alabama Press
Tuscaloosa, Alabama 35487-0380
uapress.ua.edu

Hardcover edition published 2015.
Paperback edition published 2025.
eBook edition published 2015.

Typeface: Bembo

Cover image: Mixcoatl/Camaxtli, the hunt god, from the Aztec Codex Borgia
Cover design: Michele Myatt Quinn

Paperback ISBN: 978-0-8173-6226-3

A previous edition of this book has been cataloged by the Library of Congress.
ISBN: 978-0-8173-1854-3 (cloth)
E-ISBN: 978-0-8173-8795-2

Contents

Illustrations

Figures

Table

Acknowledgments

I would be ungrateful if I didn't acknowledge the prior writings and bibliographies of colleagues and ancestors that I have read over the past twenty years. Particularly influential have been Jill Furst (1995), Stacey Schaefer (2002), James Brady (various), Lee Irwin (1994), and Robert Hall (various).

Individuals who helped me in numerous ways should be mentioned next. Thanks to Marcial Camilo Ayala, who has accompanied me on most of the Mexican rain-callings and made arrangements for us for several of them. It was he who first alerted me to the existence of annual rain-callings in Guerrero when I visited his painting studio in Cuernavaca, Mexico, in the summer of 2009. Then there are the two miraculous Appalachian State undergraduate students, Dan Polito and Josh Piercy, who knew how to do everything I needed on the very day I realized I needed them and then produced publishable line drawings and maps in good time. Chris Ellis rephotographed Figure 10 for me several times. Curtiss Hoffman of the Massachusetts Archaeological Society gave permission to reprint Figures 9 and 25.

Michael Smith of the Paleontological Society of Austin provided the fossil data necessary to create Figure 5, which he has used for a map he produced. John Gifford provided Figure 14, which Carlos Alvarez Zarikian facilitated for me by giving me Gifford's contact information. Ashley Dumas at the Alabama Archaeological Society gave permission to use Figure 17. Marilyn Smith gave permission to use Figure 32. Brandy Tunmire of the University of Missouri obtained Figure 20 and Debra Ray at Graham Cave gave permission to print it. Margaret Nelson and Michelle Hegmon helped with another, unutilized illustration. The idea for this work came from the dictionary produced by Mary Miller and Karl Taube (1993).

I also thank the authors of unpublished papers I have cited for giving permission to cite from their work. Alice Kehoe reviewed an early draft of the manuscript and gave not only useful corrective comments but praise—thank you. Thanks to the anonymous second reviewer and the various members of the team at the University of Alabama Press. Jennifer Backer was the able copy editor. Finally, thanks to Marilyn Smith for your patience and to a group of colleagues from the Anthropology Department at Appalachian State University who met with me on several occasions to discuss themes explored here and have been strong supporters of me throughout my career in the department: Diane Mines, Greg Reck, and Tim Smith.

Introduction

Like the spread of a cult, the turn of the archaeological gaze to things of a ritual nature, rather than technological, economic, environmental, or subsistence related, has advanced unevenly through time and space. My transformation from the science focus of processualism to symbolism and ritual began in the early 1990s as I began to read about and see the rich history of past and present Mexican peoples. The idea for this work, in fact, came from the *Dictionary of Mexican and Mayan Gods and Symbols* by Mary Miller and Karl Taube (1993), a work summarizing a tremendous wealth of material on ritual practices and beliefs. Mexican archaeologists have frequently given attention to rituals and beliefs, seen since 1998 in the intense work on ritual caves (Brady and Prufer 2005; Prufer and Brady 2005), domestic rituals (Marcus 1999; Plunket 2002), and landscape (e.g., Carrasco 1999). Book-length treatments of things spiritual in the eastern U.S. cultures of the Woodland and Mississippian periods have appeared sporadically since the early days of archaeology (e.g., Fundaburk and Foreman 1957; Galloway 1989; Hall 1997) and with much greater frequency in this century (Byers 2004; Carr and Case 2005; Carr and Gibson 2004; Case and Carr 2008; Charles and Buikstra 2006; Romain 2000, 2009; Sundstrom and DeBoer 2012; Townsend 2004). These studies have focused on feasting, mound use, cosmic orientation, cults, clans, and symbolism.

In contrast to later cultures, the Archaic Period in North America has no codification of beliefs such as found in the works cited in the previous paragraph or in Miller and Taube for Mesoamerica, and there is only one book-length treatment of Archaic social activities with ritual implications, *Signs of Power*, edited by Philip Carr and Jon Gibson (2004). Some previous lengthy discussions of Archaic ritual include Dena Dincauze's comprehensive review of cremation cemeteries in New England (1968), Peter Pagoulatos's 2009 excellent consideration of 55 northeastern mortuaries of the Late Archaic, John Walthall's 1999 article on mortuary behavior, and the special issue of the journal *Southeastern Archaeology* edited by Michael Russo (1994a), which reviews the case for Middle Archaic mounds. I began a discussion of specific mid-south Archaic rituals in caves as conference papers in 2005, some of which resulted in publications (Claassen 2010, 2011a, 2012b, 2012c). Other authors over the years have also interpreted Archaic ritual (e.g., Blitz 1993; Deller and Ellis 2001; Hall 1985; Hofman 1985; Webb 1971; W. Webb 1950). Most important, since 1990 we have come to realize that mound building and other made places for rituals, cemeteries, human sacrifice, trophy human body parts, plaza/mound spatial arrangement, and offering caches, all elements of Aztec, Maya, and Mississippian rituals and beliefs, *began* in the eastern United States and as a set can be found by 6,000 ya.

It should be obvious, then, why we need to problematize ritual and beliefs during the Archaic in the eastern United States and why a book such as this one is needed as a preliminary step in interrogating the archaeological record of this era. Fortunately the archaeological record is not mute about ritual or beliefs as both are materialized in many ways. As will be clear in the body of this work, archaeologists working in the eastern United States have begun to probe this materiality, particularly for the dirt mounds, the shell mortuary mounds, the shell rings, and several of the portable products of these people such as copper, stone beads, bird effigies, and cave caches.

There are several outstanding elements of Archaic ritual and beliefs that have defined the geographical scope of this guide. Burial in dirt mounds occurs in the Illinois valley and adjacent Missouri; burial in shell mounds has expression in the southern Ohio valley (SOV) from western Kentucky to northern West Virginia, in Florida, and in Georgia, as well as in shell-bearing contexts in the Northeast and Far North. Persistent use of red ocher in mortuary contexts can be found in most states north of the Ohio River and in the Far North and New England, and great piles of oyster shell–feasting debris accumulated on the Hudson River and again from South Carolina to Louisiana in rings and shellworks. Bannerstones, plummets, and decorated bone pins are found throughout much of the eastern United States, and soapstone cooking slabs, copper items, and evidence of the practices of dog burial and human sacrifice in the northern quadrant. Given the geography of these expressions, I have bounded this review of rituals at the eastern edge of the Plains but included expressions up to Hudson Bay through southern Florida. Obviously some of the Archaic beliefs and practices highlighted in this work extend beyond the eastern Woodlands, even to western Canada and Alaska.

As for the beginning of the period 11,000 ya, I have been swayed by Brad Koldehoff and John Walthall's (2009:137) argument that Dalton people were "Archaic" in lifestyle and by Kenneth Sassaman's (2010a) startling idea that they are of different ancestry than the southern Ohio Archaic peoples. Dalton people coped with a different environment than did Paleoindians and they assembled a woodworking tool kit. They also demonstrated an Archaic toolstone pattern: use of more localized stone resources and less cryptocrystalline stone. Keith Egloff and Joseph McAvoy (1990:64) see Early Archaic peoples on the mid-Atlantic slope distinguishing themselves from their Paleoindian forebears at 8,000 B.C. in additional ways: hunting smaller game; using notched projectile points; having an increased population, resulting in bigger and more sites; inventing chipped-stone celts, manos, and mutates; and cremating their dead.

At the other end of the era considered in this guide, I have included the Susquehanna Tradition of New England but not the very late Terminal Archaic Meadowood, Glacial Kame, or Red Ochre of the Great Lakes region (see Table 1). A date of 3000 B.P. has been adhered to even when the cultural manifestation continued beyond it.

Part I, "Archaic Beliefs and Rites," is an essay that considers some pertinent observations about Archaic social life and then outlines my ideas about the derivation of Archaic beliefs and the organization and structure of Archaic ritualizing including its costs and a brief discussion of the meaning of the end of the Archaic. In so doing, I offer thoughts about the beliefs that were held by the Asian immigrants and the impact of the Holocene transition, the role of visions, cults, and ritual specialists, and the specific rites that I have proposed for the archaeological record.

Part II, "Annotated Sampler of Sites," is composed of 91 alphabetically ordered entries showcasing archaeological data that lend themselves to interpretations of rituals and beliefs. The literature consulted consisted of site reports and articles specifically addressing ritual. Feature descriptions, artifact associations, numbers, and sizes, burial data, and site settings were scoured for materializations of cosmological principles. Part III, "Annotated Beliefs and Rites," contains alphabetically ordered entries on topics suggested by ethnographies and archaeologists.

It was not my goal to find every example of ritual or belief in the archaeological literature, but I attempted to construct a comprehensive list of relevant topics. Ample evidence is provided to demonstrate the link between Archaic rituals and natural topographic features—rock outcrops, caves, rockshelters, mountaintops, sinkholes, waterfalls, and springs as well as trees—and to emphasize the symbolic significance of stone, in the form of pebbles, cobbles, bifaces, fossils, blades, and even flakes, in rituals of renewal and fertility. Furthermore, as a faunal analyst myself I have seen firsthand the rote rendering of all creatures to their edible parts and calories and the dismissal of many species with documented symbolism as accidentals. An important goal of this work is to recast data previously seen only in economic or environmental terms in a ritual role where warranted or where overlooked. Finally, I have consciously pushed the boundaries of testability specifically to introduce possibilities to be pursued and to solicit additional examples from readers.

Beyond my desire to create a compendium and to stimulate the archaeological imagination (and science), Sassaman offers yet another reason for a work such as this one. "These discursive acts of interpreting the world and representing one's existence, the stuff of ritual, are perhaps better sources of data on histories of ethnogenesis, coalescence, and diaspora than are the details of concrete history" (2010a:50). The information included in this guide clearly supports ideas of agency, social constraints on agency, the power of ritual acts to transform places and social relationships, and the role of ritual in ethnogenesis. Furthermore, the search for rituals and beliefs will no doubt generate new theories and improve older ones, as well as generate new methods. The enterprise will further educate us about the real or only imagined limits of the archaeological record (Rakita and Buikstra 2008:8).

Abbreviations

ad, bc, bp	uncalibrated dates
A.D., B.C., B.P.	calibrated dates
Bu	burial
cmbs	centimeters below surface
LIV	lower Illinois River valley in Illinois
MNI	minimum number of individuals
rcy	radiocarbon years
RS	rockshelter
SOV	southern Ohio valley (region bounded by the Mississippi, Ohio, and Tennessee rivers)
ya	years ago
yo	years old

Beliefs and Rituals in Archaic Eastern North America

Part I

Archaic Social Life

Ritualizing occurs within social and physical contexts (Figures 1–4). If Ken Sassaman is correct (2010a), the social context during the Early and Middle Archaic was one of significant northward migrations of earlier southern Ohio valley (SOV) residents (Ancestry I) and the appearance of newcomers (Table 1). With the initial migrations northward of plant and animal communities at the end of the Pleistocene, residents of the Ohio valley were pulled in a northward direction out of the SOV and mid-Atlantic as they sought their standard dietary requirements. Passing through the Mississippi valley and into the empty terrain of the SOV came a western Cascades group of shellfish-eating Paleoindians introducing a new, second Paleoindian ancestry, Ancestry II (Sassaman 2010a:Figure 2.2). At first the residents of the Mississippi valley, the western Dalton people (eastern Arkansas to southern Illinois), reacted to the newcomers with large blades and by collecting their dead into a cemetery, but fairly soon thereafter many of the surrounding groups (Gulf Coast, lower Illinois valley, southern Great Lakes) as well as the interlopers materialized their presence and differences. It was the geographical closeness of all of these groups during the Early and Middle Archaic that elicited the ethnic identities that grew to be so distinct by the beginning of the Late Archaic, well after the vegetation and fauna had established their current distributions. We know the interlopers as the shell mounding people.

Shell mounding people of Tennessee seem to have adopted stone as their primary projectile material in Middle Archaic times as indicated by Webb and DeJarnette (1948a), and SOV shell mound makers in general employed atlatls, animal jaws, dog burials, turtle shell rattles, caches of heavy artifacts, human sacrifices, and mounded freshwater bivalves for their mortuary program and renewal rites. They buried at least 18,000 of their dead in shell mounds (Claassen 2010) beginning 9,000 ya at Eva and Big Sandy, both in Tennessee (Thad Bisset, personal communication with the author, April

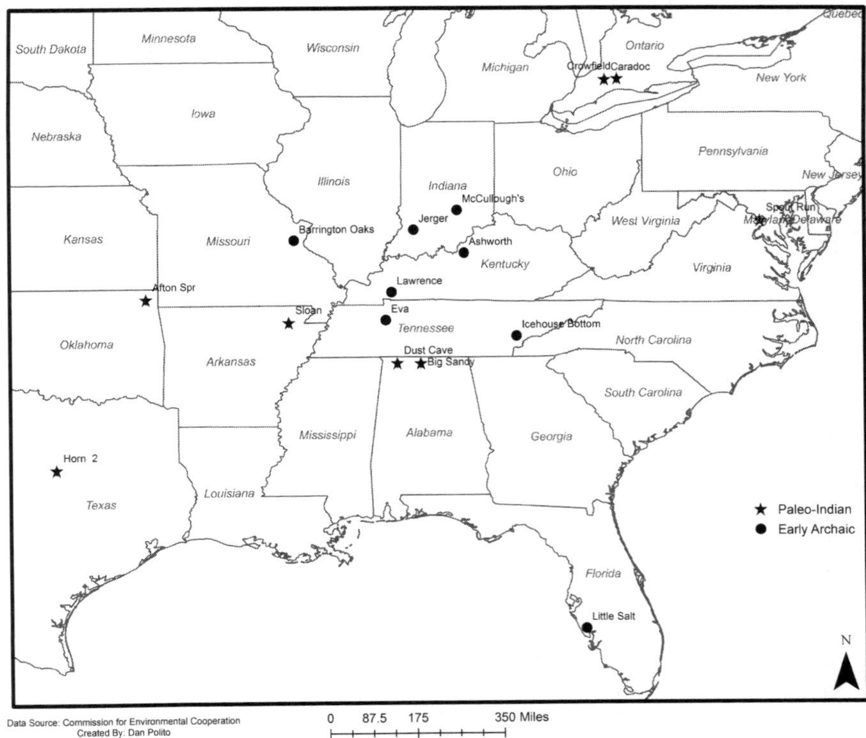

1. Locations of annotated Paleoindian and Early Archaic sites. (Data from the Commission for Environmental Cooperation. Map by Dan Polito.)

2013), many of them monumental in mass by the time they were closed (see Claassen 2010). They used caves, sinkholes, and rockshelters for rituals and fishhooks and atlatls for subsistence as well as for rituals. The indigenous population located north of the Ohio River used red ocher, cremation, and natural rises for burial, and copper, bone pins, plummets, various stone types, and cache blades for offerings to spirits. South of the Tennessee River, on the Gulf Coastal Plain, the indigenous groups used stone beads, bird imagery, steatite bowls, dirt mounds, astronomically derived measurements systems, and alignments in their rituals.

Smaller migrations have been identified for dozens of localities such as Dalton people moving northward to hunt caribou and westward to hunt bison (Koldehoff and Walthall 2009), the northward movement of Kanawha Black cherts from West Virginia into Ohio, Ontario, and Indiana (Purtill 2009:571), the cohabitation of LeCroy and Kirk point users south of the Tennessee River (Griffin 1974:94), westerners from the Great Lakes and St.

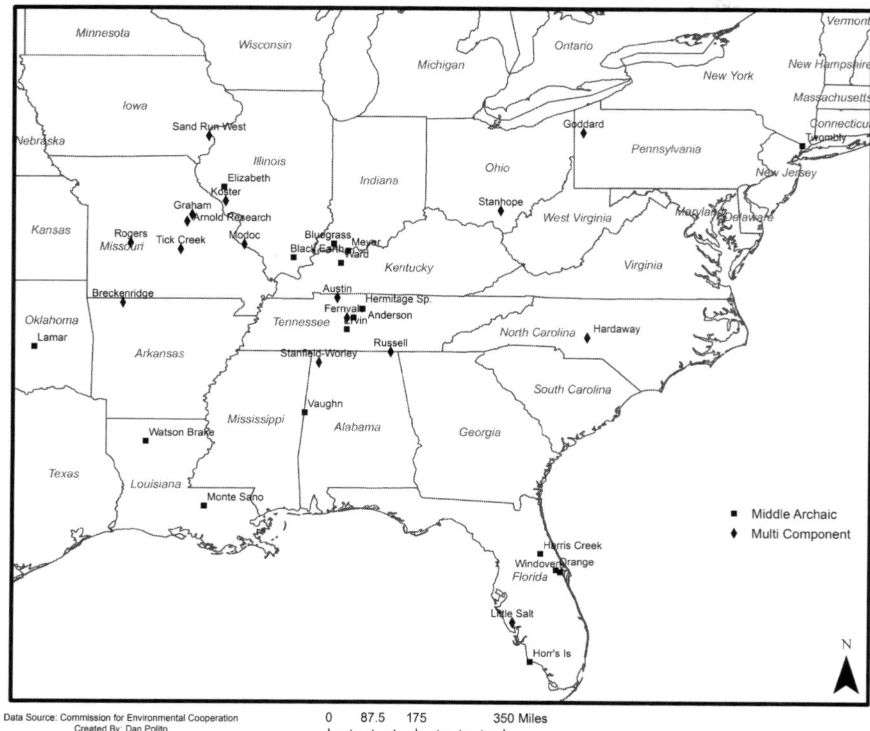

2. Locations of annotated Middle Archaic and multicomponent Archaic sites. (Data from the Commission for Environmental Cooperation. Map by Dan Polito.)

Lawrence valley moving into Maine during the Early/Middle Archaic, Arctic dwellers moving southward into Labrador, and Titterington folks expanding eastward into southern Illinois and then retreating, among many other possible examples. There also appears to have been a migration of some shell mound makers from the SOV to New York and on to the coast of Maine, where they continued the shell heap mortuary custom and several of the rites at Turner Farm, Nevin, and numerous other places.

What Sassaman's interpretation of two ancestries and cultural interaction between them and with neighbors violates the most, perhaps, are our customary thinking (1) that groups would have avoided each other in an effort to maximize the harvest of woodland resources, (2) that filling up this huge landscape would have taken most of the Archaic period, and (3) that cultures maintained fairly large territories with plenty of wiggle room. Instead, Sassaman not only has groups living close to one another but these are groups of different ancestry. The St. Johns River is not more than 40 miles

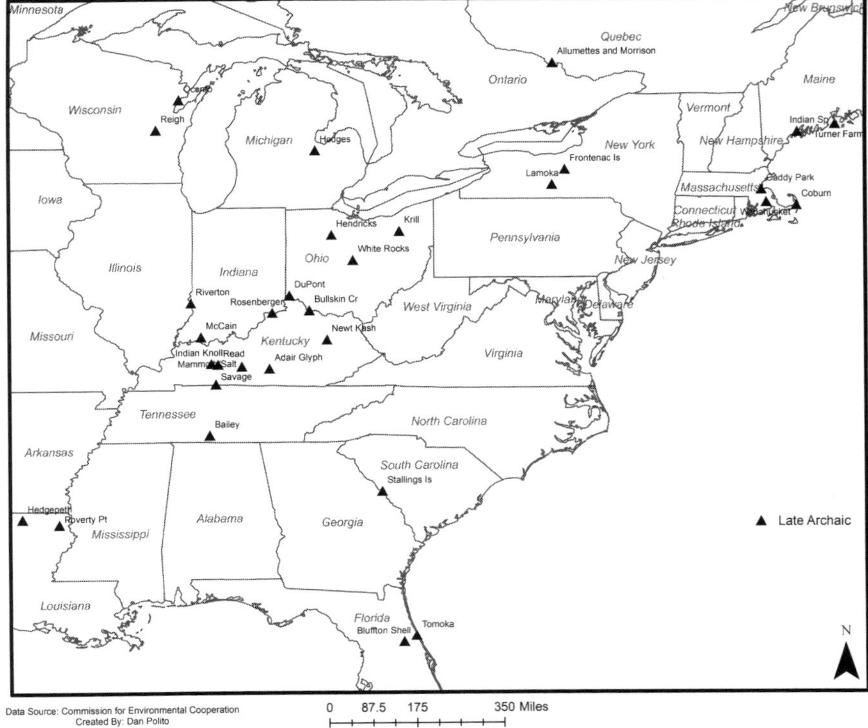

3. Locations of annotated Late Archaic sites. (Data from the Commission for Environmental Cooperation. Map by Dan Polito.)

from the Atlantic coast of Florida, but he believes there were two distinct groups living in each setting. The middle Savannah River is 140 miles from the coast, but again, different groups lived in each area. Furthermore, with less than half that distance separating them, a Piedmont group resisted pottery adoption from Stallings culture people located on the Savannah River. Even west-central Illinois is presumed to have been multiethnic (Nolan and Fishel 2009:426) during the Archaic. It looks like environmental carrying capacity was the least of the concerns for Archaic people and that trade was not about distance but about proximity (Sassaman 2010a), serving to materialize distinctions between folks and form alliances with nearest neighbors.

Resistance to change is seen in the persistence of various technologies in the new locations: hook and line fishing (Ancestry II) or net fishing (Ancestry I); steatite cooking slabs (Piedmont) or pottery (coast); and the use in burial of shell beads (SOV) or stone beads (Tombigbee), for decorated pins (LIV) or plain pins (SOV), for interments only (Green River) or cremation

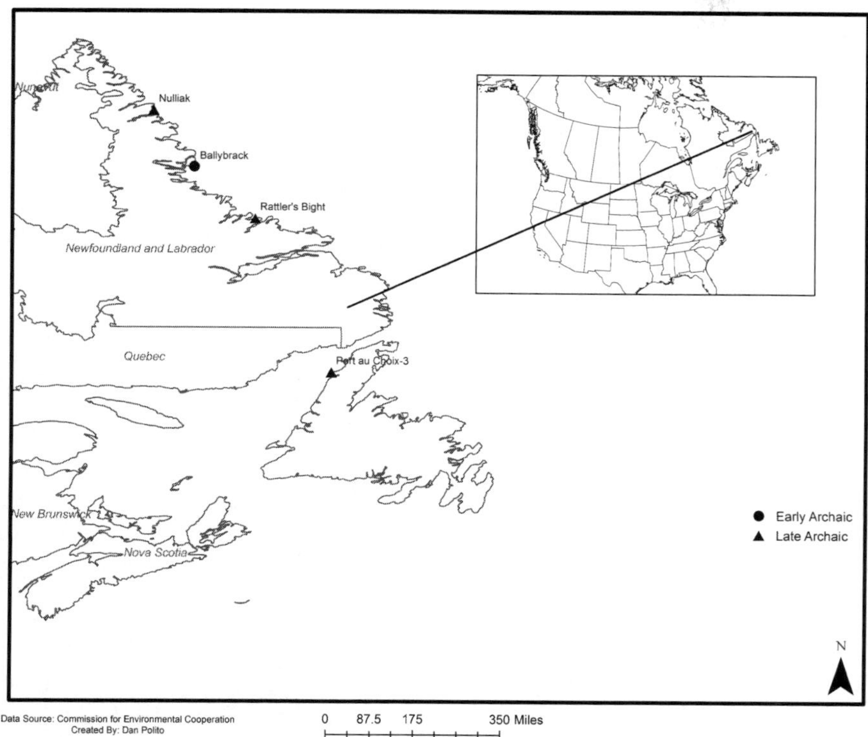

4. Locations of annotated Far North sites. (Data from the Commission for Environmental Cooperation. Map by Dan Polito.)

and interment (everywhere else), and so forth. Pottery adoption provides a good way to see agency, resistance, and ethnogenesis. "The traditional medium of exchange, soapstone, would have been rendered obsolete by technologies of direct-heat cooking, so individuals with direct access to sources of soapstone may have had an especially active role in thwarting change" (Sassaman 2010a:135). If Sassaman is right about the relationship between stresses and ritual, then these tensions around group distinction and amalgamation were causes of and opportunities for the creation, modification, elaboration, abandonment, and synchronization of rites and beliefs.

But not all was resistance and distancing. There was alliance formation perhaps conducted with competitive feasts and consistent long-term interactions that brought about new cultural synergies, as collated by Sassaman (2010a: Chapter 3). From centuries of contact between separate groups emerged Orange Culture of Florida (Atlantic coast folks + Mount Taylor), Classic Stallings culture of South Carolina-Georgia (4200–3800 B.P. Atlantic coast +

Table 1. Chronological Periods

Date	Southeast	Florida/Atlantic	Great Lakes	Northeast
			Glacial Kame	
3000	Early Woodland		Red Ochre	Meadowood
3500	Poverty Point	Stallings		Lamoka
4000		Orange		Susquehanna/ Orient
4500			Titterington	Moorehead
5000				
5500				
6000	Benton	Late Archaic	Old Copper	Laurentian
6500				
7000		Mount Taylor shell-bearing sites		
7500				
8000	Middle Archaic	Middle Archaic	Middle Archaic	
8500	shell-bearing sites			
9000				
9500	Kirk			
10,000	Early Archaic	Early Archaic	Early Archaic	Early Archaic
10,500	Dalton			
11,000	Ancestry I & II			
	Paleoindian	Paleoindian	Paleoindian	Paleoindian

Mill Branch), Orient Culture of eastern New York (Susquehanna + indigenous New Englander natives), the Frontenac phase of western New York (Lamoka + Laurentian), the Moorehead Tradition of Maine and northward (Vergennes + Maritime Archaic + Small Stemmed), and Benton people, the product of interactions between Ancestry I Gulf Coast people and Ancestry II members along the Tennessee River (Sassaman 2010a:48).

All of this movement also had an impact on place-making and place abandonment. When thinking about migrations during the Early and Middle Archaic I am reminded of the psychological trauma recorded when groups were removed during historic times. Even though many of the groups—for example, Shawnee, Seneca, Wyandot—had been removed several times and their residence was in some cases fewer than 100 years in the new locations, subsequent removal still brought about strong personal reactions. Identity formation based on landscape, or place-making, is clearly a rapid process that elicits powerful emotional connections for some individuals. The migrations of the Early and Middle Archaic must have been painful for some and may have led to (1) the creation of pilgrimages to what had become distant homeland shrines, (2) the desire to obtain and possess stone and other raw materials with familiar properties and sentimental value from the old place, as well as (3) the awakening to new spirit-filled landscape features. Nevertheless, the energetic *creation* of places for ritual in Middle Archaic times may have signaled the anomie felt by groups of immigrants as they worked to make a landscape and anchor their history in the cosmos as seen from a new perspective.

An outstanding characteristic of the social environment of at least the Shell Mound people was violence, typically cast as "warfare" and "conflict." Given that I do not think that there were scarce resources, territoriality, or sedentism in the Archaic Midwest and SOV (various chapters in Claassen 2010), I do not think that defense of territory, defense of resources, defense of burial grounds, or defense of villages was behind the violent deaths evident in the mid-south, upper New York, Maine, or LIV. Instead, I think that there were ambushes launched to capture victims for the human sacrifice needed in several types of rituals. Here again the role of visions can be invoked as demonstrated by the historic Pawnee, who performed the Morning Star sacrifice of a young girl only after a man had a dream of the rite and then went out and captured a girl from another group (Hall 1997).

The ethnicity of the victims is a tricky problem. There are people buried in the shell mounds, for instance, who have embedded antler or stone points or are missing from one body part to all limbs and head. I have assumed (Claassen 2010) that these murder victims were captive foreigners unknown to the group that captured then and conducted the sacrificial rite at the place where the victim's body was buried. Women slaves "were practically ubiquitous in North America at contact and may signal a long history of captive slaves" (Alice Kehoe, personal communication with the author, December 2012). If, however, most of the victims were kin and died away from their communities but were then retrieved by their families and buried at the shell mounds, then we can turn to the observation made by Friederici (1907; cited in Mensforth 2001:113) that the size of the missing body part was often inversely related to the distance that a "warrior" or "war party" had to travel to return to safety. This observation would mean then that the victims buried in the shell mounds were killed both near the slayer's camp (time for entire limbs and appendages to be taken before kin could intervene) and close to the victim's camp (time only for scalps, hands, feet, or heads to be removed). That these activities apparently generated little retaliation based on the few murder victims found in burial grounds outside the SOV possibly contradicts the idea of raids and warfare. Therefore, I disagree that the violence of the Archaic was identical in character to that in historic times when retaliation seems to have fueled a great number of murders (Mensforth 2001). This Archaic violence was not part of warfare. But my proposal that the individuals were sacrificial victims would not be harmed if DNA analysis were ultimately to prove that these individuals were themselves Shell Mounders and not strangers. The role these sacrifices had in Middle and Late Archaic rituals will be addressed later in the chapter.

The number of murder victims in the shell mounds is probably much higher than the count of those obviously killed. Other indications of violent death are contained in unusual burial positions, in the use of red ocher, and in the placement of marine shell with infants and children (see Claassen 2010:Chapters 6–9). Since they were buried in the same burial grounds as used by their tormentors, the genetic profiles from various Archaic skeletal populations in the regions where sacrifice was observed should be more similar than different given that they are amalgamations of different populations, captors/hosts, guests, and victims. The practice of human sacrifice and shared burial grounds tapered off after 4,000 ya, resulting in fewer large ceremonials and less genetic mixing in burial populations. Given that scenario, shared burial grounds and buried sacrificial victims, not intermarriage, account for the geographically similar genetic populations and for the fact that the cessation of these practices brought about "the pattern of isolation by distance" (Herrmann 2002:106), not the settling-in process as others have assumed. Here again we see the importance of considering the role of ritual in the archaeological record.

In addition to the distinct ancestries in the eastern United States and Canada during the Archaic highlighted by Sassaman (2010a), some other elements of community life have been uncovered for the southern Atlantic coastal plain by Sassaman (2006, 2010a:78) and others. Dual social structure detected in Atlantic coastal shell-feasting sites (Russo 2004) and in Orange Culture U-shaped shellworks in Florida may signal moiety structure during the Middle Archaic and groups of unequal ranking feasting together. Sassaman (2010b:359) posited dualist life at Poverty Point. Shared mortuary facilities such as that at Frontenac Island also suggest moieties.

Crucial to integrating moieties and probably lineages as well as communities were mound building, shell-ring ceremonies, feasting, and shared mortuary programs. The "two distinctly different people on the landscape, throughout most of the Archaic Period," engaged in practices "to materialize intercultural encounters and other interactions in assertions of identity and alterity," including mound building and elaborate mortuary traditions that "were multicultural affairs, serving to integrate people of varied heritage and disposition for purposes beyond everyday living" (Sassaman 2010a:26). Sassaman is one of several archaeologists to claim that at least some burial grounds were shared during the Archaic (2010a:141) rather than being the beacons of private property as in most interpretations. Bullseye, in Illinois, is another possible shared mortuary area (Milner et al. 2009:121). The case for shared shell burial mounds in the SOV has been made (Claassen 2010), and Ritchie (1945) argued the same for Frontenac Island in New York. Sassaman also envisioned multiethnic gatherings at Poverty Point and in the burial programs of the Far North and Northeast. Using isotopic data from people buried in Florida's Harris Creek shell mound, Tucker (2009:141) identified a group of people from the immediate region, a group (not cemetery groupings) from southern Florida, and two individuals seemingly from Tennessee or Virginia. Although the economic and labor costs of these burial programs would have been shared in these cases, they also would have been multiplied to accommodate additional participants.

Feasting was another major enterprise that created friends and united communities. "The dynamic of feasting has enormous power to alter society and impact the environment. Ironic though it may seem, rituals predicated on generosity often become institutions of selfishness and aggrandizement. . . . Classic Stallings culture may be among the many cases of economic intensification driven by ritual acts involving food" (Sassaman 2006:136). Quantifying the cost of feasting has yet to be done for an Archaic case, but costs were no doubt high given the huge piles of shells and the millions of invertebrates and even vertebrates indicated. "Enormous quantities of fish bone including large gar, suckers, bass, and catfish were found in the Classic Stallings culture pits on Stallings Is[land]" (Sassaman 2006:145).

The annual or intermittent burial events were themselves moments of consolidation and identity formation, again with costs. Hosts had to prepare camping sites, clear paths, refurbish/clean altars, shrines, and burial ground, gather food and prepare it for the various planned feasts, gather firewood for ceremonial fires, and perform pre-gathering and post-festival rites. Pilgrims had to further prepare their specific camping sites, gather firewood, set up camp, prepare offerings, and so forth (this list is based on my experience with religious pilgrimages in Guerrero, Mexico; see Claassen 2011c for partial discussion). Pagoulatos (2009:247) and I (Claassen 2010) have suggested that all of this activity was the cause of the "habitation evidence" at burial grounds, mistaken as "village" refuse.

The recognition of the various migrations of people comes from studies of artifacts and burial practices. These same studies have done much to reveal the size of these hunter-gatherer social networks. "Atlatl weight stylistic data suggest even broader connections than do the pin data. Different patterns of interaction reflected by the atlatl weight and pin data may be attributable to various social networks maintained by different categories of people (for example, female networks vs. male networks). . . . Archaeologists need to continue to collect data that contribute to the identification of Archaic social networks and to identify new attributes that can be used to expand our knowledge of hunter-gatherer social interaction" (Jefferies 2008:303). In spite of all of this socializing and ethnogenesis, these cultures were not "complex" in the sense that Hayden (1996) and others mean. They did not have scarce resources to hoard, did not live in villages, and did not engage in much social status individuation. Saunders (2004) concluded that the Middle Archaic multimound sites on the Gulf plain were equalitarian given their lack of trade, structures, burials, and storage facilities. Kidder and Sassaman (2009:675) add, "the absence of markers of permanent economic inequality or political ranking suggests that these apparently complex behaviors were embedded within cosmological or ideational realms without being manifest in permanent structures of political authority or economic control." Nothing "in the archaeological record of the Late Archaic societies who made and used [shell] rings point[s] directly to the existence of big men, big women, or any sort of chiefly elite. Rather, the evidence for social differentiation is structural and corporate, not necessarily tied to particular people or lineages" (Sassaman 2006:139–140). "Power" was in the hands of ritual specialists working on behalf of their kin and communities.

I have argued that the variation evident in grave good quantity and burial treatment, as well as the different burial places used in the SOV during the Middle and Late Archaic, primarily reflects spiritual beliefs including human sacrifice and appropriate offerings for spirits, not social differences among the living as the Saxe-Binford hypothesis would have it. Even the differences in grave goods for infants and noninfants can be explained by ritual requirements, not the status of parents (Claassen 2013a).

The few indications of social status differences that do seem to be present are found in burial positions and burial places. Some ritual specialists were apparently buried in rockshelters (witches?). The sacrificial adults who were tossed, stacked, put facedown, or weighted with stones appear to have been scorned. The individuals in the Far North under low boulder mounds and those in the initial pits in the LIV ridge-top mounds may have been specialists or apprentices. The richest burials appear to have been ritual specialists with their paraphernalia or community offerings. The one possible positive status difference in burial may be reflected in the sitting burials of Florida and the Tennessee valley, for sitting is a posture that signified a leader or deity among much later Mexican groups (Claassen 2012d).

The perspective held over much of the past century that Archaic peoples could barely feed and house themselves and had no social lives to write about when compared to that of today demonstrates a dramatic shift in the portrayal of Archaic lifeways. The extensive movement of groups and individuals to new homes or in search of desired offerings, the extensive interaction through seasonal rites, and the myriad objects deposited with the dead and crafted by the living all create a dizzying social world for archaeologists to attempt to penetrate.

Archaic Beliefs

Most of the material presented in this guide represents my particular thoughts about beliefs and rituals during the Archaic. My thinking has been greatly influenced by several authors writing about beliefs in the ancient United States (Fox 2004a, 2004b; Fox and Molto 1994a, 1994b; Fox and Salzer 1999; Hall 1976, 1979, 1985, 1989, 1997, 2006; Irwin 1994; Milne 1994; Sundstrom 1996, 2000); ancient Mexico (Bassie-Sweet 1996; Brady and Prufer 2005; Brown 2005; Carrasco 1999; Pohl 1983); ancient Andes (Classen 1993); and modern Mexico (Chevalier and Bain 2003; Furst 1995; Sandstrom 1991; Schaefer 2002). It has also been greatly shaped by my participation in a number of Nahua pilgrimages to shrines in the states of Morelos and Guerrero, Mexico, from 2009 to 2013 (e.g., Claassen 2011a, 2011b, 2013c). When I was studying symbolism for shells (Claassen 2008) I came to realize that not only do shells have a worldwide association with fertility (Maya, Aztec, Hindu, west African–get names, Nootka, etc.) but so do caves, water, snakes, trees, birds, women, men, the direction west, and so forth. Similar concordance can be found for hundreds of other objects, sounds, smells, minerals, numbers, animals, and so on, emphasizing that many of the same elements of the physical world were observed closely by *Homo sapiens* everywhere. Similarities in interpretation and even representations have been explained through ethnographic analogy, through the direct historic approach, through human cognitive hardwiring, through transoceanic contact, and so forth. Rather than working from the present backward, which does have its merits and its defenders (see Fox [2004b:47–48] for a list of scholars who have argued these points successfully), I have attempted to identify beliefs held long before the migration to the New World based on their worldwide occurrence. Furthermore, the environmental transition from the Pleistocene to Holocene and the migrations that resulted gave significant new input into the beliefs and practices of Archaic people.

The Pre-Migration Foundation

A belief in pan-American and pre-American beliefs as old as humans in the hemisphere is shared by many scholars who have wandered into discussing the cosmology of past cultures (e.g., Furst 1977:20; Levi-Strauss 1966; Whitley et al. 1999). The basis of these beliefs is human observation of the day and night sky; the life cycle of animals and plants and the behavior of animals (Lewis-Williams 1981; Linares 1977; Whitley 1994:24–28; Wilbert 1987); the biology and symmetry of the human body; the physical properties of stones, minerals, bones, clay, shells, and water; the relationship of clouds, winds, and temperature to weather; the properties of topographic features; and processes such as decay, gestation, burning, flooding, and heating and cooling of the body. Invariant characteristics of behaviors, cognition, life cycles, physical properties, and physical laws should be our route into identifying the ritual foci of the Archaic and why such similar beliefs and symbols occur worldwide. Observation—the same empirical basis so beloved for our modern science—is a basis far from irrational.

Jill Furst (1995), Constance Classen (1993), and Chevalier and Bain (2003) have written about how and why observations about the human body and life cycle have developed into beliefs and practices about the soul (two or three souls, winged flight from the body at death), infant-naming practices, eye avoidance, the use of virgins in shrines and rites, protection of fields and equipment from menstruating women, ideas about winds and frightful death, and hot-cold systems, found throughout the Americas as well as in the Old World. Around the world, segments of the human body have been standardized to create numerical systems that are multiplied to position monuments and determine sizes of sites, familiar to us as feet, inches, fathoms, and brazos. John Clark (2004) evoked this human practice to explain the spatial layouts of Middle Archaic monuments of the Gulf Coast, which used as the standard unit multiples of the distance from sternum to fingertip. Even mounds with their navels were based on the image of the human body (Knight 1989:423).

In spite of germ theory, many people around the world still believe that a breeze will bring sickness. The earth is known to bring forth new life, so cultures worldwide believe that into the earth, into the underworld, or into the land of the dead is where a corpse should go. Earth as the source of rebirth is breached by caves, canyons, sinkholes, and other crevices and through them comes new life. Christians have to look no further than the rockshelter into which Jesus was put and from which he was resurrected to see the shared perceptions across cultures. Trees are also intimately connected to human lineages worldwide as the "tree of life," the "family tree," the fertility Christmas tree, the Aztec ahuehuete tree, ceremonial poles, mortuary poles, mortuary trees, and Christian crosses (where an empty wooden cross emphasizes new life). Though ritual use of a pole or tree may vary (a Pawnee sun dance pole seems to have a very different role than a Senegalese mortuary tree), there is a fundamental belief about trees being expressed: they are or mark portals to the underworld realm of fertility and they are human-like. Umbilical cords, afterbirth, and corpses in, on, or under trees are equivalent expressions of the beliefs about this fertility role.

There are human physiological responses that have generated similar ideas and practices cross-culturally. Somatosensory effects created by trance have generated images of flight (Whitley et al. 1999:222–223), leading to a conflation of bird and pipe and even bird and smoker (von Gernet and Timmins 1987). Pauketat and Emerson (2008:79) call up biochemical and emotional states in humans that nevertheless resulted in different historical manifestations. Romain (2000, 2009) relies on arguments of human cognition to build the case for his view of Hopewell spirituality.

The physics of other materials must also have been observed very early on even if the explanations for their causes differed. Triboluminescence in quartz probably accounts for hemisphere-wide use of quartz by priests (Whitley et al. 1999:236).

Observations about the heavens were duplicated worldwide, no doubt because the same daytime sky was observed by all and the night sky was shared across hemispheres. For instance, "Among the hunting and herding peoples of subarctic and arctic Siberia, lunar and solar observation were similarly assigned to skilled specialists and keepers of the calendar and were similarly geared to periodic economic and seasonal ritual behavior. . . . [Because] the lore . . . came into the Americas with diverse groups of Asian migrants, it can probably also be assumed that these traditions formed part of the cultural preparation that helped to make the slow, seasonal, migratory movements of the dispersing hunter-gatherers possible" (Marshack 1985:44). Miller and Taube (1993:26) likewise think that several later Mesoamerican beliefs, specifically the "multi-layered heaven and earth, shamanic transformation, the moon as a rabbit, and the importance of world directions and trees, suggest a distant and ancient relation to Asia."

It is possible to go on at length here, but these few examples of common understandings and roles for the ubiquitous elements of the human experience should suffice to make the point (and other authors have provided more examples; e.g., Furst 1995). So what, then, were some pre-migration beliefs that were carried over to the New World and were emphasized in early ritualizing?

1. Cosmic dualities existed: day/night, sun/moon, above/under, right/left, male/female, dry/wet. All entities on the left of the slash are equivalents; all on the right are equivalents (see Hall 1997). Women were associated with the moon, the nighttime, and the rabbit. Concavities were "feminine."
2. Homage was due the cardinal directions and intercardinal directions. The number 4 was ritually significant. Center, up, and down were additional directions and implied added significance for the numbers 5, 6, and 7.
3. At least three levels of the cosmos were recognized: Underworld, This World, and Upper World, with resident spirits in each realm. Shells, snakes, and amphibians were dwellers of the Underworld as were nocturnal and black creatures. Raptors and white birds were dwellers of the Upper World. Creatures that crossed between worlds were especially significant.
4. Any natural feature could be the home of a spirit, as could any object. Smells, winds, and sounds could transport spirits. Therefore, there was no meaningful spatial boundary or conceptual boundary between "sacred" and "secular" space.
5. Communication routes were open between humans, other beings, and spirits. Humans could address, cajole, and bargain with other beings and spirits, and spirits were in contact with humans via visions, smells, sounds, breezes, and smoke.
6. Where the Underworld was breached, there was an excellent place to address those spirits—sinkholes, springs, lakes, caves, contact lines with sky and water—or to avoid them should one not be prepared to approach the spirit world.
7. Deities lived lives much like humans—with homes, families, hunger, and so on.
8. All entities had the potential for a soul. Souls were subdivided into two or perhaps three manifestations.
9. Bone soul, one of the souls of an animal, stayed with its bones. Through proper care of the bones (and shells) and thankfulness, the animal would be resurrected.
10. Fire, smoke, water, and shell could purify and transform an object, person, or place.

11. Expressions of beliefs were appropriately conveyed through dance, song, or other sounds (see Devereux and Jahn 1996), flowers, fire, smoke, and certain colors.
12. Rites of riddance—including the burning of bodies, breaking of objects, and burial of bodies, places, caches, feast remnants, and ceremonial regalia—were observed (Giles 2010:115–116).
13. There existed at least a 365-day calendar (solar) and a 260-day calendar (gestation period).
14. Spirits gave medicines to humans. Medicines varied greatly in their raw material source and use formulas.
15. Earlier places and people, older worlds, had existed.
16. Trees were venerable, and certain species were ritually important.
17. There was an unending supernatural struggle between the forces of the sky, earth, and water realms (Mayor 2005:30).

The Influence of the Pleistocene-Holocene Transition

In addition to these pre-migration beliefs, for Early Archaic and Middle Archaic peoples it must have been significant for their cosmology that they were experiencing both a changing and changed biological environment, even changes in topography, as the Pleistocene gave way to the Holocene and as they migrated to new places. Most important, *lost* environments needed explanation as did new environments.

The Pleistocene fauna and the Paleoindians left marks and objects on the landscape and were surely memorialized as a prior world, an earlier creation by Archaic peoples. Once Paleoindians had occupied the landscape, the materiality of their lives became an integral part of the lives of Archaic people. It is possible that Paleoindians came to serve as Ancestors in an ancestral time and their artifacts venerated through ritual location, mound building, and other acts. Paleoindian sites predictably are located near springs (Dent 1995:112–113) or sinkholes, places that would later be scenes of ritualizing. The stone tools and caches they left behind were the observable proof of an ancient creation. Indeed, Archaic people may have believed that those people either were Stone People or had been turned into stone, their souls residing inside the stones, as several historic groups believe (Milne 1994). It could be that the finding of these older stone homes was always a propitious sign and cause for place-making.

Paleoindian people also would have been the source of and focus of stories circulating among Archaic people about landscape features that were now removed from view and use, such as places drowned by rising sea level (an idea triggered by Asa Randall, personal communication with the author,

September 2012). For instance, 11,000 to 7,000 ya, waterfalls of greater volume than Niagara existed off Bruce Peninsula in Lake Huron as the lakes had much lower water levels at that time. The imposing Alpena Ridge with sheer limestone cliffs, now under the water of Lake Huron, was dry and a probable area of caribou drive lines (O'Shea and Meadows 2009). Sinkholes and caves such as Little Salt Spring and quarries such as Fossil Hole once utilized by Paleoindians on the Gulf Coast of Florida, disappeared below the water of the Gulf. Estuary formation along the Atlantic also drowned favored places for economic and spiritual activities. Furthermore, the demise of *Mammuthus* sp. would have allowed for forest regrowth over grazing lands (Dunbar 2006).

Also significant to the cosmology of the Archaic peoples must have been the disappearance of animals (either extirpated or extinguished). Stories of the giant bison, giant cave bear, giant sloth, giant tortoises, mammoth, and mastodon and their fossil remains probably morphed into accounts of an earlier creation, of deities and spirits who talked, walked, and acted in ways just like the humans telling the stories, although with more spiritual power. The real giant tortoise probably became the tortoise upon whose shell formed Turtle Island, the earth. The real mastodon may have become the Abenaki Great Elk (Mayor 2005:11) or "the grandfather of the buffalo" (Mayor 2005:50–52). Fossil mammoths and their tusks found in watery places in the east may have become the horned water monsters and the terrible swamp creature. The real giant cave bear may have become the Nya-Gwahe or Iroquois Monster Bear, the saber-toothed tiger an Iroquois cat monster (Mayor 2005:42), and the raptor *Pseudodontornis* the giant Mosquito Monster (Mayor 2005:48). (See Mayor 2005 for numerous accounts of native legends and their fossil equivalents.) With examples of drowned landscapes, the appearance of Pleistocene bone beds in bogs and lakes, and the Cretaceous sea floor visible on the Plains, no wonder the world under the surface of the water was perceived as a place of spirits and their activities and sites found nearby (Figure 5).

I propose, then, that the juxtaposition of Middle Archaic shell accumulations upon a basal record of Paleoindian points, as was often the case along the Green River, was a locational decision based on spiritual beliefs about the Stone People, not economic concerns associated with harvesting or hunting needs. Likewise, Archaic peoples' attraction to sinkholes, springs, and fossil bone beds may have been motivated by recognition of Ancient Places and spiritual connections to the older Stone People.

Migrating must also have generated memorializing and ritualizing acts referencing ancestral places. Connections to the places Early Archaic people had left would have been maintained through stories about key topographical features and perhaps replicated as best as possible in the choice of new land-

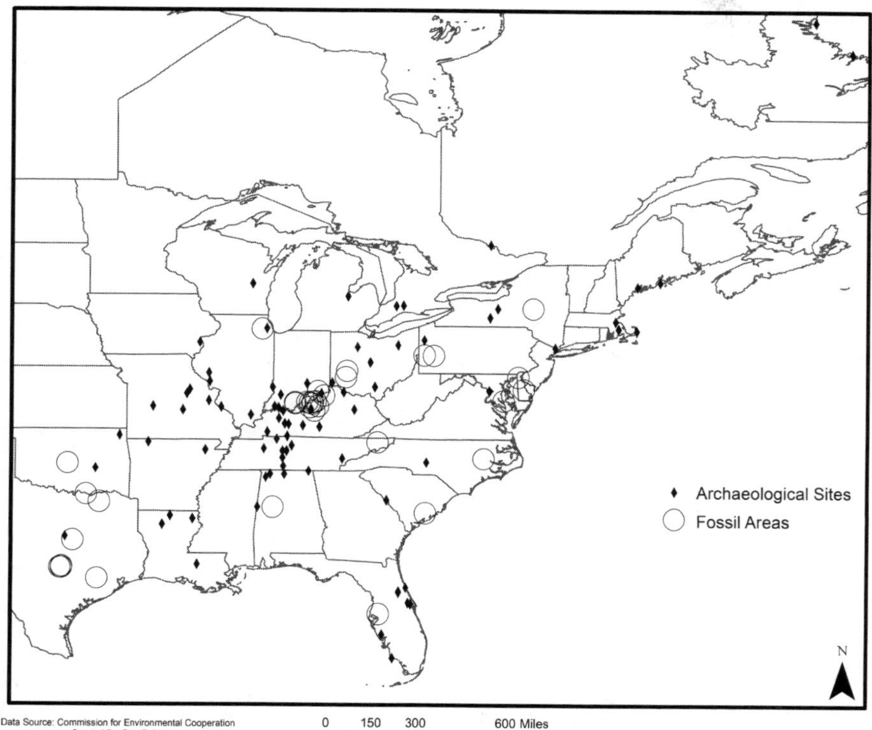

5. Correspondence of annotated archaeological sites with fossil sites. (Fossil site data from Michael Smith, "US Fossil Sites," http://www.texaspaleo.com/usmaps/paleosites.html, accessed June 1, 2013.)

scape. Connections to those ancestral places also were probably maintained through raw materials from those places. Mementos of stone are the most obvious manifestation of such concerns and connections (Gould 1980:155; Sassaman 2010a:139), and exotic lithology may well tell us to where, geographically, a group traced its origination. Rather than contracting territory as an explanation for the increasing use of local stones, the transition to local stone resources may be showing us the fading spiritual connection to ancestral places and a strengthening spiritual identification with the locale at hand.

Landscape was the context within which memorializing occurred. This memorializing has been theorized by dozens of researchers who have pointed out that the memorializing process is contentious and by no means is the outcome either predictable or stable in the mementos created, the specific places used for rites, the sequence or even the selection of particular ritualizing acts, or the elements of the past emphasized. Memorializing is such a contentious process because place-making and past-making are the mental work of individuals, asserting particularistic meanings and perspectives. I develop this idea and the tensions somewhat between short-term and long-term places in a case of modern roadside shrines and accidental death markers in central Mexico that serve to inscribe the land with family histories and teach the social responsibilities of the living to each other and to the dead. Depending on individual personality and historical accident, some of these places eventually, or even rapidly, attract cults or communities of practice.

The Historic Perspective

In spite of the number of voices that have argued for pan-American beliefs and even "the psychic unity of humans," there will be readers more comfortable working from the present backward. Here, too, there are a number of specific observations that have been made by others that either call forth Archaic evidence or imply an unbroken thread into Archaic times. Various scholars have evoked the truism that belief systems are the most conservative aspects of cultures (e.g., Whitley et al. 1999:237) to support their enterprise. A brief sampling of these comments by other archaeologists is now offered.

Fox and Salzer (1999:238) are convinced that the "shamanism" ("ritual specialist" or "priest" are preferable terms; see Kehoe 2000) of Hopewell times had been the mode of religious practice since migration into the Great Lakes region began. Giles (2010:108–109, 120) is comfortable attributing some Hopewell practices and beliefs to Late Archaic and Adena ritualizing, such as the concept of the body as a container, the use of masks to honor/address other-than-human beings, smoking, mound building and the use of multimound sites, and cyclical and repetitive ritual practices emphasizing transformation. Anne Bader (2010/11) found many points of correspondence between the burial features at the Middle Archaic Meyer and KYANG sites and those of historic Shawnee. Robert Hall pushed the antiquity of the Earth diver story back to Hopewell times in the Midcontinent (Hall 1979, 1997), and William Fox pushed it back to Late Woodland as seen at Frontenac Island (2004b). Betts and colleagues (2012:626) believe that "ethnographic records may provide insights into human relationships with animals and their body parts that are likely to be rooted in Archaic and Woodland period interactions with these animals" and explore the meaning of shark teeth in graves specifically.

Hall has also argued for the continuity of the Busk or Green Corn ceremony, among southern Indiana peoples, over 1,000 years and for its similarity to, if not genesis of, the Aztec Xipe Totec spring rite (Hall 2000). There are data to support pushing back the human sacrifice of five men, the Dickson Mounds rite discussed by Hall, into the Middle Archaic as seen at Elizabeth Mound 1 (Claassen 2010, 2012d), cast as a hunt god rite in subsequent annotations in this guide. Smith pointed out that since there was no significant interaction between the Southeast and Northeast after Hopewell times, "the similar ideas of people who live(d) in both regions are at least as old as Hopewell" (Smith 2005:166).

Moving south, Jon Gibson thinks that the Gulf coastal groups interacted for thousands of years, materializing much of the same beliefs in the archaeological record. "Historical analogs and archaeological matches are just too numerous for all to be coincidental. . . . I feel comfortable in assuming that the shared symbolism of southern historic tribes contains many elements, if not the core body, of ancient Gulf cosmic symbolism, and I do not hesitate to link Poverty Point [Late Archaic] with Gulf language speakers, if for no reason other than geography" (Gibson 1998:30).

Hall would push the interaction back quite a bit further:

> For a period beginning at least as early as the Late Archaic-Early Woodland transition in North America I recognize a circulation of ideas within the Gulf and Caribbean borderlands of southeastern North America, Mesoamerica, and Central America. I see the cosmic monster ("birdstone") form and single-hole-type atlatl grips as two products of this circulation, as I do those flutes of the vorsatz type that were prototypes of latter-day courting flutes in the eastern United States. . . . Another product would be the stone blocked-end tube pipe, which I see as a skeuomorphic transformation of the Mesoamerican cane smoking tube. . . . The cosmic monster form of atlatl grip is important as a witness to the early presence through the area of the idea of a dragon of combined crocodilian and bird form that was a personification of the sky, earth, and waters, however differently that creature came to be later perceived. (Hall 2006:470)

These seemingly ancient beliefs, mnemonic devices, and rites evident among historic Indians may well have had their origins in pre-migration experience and understanding or in the transformation of the physical environment of the Pleistocene-Holocene transition or the natural changes evident at the Archaic-Woodland transition.

Differences between Archaic and Paleoindian Rituals

The five most significant ritual introductions of the Archaic were, in the order of their appearance: (1) the conservation of the fleshy bodies of some dead in spatial concentrations (Late Paleoindian Dalton), (2) new cave and rockshelter rites addressing Underworld spirits (Early Archaic), (3) murder, which reflects rites involving/requiring human sacrifice (Early Archaic), (4) the *creation* of places for repeated conduct of rites (Middle Archaic), and (5) the concern with how people had died expressed in burial postures and grave goods (Middle Archaic, probably Early Archaic). In the following section I will discuss these topics, combining 2 and 4, 1 and 5. Even though few cultures apparently engaged in human sacrifice, the victims may have been taken from other groups and the grave goods certainly were derived from areas beyond the practice area. Details and evidence are deferred to the annotated entries on each topic found in parts II and III of this guide.

Conserving the Dead and Burial Postures

Cemeteries, or "burial grounds," began appearing in the Early Archaic in various places in the western Mississippi River valley and along the Atlantic coast of Florida. They appear over a much broader area by the end of the Middle Archaic. Pagoulatos (2009:247) thinks there is evidence in northeastern settings for the space around cemeteries to have been considered sacred precincts, and he cites low artifact densities between habitation and burial areas as evidence. Sassaman (2006) has evidence that the burial mound on Stallings Island was avoided for about 200 years while immigrants lived around it.

Most archaeologists cite territorial and resource claims as the motivation for collecting the dead, thus rejecting any version of the idea that the creation of burial grounds was an evolutionary stage in the development of human mentality. But a group could mark a territory or resource in other ways and continue whatever mortuary program that was traditional. This point, coupled with the fact there were no scarce resources in the Mississippi valley or coast of Florida in the Early and Middle Archaic, cause me to reject even that motivation for the creation of burial grounds. Instead, as Charles and Buikstra have argued in many publications but attributed to landownership motivations (e.g., Buikstra and Charles 1999), we are seeing the belief taking hold that some of the dead could be useful as intermediaries. In addition, other beliefs are implicated: that harmful spirits were released among the living by certain causes of death and needed controlling and that group identity was related to its dead. In fact, there is growing evidence that many of the Late Archaic mortuary grounds were shared, facilitating regional sociality, and were not used as socially divisive confrontational markers.

Initially, burial grounds could have arisen as part of a cult, and cult membership could explain why only subsamples of Archaic communities are found in them. Evidence of the latter point comes from estimates of the numbers of bodies buried annually. For instance, there are at least 18,000 bodies buried in several dozen shell-bearing sites in the SOV shell mounds (Claassen 2010). If that number is divided by 5,000 (Middle and Late Archaic temporal span), it amounts to only 3.6 burials per year *throughout the entire region*. The number of annual burials calculated for Williams Cemetery in northern Ohio was 1–2 people per year. Clearly, then, only a subset of the dead was gathered together in these repeatedly used burial grounds. Even fewer bodies were cremated. The vast majority of the bodies of people living during the Archaic must have been disposed of through exposure or water, a continuation of Paleoindian practice. Furthermore, based on the burial evidence presented in site reports, the burial population at many sites is filled with disconcerting deaths, not "normal" deaths, a point that will be developed throughout the annotated sections of this guide. I suggest that those people who merited placement in a cemetery or in a natural place, those people whose remains we are finding, were ritual specialists, the sacrificed, accidental deaths, the Ancestors (a restricted class) and their descendants, and a few other categories of persons.

Places for Addressing the Spirits

The animism of Paleoindian and Archaic peoples meant that spirits could manifest anywhere in the landscape. Places where there was a pattern of successful contact probably were marked with individual offerings or by group ritualizing, and even with paint by individual seekers and doctors (e.g., Rajnovich 1994). Paleoindians and people living in the Early Archaic apparently sought spirits in natural places exclusively, but beginning in the Middle Archaic people began to manipulate the spirits through landscape modification, concentrating the bodies of the dead, offering human sacrifices, and expending a notable amount of labor in the production of offerings and the accumulation of shells and of dirt into topographic high spots.

Natural Places for Rituals

The first evidence of human use of caves and rockshelters dates to early Paleoindian times in Ohio at Sheriden Cave (Waters et al. 2009) 13,000 B.P. and Dust Cave in north Alabama (Goldman-Finn 1994) 12,900 B.P. but seemingly not in the Appalachian region until 10,500 B.P. (Barber 2005). Sheriden Cave, however, was completely buried and only exposed recently during earth moving, strongly suggesting that other Pleistocene-aged caves with cultural remains exist.

Though many archaeologists believe the early use of caves in the east was for habitation, there is evidence in most of the archaeologically important caves of rituals being conducted inside beginning in the Late Paleoindian period and Early Archaic (Claassen 2012b, 2012c). Entrance chambers/vestibules and dark passages were stages for ritualizing. Vestibules show evidence of cooking, deposition of cremains, burnt animal offerings, human sacrificial and consecrating burials, four-age rites, secondary burials, burials of ritual paraphernalia, decommissioning rites for trophy parts, dog burials, and ocher powder preparation. Dark passages have fecal clusters indicative of purging, painting of walls, mining of salts, mining of chert, and passage maintenance.

A variety of rituals were conducted in rockshelters as well. The high number of violent deaths and rock-weighted bodies in the shelters annotated herein suggest that some people who were murdered or died in ways that raised concern among the living (i.e., lightning strike, drowning) were carried to rockshelters for burial. In several cases these people appear to have been ritual specialists, apprentices (both in Horn Shelter), and even witches (e.g., Breckenridge Shelter, Stanhope Cave) if the placement of the body facedown and weighted with rocks are used as criteria. Rockshelters may also have been used for ancestor or honor burial beginning in the Early Archaic. These individuals may well have been buried as bone bundles. There are cases of probable infant sacrifice, trophy part decommissioning, dog burial, swan burial, and earth renewal offerings. Menstrual and birthing rites were held in rockshelters in the Cumberland Plateau and Ozarks by Late Archaic people. Bone shrines for fauna are obvious in at least two places: White Rocks, Ohio, and Tick Creek Cave, Missouri (Parmalee 1965). Other types of fertility petitions may be evident in the "discard" or offering of sandals in places like Arnold Research Cave and textiles in Ozarks and Appalachian shelters based on the use of both footwear and textiles as offerings in central Mexico related to birth and naming of children (e.g., Claassen 2013b; Schaefer 2002).

Other rites included decommissioning of ritual paraphernalia, hematite processing, food preparation, nut stone decommissioning, trophy part decommissioning, steatite and ocher quarrying, and crinoid stem harvesting and, by Early Woodland, the initiation of boys (Crothers 2012). Rockshelters were possibly the meeting places of some medicine societies (Claassen 2011a). Many of these places received point and lithic offerings likely over centuries as well as offerings of used and old things. Rockshelters and sinkholes have emerged during this study as the most surprising natural ritual places—surprising for the wide variety of rites conducted in them.

Paleoindian artifacts are common at sinkholes in the eastern United States, and sinkholes were often reused by Archaic people. Possible shrines on rims have been excavated and rim burials found. Most interesting are the deposits in sinkholes that have caves opening off of them, such as is the case at Sheriden Cave, Mammoth Cave, Salts Cave, Wyandotte Cave, Hendricks Cave,

Austin sink, and Little Salt Spring. Human bone was found at the bottom of Hendricks sink as well as animal bone. Austin sink has extremely high numbers and density of flakes, seemingly tossed in from above.

Knolls, bluff tops, and ridges were perhaps the most important topographic features in choosing a burial area. Islands were another significant landform chosen for several of the rites already identified: bone shrines, mortuaries, and "tool" manufacture. Several springs offered up fossils and received offerings, and some springs were chosen as burial grounds. Other topographic features, as well as animals, rocks, rock formations, and trees, were potential homes for a spirit and held out the potential for the spirit to manifest from them to a human. A manifestation could occur as a surprise or could be prayed for by a human.

Created Ritual Places

In addition to utilizing and equipping *natural* places for rituals, Archaic peoples began the practice of elaborating and even *creating* places for ritual. (Perhaps Paleoindians made stone circles in Appalachian Virginia at the Spout Run site [newsleader.com, May 12, 2014]). In many cases these places appear to have been chosen because of their natural topographic attributes. For instance, it seems that the majority of burial grounds made in the Middle Archaic concentrated the dead in natural knolls, ridge tops, and bluff tops. Deposits of midden and the transport and emplacing of limestone cobbles and slabs then enhanced these chosen areas, even if only slightly. Shell mounds were often created at shoals and even on top of knolls, and dirt mounds were often erected at the intersections of creeks and rivers. Cemeteries, dirt mounds, earthworks, boulder mounds, shell mounds, shell ridges, plazas, stone cairns, and shrines constitute Archaic made places for ritual acts, often containing what authors frequently refer to as "cemeteries."

Because Archaic hunter-gatherers were rarely sedentary we should not expect all of their ritual spaces to be permanent or incised on the landscape. Nevertheless, they did return to many ritual places, leaving a permanent record in numerous cases. Swan (1995) identifies buildings, design concepts, and natural places that were used by past people for eliciting feelings of spirituality. Archaeologists have identified the use of all three of these in the Archaic, and many examples are given in the entries in parts II and III of this guide. Burial grounds should be added to Swan's list.

Whalen (2009:60) found in ethnographic reports of non-state groups that these communities used "many ephemeral and generational ritual spaces. . . . For ritual spaces housing large inclusive ceremonies, the space was outside all of the communities. Participating groups met at a dance ground or plaza that they all traveled to. When ritual spaces were the site of highly exclusive rituals, the space was within one of the communities. Here, the ritual space was a special location specific to one community, distinguishing it from the rest" (Whalen 2009:65). These comments certainly are applicable to the Archaic record and reflect the argument put forward by Claassen (2010) and Hofman (1985) that the ceremonial shell mounds were distant aggregation sites for hunter-gatherer groups. However, rockshelter use for doctoring, fertility offerings, and retreat were individual acts and are not accounted for by Whalen's observations.

Shellworks

Coastal shell rings are viewed as villages with gradually accumulating habitation and food debris whose histories were punctuated by elaborate, competitive feasting. More elaborate shellworks are typically multiple mound complexes, short and flat-topped or conical, with shell arcs, rings, ridges, and sand mounds. Many of the features found at shellworks were the result of encampments of guests (subrings, smaller mounds) and feasting debris (Russo 2004), as well as of intentional village design and facility creation (Schwadron 2010).

Plaza features were among the spaces created by the architects of shellworks and earthworks. Although typically devoid of features, the ring interior or plaza at St. Catherine's Island, Georgia, had an estimated 500 postholes, possibly derived from substantial structures (Sanger and Thomas 2010:58).

Mounds

In Classic period Mexico and since, mounds were part of a mountain cult, basically "hotels" for mountain cave spirits/deities (e.g., Bassie-Sweet 1996). However, the earliest dirt mound building in the lower Mississippi valley and in Mexico—that on the Gulf of Mexico coast in Veracruz—did not occur near mountains so mountain imagery cannot be the original symbolism of mounds. Sassaman (2010a) suggested that mounds in Florida might be the inverted image of filled ponds. The appearance of Middle Archaic dirt mounds could well have been the result of a vision and then growth of a cult centered on earth medicine knowledge.

All of the multiple mound centers as well as single mound centers created in the Middle Archaic on the Gulf Coast/lower Mississippi valley were abandoned by the late Middle Archaic. They appear to have been built rapidly, with purpose, and in auspicious places determined by premound structures or pits or astronomical sight lines, although most of them are small when compared to other mounds. The rites conducted at these places are unknown, but one at Watson Brake at least involved an initial deer feast (Jackson and Scott 2001). Perhaps we are seeing a Cult of the Earth Mound.

The shell mounds of Mount Taylor culture in Florida were earlier and as intentional as those of dirt in the lower Mississippi valley. The Florida mounds differed in a very significant way by the inclusion of burials although they do not seem to have been enlarged as mortuaries but as platforms (Randall 2015). It is surely significant that these snail shell mounds with burials were duplicated in concept and in timing by two snail shell accumulations on the Duck River and one on the Harpeth in central Tennessee. I have dubbed these mounds as the product of a Cult of the Snail Shell, a fertility/renewal cult.

Although many of the shell mounds of the SOV began accumulating as early as the dirt mounds in Louisiana and a few (e.g., Eva) even earlier, their monumentality would only emerge in the Late Archaic, after the Gulf coastal mounds were no long growing and perhaps had been abandoned. It may well be that the idea of a mound and a monument, as many of these shell heaps would become, was implanted in the minds of their users by the examples of a few southern dirt mounds and several Florida shell mounds such as Mound A at Horr's Island. The ambitions of the members of the SOV Cult of the Bivalve Feast, however, surpassed those of the other mound users judging from the human sacrifices, dog sacrifices, point offerings, grave goods, feasting, and other renewal acts that are apparent in these places.

Finally, the mounds of the Far North and LIV/Missouri appear to be low-volume domes slowly enhanced with boulders or dirt and stones after each interment. (The bluff-top cemeteries on the Iowa River may never be professionally examined [Benn and Thompson 2009:528].) Several types of ceremonies, including human sacrifice, were conducted in both regions. Again it is evident in the LIV that only a select group of people was interred in the ridge-top mounds; others were buried on the floodplain in habitation sites or in sand ridges (Charles and Buikstra 2002). Teasing out the burial place criteria should be a focus of bioarchaeologists.

Whether built gradually or in major construction episodes, many of these mounds qualify as monumental based on their size alone. The largest Middle Archaic dirt mounds are 5–7 m high and 37–45 m in diameter (Saunders 1994:133). Using a formula of cubic meters/1,000, I calculated an index for dozens of Archaic, Woodland, and Mississippian sites (see Claassen 2010:89) and found that eleven Archaic shell mounds are more massive than all Middle Archaic dirt mounds, and two shell mounds are on par with the largest mound at the Mississippian era Etowah center and the second largest mound at the Hopewell Chillicothe site. Based on volume, the largest Archaic shell mound is on the Gulf Coast of Florida, at Horr's Island, Mound A. The largest Archaic dirt mound is in the lower Mississippi valley, Mound A at Poverty Point (Late Archaic age). In fact, it is the second largest mound in the United States.

While none of the Middle Archaic dirt mounds qualifies as monumental based on volume, all are monuments nonetheless. Furthermore, "the evidence [in the Gulf Coastal Plain] suggests very old and widely disseminated knowledge about how to build large sites. This building lore persisted remarkably intact for so long [including 60 generations of non-mound-building people] that I think we can, and must, assume that it was part of special knowledge tied to ritual practices. . . . I hope to have provided sufficient evidence and arguments to raise the possibility of Middle Archaic interaction on a continental scale" (Clark 2004:201). Not only were individual mounds sited with respect to physiographic features, distance and direction from sister mounds within a single complex, but the different clusters of mounds and different sites were sited with respect to one another (see the entries for "number" and "measurement" in part III). Both Clark (2004:203) and Sassaman and Heckenberger (2004:228) speculate that the geometry and numerology uncovered for the Louisiana mound landscape will eventually be found in house spacing and camp arrangements of the region.

Clark's (2004) dissection of the numerology and calendrics underlying Archaic Gulf Coast dirt multimound complexes clearly indicates that the single mounds of the Ohio and Illinois River valleys and of the Far North were significantly different from the dirt mounds in Louisiana and Arkansas in conception and in their ritual role. This difference is further accentuated by the use of single mounds for burial in the north and the lack of burials in multimound sites along the Gulf. There is, however, a slight suggestion of a cosmic plan even among the other mound sites of the Ohio and Atlantic coastal plain and coast for the following reasons: (1) no shell rings or shellworks of the East Coast have burials, often the cosmic direction of new life; (2) shell burial mounds are found in the "west" and "south" (central and southern Ohio River valley, Tennessee River valley), often the directions of the land of the dead; (3) evidence of the use of cremation has been found in the Tennessee River mounds, to the "south"; and (4) evidence of the use of red ocher has been found more frequently in the Green River valley, or in the "north." It may also be part of this subcontinent-wide cosmology that no freshwater shell-bearing mound mortuary sites appear on eastward-flowing rivers or on eastern segments of a river. "East" was preserved as the direction of birth, not death, while west is the direction of death and, equally significant, conception. In Woodland times the Ohio valley mound center rituals apparently merged with some of the ritual of the much older mounds to become conducted, usually, at multimound centers with significant calendrical, numerological, and mortuary components.

Many Archaic peoples were not living in areas where mounds were built but participated in rites and feasts at mounds as pilgrims or guests and brought their dead to be buried in them. They surely knew about mounds even if they never visited one. One enigma in the data from the SOV burial grounds is the presence of auditory exostoses in people buried even in shell-free burial grounds, although the ear condition could reflect a lifelong steam bath regimen rather than shellfishing by men as proposed by Mensforth (2005).

Multimound configurations—existing in the lower Mississippi valley and in coastal Florida settings, and perhaps in the Big Bend of the Green River—suggest the development of cyclical rituals employing the individual mounds in sequences, in ways perhaps "analogous to the changing seasons, the movements of the sun, moon, and other celestial bodies, as well as related social and environmental events, like the migration of different birds and animals" (Giles 2010:87), which Giles thinks describes the later Hopewell of Ohio. In addition to within-site circuits, it is probable that different types of natural and made places for ritualizing were connected physically by paths by shared viewscapes, and mentally by ritual circuits, possibly even into sets of places that could be called ritual districts or ceremonial complexes. As developed elsewhere (Claassen 2010:Chapter 7), the ritual districts of the SOV, each with a different combination of natural settings and created sites, were the Green River district, the central Ohio River district, the upper Ohio River district, the Wabash/White River district, the Harpeth River district, and the upper Tennessee River district. In several cases, the juxtapositioning of natural and made places for ritualizing resulted in a ceremonial complex with a ritual circuit such as that of Dust Cave + Muscle Shoals + Perry shell mound, on the Tennessee River; Wyandotte Cave + Falls of the Ohio shoals + Old Clarksville shell mound on the Ohio River; and Indian Knoll + rockshelters with marks and mortars + Mammoth Cave, on the Green River.

Performing these circuits would certainly have occupied some ritual specialists and may have included pilgrims to all or parts of the staging places within the complex. Recorded pilgrimages for Hopi males, Panamint males, Creek males (Gatschet 1884), and Pawnee males to the Garden of the Gods (Blakeslee 2010), villagers to Virginia mounds (Dunham 1994:1–4), and Iroquois to Big Bone Lick (Mayor 2005:29) are the basis for believing that pilgrimages were a part of Archaic group rituals. In fact, "in many examples [cross-culturally,] community rituals are open to all, but occur as pilgrimages to sites located outside the community (Bauer and Stanish 2001, Gray 2001).... [Distant ritual centers] may be even more common than typically thought, especially when there is much interaction between communities in a region" (Whalen 2009:63). The historic pilgrimages within the United States and Mexico were often taken to focus the pilgrims' attention on important concepts of adulthood, understanding the cosmology and origin of the group ("this is the route our ancestors walked"), and sometimes to gather a good or foodstuff (peyote, salt, game). If various topographic features were recognized homes for important spirits in Archaic beliefs, and if abandoned places were memorialized, then it would seem that pilgrimage would have been an important way of getting to those places—whether that involved days or only hours of walking.

Murder/Sacrifice

One of the oldest cases of murder seems to be that of Kennewick Man, found along the Columbia River in Washington state dated to 9,300–9,600 B.P. (Chatters 2002). In the eastern United States these activities began in earnest in the Middle Archaic. The annotations in parts II and III of this guide provide much information about these individuals.

Why murder victims appear and continue to appear during the Late Archaic are topics too easily assigned to warfare. There simply were no scarce food resources in the eastern United States during the Archaic. Instead, it was a land of abundance (Claassen 2010). Furthermore, many of the burial grounds appear to have been shared rather than used to mark territory. The accumulation of the dead served to create intercessories for the living with the spirits and did not lay claim to territory. There was then simply no reason for "warfare."

Instead, the evidence is quite strong that most of the dead with embedded points, scalping marks, missing body parts, and in strange postures were sacrificed in various rites, particularly a four-age rite and a hunt god rite using adults as well as rain and first-kill rites using infants. Whether these victims were kin or strangers has yet to be established. Violence, yes; but warfare, no.

Structure of Archaic Rituals

Ideas for the structure of Archaic ritualizing come from historical records and my own participation in Nahua and hybrid Catholic rituals in central Mexico. Most of these rituals have involved pilgrimage to trees, caves, mountaintops, singing, praying, flowers, smoke, dancing, and offering, all aimed at group fertility in the form of rain-calling (Claassen 2011a, 2011b, 2013c). The structure for Archaic rituals, private and public, would have been imparted by visions, most of which resulted in individuals receiving medicine and instruction for doctoring but some of which grew into cults with activities orchestrated by specialists. Many rituals were no doubt celebrated with feasting if not conducted during feasts.

Visions/Dreams

Visions were most likely the major avenue for both ritual change and human agency in ritualizing, although they were not the only impetus for ritualizing. As Irwin (1994) so clearly documents, Plains Indian groups particularly, but others as well, gave exceedingly great attention to the messages and gifts given by spirits through dreams or visions. An individual ignored the message of a vision at great peril to self and even community and quite frequently created a private bundle including mnemonic devices with which to perform the instructions. Some visions that occurred to individual women, men, and youths delivered knowledge that many people wanted, resulting in collectives of people who shared and practiced that knowledge—medicine societies, warrior societies, and so forth—each with membership requirements, origin stories, advancement criteria, and paraphernalia of membership and rank. Famous examples of major sodalities—public and secret—that were the result of an individual's vision are the Native American church or the peyote cult, the Sundance, the Lenape Big House, the Iroquois League, and the Ghost Dance. Visions have played a role in many of the cultures with which readers are familiar; examples abound in the Bible. Visions led to the construction of cities such as Ephesus and buildings such as the Hagia Sophia.

Manifestations resulted in places or objects having significance for individual dreamers in all cases and significance for groups of people in some cases (when stimulating sodalities and cults). In the Archaic a few of the many possibilities for vision-inspired practices are human sacrifice, freshwater shell burial, shell-ring creation, river cleaning, tossing offerings into springs, selection of various topographic features for altars and shrines, and making effigy stone beads, Great Auk capes, dirt mounds, and even the arcurate earthworks at Poverty Point. Visions had the power to start and stop cults, initiating much about the Archaic period as we recognize it and probably causing the cessation of those same practices that lead us to see a transition into the Woodland period.

Cults

Many vision messages resulted in cults for medicine, for warriors, for alliances, and for renewal. Secret societies are examples of exclusive cults in the Archaic, but inclusive cults are also evident. Rituals centering on the earth and fertility were seen by Turner (1969) as those practiced by the most socially egalitarian. Because fertility rituals "speak to common interests and anxieties," these and other "cults of inclusiveness have a life outside of social hierarchy, class distinctions, economic control, and political centralizations. They arise in the least complex of societies" (Brown 1997:467). Indeed, cults characterize most of the spiritual activity that I imagine occurred in the Archaic.

Was there a Cult of the Ancestors anywhere in the Archaic? Certainly not in the classic sense of Incan practice where mummies were brought to the plaza once a year and entire families became custodians of the possessions of the mummified ruler for generations to follow. Charles and Buikstra (2002) argue for a Cult of the Ancestors simply because bodies were accumulated on ridge tops in mounds and could be referenced visually and physically by the living. But surely it takes much more than that to constitute ancestor worship. The move to concentrate the dead in one place was one that positioned the dead as intercessors with the spirits for the living. Rather than a Cult of the Ancestors, I see a pan-Eastern Archaic fertility/renewal religion with regional cultic variations in terms of where they focused petitions for fertility: in the SOV the renewal context was created by naiad shells, human sacrifices, and various rain-calling activities beside rivers; in the Northeast renewal was furthered by cremation primarily as well as burial in low dirt mounds, with red ocher, slate, and bird and swordfish imagery; and in the Great Lakes region renewal was ensured by cremation or dirt burial, red ocher, using copper and stone, and knolls for burial. Contrary to the statement of Hutchinson and Aragon (2002:33) that the dead "received no offerings, invocations or other ritual worship. They were left to rest in peace," large group ceremonials were held in a guest-host cycle at the large burial grounds where the dead were petitioned to help the living and the living were renewed by human sacrifice, additions of bodies and shells, and the offering of old and new tools. Stone/point offerings continued to be made at many of these places for millennia.

Ancestors surely did exist in the minds of Archaic peoples, but that category of dead persons probably referred to a very specific subset of the dead: founders of lineages and their descendants and important ritual specialists. Given that only a subsample of Archaic people who died are found in burial grounds, it may well be those individuals, then, along with ritual victims, who were interred in these special contexts, including rockshelters.

Several of the big cults that were holding sway in the Late Archaic had earlier Archaic origins. A Cult of the Blade honoring the Stone People prompted caching in the Mississippi, Great Lakes, and Saint Lawrence River valleys. The Cult of the Bivalve Feast resulted in the piling of freshwater shellfish and burial at these locations and oysters without burial on the Gulf and Atlantic coasts. This cult might have actually been a hunt god cult in most places, employing deer impersonators, bannerstones, sacrifices of four or five people and infants, atlatls, and deer as well as bivalve feasting. The Cult of the Snail Shell on the St. Johns and Duck rivers may have focused on the spiral, star, and cavern symbolism of gastropods and carried a renewal message. Other cults might have been the Poverty Point Cult of the Heavens and a Cult of the Bayonet in the Far North. All of these cults were probably concerned with fertility and were pursued in subregions. For instance, "the material manifestations of Poverty Point cosmology did not reverberate much outside the immediate region of northeast Louisiana suggest[ing] neither that it was a unifying 'religion' of all Late Archaic people nor that all regional populations were invited to participate" (Sassaman 2010a:66). Little cults may have included a Cult of River Keepers that was centered on the Green River evident in the extremely high incidence of exostoses (e.g., Mensforth 2005), as well as a Cult of the Locust (Louisiana) and Cult of the Auk (Far North).

Ritual Specialists and Priests

Ritual specialists or priests surely were at work in the Archaic. They may have structured the cults that formed around various categories of esoteric knowledge during their lifetimes and cared for the mnemonic devices that were essential to the rites.

Most communities probably had at least one resident healer, with specialties in cosmological concepts related to bad winds and soul loss, birthing, bone setting, vision interpretation, calendrical knowledge and divination, weather, finding lost people and items, and matchmaking. The weather priests were those people highly skilled in flintknapping: the cache blade makers, the Dalton Sloan point specialists (Brookes 2004:107–109), and the flint miners in 3rd Unnamed Cave, for example. There may have been lost-and-found specialists. There even may have been sacrifice specialists for humans and dogs, those who did or directed the killing and the attendant rites.

There are several burials in eastern North America whose grave goods suggest the individual was a ritual specialist; a few examples will suffice. Port au Choix-3 BuC35A was an older man with the only projectile point found in a grave, 49 beaver incisors, and a cape of 200 Great Auk bills. Rosenberger Bu144 (a Late Archaic Ohio River riverside shell-free burial ground) was an elderly woman, flexed and oriented to the northwest with 137 pieces of animal, more than in any other feature. These included worked turtle bone (carapace?) and pieces of drumfish, deer, and bird (animals from the three worlds). Short Cave woman was buried in a cave with a "variety of faunal elements and seeds that were interpreted as ritual/medicinal items. . . . suggesting that the woman was a ritual specialist" (Jefferies 2008:238). A priest's cache containing ocher, part of a great horned owl, salamander, and large pieces of antler, as well as Early Archaic and Late Archaic points, was excavated at the Bullskin Creek site in Ohio (Vickery 2008:14–15). Bu88 was found in a shell mound setting at Mulberry Creek, Alabama, an older man extended on his face with two dog burials under his feet, and on his lumbar region ten Benton blades, a piece of antler, and two bone tools (Shields 2003:93). Dogs were killed by Cherokee to guide priests specifically and to rebalance a world out of kilter (James 2006).

Among the personnel are both women and men. Fauna are important elements of their identity and include fish, deer, bird, turtle, dog, and rattlesnake. Burial contexts were shell free, shell bearing, shell mound, and cave/rockshelter; the latter context is consistent with the idea that it was not the least among them but important people who were buried in caves and rockshelters. There is also indication that witchcraft was practiced and punished by death as it was in historic times. Witches are possibly among those who died violently then were disposed of (often facedown) in rockshelters such as in Stanhope Cave, Ohio, and Stanfield-Worley, Alabama; several women in Breckenridge Shelter, Arkansas, were buried similarly. The Paleoindian people who buried the man in Horn Shelter 2, Texas, placed a Swainson's hawk talon in his mouth and four unperforated claws of a Swainson's hawk near his neck, as well as a youth in the same grave. Both bodies were stone weighted.

Apprentices would have been important for generational transfer of the esoteric knowledge that enabled the correct relationship with spirits and for the continuity of practice. Actual apprentices may include the boy who died inside Salts Cave, Kentucky, the young individual laid beside the older adult man at Horn Shelter, Texas, and the juvenile on top of the adult at the back of Stanfield-Worley. (See annotations for more information.)

In the debate over whether shamanism was present in Archaic cultures (there is no other choice in the classification of Joraleman 1996), we have lost track of the fact that a great deal of ritualizing was likely conducted by nonspecialists. Household heads, mothers, mourners, hunters, gatherers, fishers, net-makers, clay diggers, medicinal plant seekers, youths completing a first basket or first kill, and so forth conducted private rituals and household rituals (e.g., Marcus 1999; Plunket 2002; Schaefer 2002). Everyone was a potential visionary, but some collected more visions and more animal allies than others, and some were called to be ritual specialists by surviving a serious illness, lightning strike, or other sign, but most people were not. All of this is to say that there was no dominant ideology that was controlled by or obscured by an elite for selfish purposes. Nonspecialists understood and were agents in all of the elements of the Archaic spiritual structure, and they introduced a great deal of variation in materials and features and innovation in ideas and mnemonic devices. The variety of religious practices during the Archaic was

6. Preparing the feast to follow the 2013 rain-calling pilgrimages of San Andres de la Cal, Morelos, Mexico. (Photo by author.)

great. All I can hope to do in this project is to alert readers to the potential and suggest types of data that might imply ritualized activities when viewing the archaeological record.

Feasting

Feasting was an important part of ceremonials in the Archaic, a conclusion supported by the arguments of Russo (2004), Saunders (2004), Sassaman (2006), and Jackson and Scott (2001) and the evidence from sites such as Stallings Island and County Home. Pilgrims, guests, hosts, and kin probably attended the large feasts during which ritual specialists conducted rites, hosts and guests gave speeches, and gifts were exchanged. Facilities related to feasting can be cited and even the adoption of pottery, and soapstone bowls may have been in service of feasts; they and bone pins may have been circulated among feasters. Equally important was the labor pool that gathered at the feast site who could then be expected to help gather firewood, prepare and serve the food (Figure 6), clean up, build shellworks, and mound dirt (Saunders 2004).

Facilities for Ritual

Archaic peoples created a variety of facilities to enable their ritualizing such as very large hearths, baked-clay floors, clay-lined ovens, deep pits, bedrock mortars, shrines, screens, altars/platforms, cairns, rock walls, and so forth, all annotated in this guide. For example, a Middle Archaic hearth at Campbell Hollow, Illinois, had a volume of 84.79 liters. At Mulberry Creek in Alabama an "unusually fine fire hearth was composed of at least four and possibly five layers of clay, superimposed each one on the preceding hearth. The entire area was brick red and extremely hard. It was nearly 6 feet in diameter, and dome-shaped, the center being nearly 1 foot higher than the edges" (Webb and DeJarnette 1942:238). A mortar at Tick Creek Cave in Missouri weighed 52 kg, and bedrock outcrops with multiple mortar holes appear in the Cumberland Plateau in the Late Archaic (Franklin 2002). The largest measured pit in the SOV was found at the bluff-top Ward site (23,524 liters), and another large pit was excavated at Kirkland (13,942 liters) with a dog skull at the bottom. Huge roasting pits were found at two eastern Iowa sites, McNeal Fan and Sand Run West, representing "substantial labor investment in collecting large volumes of resources, digging large holes, and redistributing the heated products to large groups" (Benn and Thompson 2009:524). Finally, the baked-clay surfaces found primarily in the Tennessee River valley were cooking facilities in most cases (Sherwood and Chapman 2005), but some may also have been shrine floors.

Shrines may have been house-like post outlines or even cairns. Possible shrines could be the large structures at Goddard, Pennsylvania, a pithouse at 9Wr4 (Ledbetter 1995), a posthole feature at the Higgs site (Hofman 1986), a round structure at the Bailey site (Bentz 1988), structures at Go-Kart North (Fortier 1987:49), McLean, Illinois (McElrath 1986), and Harris Creek (Aten 1999) (see site annotations for details). Cairns and posts are other features that would have had a ritual role, and several examples exist on graves (Port au Choix-3 cemetery) and on mountain slopes and mountaintops in Arkansas, Missouri, and Tennessee (Deter-Wolf and Hockersmith 2007; House 1965). Crematories may be considered shrines as well although they are rare, truly surprising given the very high incidence of cremation.

Offerings and Mnemonic Devices

The raw material chosen for an offering or mnemonic device was as much a part of the meaning as was the object fashioned or the motifs engraved. Stone, bone, wood, and fiber all had their special symbolism and links to specific spirits and to past time. Robinson (2006:344) seems to espouse the same perception.

Robinson (2006:352) identifies a bone to stone transition in the Moorehead Archaic Tradition for a number of grave good types. Earlier complexes, those prior to 6800 B.P., contained few flaked bifaces (Sassaman 2010a:82) while later ones had considerably more flaked stone. There is a similar transition in the Tennessee River shell mounds as discussed by Webb and DeJarnette (1948a:49), specifically referring to Little Bear Creek in Alabama: "In the lower three feet of this midden, from the 9.5 foot level to the 6.5 foot level, very little flint was found. It is in exactly this region that the bone points are most numerous. It appears that in the history of this site, when the 6.5-foot level was laid down there was a sudden desire for flint artifacts, resulting in their very rapid increase. This seems to have been connected with the appearance of shop sites in the midden. . . . These work shops, which produced rough blades by percussion only[,] seemingly gave rise to [point types] which are the dominant types in this midden."

Bone points give way to stone points. Both are found embedded in human bone. Is this transition at Little Bear Creek, Perry, and O'Neal indicating the rise of a cult that placed new emphasis on stone? Perhaps the beliefs about Camaxtli, the hunt god and giver of fire and first flaker of flint, began at this time, spawning the move to stone points. Do the workshops in the Alabama shell mounds mark the beginning of these beliefs, the crude percussion flakes produced as part of a hunt/fertility rite? If so, then after three feet of accumulation, these shell mounds seem to have been the sites of major feasts and ceremonials. This transition to greater use of stone and increased numbers of stone points then is not the result of expanding population but of ritual. During the Middle Archaic the meaning changed behind the use of stone, stone knives, stone points, chips, and flakes.

A similar case might be made for a documented move from bone to antler. Webb (1974:330–333) called the earlier wooden atlatl and the later antler atlatl "another step in refinement." Was this transition motivated by a desire to strengthen the visual and tactile association between the hunt god and deer?

Much of the movement of exotics and grave goods found in Archaic contexts should be understood as offering driven. The premier raw material for offerings was stone, in raw, chipped, or ground form, particularly projectile points, knives, blades, and pestles. There are numerous reasons for believing stone was used in offerings, among them the sometimes extraordinary number of flakes or points/bifaces in some settings and the highly popular caching of blades.

O'Brien (1998:26) wonders at the tenfold increase in the numbers of Dalton points over Clovis points even though Dalton culture lasted only 1,000 years. Rather than explain the increase as an explosion in human population, might it signal the beginning of the use of chipped-stone bifaces as offerings, offerings placed both in burials and left at auspicious locations by ritual specialists or pilgrims? Some Archaic sites have truly incredible quantities of bifaces such as Indian Knoll (9,424), Perry (7,200), and Carlston Annis (2,101) (numbers in Watson 2005), closely paralleling the rank order of these sites in number of burials (Claassen 2010:Table 6.2). Stanfield-Worley excavations netted 2,500 points from less than 50 percent of the shelter, and the Hardaway site (North Carolina) had 5,000 points. Olive Branch (Illinois) has at least 4,500 points, and James Creek (West Virginia) 815 points. Austin, a Tennessee sinkhole, yielded 462 points in 4 m^3 of excavation. But in spite of extensive excavation at Meadowcroft Rockshelter only 44 points were recovered, suggesting a very different use for this famous shelter.

What other cultural or natural formation process besides offering could explain the tremendous number of points at these sites? Do we really think the men at James Creek lost 250 points during the Early Archaic even when the site was reused during the Late Archaic? Wouldn't later people have collected or used those points? Yet they, too, "lost" another 250 points there. "Loss" of 9,424 projectiles/knives at Indian Knoll?

Deposition, as offerings, is the far more likely explanation for the high number of points/knives. In total these worked stones represent a significant amount of raw material and human labor. Lithics as offerings have been documented in numerous historic circumstances in the Great Lakes, Plains, and Southwest (Rajnovich 1994; Selig 2010; Sundstrom 1996, 2000). Older points in younger settings also suggest offerings. Could it be that thousands of multicomponent sites we've identified based on the mixture of projectile types were not actually occupied during those various time periods but attracted offerings because of their landscape setting or the presence of burials? A simple count of points, and of flakes, which are also apparently used in offerings, will quickly identify ritual locations.

Numerous other substances and items were employed as offerings, including many that would not preserve in most archaeological contexts. Some of the mnemonic devices used in rites, collected into sacred bundles, or gifted at feasts were buried or cached, broken, burned, marked, or shaped. Rock art, bannerstones, shell masks, red ocher, animal jaws, copper items, atlatls, quartz crystals, and hypertropic blades and bayonets are outstanding examples. Less apparent to archaeologists are rounded pebbles, bedrock mortars, pestles, bones of songbirds or white birds, shell spoons, human bone objects, and fossils,

7. Fertility rockshelter shrine at Chalma, Mexico, June 2011. (Photo by author.)

among a few of the possibilities. In fact, much of what we find may be classified as mnemonic devices—the projectile points, drills, adzes, birdstones, bannerstones, colors of stones, pebbles, counts of items—so commonly used that we should think of the peoples of the Archaic as literate, reading these items as we archaeologists now wish to do (Giles 2010:37). Giles (2010:45) says that "the development and utilization of symbolic systems is a cumulative process because one symbolic system is not simply replaced with another." Numerous ways of identifying the offerings from the trash have been offered (e.g., Claassen 2010, 2012b, 2012c) and are elaborated in parts II and III.

The variability in offerings evident in today's rites in Mexico probably replicates that of the past. For instance, to a rock face in Chalma, Mexico, pilgrims bring photos of children, wooden crosses, umbilical cords in baggies, baby socks, candles, and flowers (Figure 7). The offerings in the sinkhole at Hendricks Cave likewise show variability in that flakes, points, and bones of different animals were thrown in. Live offerings were also made into the Mexican sinkhole of Ostotempan (Claassen 2013c).

Contemporary examples of offerings at shrines also demonstrate that an exchange occurs at those places. When Wixárika women take an offering of a weaving to a shrine they usually exchange it for one left previously by someone else and then copy the design weeks or years later (Schaefer 2002). This exchange is a major avenue through which designs spread. The pilgrims to the Chalma rock face also take away something from their visit—holy water running out from the hillside, a crown of fresh flowers, photos, tactile and visual memories of wetness and rock, a chunk of edible rock, a bottle of mescal, some plastic memento, and/or information from conversations with other pilgrims. Similar exchanges in the past could account for a great deal of trafficking in raw materials and information and would have generated mnemonic devices, essential in ritual. A useful distinction for archaeologists might be fine-scale and grand-scale memorializing with the former tracking previous placements of altars, bodies, caches, doxa, poles, regalia, ritual grounds, paths, and life stories, and the latter tracking ancestry, migrations, culture heroes, ritual history, medicinal formulae, and so forth.

What archaeologists label debris or "trash" was apparently an essential element of ritual in Archaic times as celebrants left behind old items and camp "trash." Cameron (2002) and Knight (1989) have explored the nature of "trash," and Knight reported that plaza sweepings were put on mounds, but Clark (2004:213n7) knows of "no evidence that Archaic mounds were built or augmented in this way." However, trash is the basis of the argument over whether the SOV shell mounds were ritual places or villages. The thousands of pieces of points and flakes, groundstone, fire-cracked rock, bone, antler, and so forth were perhaps only the mundane refuse of village life (Milner and Jefferies 1998), or perhaps they were the products of acts of renewal during major ceremonials. Breakage and burning were common characteristics of offered items as well.

The Rites

Rites and their pertinent rituals have been discussed by anthropologists for over a century. Catherine Bell (1997:185–192) lists four categories of rites: (1) rites of passage or transformation, (2) calendrical rites, (3) rites of exchange and communication, and (4) rites of affliction. Anthony Wallace (1966) gives five categories with subsets. Others divide religious rites into those planned according to some sort of time schedule and unplanned performances based on some immediate need. This simple division seems the most appropriate at this point in the study of this subject.

Public rites that seem to have occurred during the Archaic based on the evidence in site reports and that are presented in the annotated part III include the following: four-age rite, hunt god rite, dog sacrifice rite, dog with human burial rite, bone soul rite, commissioning rite for a place, decommissioning rite for a place, infant sacrifice, cache offering rite, first-kill rite, rebalancing rite, trophy part decommissioning rite, turtle shell rite, and spirit release rite (breakage and burning to point of calcification). Some of these rites overlapped or were combined, such as a four-age rite used in commissioning and decommissioning the shell heap at 1Ct17. All of these rites serviced, in one way or another, a basic concern with fertility and world renewal as would the later Hopewell rites (Romain 2009). As Giles points out, even opening a sacred bundle, repeating an origin story, singing an old song, and the procession of spirit impersonators were acts of renewal generating possibilities, fertilizing the future.

This survey of Archaic sites, features, burials, and artifacts has uncovered variation in several of these rites that is instructive for understanding the degree to which personal agency (visions? apprenticeship?) shaped and influenced Archaic ritualizing. This latitude in variation can be illustrated with the turtle shell rite and the hunt god rite, the latter perhaps the most significant finding of the research for this guide.

The turtle shell rite as it was practiced at Read, Kentucky, consisted of stones encircling two carapaces near a rockshelter at the base of the bluff-top site. At Eva, an earlier example shows that the rite was conducted in the shell-bearing layer. It started with a prepared bed of mussel shells upon which four shells were placed at the cardinal directions. In the center of this arrangement a single carapace was placed. With these two examples, we see variation in the context for the rite, in the encircling materials, and in the number of carapaces but with the central position for a carapace remaining constant. Actual turtle shells were also found covering the face of infants and adults as were *Busycon* shells, incised so as to mimic carapaces. These examples seem to indicate that one could convey similar meaning with rock shell, or carapace, and a covered face of an infant or an adult.

The differences between the various examples of hunt god rites also illuminate the latitude exercised by individual priests. First identified in the archaeological record by Hall (2000) in Mississippian contexts where four individuals were killed and buried together, the hunt god rite can now be pushed back to the Middle Archaic (Claassen 2012a) and referenced a god much like Camaxtli or Kanati, who gave the fire drill to humans and was god of the Milky Way and of the deer hunt. In the Archaic examples the rite could employ snail shell belts and bracelets on some but not all sacrificial victims, using freshwater or marine snails in the belts; adults arranged side by side or forming a square or "encircling" a focal point; four bodies or five bodies; all men or a mixture of women and men; and either the deer symbolism (headdress of antlers) or the Milky Way symbolism (snail shell belts) expressed. This degree of latitude in mnemonic devices is evident in numerous other examples, such as in the caching of blades, the use of ocher, and so forth. Hall (1997) made the use of analogy and simple substitution of referents by native peoples quite clear, and it was no less important in ritualizing during the Archaic.

Even a brief survey of Archaic peoples' beliefs about what to put into a grave and where to bury the dead indicates that the overarching concern of Archaic ritualizing was with renewal. Whether the concern was the renewal of the family, clan, lineage, animals, plants, toolstone, or seasons, bodies were used to solicit the favor of the Upper World or the Underworld spirits through rebirth of the dead via their descendants. The desire for continuity of families and humanity was expressed in various ways including the protracted juxtaposition of bodies in the same burial ground, the inclusion of stone grave goods, a material that housed the most ancient of spirits, and burial settings among shells or in dirt or in rocky surroundings, all laden with renewal symbolism.

Concern with human reproduction was expressed in myriad fertility rituals and practices. This survey of ritualizing has convinced me that rain calling or weather controlling, communicating with thunder and lightning deities, and the fertility symbolism implied by water were of paramount importance to Archaic fishers, gatherers, and hunters as well as all subsequent peoples regardless of their subsistence base. The cyclicality of weather phenomena that perhaps is best bracketed by spring tornadoes and fall hurricanes or summer heat and winter cold determined the timing for weather control activities. My own participation in Nahua May rain-calling ceremonies has attuned me to this actuality, as has reading about such ceremonies and practices in U.S. cultures, particularly the acorn gatherers of central California. Those gatherers refer to and use "rain rocks" to produce the sound of thunder, and rock powder is eaten and rubbed on one's body for fertility. Rain, terrestrial water, growth, offspring, and renewal were and continue to be concerns for (nonagricultural) Plains Indians hunting groups and the Apache. Concern with rain, water, and the fertility implied therein can be seen in the cases included here of abundant lithics, abundant fauna, faunal renewal pits, activities in caves and rockshelters, and so on. Indeed, even the modern agricultural Nahuas seek rain for the fertility and abundance of all things important to humans.

Weather control activities in the Archaic probably involved, in some cultures, the use of: reptiles; egg-shaped stones; infantile/small fauna (young or small bodied) and humans; miniature objects; marine shell; stone powder; and actions that could simulate the sound of thunder like pecking bedrock mortars, rolling stones, beating water drums, or the sound made by cicadas (Blitz

1993). Arrows probably were connected to rain calling in the past as they are today for the Apache (Alan Houser sculpture "Sacred Rain Arrow"). Alternative viewpoints abound, but archaeologists should consider the potential fertility import of these items.

Schedule of Ritualizing

One can predict a fixed timing for many group rites, and even private rites, based on plant life cycles, heavenly movements, animal migrations, and so forth. To argue that plant growth—and thus rain, or springtime—would have been less important to hunter-gatherers than to horticulturists is to misunderstand the vital role of plants in spiritual life and to perpetuate the error that hunting, more than gathering, provided the nutritional mainstays.

Many plants were medicine. Their greens, flowers, fruits, and seeds were key offerings, and feasting foods and fruits or flowers may have governed when a rite was scheduled. For instance, the florescence of the fern *Osmunda regalis* with its ethnographically attested gynecological applications seems to have governed the timing of rites at the later Blood of the Ancestors Grotto (Stelle 2006).

The completion of cosmic units of times was also probably a cause of celebration. The sun's position in December and June and equinoxes in September and March may have been observed by most groups as probably was the monthly cycling of the moon. The unit of time in which Venus appeared as morning star and then evening star may have been important, and the hunt god rite may have been performed at the completion of five Venus cycles (eight years) as it was among Nahuas. The movement of various stars, constellations (Gartner 1996:144–145), and planets (Dipper, Hand, Pleiades, Venus) may have triggered other ceremonies on behalf of a group. Some Gulf coastal mounds' construction histories suggest a ritual cycle of multiples of these cosmic units of time (e.g., Clark 2004; Clark and Colman 2012).

Clues to the timing of other rituals can be found in feces, flora, fauna, and pollen. Floral and pollen elements in fecal specimens found in Mammoth Cave and Salts Cave support the idea of two periods of work inside these caves, May (Crothers 2012) and fall. If cave rites were part of a ritual cycle, then we have hints here that caves may have been visited prior to summer and winter solstice–related events. Similarly, the Aztec Earth Goddess, Tonantzin, was celebrated annually in a cave rite held on December 12.

The Consequences of Ritualizing by Archaic Peoples

The benefits and consequences of the ritualizing evident in the Archaic would have included the following: ethnicity formation; alliance making; the spread of ideas, genes, objects, and technologies; the movement of raw materials; migration; expenditures of raw resources and human effort; the rise of "labor"; and violence. Dent (1995) and Sassaman (2010a) have probed the consequences and many archaeologists have addressed the benefits. The actual costs in materials and time, however, have yet to be approximated (see Brady 2005 for an example in a Maya region), but they must have been substantial with respect to all other types of productive activities given the thousands of burials with copious quantities of ocher powder; the tons of stone raw material; the production of thousands of hypertropic blades, bannerstones, heavy grinding tools, slate items, steatite items, and marine shell objects; the capture of birds and removal of beaks and feathers; and the capture of swordfish—and all of this is just what has been left for us to count. Tremendous amounts of preparation time are indicated.

Richard Dent (1995) has begun an exploration of the growth of "labor" in the Archaic, focusing on the Susquehanna culture. Toward the close of the Archaic period, flooding and sea level rise occurred, causing migrations. Perhaps the best-documented migration in the archaeological literature of the Late Archaic is that of the Broad Blade users who moved northward along the Atlantic coast into formerly only Narrow Blade users' territory and as far north as Turner Farm, Maine. In the mid-Atlantic area this migration lasted 2,000 years: 5,000 to 3,000 ya (Dent 1995:160). These Susquehannans introduced steatite, atlatls, and grooved axes to the northerners, but still more important was, in Dent's perception, the replacement of work with labor during the intensification of resource exploitation (Intensification Period, 4200–3000 bp). This labor, this intensification, "was less an economic phenomenon and more a set of social relations and the ideas that sustained them. . . . In the name of larger goals, nature was no longer accommodated. It was now beginning to be socially appropriated. . . . Constraints were placed on individual autonomy by new social entities. Work became labor as individuals were more interdependent within social entities that moved beyond kin groups" (Dent 1995:211–212). In support of this scenario, Dent pointed to "increased interdependence, increasing restriction of knowledge and increasing transportation costs," as well as the technological innovations that "had to be absorbed by a group larger than the collection party. . . . People were left to the make the best of their situation through small individual acts of resistance, group mediation, and ritual" (Dent 1995:213).

To the south of the Susquehannans were the Classic Stallings people. Ritual activities began well before their arrival in the Savannah River valley, including the establishment of an island mortuary and feasting. "Classic Stallings society required ritual to stay afloat; and the costs of ritual practice were real, if not substantial. It is difficult to judge the relationship between the price of ritual and the budgets of day-to-day living in Stallings communities" (Sassaman 2006:153).

At Poverty Point, the effort of building the rings may have resulted in the suspension of most other productive activities. "It seems the builders were curating tools and conserving rock supplies when they were working on the rings, suggesting that construction work kept them pretty busy. The building project evidently curtailed toolmaking and economic exchange and may even have temporarily shut down exchange entirely. Economic inflation, precipitated by construction's drain on resources and labor, was even felt at small contemporary sites nearby" (Gibson 1998:22). Gibson's evidence came from the rings themselves—there was a high percentage of broken tools, recycled stone, and informal flakes and blades, the opposite situation to that found in the dark surface midden.

The price of ritual for the SOV can be addressed in several ways: the number of burials, the expenditure of objects in burials, the expenditure of objects during ceremonies, the expenditure of people during ceremonies, the quantity of rare items deployed, and the scale of feasts, among other parameters. An estimated 18,000 bodies were buried over the 5,000 years of the Middle and Late Archaic. Although this is a large number of dead, if they were spread out over just the 3,000 years of the Late Archaic, burial activity would amount to six burials a year in all of the shell heaps of the entire SOV. By this measure there was little cost, it would seem, incurred in those events.

How do the counts of items in burials compare to the counts of items in the "middens"? Or put another way, what proportions of the labor and raw materials evident in the Green River sites were expended in grave goods? (Weights of items would be useful in such an enterprise but are not available.) Based on counts published for Indian Knoll (Webb 1974:230–235), one can see that 0.8 percent of the flint artifacts were found in burials, 3.4 percent of the bone artifacts, 5 percent of the groundstone items, and 2 percent of the antler objects, but 100 percent of the copper items (n = 6), 99.4 percent of the marine shell items, and 38 percent of the fossils. Turning to Carlston Annis (Webb 1950:298–303), nearly as important in Late Archaic life in the Green River valley as was Indian Knoll, we see that 100 percent of marine shell and copper items (n = 2) and 0.8 percent of the flint points were in burials, and 0.8 percent of all siliceous stone pieces, 8 percent of all groundstone items, and 1.3 percent of antler items were in graves, but no fishhooks, gorges, or bone pins.

Marine shell use can be examined more closely and will be based on the counts I made at four repositories visited in the mid-1990s (Webb Museum, McClung Museum, Moundville Museum, Smithsonian). From the period

7,000 to 3,500 ya come 17,329 probable Busyconid shell beads in six river valleys (11,891 Green, 2,113 Savannah, 2,261 Tennessee, 1,013 Harpeth, 20 Cumberland, 25 Wabash, 6 Duck). Of course, the number of beads that can be cut from a *Busycon* sp. shell depends on the size of shell and the skill of the artisan, making a count of individual shells very difficult. Using a random number of 50 beads per animal would implicate 367 shells. The number of columella items, large pieces of lips, and nearly complete shells found in the collections suggests fewer than an additional 100 whole Busyconid shells, for a total of 467 animals. Even if this number were increased tenfold to 4,670 shells, when divided over the probable 1,000 years of most intensive use, the harvest is miniscule and would not have supported trading relationships between individuals at the coast and in the Green River valley. I take these numbers to be further evidence that we are not looking at trade but at cult/ritual activities involving offerings.

The cost of raw materials for rituals in the Green River valley sites appears to have been far less than, for instance, that of the Great Lakes copper and flint and that of the bird parts, swordfish parts, and slate used in the Far North. The supply of swordfish and flint would not have been significantly impacted by these endeavors. The supply of steatite, particularly in the southern Appalachians, may have been noticeably diminished as may have been the readily available copper and some stones in quarries.

The most expensive ritual items, in terms of labor, were not those made with marine shell, animal bone, or copper, all easily worked or minimally worked, but must have been the stone blades in the Mississippi valley, steatite bowls along the Gulf and in the Northeast, bannerstones in a variety of places, and slate bayonets in the Far North. Perishables must have been even more abundant. When considering labor, it is clear that to focus a cost analysis on the grave goods alone is incomplete. Still more significant were the costs incurred by the feasts and the labor put into building up shellworks and earthworks. While the people of the Far North seem to have expended far more labor in grave good production than did people to the south of them, Southerners expended far more effort in ceremonials and feasting if shellworks are our measure. The person hours spent harvesting mollusks and mounding them were tremendous. And it was this labor and its self-consuming cycle—feasts were needed to amass the labor—that ultimately seem to have discouraged participants.

Many of these ceremonials also seem to have demanded human life, which itself was costly in social terms. Included among the burials of the SOV were 160 victims of violence based on obvious criteria, but as many as 318 additional people may have been victims based on unusual burial position or burial in a mass grave (Claassen 2010:Table 6.6). Among the 6 non-shell-bearing burial grounds in the SOV considered by Claassen (2010:119), at least 12 obvious murder victims exist and there are possibly 18 more. Altogether we could be looking at a *minimum* of 500 adult sacrificial victims, not including the victims identified in rockshelters (see entries in part II). There may be hundreds of infant and child sacrifices in these sites as well. These practices, coupled with feasting costs, and the other work involved in fortification of the extrafamilial social networks were a lot to sustain and may have been the undoing of the cults that disappeared at the end of our Archaic period.

End of the Archaic

In many areas of northern North America the periodization of Archaic and Woodland now seems artificial because cultural practices continued uninterrupted, often particularly in the mortuary programs. The Susquehanna Tradition, for instance, begins in the Late Archaic around 4,000 ya and ends in the Early Woodland, at around 2500 B.P. (Pagoulatos 2009). Although burial practices are somewhat different over this span of time, they are nevertheless elaborate and recognizable as a tradition. The same can be said of the continuum from the Old Copper complex to Red Ochre and Glacial Kame in the eastern and southern Great Lakes region, or the period from 6000 B.P. to 2600 B.P. (Pleger 1998).

Unlike the situation in the area north and east of the Ohio River, there was a dramatic end to the Archaic and break with the Early Woodland periods in the Southeast, thus reifying the archaeological divide. The shell rings of South Carolina and Georgia were abandoned in three waves. Sanger (2010:214) has shown that each interval correlates with either a sea level drop that left a ring too far from the oysters or a sea level advance that drowned the ring. In Florida, the transition to the Early Woodland has been most closely scrutinized in two regions, southwestern and northeastern Florida. For northeastern Florida the shell-ring phenomenon was over by 3600 B.P. (Russo 2010), and in the middle St. Johns River valley snail shell mounding had ended by 3800 B.P. (Sassaman 2010b). Life lived in circles, and competitive feasting and its monuments ended as may have dualistic societies. Ritual life shifted away from elaborate feasting, leaving only obvious mortuary (sand) mound ritual (Russo 2010).

In the Everglades there is also evidence for the abandonment of the interior tree islands by 3800 B.P., precipitated by flooding (Russo 2010). Schwadron (2010) thinks that these Archaic people moved to the coastal Ten Thousand Islands area, melding into a resident Late Archaic population that had been living in rings and creating shell works sites like Horr's Island for thousands of years.

Poverty Point and its sphere of influence offer one of the better examples of an abrupt cessation of ritualizing. Kidder (2010:25) has commented that there were "no sites in Upper Tensas basin . . . where there is a direct stratigraphic continuity between Late Archaic Poverty Point related materials and Tchefuncte Early Woodland." Both radiocarbon dates and geoarchaeological data indicate a hiatus in occupation of the area from 3100 to 2500 B.P.

Two causal mechanisms proposed to explain the end of Poverty Point are megaflooding and a sea level drop brought about by a global weather phenomenon (Little 2003; Kidder 2010). The cumulative effects were felt earlier in some areas and later in others and may be bracketed with environmental data of one kind or another from 3600 to 2600 B.P. (Kidder 2010). Megaflooding does seem to fit well with Poverty Point and the shell rings of the Atlantic records. Megaflooding (frequent, grand floods) would not have reached the actual Poverty Point center and may have even stimulated the growth of Poverty Point (Kidder 2010), but by 3000 B.P. flooding would have inundated the lower-lying communities from which honor, offerings, and pilgrims derived and may have caused the catastrophic failure of the basin enclosing Lake Macon upon whose fish and waterfowl Poverty Point residents had been dependent (Gibson 2010). Kidder identified what he thought was a pan-Eastern phenomenon of flooding by citing Early Woodland settlement data that show an increased number of upland sites in Kentucky and the upper Tennessee River valley, presumably caused by people escaping the flooding in the floodplains. To him, this megaflooding phenomenon would explain the end of the Cult of the Bivalve Feast in the SOV.

For all of the reasons discussed previously in connection to the Hypsithermal and intensive harvesting of naiads (Claassen 2010:51–83), high water simply is irrelevant to shellfishing and megaflooding thus irrelevant to the end of the Cult of the Bivalve Feast for one. Ed Curtin, who weaves an engaging picture of the changing upper Hudson-Mohawk valley at the close of the Archaic, does not mention greater flooding—quite the contrary. "I offer the suggestion that substantial sections of floodplain, which were at least somewhat protected from high-energy flood processes, increasingly became significant new landscapes for human use during and after the Late Archaic period. . . . Moreover, as the floodplains increasingly became occupied, the rivers increasingly became pathways" (Curtin 2011:3).

The same can be said of the Delaware River valley. "In the Delaware River valley, archaeological activity intensified during the Terminal Archaic period. . . . Land surfaces by this time (3500 BP) were rarely inundated, except during major floods. The Delaware River was entrenched in its channel . . . [and] prehistoric occupation intensified as the uppermost surfaces were no longer actively aggrading by alluvial inputs" (Bergman and Doershuk 1998: 53). Turning to the opposite end of Pennsylvania, we see that the floral record, the terrestrial gastropod record, the femur length of various animals, and the general faunal record at Meadowcroft Rockshelter fail to show any evidence of unusual flooding after or before the Late Archaic (Adovasio et al. 1998). Furthermore, there is a decline in high-elevation sites from Middle Archaic to Early Woodland, and all base camps are found on floodplains in the Early Woodland, not along the tributary of Cross Creek drainage, the opposite situation from that indicated by the Green River data.

Nor does the flooding and sea level drop explain much more than a hiatus in regional occupation in Florida. While the four big shellworks sites on the southwestern Gulf seem to end by 3700 B.P., new ones appear on the same coastline and a new one appears on the southern Atlantic coast of Florida at 3500 B.P. (Russo 2010). The Everglade tree islands were reoccupied by 2700 B.P. with sites looking exactly like they did before abandonment (Schwadron 2010:121).

Sassaman assessed the end of Archaic activities in the middle St. Johns, the middle Savannah River, and the middle-upper Tennessee River and found two "inflection points" in practices, one at 3800 B.P. when there were "major cultural realignments in the middle Savannah and middle St. Johns" and in the Tennessee valley, a "surge in soapstone vessel production," and adoption of pottery (Sassaman 2010b:235). The second inflection point was at 3,300 B.P. when there was "an overall dispersal of settlement into upland units across much of the lower Southeast" (2010b:235). To add to these cultural changes that seem to have had little to do with flooding, the Cult of the Bivalve Feast was fading well before 3,500 ya.

When I started this project I occasionally found myself wondering if *all* Archaic peoples were believers, devout participants in rituals small and grand, or were there apathetic people, even atheists? My conclusion is that yes, as in our own societies, there were doubters, detractors, and people who adhered to idiosyncratic explanations for events and circumstances. And it is in thinking about the end of the elaborate ceremonies in the LIV, SOV, South Carolina to Florida, and in the Susquehanna area where these doubters emerge most clearly. If there were pilgrimage centers and major ceremonial centers around the eastern Woodlands and coasts that stimulated the movement of goods and social gatherings, if Ken Sassaman is correct in thinking that ethnogenesis was *the* social activity of the era, then the loss of faith and practice in any one geographical area would have had ramifications for the surrounding areas. Sassaman (2010a:192) reviewed "some of the relational consequences of climate change at the close of the Archaic period by considering how local effects set off chain reactions that encompassed entire regions, even subcontinents, as groups experienced realignments of personnel and places."

Perhaps the practice of human sacrifice was the breaking point. Perhaps the weeks given over to preparations for megafeasts and ceremonials were too taxing. Perhaps the incantations and offerings proffered during the ceremonials failed in the face of multiple-year hurricanes, earthquakes, or ruptured social relationships. Perhaps a visionary preached a message that contradicted popular ritual practice. In short, it seems that there was some failure of the belief system, the cult concerns, that resulted in the abandonment and then avoidance of previously honored persistent places. Some Navajo people have expressed such an idea about the abandonment of Chaco Canyon, that dark powers accumulated in the canyon, causing it to be abandoned (*Mystery of Chaco Canyon* 2003). David Anderson has proposed something similar: that the lack of interest in Poverty Point after it was abandoned might be because something bad had happened there (2010:300n22). Less sinister for the shell-ring feasters is that perhaps the competitive feasting finally resulted in a winner, the last group standing so to speak, the other groups having dropped out over the generations because of the escalating cost of participating (exacerbated by a receding shoreline and its oyster resources). Whatever the explanations for culture change may be, there were rites and beliefs at the close of the Archaic that would continue to hold sway for the next 3,500 years and others that seem to have dissolved.

A partial list of the dozens of ideas that were present at the close of the Archaic and were still visible in Mississippian times includes the following:

1. caves/sinkholes as portals to the Underworld and places for renewal rites
2. the taking of tonali via limbs, heads
3. the association of the four cardinal points with life stages
4. the belief that menstruating women were so powerful as to need to retreat
5. the association of women with weaving, braiding, and reproduction
6. the use of the foot motif as fertility symbol
7. the shell as a renewal, adoption, fertility symbol
8. gastropods as spiraling symbols associated with beginning time and the importance of the counterclockwise direction seen in the use of the left-spiraling *Busycon contrarium* shell throughout eastern North America

9. the use of bone shrines
10. the use of points and chips in offerings
11. the use of the Standard Unit and triangular layout of sites
12. the C-shaped ceremonial earthworks and shellworks
13. the recognition and significance of the numbers 13, 20, and 52
14. the use of plazas
15. the creation of dirt mounds and sand mounds
16. the dog as leader of the dead, of priests, and rebalancer
17. the symbolic import of copper
18. the use of limestone in burials
19. the hunt god rite
20. the recognition of a prior creation

The end of the Archaic did signal the end of several rituals and beliefs and, what is more significant, the major cults. One can hardly imagine what the social life of Early Woodland people became in light of the absence of these big cults. There must have been long hours of storytelling. Archaic-like rites of renewal did continue, many of the mnemonic devices continued to be duplicated by later priests (shell beads, large blades), and some of the places were honored with point offerings, reused for burial, or avoided. Any effort to understand Hopewell or Mississippian ritualizing must start in the Archaic.

Part II

Annotated Sampler of Sites

Part II contains 91 alphabetically ordered annotations of a biased sample of sites that emphasize not their dates or projectile point styles but rather what appear to be supporting data for rituals and beliefs. Figures 1–4 provide the location of each site annotated. The sites annotated in this part are by no means the only sites where evidence of ritual behavior can be posited, and twice the number of sites discussed here are mentioned in parts I and III.

Adair Glyph Cave, Kentucky

Torch charcoal within this cave returned a date of 3560+/-110 B.P., or Late Archaic. Mud glyphs were found on the floor of a passage more than one kilometer inside the cave. These glyphs were "'geometric' symbols including trailed lines, zigzags, hatching and cross-hatching, and chevrons" (Faulkner 1997:151).

See *cave, design elements*

Afton Springs, Oklahoma

This sulfur spring in northeastern Oklahoma contains mammoth and mastodon bones buried under thousands of lithic pieces, primarily post-Pleistocene in age. "A deer antler from the springs has been radiocarbon dated to around 3,000 years BP" (Ray, Lopinot, and Hajic 2009:188), and Afton points have a date range of 3000 B.C. to 1000 B.C. (http://www.arrowheadology.com/forums/typology/8315-afton.html, accessed June 14, 2014). The association of Pleistocene fauna with lithics in a spring is suggestive of offerings and is duplicated in other springs and sinkholes.

See *fossil, mammoth/mastodon, paint/powder, spring, sinkhole*

Allumettes and Morrison Sites, Quebec

These two island sites on the Ottawa River appear to have been bone shrines given their density of bones: 82 bones/m^2 and 40/m^2, respectively. Human burials were added to the bone collection, 18 and 21, respectively. No hearths were encountered at either site, indicating to the authors that there was neither a fire included in the mortuary program nor a habitation site present. There is an "exceptional number of abrading stones" in both sites, and there is much "variability exhibited by the bone, copper and chipped stone tools" (Chapdelaine and Clermont 2006:198).

Fabrication of bone and copper items appears to have occurred at both places. Allumettes is the older and the bigger of the two bone shrines, dating to 4200 B.C. with a higher bone density, two times the artifacts, and four times the copper wastage material of Morrison, which dates to ca. 3500 B.C. Allumettes has "amazing numbers" (Chapdelaine and Clermont 2006:198) of conical copper points while there are none at Morrison. Copper bracelets, rings, and heavy tools are absent from Allumettes, but there are more fragments of ulus and bannerstones there. People visiting both island shrines brought in Onondaga cherts and Lake Superior copper.

Expended bifacial tools dominate the chipped-stone items with most chert points made elsewhere, suggestive of offerings. Hundreds of abraders made of local sandstone were recovered. Beaver incisors and bone tools occur in large numbers.

Morrison visitors buried their dead as extended bodies in shallow pits of 75 cm or less in the copper workshop areas. Grave goods were rare, but red ocher was frequent. "There is no pattern regarding the body orientation, and the nature or quantity of offerings associated with age and sex. A similar pattern can be recognized at Allumettes" (Chapdelaine and Clermont 2006:198).

Among the 45,000 bone specimens and 30 taxa at Allumettes and the 15,100 specimens and 45 taxa from Morrison, mammalian remains rank first followed by fish and reptiles. Morrison deposits were dominated by eel bones, but beaver bones were also important. Deer might have been more important at Allumettes. These differences in Underworld and This World creatures could indicate that the two shrines were actually paired, expressing a cosmic duality. Birds and amphibians were relatively rare in both shrines (Chapdelaine and Clermont 2006:196).

See *bone shrine, bone soul, island*

Anderson, Tennessee

This early Middle Archaic shell-bearing site had a distinct mortuary area containing at least 73 people, among which were flexed burials, infants, three cremations, and three individuals with red ocher. Twenty-three graves had grave goods including marine shell items, shell and stone atlatl weights, stone beads, bone pins, and lithics (Dowd 1989).

The most interesting of the burials were those of Bu53 and Bu73, both cremations containing antlers and atlatl parts. A hunt god rite could be represented in these two cases, although without better contextual information it seems that the expected associated burials are missing. Perhaps the inclusion of an atlatl and cremation were sufficient to hold the rite.

Other interesting burials include a woman with a pipe, several bodies with vertebral compression fractures, and two bodies placed in opposite directions in the same pit (Dowd 1989). Several of the burials here were in undersized pits, forcing the head into an unnatural position, or were found in strange, even "grotesque" positions, including the rare torso-twisted position. The twisted burial, Bu18, is also interesting for the use of limestone slabs. This young male was buried in a refuse pit, tightly flexed with head twisted or slumped and "the knees touching the back of the head. Three large limestone slabs rested directly on the skull area and three other large slabs covered most of the skeleton. Evidently, after burial, the pit had been covered with limestone slabs as protections against predators" (Dowd 1989:86). Perhaps the slabs were more about containing a potentially wandering soul. Grave goods with this burial were plentiful, including two deer long bones, an awl, a drilled bone bead, and an antler shaft straightener.

An intense burn, labeled Feature 5, suggests a communal rite around a fire. Level 3 contained a dramatic increase in the number and species of birds. Among them were cardinal, prairie chicken, two species of owl, grebe, goose, swan, two species of duck, crane, turkey, quail, pigeon, and crow. There are numerous collections of limestone at Anderson including several revealing a circular form, some weighing 40 pounds (Dowd 1989). Several types of burials and Feature 5 indicate one or more ceremonies at this site.

See *bird, bone pin, burial—under limestone, burial—posture, hunt god rite*

Arnold Research Cave, Missouri

Arnold Research Cave is a single, large, vaulted area on the north bank of the Missouri River, nearly identical in outward appearance to Graham Cave. It has mixed deposits spanning late Paleoindian to later prehistoric material.

Arnold Cave provides the best example of a cave used for fertility offerings, in this case in the form of footwear. As explained in the entry "feet/footprint/track," feet, tracks, and footwear were probably fertility symbols used in petitioning for pregnancy. At least 32 sandals were recovered from mixed strata inside and along the talus slope outside the shelter. Three of 18 sandals/slippers examined by Kuttruff and colleagues (1998) were complete, and five specimens were less than half complete. All showed use. The oldest sandal dated to 8325–8100 B.P. and the most recent to eight centuries ago, demonstrating a long history of this petitioning and that the petitioner did not need to offer a complete or new slipper or pair of slippers.

The presence of copious sandals in this cave and at Mammoth Cave is unique in the eastern United States but reminiscent of caves surrounding the Great Basin that contain dozens of individual slippers or sandals. I propose that this western practice is in evidence here in Missouri and offers support for Sassaman's Ancestry II migration (2010a).

See *cave, feet/footprint/track, rockshelter, sandal/slipper*

Ashworth Shelter, Kentucky

Ashworth is an east-facing shelter on Floyd's Fork, a tributary of the Salt River in Bullitt County, where salt licks abound. It is of interest for three reasons: the discard of naiads in Early Archaic context, the human burials, and the deposit of most of a dog. Not only is this dog one of the oldest dogs found in the east, but it is also of interest because it was deposited in a rockshelter and had been butchered rather than buried, suggesting that it was consumed (Phil DiBlasi, personal communication with the author, 2009).

Ten human burials were recovered from inside the shelter, two of which may be Early Archaic in age and the other eight may be Late Archaic (DiBlasi 1976). Bu4, a woman, was found facedown, head to the southeast, in the Early Archaic stratum, with an Early Archaic point embedded in a vertebra. A second point was found near her knee. Once in the ground at the back of the shelter, her body was covered with limestone slabs. She was 27–30 yo with significant upper and lower jaw abscesses. Bu4 is one of the oldest examples of a shooting victim in the east. It is interesting that this was a woman and her body was placed in a rockshelter. Unlike Bu4, Bu9 consisted only of two patellas and eight phalanges.

The early Late Archaic burials, 4000–3000 bc, included two men, a toddler, three infants, an adolescent, and another adult. (Was there a four-age rite conducted or buried here?) Bu2, a 45+ yo male, was facedown, head to the east and covered with limestone slabs. Bu5 was a toddler on its back with three turkey phalanges at its right wrist. Bu6, an infant with a displaced skull, was covered with rocks. DiBlasi (1976) thought that infants Bu3 and Bu6 might have been twins, interred together, and were later intruded upon by an adult burial. Bu8 was on its back, skull to the west, 15–17 yo and radiocarbon dated to 1900+/-165 bc. Bu8 was an articulated youth but damaged and charred by the construction of an adjacent hearth.

Two other individuals were represented by a newborn's maxilla and the stray vertebra and phalanges of adult. The facedown position is most unusual and with the addition of limestone slabs suggests that the living wished to keep the souls of these three individuals contained in the pits and in the shelter.

See *burial—under limestone, burial—posture, dog, rockshelter*

Austin Cave, Tennessee

The east-facing Austin Cave is a double entrance cave on the western Highland Rim in Tennessee. The fields surrounding the cave have yielded numerous Paleoindian and Archaic lithic tools as has the area immediately in front of the cave. Springs, sinkholes, and caves are prominent features of the landscape around and adjacent to Austin Cave.

One-meter-square units were placed 4 meters out from the center of the cave entrance and at the basal level of a small sink, as well as uphill and to the north of the cave, and 4 other units formed a trench southwest of the cave to sample "midden" in the sink (Barker 1997). These 6 m^2 of excavation yielded 52,952 flakes and formal tools, 97 percent coming from the trench and a feature; 45,519 items were bifacial thinning flakes, tertiary flakes, and broken flakes, 97 percent from the trench. The trench also held most of the 462 points, 24 refashioned point scrapers, and 93 cores. Blocky debris (4,327 pieces) and cortical flakes (2,240 pieces) indicate that some raw materials were worked here. The diagnostic points span the Archaic era (Barker 1997).

Other items recovered were half of a banded green slate bannerstone (parts of 6 others are in private collections), 5 hammers, 3 bell-shaped pestles, and 8,693 pieces of bone, 99 percent from the deepest level in the trench. Nineteen percent of this material was identifiable to at least family level. Pieces of a minimum of two people were included in the trench sample and of one person in other units (Barker 1997:210).

The identified faunal sample from the 4 m^2 of trench is remarkable in the variety of animals and the minimum number of animals yet represents only 19 percent of the bone collected. The middle stratum, Stratum II, yielded a minimum of 2 deer (25 bones) and then 1–7 bones of 8 other mammals, 2 birds, 1 snake, and 2 turtles. Stratum III yielded a minimum of 9 deer, 16 gray squirrels, 5 raccoons, 5 passenger pigeons, 4 fox squirrels, woodchucks, and rabbits, and 9 minnows in addition to 1–3 individuals of 35 additional species. Among the birds found throughout the 6 units were 3 sandhill cranes, 1 hawk, 1 trumpeter swan, and 4 geese. Aquatic gastropods were found in all strata of the trench (Barker 1997).

Radiocarbon dates and diagnostic projectiles emphasize Middle Archaic activities, or 6650+/-80 rcy to 5990+/-90 rcy, and a rough span of 500 years at this cave. Barker has noted that four fluted preforms were recovered in Stratum III of the trench, that Clovis and Dalton artifacts had been collected from the surface, and that Stratum I in the trench contained items dating to Late Archaic and Early Woodland activities.

Several themes repeated throughout this guide are applicable to the interpretation of the archaeological record at Austin Cave. One is that the bulk of the material comes from the bottom of a sink off of which the cave mouth is found. Five square meters excavated in this sink yielded extraordinary quantities of flakes, points, and individual animals. A single square meter unit and eight shovel tests that sampled the rim of the sink revealed bones, points, and flakes. Another theme is the deposition of projectile points and flakes as offerings. A third theme is that of bone soul and faunal offerings at bone shrines.

The Austin Cave site can be interpreted as a "Mid-Holocene base camp used throughout the year" (Barker 1997:217) with later items washed in from the sink's rim and surroundings or as a fertility shrine. The extremely high number of bones, flakes, and points, as well as the variety of animals, suggest another scenario: the sinkhole shrine. In this interpretation, the fauna, points, and flakes were offerings, the sinkhole a focal point for the concerted efforts of people to solicit Underworld patronage. Given the emphasis on flakes and the possible association of flakes with children and lineage, this sinkhole was perhaps even a destination of ritual practitioners conducting a fertility ritual to call out the resident spirit of rain using flake and point offerings. This shrine was chosen not only because of the sinkhole-with-cave configuration but also because of the remains of the Stone People found here, seen in the fluted points. It was visited most often during the Middle Archaic but pilgrims continued to solicit the Underworld spirits here into the Early Woodland. In this interpretation, Austin Cave is more appropriately thought of as Austin Sinkhole and is somewhat similar to Hendricks Cave (Sinkhole) in Ohio although it lacks the human body offerings of Hendricks.

See *bone shrine, flake/chip, Hendricks Cave, projectile point, sinkhole, Stone People*

Bailey, Tennessee

This site in south-central Tennessee with a radiocarbon date of 4450+/-80 rcy (Bentz 1988) is a good candidate for a Late Archaic ritual center with both lithic shrine and bone shrine functions. A possible circular temple/shrine or ritual house had an internal screen, hearths, and large-volume pits

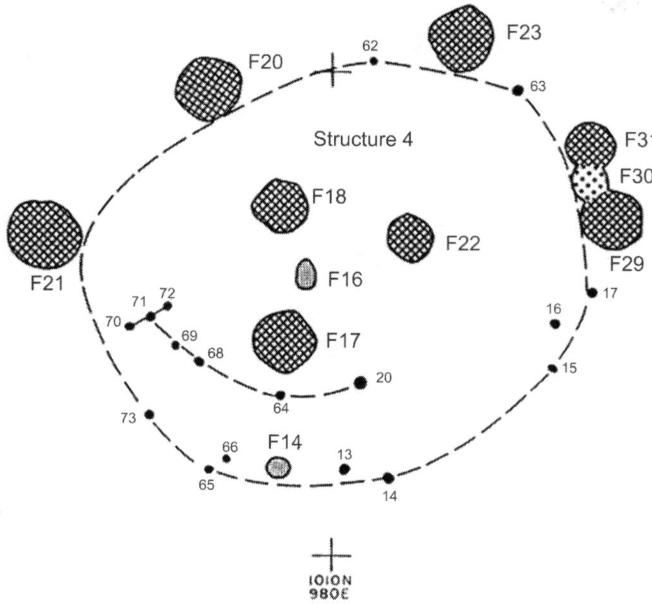

8. Structure 4 at the Bailey site with exterior pits and interior windscreen (• = postholes, larger circles = pits, medium circles = hearths). (Reprinted from Bentz 1988, TDOT Publications in Archaeology 2, with permission of Tennessee Dept. of Transportation and Charles Bentz.)

(Figure 8). "This structure was approximately four times larger than the average shelter size. A hearth flanked by three deep storage pits was positioned in the center of the structure and a second interior hearth was adjacent to the south wall. Six additional [large, deep, and medium] storage pits [and shallow hearths] ringed the north half of the structure just outside of [the house] and adjacent to the wall" (Bentz 1988:8). Structure 4 had a floor area of 73.4 m^2. A partial interior wall may have served as a screen. Three other structures at the site were open-ended rather than closed (Bentz 1988).

One hundred forty-six pits yielded a total of 347,000 pieces of chert debitage and 1,530 chert tools, primarily local Ft. Payne cherts. One feature had 13 Ledbetter points. Twenty-two thousand bone and antler pieces were recovered including those from a Canada goose, a snake, and a dog burial in a pit. At least seven of ten flexed human burials were in Late Archaic contexts and none had grave goods. This might be an example of the combination of bone shrine and lithic shrine, both of them focused on fertility (Bentz 1988).

See *bone shrine, dog, flake/chip, shrine, stone*

Ballybrack Mound, Labrador

Two boulder mounds at this site once covered the remains of humans. Mound 1 was 5 m in diameter and hid a conical pit filled with red ocher–stained sand and more boulders and several broken bifaces. At the bottom of the 1-m-deep pit was a shallow oval depression containing a thick deposit of red ocher. Mound 2 was very similar in shape and pit contents with charcoal that yielded a date of 7065+/-70 B.P. (Fitzhugh 2006).

See *mound—boulder, Nulliak Mounds, Rattler's Bight*

Barrington Oaks, Missouri

Feature 2 at this site was a basin pit 12 x 36 x 10 cm. It contained a cache of 5 Early Archaic points facing the same direction (southeast) but all of different types with shaped rock forms at each end of the cache. Softrock had been carved into a fish shape and rested underneath the stack. A 6-ounce lump of melted lead was positioned next to the cache. A geode and an hourglass-shaped piece of dolomite as well as witch hazel seeds rounded out the cache, interpreted as a ritual specialist's bundle (Harl 2009:379).

See *medicine, medicine bag, ritual specialist/priest*

Big Sandy, Alabama

This "site occupies a small knoll overlooking the southern portion of a diminutive, yet deep, sinkhole in the center of a large cultivated field a few hundred meters from a creek. . . . The terrain is very rocky, made up of quartzite pebbles and chalky limestone cobbles" as well as red soil (Cole 2006:37). Collectors have recovered 13 Clovis, 14 Cumberland, and well over 100 Big Sandy points and "nearly as many Daltons." In the vicinity of Big Sandy are over a dozen camps ranging from Dalton to Early Archaic with "at least that many of each [point] type . . . recovered in various other portions of the district" (Cole 2006:37). Cole also recognized that the sink itself was important: "[P]erhaps the sink could also provide an interesting study" (2006:37).

Cole's unique study of Paleoindian point colors led to the conclusion that Big Sandy had more connections to other Paleoindian sites in Limestone County during Clovis and Cumberland point use times than any other site in the county. Here is fodder for theories about the long-term attraction of some sinkholes for surrounding populations and about points as offerings, their color being an important element of the offering.

See *color, projectile point, sinkhole*

Black Earth, Illinois

Excavations in three areas of this site near the Indiana border in the Saline River valley revealed much about Archaic ritual and beliefs. Area B had 18 graves with 24 bodies. Area A had 201 burials with 223 bodies in the Middle Archaic component, 124 of which could be used in analysis. All were dated to 3955 B.C. or more recent (Jefferies and Butler 1982). This site is interesting for the evidence of violent death, a four-age rite, and the burial of a ritual specialist.

Evidence for violent deaths is found in the burial positions: extended, facedown, and multiple burials. A surprising 47 percent of the bodies were extended, the highest percentage of such burials in the Midwest. This posture that in the SOV signals violent death was most frequently associated with infants, subadults, and young adults. Twice as many extended bodies as flexed bodies had grave goods (Jefferies and Butler 1982:190).

Three bodies were placed facedown, a probable violent death position. Seven adults and one subadult were covered with clay caps, four of whom had ceremonial items and all of whom were interred on their backs. Seven of them were extended. (The nearly equal proportion of extended and flexed bodies is repeated only at Frontenac Island burial ground in New York, where that trait suggested a shared burial ground between at least two groups with different burial practices.)

There were nine multiple burials in Area A, one with four individuals, two with three bodies, and six with a pair of skeletons, accounting for 22 people. Thirteen of these people were flexed. The four-body grave shows the four-age distribution that has been suggested as a rite: infant, child, young adult, and mature adult. One person was extended. Only 9 percent of the multiple-burial individuals had grave goods compared to 31 percent of single interments (Lynch 1982:1160). As in the Green River area, there were no cremations deposited in Black Earth.

Head orientations showed a strong preference for cardinal west for subadults and men. When the burial area was divided into quadrants, there were no discernable patterns in burial form, age, or sex distributions (Lynch 1982: 1137–1139).

Grave goods included single mussel valves, animal jaws, awls, utilized flakes, tines, anculosa beads, bone pins, needles, carapace cups, red ocher, and quartzite pebbles. A few cases of elk antler cups, fluorspar crystals, crinoid beads, and banded slate, as well as a gorget, were noted. According to Nance, single mussel valves "must be assigned some kind of ceremonial status" (1986:11). A carapace rattle with quartz pebbles was like the "Indian Knoll" rattle (Breitburg 1982).

One man, Bu137, the richest burial, has been interpreted as a ritual specialist based on the 45 grave goods including a miniature ax, eagle talons, bear phalanges, and an elk antler cup (Lynch 1982:1151).

The 197,844 pieces of fauna from Area A were, like the collection from Indian Knoll, rich in deer remains, suggesting that this area of the site had a bone shrine function and/or deer feast use. Eleven percent of the deer bones came from the axial skeleton, 24 percent from the head, 13 percent from the foreleg, and 21 percent from the hind leg; in addition, 7 percent were metapodials, and 24 percent were feet.

See *bone pin, bone shrine, deer, cardinal direction, four-age rite, Frontenac Island, gambling, miniature, ritual specialist/priest, rattle*

Bluegrass, Indiana

Bluegrass was a Middle and Late Archaic shell-free burial ground and encampment with 138 pits, 80+ human burials, and 11 dog burials. The high number of dog sacrifice rites marks this site as an important ceremonial center (Claassen 2010), but the confusion over component attribution for the dog rites (and the human burials) frustrates efforts to understand this ritual. One adult human–dog pairing was found in the center of the site near the highest point while the other 10 dogs were buried outside the cemetery area to the southeast (Stafford and Cantin 2009).

Bluegrass is distinctive among SOV shell-free burial grounds not only for the high number of dog burials but also for the inclusion of animal jaws in 7.3 percent of the graves (Claassen 2010). Atlatl parts and carapace rattles were included in a few graves (Stafford and Cantin 2009:308), which may have been elements in first-kill rites, hunt god rites, or other rituals. Also surprising was that 4 percent of the identified fauna were rattlesnakes and racers, animals typically found in only trace quantities and associated with Underworld and rain rites in ethnographic examples. Bluegrass people participated in the engraved bone-pin circuit of the Midwest (Jefferies 2004) possibly indicating mortuary gambling.

See *bone pin, divination, dog sacrifice rite, first-kill rite, gambling, paint pot, snake*

Bluffton Burial Mound, Florida

The base of this mound was a freshwater gastropod matrix, in the center of which was a shell ridge. Above this was a one-meter-thick layer of sand with some shell mixed in, with successive layers of shell, black organic muck, sand, and brown sand with shell at the surface (Aten 1999). Burials lacked grave goods. A recent AMS date on human bone returned an estimate of 5660–5320 B.P. (Randall and Tucker 2012:222).

Sears (1960) found a single burial on top of a preexisting shell floor that had been burned. Sears offered the following sequence of events. First, a fire was built on the floor and then the body put on the old shell midden. Next it was covered with what might have been alligator feces. Then basketloads of sand were put on top of that followed by alternating sand, shell mix, sand, a layer of "gumbo," sand, and finally a large deposit of shell and a second burial at the mound's edge, "all constituting a single event" (Randall and Tucker 2012:222). Was this individual a ritual specialist?

Today this mound is 30.5 m in diameter and 4.9 m tall. The shell it contains is primarily the freshwater gastropod *Viviparus georgianus*. It is part of a large shellworks, including a shell ridge and shell dome (Randall and Tucker 2012:221).

See *Cult of the Snail Shell*, *feces*, *ritual specialist/priest*, *shellworks*

Breckenridge Shelter, Arkansas

This large overhang in the Ozarks opens to the south at the base of a steep limestone bluff above the White River. Of probable ritual significance are an intermittent spring located 500 ft (152.40 m) east of the shelter and a small waterfall that flows over the middle of the shelter's overhang during heavy rain.

Deposits here are exceptionally deep. Perishables were recovered in the center of the floor area and pits were found lined with grass secured by strips of split cane or basketry (Wood [1962] 2000:56). A stone pipe, a shell pendant, a wooden hoop, and a cane flute were among the remains in this section as was a low stone wall 18 ft (5.49 m) long in the west end of the shelter.

In addition to isolated phalanges and a skull, five burials were recovered, three at the back wall in each third of the shelter and two in the western end. Bu1 was an infant found in a crevice between slabs, skull missing but oriented to the west. Bu2, an extended facedown adult, was in a crevice under limestone fall rock. The skull was charred. "There were large numbers of animal bones around the body: 135 pieces, including deer, terrapin, mollusks, bear, elk (?), squirrel, and turkey. These bones, all of them broken, were largely on the right side of the body. A modified deer skull and a mandible; a chert knife and a chert hammer; and an arrow point, dart point, and chert knife were on the left side of the burial" (Wood [1962] 2000:59). Bu3, 5 m northeast of Bu2, was found between two large limestone fall rocks 66 cmbs. This flexed adult on its left side was covered by a fine gray ash, but there was no sign of burning. A scraper and deer ulna awl were near the left hand. Bu4 was a desiccated infant strapped in a cradle put on a bed of grass over a bed of dense ash 30 cmbs and probably was an Archaic burial. Bu5 was a flexed, facedown adult near the back of the shelter 100 cmbs, represented by a portion of the skeleton. Two highly polished awls were at the distal end of one humerus (Wood [1962] 2000:72).

Of these five Archaic individuals, two infants and three adults, infant Bu1 may have been a sacrifice, and adult Bu2 and infant Bu4 appear to have died under unusual circumstances given their facedown positioning. Bu3's posture, between and under large rocks, also suggests a disturbing death in the view of the person's contemporaries.

See *burial—posture, burial—under limestone, rockshelter, Russell Cave, sacrifice—infant and child*

Bullskin Creek, Ohio

Vickery (2008:14–15) believed that a priest's cache was found at the Bullskin Creek site in southern Ohio. Occurring in a pit were "a deer antler atlatl hook, a box turtle carapace cup, the articulated remains of the forearm and talons of a great horned owl, a hematite rubstone, a concretion, an unmodified amphibian bone, and deer antler tools that included a tine flaker, projectile point, and awl. At a lower level, but having been placed on the ground surface . . . were a piece of limonite, a large worked deer antler, an Early Archaic projectile point, and a McWhinney point" (Vickery 2008:14–15). It seems this priest had collected an old point. Elsewhere in this site barred owl and red-tail hawk were found (Vickery 2008:22). The contents of a second cache were given as "hardstone roller pestle preform and associated chert hammer near the edge of a roasting pit" (Vickery 2008:15).

Three tightly flexed burials were found in a roasting pit (4051–2213 B.C.), none with grave goods or any indication of age or sex. One of these bodies had an embedded point.

See *antler, atlatl, awl, deer, DuPont, owl, rattle, ritual specialist/priest*

Caddy Park, Massachusetts

An hourglass-shaped feature outlined in red ocher was 1 m x 2 m in size, oriented slightly west of north and was found on top of the glacial till in Quincy, Massachusetts (Figure 9). Its 256 artifacts included flaked-stone tools (140 quartz tools and preforms), 4 unique large blades, groundstone tools, 6

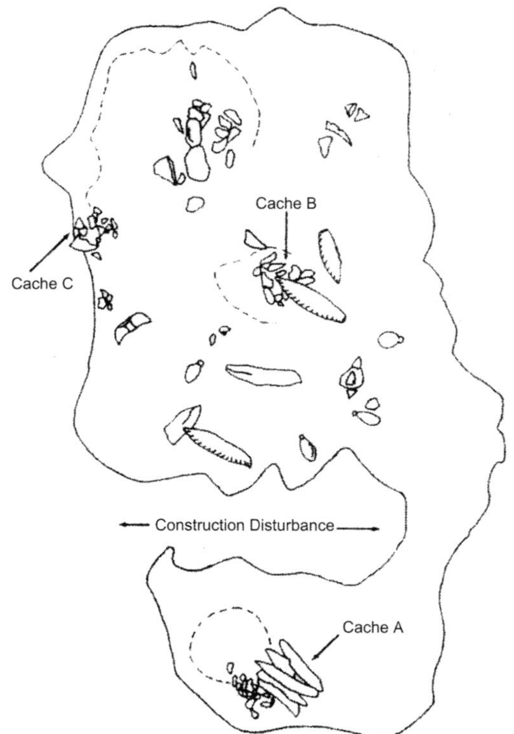

9. Caddy Park, Massachusetts, floor plan of feature. (Reprinted from Mahlstedt and David 2002:Figure 2, with permission from the Massachusetts Archaeological Society.)

plummets, 1 whale tail atlatl weight, and stone ornaments (Mahlstedt and David 2002). The only broken item included in the feature was a whale tail pendant. A third whale-related object was an effigy gouge.

Several caches were placed inside this feature. Red ocher was sprinkled on the ground before a cache of adzes was made and then on top of all of the caches. Four biface and preform caches found in this feature had 66, 42, 24, and 7 items, respectively. The larger two caches seemingly had been contained in bags. A smaller cache was positioned next to a possible stone-polishing kit.

Mahlstedt and David argue that this large, deep feature outlined with red ocher and containing giant blades and whale images was an offering to Maushop, "accredited with forming much of coastal southern New England, including Quincy Bay. . . . a benevolent giant who drove whales onto the shore as food for his followers" (2002:21), and that many of the cached tools had been made specifically for this offering.

See *cache—blade, number, ocher, offering*

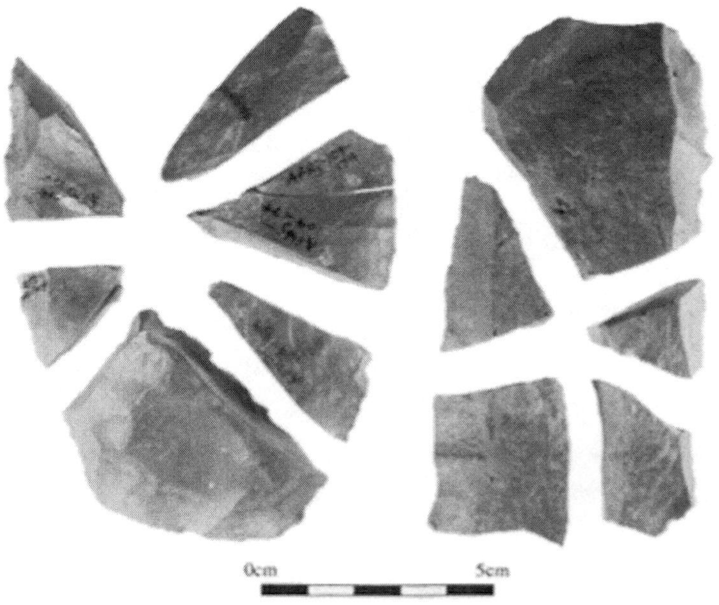

10. Ritually broken bifaces in the Caradoc cache. (Photo courtesy of Chris Elliss.)

Caradoc Site, Ontario

This isolated late Paleoindian blade cache was found 4 km from the older Crowfield site. Some 75 tools, 67 of them thick, rudimentarily shaped siliceous stones had been smashed or sacrificed by one to three blows to their midpoints and the pieces placed on the southeast side of a knoll on the surface (Deller and Ellis 2001). This knoll was set back from a third-order stream in a remote setting. Only four of the tools were finished. Sixty-two refits showed that the pieces had dropped within a constrained area, suggesting a possible structure or shrine. The authors call this cache an offering (Figure 10).

While the dominance of unfinished forms is common in early Great Lakes caches (Deller and Ellis 2001:275), some of the significant differences from those caches include the following: (1) these pieces at Caradoc were not burned, (2) they were intentionally broken, (3) the stone source was 175 km away, and (4) the set weighed 2.6 kg, representing a heavy load to transport this far—an expensive offering to make.

In addition to the oval chunks of Bayport chert, there were 10 nonsiliceous items, 5 sandstone pebbles, an iron pyrite nodule, and 27 unifacially modified flakes. Here again is evidence that flakes and pebbles were a part of offerings.

See *breakage, cache—blade, Crowfield, offering*

Claiborne, Mississippi

Claiborne is a shell arc with abundant soapstone vessels. A cache containing twelve soapstone vessels, two copper sheet bracelets, one copper pendant, and a cube of galena was found in sand near the peak of the shell arc. A short, conical earthen mound was sited to the east of this cache. These constructions are separated by the Standard Macro-Unit (86.63 m). This cache recalls a similar cache at Poverty Point (Sassaman 2010a:63). It may also be viewed as paired with the nearby Cedarland site in an oppositional dualistic relationship.

"Claiborne is, in some respects, a one-sixth model of Poverty Point in reverse. [When enlarged six times] the spatial articulation between Poverty Point and Claiborne is uncanny. Besides their geometric conformity, the line of sight between the low mound and the soapstone cache at Claiborne is very close to the reciprocal line connecting Mound A to the central plaza at Poverty Point" (Sassaman 2010a:63). Sassaman believes that people from Claiborne were part of the team that laid out the Poverty Point enclosure after 3600 B.P. "Claiborne delivered to Poverty Point not only soapstone but also the idea of arcuate compounds, residences on ridges, and mounds placed to the backside of the arc" (Sassaman 2010a:63, 65).

See *duality, geometry, measurement, Poverty Point*

Coburn, Massachusetts

A single pit on Cape Cod with four greasy black stains located roughly in the cardinal directions was presumably the final resting place of four or more cremated individuals although the bone evidence was lacking (Dincauze 1968). The southern stain contained 132 items including many points, adzes, axes, and plummets, a few of which were burned. The western stain lacked blades but contained 2 of 3 recovered pestles and 43 other items. The northern area had 4 caches of points, 1 in red ocher, plus 8 random items. The eastern blackened area had 1 point cache and 28 other items (points, adze, pestle, ax). The general fill of the pit held few burned items.

The 300-plus items were indicative of fishing, hunting, woodworking, and grinding activities, using locally available stone. Dincauze (1968) concluded that the cremations were deposited simultaneously and were accompanied by the worn-out, unfinished, or broken objects of their community. The five caches, although unburned, were also comprised of used blades and points. This burial rite occurred late in the Late Archaic. The numbers of associated items are fodder for a study of numerical symbolism.

See *breakage, burning, cache—blade, number, offering, trash/midden*

Crowfield, Ontario

Sassaman (2010a:79) noted that 4,500 burned fragments formed an estimated 200 complete tools found at Crowfield. Parts of 29 fluted points were found in a probable cremation pit, 1.5 m in diameter by 20 cm deep. The lack of debitage and the fact that all tools had been whole at the time of burning and showed no manufacturing error or use breakage indicated that these 200 tools were elements of a ritual cache. Furthermore, there were, for an assumed habitation site, several rare types of tools (Deller and Ellis 1984:49). "At least one tool had been broken by a blow to the center. No end scrapers were included in the feature although unheated endscrapers were found outside it, suggesting a possible male cremation" (Deller and Ellis 1984:51). The tools appear to have been utilitarian.

Deller and Ellis (1984) suggest that this feature had been associated with a Paleoindian cremation. If it was a cremation, this would be one of the oldest cremations in the New World and the oldest associated with fluted points although it is apparently a late Paleoindian deposit.

See *breakage, cache—other, Caradoc Site*

DuPont, Ohio

DuPont is a Late Archaic "midden" in southern Ohio with 30 burials, one of which was sitting (the rest flexed), and two of which had embedded points. In addition, there were platform burials unique in the Archaic (Vickery 2008:11). One of the victims, a 25 yo man, had four embedded points that had entered from behind, a marine shell and cannel coal bead necklace, an antler atlatl weight, a drill, and a box turtle carapace with a lump of red ocher inside, constituting a possible hunt god sacrifice (given the atlatl weight) or witch killing (given the possible indication of a ritual specialist's equipment). Red ocher had been sprinkled on his face. A second individual had been sprinkled with yellow and red ocher and had a bird bone flute and bone beads. Other grave goods were limestone or dolomite roller pestles, scraper planes, pieces of worked antler, a marble atlatl weight, perforated bone shuttle, perforated raccoon canine, a three-quarter grooved axe, another carapace container, various projectile points, a small mammal, and deer toe bones (Vickery 2008:12).

Huge earth ovens connected to each other with ventilator shafts suggested to Vickery (2008) that large groups had been present. At least one dog had been baked in clay, and numerous mussels apparently were as well.

See *antler, atlatl, ax, carapace, dog, hunt god rite, ocher, turtle, witch*

Dust Cave, Alabama

Utilization of this cave began around 12,900 B.P., indicating Paleoindian cave interest. Although the remains in this cave have been cast as habitation debris left by the Paleoindian, Early Archaic, and Middle Archaic peoples of the region (Hollenbach 2009; Walker et al. 2001) and the floral remains as evidence of general diet and foodways (Homsey, Walker, and Hollenbach 2010), there are several aspects of the setting and the data recovered that suggest ritualized use of the cave throughout the sequence.

One characteristic that makes this cave unlikely to have been a simple habitation locus was its very close proximity to the Perry shell mound, the mound with the highest number of human burials and dog burials in the Tennessee River valley. The adjacent Muscle Shoals may explain why this particular cave was selected and why the shell mound ceremonial center was later formed here. It is likely that sequestered activities associated with major rituals at the Perry shell mound took place in Dust Cave. Those activities would have been ones related to general seclusion of ritual specialists between rites, rites directed at an earth deity, feasting associated with rites removed from sight of the general audience gathered at the shell mound, burial of the founding ancestors, and rebalancing rites. Given that the dark zone was particularly dangerous for all but the most prepared specialists, the entrance chamber and outside the mouth of the cave were where pilgrims would have observed some rites. Inside the cave was the domain of specialists (including archaeologists). These two places—cave and shell mound—then should be viewed as a ceremonial complex starting in Middle Archaic times.

The excavations in the entrance chamber opened 100 m^2 of floor to reveal seven deposits 5 m thick (Homsey, Walker, and Hollenbach 2010). Entrance chamber activities included clay floor preparation, food preparation, cooking of fish, meat, and shellfish, cleanup activities (covered in Homsey, Walker, and Hollenbach 2010), nut oil rendering, nutmeat extraction, and burial of the dead (33 features). Features were most dense during the Middle Archaic.

One of these features contained a cache of goose humerii (Walker and Parmalee 2004). Clay floors appear as early as 12,000 B.P. but were most common in the Early and Middle Archaic, 12,000 to 6,000 ya (Sherwood and Chapman 2005:71). Four dog burials were found.

Nineteen individuals were apparently buried as corpses in Dust Cave and parts of eighteen others were recovered, all Middle Archaic in age (Turner 2006). A probable five-year-old child was the initial burial, in the Kirk Stemmed level, reminiscent of the initial infant burial at Russell Cave. The dead sorted into 18 adults, two subadults, one juvenile, nine children, and seven infants. One dog burial seemed to accompany the juvenile.

Thirty-two percent of the dead in this cave had violent deaths and another 16 percent probably did (Turner 2006:81). Six had cranial depression fractures (Turner 2006:130). The incomplete skeletons are not surprising given the similar record at Salts Cave.

Late Paleoindian fauna were 69 percent avian remains, half of those waterfowl and the highest percentage of any component in the cave, plus 19 percent mammals, 9 percent fish, 2 percent reptiles, and 1 percent amphibians. There was a high proportion of calcined bone (30 percent of all bone recovered), particularly for birds and mammals (Homsey, Walker, and Hollenbach 2010). In light of the high percentage of birds and low percentage of deer in the earliest levels, Driskell said, "Dust Cave may well represent an unusual site type whose faunal assemblage is not very indicative of overall subsistence activities during this early period [outside this cave]" (1996:323). As stated earlier, it would not be unexpected for the burial of particular ancestors, and the dog sacrifice rite in this cave, to have been associated with the rites conducted at the nearby Perry shell mound and for the two places to form a ritual complex.

See *baked-clay surface, burning, cave, dog sacrifice rite, mound—shell, sacrifice—adult*

Elizabeth Mounds, Illinois

These are bluff-top mounds overlooking the Illinois River valley with Middle Archaic and Woodland mortuary features. The location of this group of mounds is west of the Illinois River at the top of a steep bluff face with a commanding view toward the east and both upriver and downriver. This and other Middle Archaic mounds in the Illinois valley indicate that the land of the dead was conceptually "west" and that bluff tops were symbolically charged locations.

Of the 17 mounds and knolls at Elizabeth, Mound 1 alone contained Archaic burials. Mound 1 was a natural knoll on a high point on top of the bluff made of redeposited dirt, creating a long, low mound. "At least 68 individuals in enumerated burials and an additional 30–40 represented by isolated bones scattered through the mound fill were deposited in an area of less than 50 m^2" (Albertson and Charles 1988:29). Three burial episodes were evident in Mound 1: two large pit features with multiple burials and a third "flat cemetery" with single and multiple interments in shallow basins.

Pit Feature 4, possibly the first burial ritual, cut into a natural knoll and was stopped by the B horizon soils. The deepest burial (Bu32) contained five articulated skeletons lying on the B horizon, four teenagers and one man, a possible hunt god rite deposit. These bodies were aligned side by side and outfitted with *Leptoxis* (Milky Way) belts around their waists (but turned outside in), shell bead bracelets, and possible bear canine earrings on two skeletons. Two Middle Archaic points were inserted into the chest cavities of four of them sometime *after* decomposition began; we know this because (1) there was no damage to the surrounding ribs, (2) the points were put in base first from below the rib cage, and (3) "the inferiorly directed tips of the points with Skeleton 8 indicate that they were not hafted" (Albertson and Charles 1988:35). Bones from each individual were combined for a radiocarbon sample, returning an event date of 6340+/-90 rcy. Bones from an additional eleven individuals in Bu32 were recovered above the burial site: five women, two men, and four adolescents.

Above Bu32 at the southwest corner of Feature 4 was a headless man 25–30 yo with disarticulated elements of other individuals, covered with a large limestone slab (Bu31). The lack of cut marks on the vertebra indicated that his head had been removed after some time in the ground. Overlapping this man was a grouping of disarticulated elements (Bu24) from another five individuals: three men, a teenager, and a young adult, another possible hunt god rite. Intermingled with the bones were a ¾-grooved ax, an antler haft, two Godar plummets, and an Osceola point. "The extreme disarticulation of all bones and the differential representation of skeletal elements indicates that Burial 24 was an ossuary containing the remains of individuals who had been exposed long enough for the flesh to have decayed, buried elsewhere, or perhaps intentionally dismembered" (Charles, Leigh, and Albertson 1988:248). Elsewhere in Mound 1 was a loose cluster of isolated bones from three young adults (Albertson and Charles 1988:35–36). Feature 4, then, consisted of five interment events including two possible hunt god rites.

Along the original ridgeline was a series of pit burials comprising the

Flat Cemetery. The excavators were uncertain as to whether the incomplete skeletons were interred in that condition or disturbed by later digging for other single burials and a large burial pit, Feature 7. At least one burial in the Flat Cemetery was older than those in Feature 4, and several appeared to be contemporaneous with Feature 4. Fourteen bodies were definitely in the cemetery and six more may have been.

Feature 7 was a large basin, 6 m x 4 m, dug into the knoll itself and through the Flat Cemetery, and represents the last Archaic rite performed on this bluff top. Originating at the base of this feature were several burial pits holding eight skeletons. One of these eight burials had an Osceola point. One adult male was buried with an infant and crescent bannerstone on his pelvis. One male had the bones of another male and of a child with associated drill and Matanzas point. In addition to those eight bodies, seven more bodies were probably there as well, including two infants, two men, and one woman. The basin was then filled with reddish-brown soil, possibly stained by red ocher and possibly forming a low domed mound above the original surface level.

Here is a clear example of how spirit-filled places continued to stay present in the minds of later generations who saw the older facilities as auspicious places to be reused—in this case for later burials. Mounds 6–7 covered an Archaic habitation, suggesting that all of the later mounds may have used Archaic habitation midden for fill.

See *bluff, hunt god rite, Leptoxis/Anculosa, Milky Way, mound—dirt, sacrifice—adult*

Ervin, Tennessee

Ervin contains several features that demonstrate Middle Archaic ritualism. It is one of only two interior U.S. shell mounds, both on the Duck River, which are comprised primarily of riverine gastropods (Hofman 1986). It is located within an easy walk of Cheek Bend Cave downriver and a significant waterfall upriver. In addition to human burials in the shell, there were at least three earth renewal deposits left at the locus. Feature 22 contained a cremated human along with 18 other species, including burned bones of deer, raccoon, rabbit, mole, and turkey. Feature 35 contained bones of *Homo sapiens*, striped skunk, and four other species with burned bones from fox squirrel and humans. Feature 36 also contained burned human bone and 16 additional species. Some of the rabbit, woodchuck, squirrel, and gar bones were burned (Hofman 1986:112). In these offerings we see the use of fire, the inclusion of humans, the equality of humans and other animals, the importance of small animals, and the association of burning with particular species. These were probable world renewal offerings.

See *burning, gastropod, offering, world renewal rite*

Eva, Tennessee

Eva is a Middle Archaic shell-bearing and Late Archaic shell-free site on the north-flowing section of the Tennessee River. One hundred ninety-eight burials were uncovered, some with bone grave goods or ocher. The Eva stratigraphy gives us some evidence for the relative ages of different practices in the SOV. In the oldest, or Eva component (now dated to the Early Archaic; Thad Bisset, personal communication with the author, May 2013), as well as the subsequent components tight flexure is the norm for adult burials (137 of 152 bodies) but for only half of the infants and children. A flexed, head-first burial is among the Eva component burials as is a facedown, flexed burial. The head-first posture and the facedown posture are indicative of a violent death (Claassen 2010). Activities, then, began at Eva with two very unusual burial events. An initial large feature with antler and much faunal debris (Lewis and Lewis 1961) suggests a founding feast.

The early Late Archaic (Three Mile phase) gives us the first dog sacrifice rite, a sitting human burial, an extended burial, a turtle rite, and the use of ocher in burials. Green slate gorgets and copper beads appeared first in the late Late Archaic Big Sandy component as well as the burial of a ritual specialist with a rattlesnake necklace (Bu62). Eva differs from contemporaneous shell-bearing sites in the SOV in the complete lack of marine shell items and cremations and in the low frequency of projectile points and awls in graves. There also are no group burials. Two individuals were buried with atlatls in the Middle Archaic Stratum II and two were the rare torso-twisted burials, possibly associated with the hunt god rite.

Other evidence of ritual at Eva may be seen in a large deer feast preserved in the deepest stratum and covered over by the densest part of the subsequent burial ground. This Eva phase feast resulted in ash and charcoal under a mass of fire-cracked rocks, bones, debitage, artifacts, and large sections of unburned antler. Of the 884 identifiable bones, 770 were deer. The artifacts discovered there were two points, a drill, four blades, seven large choppers, an antler handle, a wide-bit antler scraper, and an antler flaker (Lewis and Lewis 1961:15). The excavators collected 14,000+ pieces of fauna from the Early Archaic Eva component and only 3,200 pieces from the rest of the site. This feast may have accompanied the two unusual burials and indicate a hunt god rite.

See *burial—posture, deer, feasting, hunt god rite, ritual specialist/priest, turtle shell rite*

Fernvale, Tennessee

The Fernvale site along the South Harpeth River is a multicomponent site with Middle Archaic through Mississippian components. Two burials are of interest. One, a cenotaph, had a marine shell gorget and collection of shell beads carefully stacked at one end. Cenotaphs are unusual in Archaic sites of the SOV and suggest later bone collecting.

Fernvale also had a burial of an adult male that included a bundle of artifacts: sharpened turkey bone awls and other modified bone tools, modified antler tine, disarticulated and stacked bivalves, stone tools, projectile points, the remains of three partially articulated dog paws, small nodules of raw pigment, evidence of degraded red ocher, and a possible tattoo tool kit (Deter-Wolf 2013). This individual may have been a ritual specialist.

See *dog, ocher, ritual specialist/priest, projectile point, tattooing*

Frontenac Island, New York

Key to understanding the symbolism of the mortuary rituals carried out at Frontenac Island from Late Archaic (4500 to 4000 B.P.) through Middle Woodland times is its setting on an island, "the only island in the Finger Lakes" (Ritchie 1945:2, quoted by Fox 2004b:52), and the fossiliferous character of the limestone. This lacustrine island has a fossiliferous limestone bedrock "storm beach backing a lower energy foreshore deposit" (Fox 2004b: 52). Both of these characteristics call forth the creation and long-ago time. Furthermore, the Frontenac Island shoreline seems to have been copied in Middle Woodland non-island burial mounds of the Lake Ontario area that began with an outer perimeter of river pebbles and then an inner perimeter of limestone slabs encircling a single central, often female, burial (Fox 2004b).

The mortuary area was located on the top of the mound and contained 163 burials in three groupings, three burials with box turtle shell rattles (Fox 2004b:53), several adult males with dogs (Strong 1985:33), and one eagle burial. Pits, hearths, and clusters of fire-cracked rock were also present.

What makes Frontenac Island unique during its milieu are (1) the inhumation of 162 people and cremation of but one person where the norm was cremation, (2) the large number of extended bodies, and (3) the mixture within the burial ground of both Lamoka and Brewerton artifacts and "head shapes," each with its distinctive burial postures. One group of flexed burials had Lamoka utilitarian grave goods. The second group of bodies was extended brachycephalic skeletons like those from the Brewerton sites, with artifacts of Brewerton affiliation. The third group was comprised of extended burials. Here is evidence of a shared burial ground.

In addition to objects of both Brewerton and Lamoka origin, these graves contained artifacts either not found in Archaic complexes of New York or modified from forms of the Lamoka and Brewerton phases. Among the new traits found with these and certain of the other burials were "antler spoons, an antler cup, turtle carapace dishes, an eyed bone needle, a bird effigy antler comb, and shell pendants" (Ritchie and Funk 1973:45).

Among the rites conducted at Frontenac Island may have been human sacrifice. According to Mensforth (2007), six men, a child, and an adolescent were headless and missing one or more limbs (two were torsos only), another man was headless in a group of three men, and two women were headless. One man had an embedded point in his forehead and attempts to remove it were unsuccessful (Mensforth 2007:218).

See *antler, burial—posture, fossil, head removal, island, rattle, sacrifice—adult, skull, trophy part, trophy part decommissioning rite*

Goddard, Pennsylvania

This large site on the top and southwestern slope of a large glacial kame overlooked a valley. Two possible Early Archaic structures were found on top of the kame. "A hearth and ca. 20–30 small post molds, forming two concentric semi-circles on the northern edge of the hearth area" (Koetje 1998:29), constituted Structure 1. That hearth had a date of 9180 B.P. and an associated MacCorkle point. Structure 2, much larger, is evident through six postholes, all 15–20 cm in diameter in two lines about 1.5 m apart. A large hearth sat just outside the structure, and another oval depression with reddened sediment lined with slabs on the bottom was located just inside the west end of the structure as defined by the postholes.

Two other large hearths make up part of the Late Archaic features found in a separate area of the kame. Near the edge of the knoll was a large burned basin that gave a radiocarbon date of 5130+/-200 rcy with a single heat-treated chert cobble inside (Koetje 1998:35). Koetje thought this pit had been a heat-treating facility; the three heat-treated flakes and all heat-treated points recovered came from this area.

Artifacts were sparse in the Early Archaic area yet the features were quite large and relatively substantial. Most of the flakes were tertiary flakes. Koetje found these characteristics to be contradictory. "There is a serious disjunction here between our expectations for a brief occupation . . . and the substantial energy investment evident from the features" (Koetje 1998:42).

The Late Archaic situation was also puzzling: heat-treating facilities and activities, a substantial hearth, several points, primary and secondary core reduction, groundstone, and artifacts associated with fishing but no structures. Again, only short-term stop-overs are indicated. "There are several other Late Archaic features that show a distinct pattern of apparently small, short-term occupations occurring within a large area centered on the knoll" (Koetje 1998:43).

What Koetje may have excavated was an Early Archaic shrine (structures) with hearth. The location was auspicious, the large size is appropriate, and the western internal hearth in the largest structure is located where groups in historic times located ritual hearths. Thus the entire knoll may have been a staging area for ceremonies.

See *shrine*

Graham Cave, Missouri

This cave is actually a shallow rockshelter (Figure 11) with large fireplaces, stone features (Figure 12), hematite processing, and burials that provide information on Archaic rites and beliefs.

The 1949 excavations (Logan 1952) revealed several burials of interest. Bu1 may be the deepest, in levels 5–6, and was possibly dismembered or secondarily deposited. A slab of limestone was under the scapula, another was on edge leaning over the skull, and a perforated wolf canine was in the area of the knee. An awl, a tine, a hammer, a point, and worked hematite were nearby. The head pointed west. Bu5 consisted of an infant femur and a few other fragments. Several fluted points came from these levels.

Other burials dated to the Late Archaic. One primary burial was found at 4 feet (1.22 m) below the surface, semiflexed on the face. "The legs were broken just above the ankles and no foot bones were present" (Logan 1952:26). Red ocher was on the pelvis and skull. At the fingertips of the right hand was a single naiad valve. Elsewhere in the pit was a piece of worked hematite and a scraper.

Secondary bundle burials were present. Infant Bu3 was represented by a few bones and was associated with three rocks, a chopper, a point, a broken point, and a broken ax. Several long bones, phalanges, skull parts, and an upper jaw were numbered Bu7. A hammer, broken mortar, and mano, both of the latter with red ocher, were associated. Bu10, a skull, femur, phalanx, rib, right humerus, and right ulna, may be a trophy part deposit. To the north of

11. Graham Cave. (Photo by author.)

12. Stone circle inside Graham Cave. (Photo by author.)

this burial was a pile of 10 rocks, four manos, and three mortars, most of them showing red ocher (Logan 1952:27).

The quantity of hematite evident in the deposits inside Graham Cave has been commented on by several archaeologists (e.g., Klippel 1971). Logan reported 69 ocher fragments and a cairn that covered mortars and manos in levels 4–5. A circle of large stones was also uncovered inside the cave. Several stone balls were found inside and outside the shelter. The 13 cupstones found had 4–8 very round depressions. A calcite crystal, found in level 4, had been ground and incised.

Baked-clay surfaces seem to have been present since Logan mentions "textile and basketry impressions on burned clay" (1952:58) and matted grass impressions. Shell objects were rare and included one possible piece of marine shell and three modified naiad valves. Finally, large quantities of split and charred bone were recovered as were several bone pins.

See *baked-clay surface, bedrock mortar/nutting stone, bone pin, burial—posture, crystal, feet/footprint/track, ocher, trophy part, trophy part decommissioning rite*

Grandstaff and Davis Cache, Ohio

Found in Ross County, Ohio, this cache was in a sandstone-lined circular pit 2 m in diameter and 30 cm deep in a field of the Paint Creek floodplain. Although containing Turkey-Tail bifaces and stone tablets, this cache returned an Archaic date of 4860 B.P. "Seven complete Turkey-tail bifaces, all oriented north to south, were situated on top of one of the gneiss tablets in the approximate center of the feature. Abutting this tablet was a gneiss bar amulet that was heavily burned and fragmented" (Purtill 2009:591). A second gneiss tablet was found north of the first tablet and was intensely burned on one face. This second tablet was on its side and lying perpendicular to the first tablet. Fragmented pieces of a third gneiss tablet, along with several pieces of charcoal and bone, were found south of the first tablet. Pieces of bifaces were found between two of the tablets, and red ocher had been sprinkled over many pieces.

See *amulet/charm/talisman, cache—blade, cardinal direction, Turkey-Tail blade, Caradoc Site*

Hardaway Site, North Carolina

The Hardaway site has a formative role in the understanding of the chronology of the Archaic of eastern North America (Coe 1964). It also offers information about Early Archaic rituals and beliefs.

The Hardaway site occupies a saddle, bluff tops, and northern point of land 280 ft (85.34 m) above the Yadkin River in central North Carolina. A springhead can be found in the saddle and may have formed a pond. The bluff-top location, the central location in the saddle, and a spring make for an auspicious siting. So do the artifacts recovered.

The 3,000 projectile points (particularly Palmer-like points) and 1,930 scrapers found here (Coe 1964) suggest something other than lost points and scrapers. They suggest lithic offerings as do the dense but abandoned lithic workshops that typify the Kirk zone. These features suggest a possible hunting shrine, as do the 237 bannerstones found here, most of which are unfinished or broken.

Two hundred and thirteen engraved slate fragments were retrieved from the surface and 16 from excavation. Forty-six engraved water-worn pebbles were also recovered on the surface of the Hardaway site (Coe 1964) and 16 slate and 5 pebbles more from excavation. Designs range from lines to intricate images. Only two other sites—Doerschuk site, also in the Piedmont of North Carolina, and the Gault site in Texas—have comparable numbers of engraved stones. These engraved stones and bannerstones might be related to a hunting or fertility cult for which the 78 mortars may also have been appropriate offerings.

See *bannerstone, bluff, center, pebble—engraved*

Harris Creek, Florida

An artificial ridge was the foundation for two mortuaries in four mounds: a large mound, possibly 35 ft (10.67 m) high, and three small mounds, each with one burial (Aten 1999:136). "Throughout its construction history, the mound was oriented north-south and apparently faced west" (Aten 1999: 147). The large Mount Taylor mound at Harris Creek (once called Tick Island) was primarily a platform mound with burials located in a few sectors (Aten 1999:147).

The first mortuary in the largest mound used white sand to fill burial pits. A possible pole structure was associated, but a charnel house function is negated by the lack of secondary burials. All 20 burials in the white sand were found on the northern and eastern portions of the underlying ridge and in the center but not in the western sector, duplicating the arrangement seen at Hontoon Dead Creek, also on the St. Johns River. A date of 4310 B.C. came from Bu12 in the base of the first mortuary. One of the bodies had embedded points, and several had perimortem crushed skulls (Aten 1999:135).

A mass grave measured 4.7 ft (1.43 m) x 3.5 ft (1.1 m) across the top and 3 ft (0.91 m) deep into shell and dark brown dirt. In the upper 6 inches (15 cm) of fill were eight skeletons tightly flexed and lying in white sand with charcoal bits. Two feet (61 cm) into the fill were cemented together parts of three more individuals, a child, and skulls with pieces of postcranial material of two adults, sand, and shell. There may have been a small mound of white sand built over this pit, and there may have been a post structure outside the feature. Although Aten (1999:174) explained that intersecting individual graves accounted for this mass of semi-articulated body parts of four or more people, there is precedence for such a deposit of trophy parts or secondary burials in other Archaic sites: "The absence in Layer 3 of any burials above the large grave pit . . . as well as the apparent rectilinear fence or building around this grave further reinforces the interpretation that prehistoric concepts of spatial structure and boundaries were in use" (Aten 1999: 173). The fact that no later burials were placed over this area suggests that it was marked and remembered. Other postholes suggest two arcs (Aten 1999: Figure 16) or two quadrilateral structures.

The second mortuary, Mortuary B, did not use white sand but rather brown sand in the matrix and burial pits. Layer 4 had 67 burials and layer 3 had 78 burials, found as individuals or in groups of 2 (n = 3), 3 (n = 2), or 4 (n = 1). In some of the multiple-body graves the bodies were separated by white sand. In four graves in each layer, the dead were placed atop hot coals and subsequently buried (Aten 1999). Shells were burned as well. Grave item variety was much narrower than in the first mortuary but more bodies had grave goods. Two Mortuary B individuals were murdered when facing their attacker(s) and one possibly beheaded while two other murdered individuals had no provenience. One individual had a miniature celt and adze/gouge, and one had eleven tubular bone beads. Each mortuary may have been used for a century or two.

A so-called charnel house at Harris Creek was reinterpreted by Aten as two superimposed arcs. The first arc, in level 4, suggests a structure with area of 11.3 m^2 and that in level 3 a structure 7.1 m^2. "The lowest posthole level contained two rectilinear structural segments, one of which may represent an enclosure of the large grave pit by a fence, shelter, or building" (Aten 1999:170).

After the two mortuaries accumulated, layer 5 enlarged the east, rear, and side of the mound, expanding its base. Layer 6 augmented the east side and raised the mound's height (then 43 m x 25 m x 2 m and summit 265 m^2), as did layer 7. Layer 8 is a new, lower platform created on the west side of the mound when the top platform was further enlarged (5000 to 5300 B.P.). Four burial pits may have been dug then. The final act was to cap the mound with muck, a post-Archaic act (Aten 1999).

All bodies were either loosely flexed and placed on their side (38 percent) or tightly flexed and put in a seated position (60 percent) (Aten 1999). The loosely flexed burials may have been interred shortly after death (primary burials) and the tightly flexed vertical burials interred after an extended period of exposure aboveground (secondary burials), according to Aten. "Additionally, some bones in tightly flexed burials were associated with the remains of small fires and some bones show evidence of charring, indicating that these bodies were desiccated and partially decomposed prior to burial" (Tucker 2009:40). Tucker (2009:49) found statistically significant differences between these two burial postures based on $\partial^{13}C$ and $\partial^{18}O_{IW}$ values and interpreted the data to mean that the loosely flexed individuals were from "away" (south of Harris Creek) and the sitting burials were the local population. At least 50 percent were oriented to the south-southwest-west and 33 percent were oriented to the north-northeast-east.

Bu94, with an internal projectile point, was also headless. No infants were present with the one exception of fetal remains in a pelvic cavity of Bu142. "Although 184 individuals were documented in the field, there were a great many more than this originally in the site" (Aten 1999:170).

"Shell midden apparently continued to accumulate over the basal mortuaries" into Woodland times such that "the resulting mound, with its veneer of late-period midden, was a massive construction some ten meters high in a mound and ridge complex covering five acres" (Sassaman 2010a:69). "Spirits seem to be reflected at this site in four ways: 1) in the general shift that may have occurred in beliefs relating to the transition from water to land burial; 2) in the storage of tightly flexed bodies for a time prior to interment . . . 3) in the preparation of the grave itself . . . and 4) in the implications of burial disturbance for 'the near dead' versus 'the long dead'" (Aten 1999:179).

See *burial—head direction, burial—posture, capping, color, mound—shell, shellworks, violence*

Hedgepeth Mounds, Louisiana

These are the oldest known dirt mounds in Louisiana. Mound A is conical, 45 m in diameter, and 6 m high and was constructed in two stages. Mound B is domed, 25 m in diameter, and just over 1 m high. Both mounds were constructed on the edge of a floodplain. A test unit from top to bottom of Mound A revealed only 13 artifacts. The paleosol under Mound A concealed a hearth that radiocarbon dated to an unexpectedly late 4270+/-100 rcy. Four trenches between the mounds and excavation under Mound A revealed copious artifacts (Saunders, Allen, and Saucier 1994:148). Did the building of Hedgepeth Mounds trigger the start of the Mayan calendar (see Anderson 2010:299n12)?

See *monument, mound—dirt*

Hendricks Cave, Ohio

This is a vertical sinkhole 30 ft (9.14 m) deep and 15 ft (4.57 m) in diameter with three chambers radiating outward from its bottom and seems to have been a sinkhole shrine. These chambers—A, B, C—had roofs 6–10 ft (1.83–3.0 m) high. Chamber B is entered through a passageway 5 ft (1.5 m) from the floor of the sinkhole (Pedde and Prufer 2006). Chamber B contained 137 pieces of human bone (31 leg bones, 33 skull pieces and mandibles) representing an MNI of 14 humans—a child, 3 subadults, and 10 adults (at least 2 men and 4 women)—all represented by incomplete bodies. These bones were located in and near a rock-lined hearth that yielded a date of 2503+/-220 bc. One large adult skull fragment had been altered and placed upright on the ground surface (photos in Prufer and Prufer 2006).

Faunal remains were equally incomplete and came from bear, elk, deer, canid, fish, naiads, squirrel, skunk, raccoon, snake, and turtle. These isolated bones and shells were placed in the chamber or dropped into the sinkhole. McKenzie and Prufer (1967:130) argued that the sinkhole had been artificially filled to seal the deposits in the chambers.

See *Austin Cave, Big Sandy, Lawrence, offering, sinkhole, skull*

Hermitage Springs, Tennessee

There are several aspects of this shell-bearing burial ground that suggest it was the scene of various rituals. One curious aspect was that among babies with actual aging, there were no infants but there were 12 newborns and 5 fetuses, several suggesting ritual death. One newborn was buried with red ocher, one with atlatl, and two with marine shell, including a possible Milky Way belt—all possible elements in a hunt god rite. One newborn was buried with a dog in a possible renewal or rebalancing rite. Another newborn was buried facedown, and yet another was put inside of a large marine *Busycon* sp. shell (data from burial files).

A mother with fetus in utero was found with an antler point in her thorax buried on top of a child (Bu268) who was placed in an extended position. A group burial consisted of a fetus, a woman, and a man, which could have been an adultery killing (Claassen 2013a).

See *adultery killing, atlatl, dog sacrifice rite, first-kill rite, hunt god rite, sacrifice—infant and child*

Higgs, Tennessee

Higgs is on the Duck River just east of Ervin. Both of these sites (as well as the lowest levels of Anderson site) are unique in the deposition of freshwater gastropods to the near exclusion of bivalves. The Middle Archaic "floor" in Stratum VI and a higher Terminal Archaic "floor" feature in Stratum IV might best be interpreted as ritual features. The remnant Archaic floor was 275 ft^2 (25.55 m^2), unwalled and 0.2 inches (5 mm) thick with four features: 3 hearths aligned 10 ft (3.05 m) apart and a flintknapping area. The easternmost hearth had an inordinate amount of fire-cracked rock, quartzite cobbles, and charcoal. The westernmost hearth had a heavy concentration of charcoal and burned rock but an unburned deer mandible in the center. It also contained or was surrounded by calcined drumfish teeth and postholes. Two additional deer mandibles were 2.7 ft (82 cm) northeast of this hearth. The central and western hearths and the area between them and the knapping locus contained several hammerstones and 6,600 pieces of chert, from four cores. The large size of this floor and the various objects and features lead to the conclusion that a Middle Archaic shrine or ritual locus was encountered.

The Terminal Archaic floor of 130 ft^2 (12.1 m^2), 14 ft (4.3 m) in diameter, was located near the highest elevation of the site and had six postholes on the southern side, a possible windscreen (Figure 13). McCollough and Faulkner concluded that if this were so, then the southwestern winds off of the river would mean that this feature was utilized in the spring months (1973:57). An irregular shallow "trash pit" was centered in the shelter floor, and contained a mass of faunal remains. A formal earth oven was dug into the north edge of the shelter floor, filled with cedar-wood fuel and abundant charred remains of domesticated sunflower seeds, chenopod and acorns. In the southern half of this 4 ft x 6 ft (1.2 m x 1.8 m) pit were densely packed shellfish and small quantities of unburned drumfish, catfish, bullhead, sucker, deer, crane, and fire-cracked rock. The northern half had more unburned deer bone, fire-cracked rock, and large fragments of charred wood. This "trash-pit" was "strangely placed near the center of the small intensively occupied

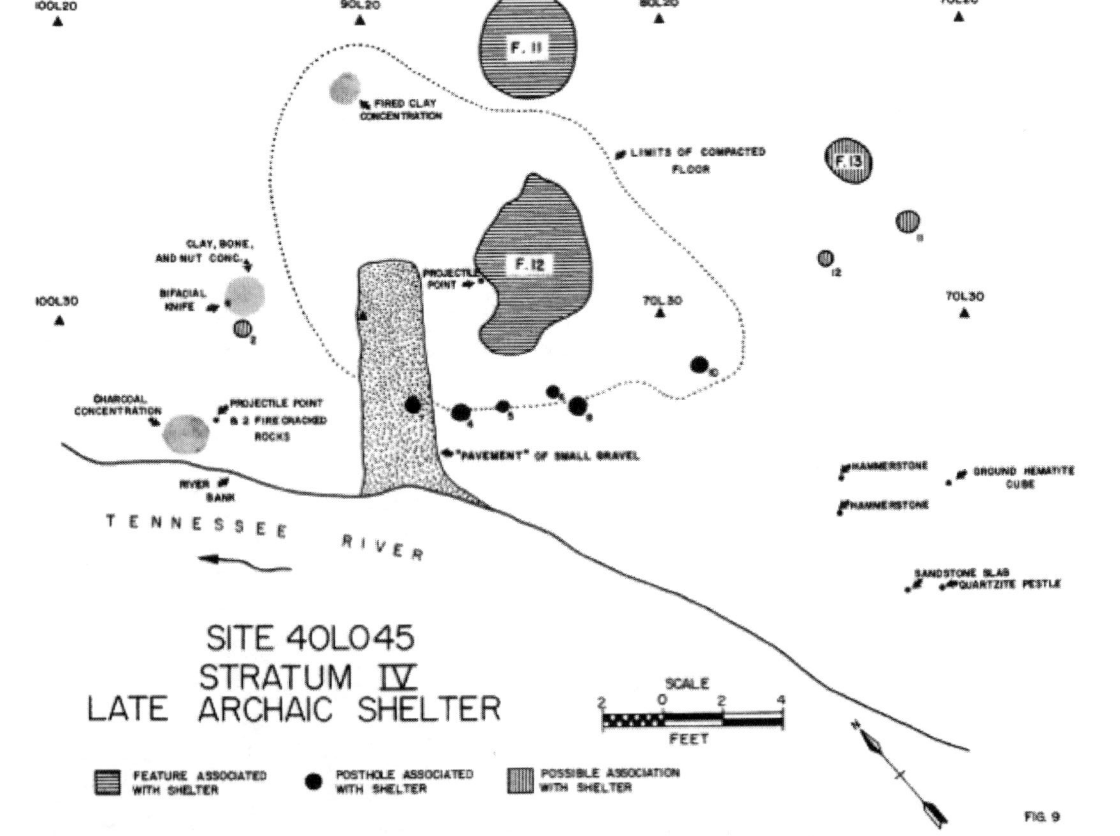

13. Shelter plan at the Higgs Site. (Reprinted from the Tennessee Anthropological Society publication of McCollough and Faulkner 1973:Figure 9, with permission from Charles Faulkner.)

floor where a protected principal hearth could be expected to be situated" (McCollough and Faulkner 1973:59–60). This floor dated to approximately 900 bc.

What recommends this set of features as a ritual facility are the high terrace location, the screen hiding the area, the mass of bones (a decommissioning rite after a feast or a renewal offering?), the crane, the cedar, and the formal earth oven, in a place that looked used for no more than one season (McCollough and Faulkner 1973:58).

See *crane, decommissioning rite, deer, drumfish, flintknapping, offering, shrine, trash/midden, world renewal rite*

Hodges, Michigan

Hodges gives us a rare look at a late Late Archaic/Early Woodland cremation pit in a sand knoll. The pit measured 5 ft, 6 inches x 4 ft, 2 inches (1.67 m x 1.3 m). The base of the pit consisted of sand and silt particles fused together and overlain in the southern half of the pit with fire-cracked rock, calcined bone, and burned artifacts in a very dark, organic-rich soil. The northern half of the pit above the burned sand had unburned artifacts and a concentration of red ocher. The contents of one of the numerous dark pits in the yellow sand were inventoried (Binford 1963). Pieces of limonite and "triangular scrapers" in the pit were interpreted as elements of a firemaking kit.

Nineteen siliceous stone items were included in the pit made with six types of chert. Among the groundstone items were a refurbished gorget, adz fragment, and several burned gorget fragments, and two copper awls. Several of these items were burned.

Recognizable charred human bone fragments in 324 grams of burned bone suggested an entire corpse had been cremated. One raccoon tibia, five songbird-size bones, and five fragments of turtle carapace seemed to have been included in the dry state in the fire. Several small mammal bones indicated burned carcasses. Several pieces of sinew or gut that escaped the fire were retrieved from the dark soil of the pit (Binford 1963:138–139).

Flora material from the pit soil included 68 *Chenopodium* seeds and three *Polygonum* seeds, indicative of fall seasonality. There was also red maple charcoal.

Four clusters of items were found in the north, central, southwest, and south parts of the pit. The central cluster had 10 chipped items and the other three clusters had only two. Unique lithological types occurred in each cluster leading Binford to conclude that multiple individuals or social units had contributed items, including a one-quarter section of a refurbished gorget. The burned items were believed to be the personal effects of the deceased. Binford further surmised that the crematory had been raked after the fire died down, leaving the bone in a pile at the south end, after which a few burial goods were added. Other goods were placed in the north end of the pit upon an ash layer.

See *burning*, *cardinal direction*, *center*, *Chenopodium*, *crematory*, *number*

Horn Shelter 2, Texas

Like Russell Cave in northeast Alabama, Horn Shelter is a double rockshelter, one side of which has yielded significant information about ritualizing (http://www.texasbeyondhistory.net/horn/, accessed June 30, 2011). A Paleoindian/Early Archaic grave with two limestone-weighted bodies was found in the center of this rockshelter on the Brazos River in central Texas. This burial event, located in Stratum 5G, occurred around 9,700 ya, confirmed with Saint Patrice and Wilson points. One burial was a man about 40 yo, and the second body, nestled against the back of the man, was a juvenile 10–12 yo with one extremely worn molar. Both skeletons were in excellent condition, flexed on their left sides, heads to the south, and their postcranial remains covered with 19 limestone slabs.

The grave goods were extensive. A bag of items had been placed under the head of the man that contained "three modified turtle shells; two deer antler butts . . . ; two thin sandstone grinding stones with slight use-wear; a square fragment of fine red ocher; a crude chipped-stone biface; and a long, slender deer bone" (http://www.texasbeyondhistory.net/horn/burials.html, accessed June 30, 2011). One turtle shell was inside another, and those two had been placed on top of the inverted third shell. All carapaces had been scraped smooth inside. Three perforated coyote teeth and four unperforated claws of a Swainson's hawk were near his neck, and four badger claws were in front of his skull. Inside his mouth had been placed the talon of a Swainson's hawk and the claw of a badger. A fourth carapace had been placed over his face and a fifth, under his pelvis, contained an antler fragment and two marine gastropod beads, one of which was an *Oliva sayana* shell. Near one leg were a shaft straightener and three Neritina snail beads. The juvenile also had grave goods—an eyed, broken, bone needle and 17 marine shell beads using the gastropod *Neritina reclivata*. Taken from the grave fill were 63 additional *Neritina reclivata* beads (a broken string?), chert flakes, turtle skull bones and other parts, worked antler, and fragments of bird, rodent, snake, frog, fish, and deer bones.

There was no apparent cause of death for either individual. The various grave goods suggest that the man had been a ritual specialist, the youth a possible apprentice. One reason a specialist and apprentice might have been buried simultaneously is if they had been killed for witchcraft. Their burial in a rockshelter suggests that this setting was particularly appropriate for murder victims and for ritual specialists dealing with Underworld spirits.

See *burial—under limestone, hawk, ritual specialist/priest, rockshelter, shell bead*

Horr's Island, Florida

On Horr's Island (also called Key Marco), in coastal southwestern Florida, is a Middle Archaic shellwork of four marine shell and sand mounds, a large shell arc, several shell ramps, and an adjacent habitation area. Three of the mounds are clustered with a shell arc and shell ramp and have heights of 1 m to 6 m. The fourth mound is 4 m high and offset to the east. They are made of alternating layers of marine shell and sand. Two dates in Mound B bracket the period 7600 to 6700 rcy (Russo 1994b: 102), making these the oldest marine shell monuments in eastern North America, if not all of the Americas.

Prior to Mound A's construction, a living floor over a meter deep had accumulated. That surface was leveled and burned ca. 5,000–4,600 ya. Two meters' worth of height was obtained by quarrying sand from the lagoons around the island and mounding it. "The extra labor and resultant technological problems associated with mining submerged deposits and transporting them across estuarine waters through mangrove swamps and up the steep-sided dunes may imply a symbolic significance to the source" (Russo 1994b: 100). This significance was no doubt that of material from the Underworld and specifically the primordial sea. Lagoon sand was then capped with 1–2 m of clean oyster shell deposited directly onto the sand. Before a soil could form, another layer of multicolored sands was put on up to 1 m thick. This dune sand had been colored with a different amount of charcoal, expressing obvious color symbolism with light and dark tan, gray, and black sands. A pit was then excavated into the mound at its base and filled with white sand, found nowhere else on the island except in root casts for some ritual purpose. Next, the entire mound was given another sand mantle up to 50 cm thick. The final act in the construction of Mound A was a cap of oyster shells 1–2 m thick. Subsequently, a burial was made into the top of the mound around 3500–4000 rcy (Russo 1994b: 102).

The ritual construction of this mound included color symbolism, Underworld symbolism, mound symbolism, shell symbolism, and human burial. Although there are abundant sherds surrounding the mound complex, no sherds were found on or between the mounds (Russo 1994b:104), a situation that suggests avoidance of the ceremonial complex by later peoples. Lithics objects were absent.

These features were part of the landscape of this Middle and Late Archaic permanently occupied habitation site where numerous mass-feasting ceremonies and ritualized construction events occurred. Similar activities were under way at Bonita, at Hill Cottage, and in several places in the northern Ten Thousand Islands.

See *Bluffton Burial Mound, capping, color, Harris Creek, mound—shell, shellworks, site avoidance*

Icehouse Bottom, Tennessee

Located in extreme eastern Tennessee on the Little Tennessee River is this now deeply buried Archaic site. During the Early Archaic it possibly functioned as a residential camp based on a large collection of flora, features, and lithics (but no bone). The most frequently encountered Early Archaic feature was the baked-clay "floor" (n = 167 of 396 features), a pancake of reddish-brown clay averaging 0.67 x 0.42 m and fired on top of the alluvial sandy loam ground surface. Twenty-nine of these pancakes had textile or net impressions and all were found in the Kirk Corner Notched levels (Sherwood and Chapman 2005:72). Also associated with the Kirk Corner Notched levels was one redeposited human cremation. Another was found in the Bifurcate Phases (Chapman 1977:112–115). In spite of the extraordinary amount of hematite found here, few burials had it. Icehouse Bottom appears to have been a rare open-air site for hematite processing.

See *baked-clay surface, Graham Cave, hematite, ocher*

Indian Knoll, Kentucky

Indian Knoll may have been founded about 5585 B.P. and used until 3639 B.P. This Late Archaic shell mound is unique in eastern North America both in individual characteristics and in the combination of characteristics, all related to ritualizing. Its distinctive traits include the large number of burials (1,100+), the high number of murder victims, the extraordinary prevalence of auditory exostoses, the extremely high minimum number of deer (500 based on distal humeri or 1,000 based on scapulae), the huge number of bifaces (n = 9,424 from 60 percent of the site), the greatest concentration of atlatls and rattles in eastern North America, and the greatest number of human-dog burial pairs. Rather than a village, Indian Knoll was a major, if not *the* major, ceremonial center of the SOV in these two millennia and was probably recognized as such by people outside the valley. It is relevant to the siting of this ceremonial center that when the Green River floods, Indian Knoll becomes an island (Webb 1974).

Marine shell was procured and deployed for these rites, including use in Milky Way belts and shawls for the fertility sacrifices and a new year rite. Twenty percent of the burials were accompanied by marine shell items (Claassen 2010:129), and millions of freshwater naiads—fertility food—were consumed during feasting. The shells were discarded in heaps, creating a renewal context for the burials and a memorial to each event. Deposited with the shells were the contents of old tool kits and the material homes of spirits, as well as items used during ritual preparation and conduct, all discarded as part of the renewal rites.

High counts of *Leptoxis* and *Busycon* shell beads in the pelvic regions of four infants and children, two subadults, six men, three women, and one unsexed adult imply Milky Way belts and rebosos on these 16 people, deaths related to the hunt god rite. These belts and the facedown or on-the-back position of most of these people suggest sacrifices.

The number of adult murder victims in Indian Knoll is at a minimum 64, based on obvious signs of trauma, plus 46 additional individuals based on burial postures (Claassen 2010:Table 6.4, Table 6.5), including those people in at least two hunt god rites (Bu55–58, Bu611–614). In one of these groups, each burial was accompanied by atlatls, bannerstones, human femoral awls, shell beads, rattles, and points. Possibly 30 infants were sacrificed (Claassen 2013a). There were thus 140 victims in a minimum of 64 sacrificial rites. There were probably many more of both.

Indian Knoll has the highest proportion of dogs buried with humans of any Archaic site (Claassen 2010) (13 of 21 dog burials were paired with a human), suggesting, as Webb (1950) implied with his medicine bag study, that there were several ritual specialists buried among the dead. In addition, there is evidence for the burial of at least 13 people, including infants, in textiles of woven bark and possibly all in one portion of the site. A minimum of two cults operated from this center—the Cult of the Bivalve Feast and the little Cult of the River Keepers—whose members were buried here more often than anywhere else in the region. These cults had as their goal the renewal of life and lineage.

The Cult of the Bivalve Feast apparently conducted several different types of rites here such as the sacrifice of single adults, the four-age rite, the hunt god rite, and the sacrifice of infants and children in fertility rituals. A rattle dance for this latter rite may explain the 32 rattles found with burials and the several flutes recovered; the flute was a fertility instrument as well (Hall 1997). Numerous ancestors were interred here over a 2,000-year period in addition to the sacrificial victims at a rate of one every 15 months (Claassen 2010:122). The attendees were restored to balance after human and dog sacrifices and the souls of kin and victims were led away by dogs. The deepest burial, possibly a consecrating burial, may be Bu492, a young adult on its back with an extinct tapir tooth and six jaws of a lynx, an animal found far to the north of this place. Did the founders of Indian Knoll trace their origins to the Stone People and a northern forested area?

See *auditory exostoses, dog sacrifice rite, dog with human burial rite, first-kill rite, hunt god rite, jaw, island, Milky Way, sacrifice—adult, sacrifice—infant and child, shell bead, world renewal rite*

Indian Spring, Maine

Three mortuary features led excavators to call this Susquehanna Tradition site in the Merrymeeting Bay region a ceremonial site. One feature was a "small cylindrical pit just large and deep enough to hold seven Susquehanna bifacial preforms overlain by two small adzes and a shallow, fully grooved gouge" (Bourque, Cox, and Lewis 2006:316). A second feature held a ¾-grooved ax, a pecking stone, and charred wood dating to 3558+/-135 B.P. The third feature revealed a discoidal pecking stone and a bipointed biface.

See *ax*

James Creek, West Virginia

The James Creek site in West Virginia spans two bearwallows and adjacent rim area and the saddle between the two tops of Cherry Pond Mountain. Excavation yielded over a dozen hearths, 800+ projectile points, and dozens of hand-sized nutstones with multiple pits (Wilkins 1978). One bearwallow alone yielded a coal bead, gorgets, rubbed hematite, a soapstone fragment, a grooved ax, pitted sandstone, an atlatl weight, hammerstones, fire-cracked rocks, and 181 points (including Kirk points). From one unit outside the wallow came 22 points including a fluted point and several hearths. The second bearwallow at the site yielded 10 hearths with Woodland and Archaic artifacts. In the adjacent rim excavation 59 points and 2 hearths were encountered. Pestles, mortars, endscrapers, drills, knives, nutstones, and mullers were frequently found (Wilkins 1978). The large number of points found here suggests point offerings.

One-third of the 800+ points found dated to the Early Archaic, and these used local Kanawha black chert and exotic Carter Cave chert from Kentucky. A decrease in the number of Middle Archaic points may signal a decreased use of bearwallows, but by Late Archaic times the large number of points reflects a resumption of use equal to Early Archaic use (Wilkins 1978:34–35).

Several aspects of this site suggest ritual. One aspect is its location (in a high elevation), another is the abundance of tools left inside the bearwallows, and the third is the great number of points—possible offerings. There are examples from Plains cultures of men seeking visions lying in depressions and in high elevations (i.e., LeBeau 2009).

See *dream/vision, mountain, projectile point, sinkhole*

Jerger, Indiana

Jerger is on a sand ridge in the White River valley, overlooking what was once a marsh. Burned and unburned animal bones, human bones, bifaces, and drills were mixed in this Early Archaic mortuary site with cremations and red ocher. Fauna identified were deer, raccoon, turkey, canine, and turtle. Perforated animal teeth and awls were also recovered (Tomak 1979:65; Schmidt et al. 2008).

All excavated pits contained burned human bone, broken bifurcate points (MacCorkle and St. Albans), modified pieces of bone (spatulate-like and awl-like), marine shell beads, and red ocher. In the fill of Feature 3 (1.8 m x 1.4 m x .01 m) were cremated bone, polished bone, a piece of shaped red ocher, and five small, burned *Olivella* sp. shells, with apex missing (Schmidt et al. 2008:228).

Examination of a sample of the cremains yielded information on 9 subadults ranging in age from newborn to roughly 15 yo and 5 adults, 3 with extensive tooth wear. Eighty-two percent of the burned bones were calcined or nearly so and extremely fragmented, consistent with pulverization in modern experiments (Schmidt et al. 2008:232–233). Of great interest for ritual practices is the discovery that Feature 3 at Jerger contained the remains of 4 individuals, one 0–6 months, one 5–6 years, a young adult, and an old adult. This age distribution reflects a four-age rite and gives Jerger the oldest record of this rite.

There is no evidence of the crematory at Jerger and no non-mortuary type of feature occurs here. "The known Jerger Phase cemeteries were in special mortuary locations. There is no evidence that Jerger people used these sites for any other purposes [than mortuary] and there is little indication that these sites were used much by any other American Indian group" (Schmidt et al. 2008:229). The dates offered are 10,000 to 7000 B.P.

See *cremation, four-age rite, Olivella, shell bead, McCullough's Run*

Koster, Illinois

Early Archaic Horizon 11 had nine burials, five flexed adults (two women, a man, a probable man, and an unknown), only one with a grave good, and four flexed infants. Limestone was found over some of the adults. Several dog burials were found, one with its head resting against a mano and metate, suggesting that this dog was part of a hearth rite or rebalancing rite (James 2006) conducted 8400 B.P.

Horizon 8C (Middle Archaic) has several deep post molds—too few for a structure. Brown and Vierra (1983:184) see the posts as substantial wall supports. Could these instead be ceremonial posts?

See *burial—under limestone, dog with human burial rite, pole/post, rebalancing rite*

Krill Cave, Ohio

This cave in north-central Ohio contained 150+ bones representing at least four infants, four children, two adolescents, and five adults (Prufer and Prufer 2012:228). The majority of bones were hand and foot digits, suggesting trophy parts. One cranial bone was covered with red ocher, and the ocher-stained lower legs of two individuals were "placed" (Prufer and Prufer 2012). Radiocarbon dates were 1390+/-65 bc and 2030+/-130 bc.

See *feet, Hendricks Cave, Stanhope Cave, trophy part, trophy part decommissioning rite*

Lamar, Oklahoma

Lamar was an apparent Middle Archaic/Late Archaic burial ground on the Washita River, near its confluence with the Red River. Twenty-five burials were excavated, including Bu14 with an artifact cache containing 38 stone items (Neal 1994). This burial was slightly flexed with head to the northwest. The cache was positioned where the rib cage should have been and contained a mixture of usable, reworked, and broken items. The raw materials of the cache, the high incidence of heat treating, the large flakes, and the biface forms in the cache were unique at the site. Neal reasoned that the cache was a personal tool kit (1994:178).

See *stone*

Lamoka Lake, New York

Evidence for Late Archaic ritual activities at this site is ample including the presence of red ocher and burials. Sixty-four burials were tabulated by Ritchie (1932:117) with flexed position being the norm. No cremations were recognized, and grave goods were few in number and infrequently given. All ages were present.

A double burial appears to have been a ritual kill. It included one young man with four points in or on vertebrae and a severed head, hands, and left foot. He was weighted down with five slabs. The second body was also resting on the back and was missing skull, hands, and feet. The arms appeared elsewhere in the grave, one charred, placed at the edge of a hearth. The men's heads were to the south or southeast. A woman was a third victim of mutilation and burning.

Some of the 13 fire features found here, called "fire-beds" by Ritchie, are quite large. "These large and important structures were in some cases over 55' long, 10' wide [16.8 m x 3 m], with a thickness of several feet of pure white and buff colored ashes, flecked with charcoal granules, in which hearths were profusely scattered at various elevations. . . . Very seldom were refuse bones or artifacts encountered in the fire-beds" (Ritchie 1932:86). Ritchie thought that these features might be fish-drying areas, used to destroy offal or smoke the air to repel mosquitoes, or burned to provide warmth.

Hearths were numerous and large with "pure charcoal averaging six quarts in volume. . . . In only a few instances did hearths contain implements and these were confined to arrow points and charred awls"; scrap bone was equally rare. "The intense heat generated in many of these hearths was responsible for a discolored induration of the enveloping soil . . . and reddish gravel often completely enclosed the charcoal and required considerable effort to displace with the pick" (Ritchie 1932:86–87). Were these mortuary fires? In addition to the large fire-bed and hearths, the 380 pits were 3–7 ft (0.9–2.7 m) in diameter and 3–6 ft (0.9–1.8 m) in depth with hearths located in the bottom of many of them and higher up in others. Fire-beds, hearths, and pits this size surely reflect the activities of large groups of people rather than those of small family units.

Yet more indication of ritual rather than mundane activities at Lamoka Lake can be seen in the "immense quantities of refuse bones and shells that were taken from the pits and village layer, over 500 pounds being reserved for study" (Ritchie 1932:113). Deer and bear were found in groups of 50+ bones in several cases that Ritchie interpreted as feasting refuse. Bones of bobcat, lynx, swan, great horned owl, and golden eagle indicate ritual activities as well. Ritchie points out that tools, particularly projectile points, were left as offerings: "Arrowpoints, awls and celts were the most common, and these occurrences seemed to relate to the custom . . . of appeasing the spirit of the slain animal by a minor sacrifice, an implement, a pinch of tobacco, etc." (Ritchie 1932:113).

See *bear, bobcat/lynx, deer, feasting, owl, projectile point, sacrifice—adult, trophy part*

Lawrence, Kentucky

Lawrence is located on the edge of a sinkhole in the uplands east of the Cumberland River in Trigg County with a sizable Early Archaic record (Mocas 1985). This component was preserved in a 17-cm thick midden that had numerous pit features. Kirk-like points were the principal diagnostic Early Archaic artifact.

Mocas (1985) concluded that the midden and features resulted from a series of sequential occupations rather than one of extended length. Feature 72 was an Archaic mortuary facility containing two males and associated grave goods located at the edge of the sink (5,375 + 125 B.C.). Both men, estimated to be between 22 yo and 28 yo, were flexed. Grave goods associated with one burial consisted of a heavily utilized and resharpened Kirk-like serrated projectile and a cache of projectile points, drills, and scrapers larger and less used than others recovered elsewhere in the site. Both burials contained necklaces made of domesticated dog canines and beaver incisors (Mocas 1985:82–89). The materials, the burials, and the sinkhole locality suggest a ritual site.

See *Austin Cave, Hendricks Cave, Little Salt Spring, sinkhole, teeth*

Little Salt Spring, Florida

This burial site today consists of a slough draining into a sinkhole, the slough containing between 100 and 1,000 burials. The sinkhole proper is 60 m deep and filled with water and additional human bodies (Figure 14). This sinkhole constitutes one of several Florida Archaic sinkhole mortuaries, suggesting a special role for sinkholes. In addition to human bodies the slain remains of giant ground sloth and giant tortoise have been recovered.

Hundreds of disarticulated and several articulated bodies were found in

14. Aerial photo of Little Salt Springs sinkhole. (Photo by Peter Masa. Reprinted with permission from Elsevier.)

the muck-filled slough and midden adjacent to the sinkhole and the spring itself. Most were extended and many were covered with vegetable matter from mats, boughs, or shrouds.

An apparent double burial of a man and a woman is of interest. The woman was extended with head west, wrapped in layers of plant fiber and accompanied by a chert knife and a wooden digging stick. She was then covered with layers of grapevine, each layer oriented in a different direction (Wentz and Gifford 2007:334). Small postholes were found near her body. Beside the man was a pair of feet wrapped in grass. "Other [bodies] appear to have been placed inside small structures or surrounded by posts" (Powell 1995:118). Grave goods were stone points, baskets, wooden tools, and one carved wooden tablet. Many of the slough burials were oriented to the west.

Excavation in the spring basin has yielded artifacts of deer bone, antler, and oak in strata dating to 9500 rcy. No human bones were found there. However, the spring itself contains hundreds of bones, among them a Pleistocene male skeleton and 2 in situ burials, one 2 m deep on a ledge, the other 8–9 m deep, both on the western half of the sink. One of these bodies was a young female with brain tissue dating to 6860+/-110 rcy (Wentz and Gifford 2007:331) and the other was a juvenile. A wooden item gave a date of 12,030 B.P. A Pleistocene man was trapped apparently in the sinkhole and drowned. Mineralized bones remain in the sink "and appear to be derived from burials that were interred around the circumference of the spring basin, between 1 and 2 m below the present surface" (Wentz and Gifford 2007:331). A complete skull of a juvenile burial and 3 facial portions suggesting masks were found. Twenty-two pelvises were sexed as 18 females and 4 males.

The findings of femurs and majority of women in the collection of bones from the sinkhole are intriguing given the role of the femur in ancestral claims in Mexican cultures and the use of women in water-related sacrifices. Wentz and Gifford (2007) see similarities with Windover and Bay West pond mortuaries, including the presence of possible effigy and mortuary poles around some bodies. While the Florida mortuary pond affiliation is emphasized by Wentz and Gifford, it should be recognized that Little Salt Spring is also part of a larger class of sinkhole shrines and of spring shrines.

See *feet, femur, pole/post, sinkhole, spring, Windover*

Mammoth Cave, Kentucky

Mammoth Cave and the connected Salts Cave are part of the Flint Ridge cave system of southern Kentucky "marked by sinkholes, valley sinks, blind valleys, disappearing streams, and numerous caves" (Watson 1969:2), a landscape of mystery and surely orenda. The oldest date from the cave is 4120+/-70 rcy, but most of the activity evident in these two caves occurred during the Early Woodland when salt mining appears to have been the motivation. "The remains in Mammoth Cave interior are, in general, identical with those in Salts Cave although the Mammoth Cave material was apparently more abundant and the cave more intensively used than Salts" (Watson 1974a:183). Remains of interest in Mammoth Cave that may be Archaic in age are a desiccated body, a burial, cane torches, feces, rock markings, world renewal offerings, and surface fauna.

A flexed young woman in a grass-lined pit was interred in the vestibule of the cave. Work in the vestibule found various skeletal fragments of an adult femur and patella, a female pubis, a child's mandible, and remains of a fetus (Robbins 1974:146–147), hinting at a four-age rite. A sample of faunal material from the vestibule included black bear, opossum, porcupine (nonlocal), brown bat, turtle, elk, and crane (Nelson 1917). A man 45+ yo was the victim of rock fall much deeper inside the cave. Was this man a cave priest? Artifacts found in the cave systems seemingly not related to mining were bone tubes, awls, bone punches, and more than 60 slippers. Bone tubes are often attributed to doctoring by archaeologists. Slippers may have been fertility petitions.

The Early Woodland salt mining in the cave appears to mark a short-lived era of boys' initiations in the cave and to be related to the 100+ fecal remains found in this and Salts Cave (Crothers 2012). Analysis of 12 fecal specimens indicated male origin (Sobolik et al. 1996). Plant pollens recovered in the fecal specimens were dandelion, maygrass, liliaceous plants, sumpweed, sunflower, and chenopod, as well as flowers of sweetflag, suggesting spring and fall entradas (Bryant 1974:209).

There are other aspects of the cave that are relevant to a ritual use (Claassen 2012b, 2012c). For example, a handful of markings in Mammoth Cave are found at some distance from any entrance, including on a rock just out of sight of a significant underground waterfall. Recalling beliefs that caves are the origin of water and thus that the water in them is the purest of all water, it makes perfect sense that the priests/initiates/pilgrims would purge themselves at this place (where a high density of fecal remains have been recovered) after eating the mirabilite on the walls (the focus of the mining activity) in preparation for rites at the waterfall and collecting water.

See *cave, cave mineral/mining, Chenopodium, feces, ritual specialist/priest, sandal/slipper, world renewal rite*

McCain, Indiana

This is a shell-bearing site on a ridge top with 16 burials. Bu16 was flexed and lying on its left side on the sandy clay subsoil, "some of which had been mounded over part of the body" (Miller 1941:22). A biface had been placed at the head and at the foot. "The entire top shell of a land turtle . . . had been placed under the head as a pillow, and the shell in turn rested directly on a deer skull" (Miller 1941:23). Perhaps related to this burial was a cache of heavy, pecked stone implements "completely covered by a small mound of the same sandy clay" (Miller 1941:23). This individual should be considered a possible ritual specialist. Several other piles of stones were possibly associated with other burials. Awls, needles, pins, and a great number of axes (limonite, granite, gneiss) of different sizes were encountered between the burials.

See *ax, cache—groundstone, deer, ritual specialist/priest*

McCullough's Run, Indiana

McCullough's Run is an Early Archaic Bifurcate Tradition habitation site and burial ground in western Indiana, 75 miles northeast of Jerger with 10 individual circular cremation disposal pits. Red ocher was found with several bodies as was a MacCorkle point. St. Albans points were found with two cremations that lacked red ocher. Several pits showed that the contents had been emplaced in containers.

Feature 25, a mixture of burned human bone from at least three individuals (infant, child, and adult) and burned lithics, "also contained a cache of 47 bifaces, three chunks of red and yellow ocher, a sandstone abrader and a bivalve shell" (Cochran, Knight, and Bush 1997:10). The bifaces had fewer than 10 flakes removed. The fill also contained a beaver tooth, a worked deer bone, a bone perforator, faunal remains, and wood charcoal. Unburned points (one Early Archaic MacCorkle) and stones were found above and below the cache.

Feature 34 (80 cm x 90 cm x 35 cm) had a cache of four deer leg bones at the top and a cache near the bottom containing two bifaces, a deer bone awl, drilled drumfish operculum, and a stone. Feature 38 was very similar.

These people were cremated in the flesh, and 92 percent of the bone was completely incinerated. The ten pits contained a minimum of 18 individuals ranging in age from 18 months to older adult. Three pits had remains of at least three individuals, each of a different age category (Cochran, Knight, and Bush 1997:10) and are potential candidates for four-age rites.

See *cache—blade, cremation, deer, four-age rite, Jerger, ocher*

Meyer, Indiana

This is a late Middle Archaic–Late Archaic burial ground located on a ridge spur overlooking wetlands along the Ohio River. Twenty-seven primary burials were found in 900 ft^2 (83.6 m^2) as were numerous thermal features and large shallow pits in a thick black midden (Bader 2010/11). Chert debitage was rare. Burial pits were richer in artifacts than was the midden, including such items as bone pins, tubes, beads, awls, modified canine teeth, cut antler, stone points, drills, hafted scrapers, groundstone tool fragments, and turtle carapaces.

Each of the Middle Archaic burials had one or more smudge pits located at the feet, knees, or skulls of flexed burials while none of the Late Archaic burials had these fire features. One infant burial had four smudge pits, each located in a cardinal direction (Anne Bader, personal communication with the author, 2008). No wood charcoal was found in the examined smudge pits. Sedge seeds were found in one pit. Fired earth stains constituted a second type of intense burn feature associated with the burials in the Late Archaic component. No stain contained charcoal, ash, or fire-cracked rock. The third feature type at this burial ground was the shallow basin, eight in all, most of which contained hematite and limonite, burned and unburned animal bone, and shells.

The 27 burials included infants, subadults, men, and women, moderately to tightly flexed. Two of the burials were positioned facedown. One subadult may have been shot or stabbed in the shoulder, and one subadult appears to have had the tongue cut out and the head removed. Bone pin locations suggested that most bodies had been wrapped. Most graves had at least one large naiad valve included, and one grave had a stack of them. Bader thinks that these were digging implements. Several graves had well-preserved bodies lacking a body part—primarily upper arms, vertebrae, and ribs—and seven pits contained only parts of bodies—vertebrae, skull fragments, and phalanges, possible trophy part decommissioning rites.

See *bone pin, burial—posture, gambling, shell scoop/spoon, trophy part, trophy part decommissioning rite, violence*

Millbury III, Massachusetts

Excavation and analyses have brought to light several aspects of ritual at this Susquehanna cremation cemetery (Leveillee 1999), including 26 features sorted into three types: deep pit cremations (n = at least 7) with lithics, bifaces, groundstone, seeds, nuts, wood, and red ocher, often suggesting bundling; shallow basins/bowls with burned soil, artifacts, or floral matter but no bone; and shallow pits with low densities of both bone and artifacts, and no indication of burning.

Feature 1A yielded 7,900 pieces of bone and 315 pieces of lithics, all of which were clustered. These lithics were fragments of points, flakes, complete points, and drills, fragments of pestles, and fragments of axes. Groundstone items were generally found along the outer edge of the feature, and the bottom of the feature was lined with rocks.

Feature 1B, the second largest feature, contained 554 calcined bones and 83 lithic pieces. Interesting for the possible symbolism of wood was the finding of oak, willow, and elm among the charcoal. Elsewhere these three woods were complemented by a fourth, a conifer, suggesting associations with the cardinal directions.

Among the animals (n = 9,937 pieces) cremated with the humans (n = 11,425) were deer, box and painted turtles, and birds. Nonhuman bones were more frequent than human bones in all but three of the bone-bearing features (all of which had animal bones) and the bones were always completely calcined (Leveillee 1999:173).

Among the human bones, dry as well as wet bodies were cremated, and all bones were completely calcined. While Leveillee assumes that the dry bones were from secondary burials, there is no evidence that these individuals had been interred prior to their cremation. All parts of the body are present, and both women and men, young and old, are represented.

Hazel and hickory nut meat seem to have been burned on some occasions, and shells of both plus acorn were burned. Huckleberry and blackberry were present in several features with cremains, and a single strand of two-ply, S-twisted cordage was recovered in one feature.

At least 25 percent of the stone items were significantly worn—as though water rolled—when deposited. Leveillee thinks that they might have been carried long enough to produce this effect. Several items were obviously broken at the time of interment. "[I]t is clear that 'old' tools and tool fragments were introduced into the cremation features. In some instances, worn artifacts were re-worked before they were included in the cremation context" (Leveillee 1999:178).

See *cremation, tree*

Modoc Rockshelter, Illinois

There are two shelters here, Main and West, both opening to the southwest and 4.8 km from the Mississippi River, although the river was closer during the Archaic. It is one of many shallow limestone rockshelters in a 30-km stretch of the Mississippi bluffs. A small creek is 200 m west of the shelter. Both Ste. Genevieve and Burlington cherts were abundant in the surrounding limestone.

Although Dalton points cluster in the West Shelter over a large projecting bedrock shelf, C14 dates indicative of Dalton did not appear in the suite of dates. Ahler et al. (1992:12) offer scavenging of older points and deposition here as an explanation for the presence of Dalton points.

Stratum 9E was interesting for several reasons. Pigment production was intensive in this component, and the greatest proportion of aquatic versus terrestrial resources was removed from this stratum. Stratum 9E had cherry, *Cucurbita*, bedstraw, dogwood, and persimmon. Exhausted items are twice as common in Stratum 9E as in other strata. One burial in Stratum 9E was a headless female, 45–50 yo, flexed, and on her left side.

It is most curious that Stratum 8E, said to be essentially sterile and a stratum that delineated two essentially single components, Strata 9E and 7E, has birds with ritual significance including passenger pigeon, northern flicker, Canadian goose, sandhill crane, the only hawk (*Buteo lineatus*), and a yellow-billed cuckoo or "rain crow." It also has a number of reptiles (Ahler et al. 1992:60) and the lowest percentage of burned bones among all strata. Each substratum of level 8E was dominated by a different class of animal. Four marine snail *Marginella* sp. beads came from Stratum 12 with an 8,000-year-old date, and 3 from Stratum 7/8 with a date of 7,200 ya (Ahler et al. 1992:6). Stratum 8E also had the highest proportion of unifaces among all strata, demonstrating an emphasis on expedient tools rather than curated tools.

From the Late Archaic Stratum 7E came 68 features, 40 with partial excavation. A large rock with "major pitted and battered areas on its upper surface" was found in one of the pillars of sediment (Ahler et al. 1992:24). Ash lenses made up the majority of the features, suggesting cooking and heating functions. "All of the Late Archaic strata (4890–4100 BP) appear to contain more species than would be expected for the specialized Late Archaic hunting camps" (Ahler et al. 1992:78). The most common Late Archaic seed was wild chenopod. Two wild *Iva* seeds and squash were recovered.

Among the 28 skeletons recovered from this site, the majority were 30+ yo with evidence for fractures in all but one woman. Bu11, Bu20, Bu23, and Bu24 at Modoc were missing either the skull or mandible; in these cases the skeletons were either disarticulated reburials with other elements also missing or had been disturbed by animals. Bu21 was a skull only. Many were older than 45 years and quite unhealthy (Neumann 1967). Only five people were 20 yo or younger. Several other subadults were identifiable only by loose teeth and were not in the count of individuals (Powell 1995).

Although Charles and Buikstra (2002) have argued that burial populations found in places other than ridge-top mounds are made up of nonproductive individuals, it is just as easy to argue that honorable dead—the elders and priests—were placed in this rockshelter as secondary burials, given the importance of caves, rockshelters, and elders. In the process of primary or secondary interment in rockshelters such as Modoc, funeral fires were burned (Modoc had five times the charcoal of all but one other LIV site), and birds, aquatic fauna, and stone points were offered by kin and by descendants.

See *ancestor, bird, gastropod, ocher, point reuse, ritual specialist/priest, projectile point, shell bead, trash/midden*

Monte Sano, Louisiana

An important window into Middle Archaic ritualizing in the lower Mississippi valley is available at this early two-mound site in east-central Louisiana with burials. Mound A was 5 m x 45 m in diameter and Mound B 2.5 m x 35 m in diameter. "A rectangular structure measuring 10 m on a side was built on the ground surface. This building was dismantled and a low rectangular platform roughly .5 m high was built covering most of the rectangular structure. The surface of this platform was burned and was overlain by a layer of charcoal and burned bone, 'most probably the remains of human cremations' (Kuttruff 1997:5). A small (ca. 4 m high by 1.5 m diameter) dome-shaped mound was built on this platform" (Kidder and Sassaman 2009:673). This small mound was composed of two layers of charcoal and redeposited cremated human bone. "A final mantle covered the primary and secondary platforms. Artifacts included an oversized biface of northern flint, two tubular jasper beads, and a jasper 'bird' effigy bead" (Kidder and Sassaman 2009:673).

See *burning, capping, cremation, Hedgepeth Mounds, mound—dirt, stone bead*

Newt Kash Shelter, Kentucky

This shelter in eastern Kentucky is one of several in the Cumberland Plateau that seems to have been used as a menstrual retreat, birthing shelter, and possibly a medicine society meeting place (Claassen 2011a, 2013b). It faces due south and is at the head of a deep sandstone ravine. Activities may have begun here in the Late Archaic. In addition to the famous stashes of goosefoot and sumpweed seeds, nuts (acorns, hickory, walnuts, chestnuts) in great quantity had been pulverized, and two mortar holes were found in one boulder in the shelter (Webb and Funkhouser 1936). Along with the seeds, quids, sheaves, wood, and nuts, there were hundreds of pieces of fabric, string, and cordage. Caches of textiles were found in several places. Freshwater valves, shell spoons, antler points, awls, needles, a few sherds, gourds, nutting stones, a large number of fecal specimens, small pits, and postholes, a few animal bones, and a cradleboard were found. These seem to indicate special utensils and a particular diet for menstruating women (low in meat), as well as the activities they undertook while retreating: nut oil and dye production, gathering and processing bark and fibers, and making string and cordage.

Doctoring also seems to have been undertaken in the shelter. The vast majority of the plants recovered had medicinal properties including astringents, abortatives, gynecological aids, purgatives, and kidney aids (Claassen 2011a). The shelter may have had a separate use as a meeting locus for a medicine society.

Perhaps the best evidence for regulated/ritualized activities can be found in the three groups of pits and the 15 postholes uncovered. The first group consists of 8 pits, nearly equally spaced against the back wall of the shelter. Their volumes range from 60 to 1,248 liters with uniform spacing of the larger pit subset and of the smaller pit subset.

A second group of pits forms a quincunx approximately in the center back of the shelter. The quincunx is associated with earth creation and earth renewal at least by 1,700 ya (Hall 1997). Equally pertinent to the understanding of the significance of the quincunx is that the days with the number 5 in the Aztec calendar were associated with handcrafts and with women dying in childbirth (Anders et al. 1993:250). Finally, the roof fall rocks had been pushed to the drip line, making an amphitheater facing the central quincunx and altar stones. The burned bones of an infant were found between and beneath these two rocks.

See *altar, bedrock mortar/nutting stone, medicine, menstrual retreat, number, rockshelter, sacrifice—infant and child, shell scoop/spoon, textile/weaving*

Nulliak Mounds, Labrador

This boulder burial mound site dates to the later half of the Late Labrador Archaic, 4000–3500 B.P. Mound 1 was an oval 10 m x 8 m pile of boulders 5 layers thick. Under a stone chamber with lintel constructed in the eastern side was a huge red ocher–stained cap slab. Under that lintel was an oval burial deposit (150 cm x 120 cm) with 7 clusters of grave goods, "including groups of Ramah chert points, large bipoints, a quarry blank, and other tools, many of which had been killed, resting on sheets of red ocher–covered mica and birch bark" over charcoal (Fitzhugh 2006:57–58).

A second tomb was indicated as an 8-m-wide boulder pavement. The pavement covered Ramah chert bifaces, a ground slate knife, and, deeper, a walrus tusk, red ocher, charcoal, and fragments of mica and bone. "Large sheets of mica lined the pit walls and floor. The mica sheets, a native copper pendant, and a Ramah stemmed point dated the burial to the Rattler's Bight period, ca. 4000–3500 BP" (Fitzhugh 2006:57–58).

The burials were either single and flexed or possibly bone bundles. Fitzhugh (2006) envisions these dead to be of importance to a community larger than a family, given the richness of Mound 1. Perhaps they qualified as "ancestors."

See *ancestor, breakage, cache—blade, mound—boulder, ocher, Rattler's Bight*

Oconto, Wisconsin

This early Old Copper cemetery with 53 excavated bodies and an estimated 150 more people is situated on a gravel knoll near the Oconto River. Pleger (1998:80) argues that the cemetery was on an island at the mouth of the Oconto River and visible from Green Bay when it was being used 4000 to

3000 B.C. Here was found not only a burial ground but a rare crematorium with remains from at least 5 individuals. Numerous post molds in the burial ground were reported.

Among the dead in the burial area were 9 extended bodies (2 facedown), a posture that probably indicates a violent death, 12 bundles, 11 flexed skeletons, and 8 cremations. Four of the dead were infants, 9 were juveniles, several were adults, and 8 were of unknown age. Other types of burials found were superimposed burial, bundle of a man with children, isolated body parts, mother and babe, and groups of 5 or more individuals.

Feature 7 had evidence of multiple individuals, including a female cranium, a disarticulated male, several sets of long bones, a woman with grave goods, an infant, and miscellaneous bones from at least 3 individuals, perhaps people represented elsewhere in the feature (Pleger 1998:90). Numerous burial pits at this site contained only parts of individuals such as Bu14, which held the cranium and feet of a juvenile 6–8 yo (a trophy part disposal?) and the cremated long bones and skull of another individual.

One burial had marine shell and 2 naiad valves. Two to six percent of the dead in each age category had grave goods, adults most frequently. Pleger (1998:112) handled 329 g of copper items. Copper, chipped-stone, bone, and shell artifacts were associated with some burials and included a copper fishhook and an open-clasp bracelet. There were no signs of violence on any bodies, but plenty of isolated parts (crania, long bones, foot) were encountered.

Much about this burial area suggests an unusual collection of individuals. Several treatments of the dead are quite different from what is typically seen. The extended bodies, mass cremations, and body-part deposits suggest a burial ground filled with the remains of victims of perhaps murder, accidental death, or trophy part decommissioning rites.

See *burial—posture, crematory, island, trophy part, trophy part decommissioning rite*

Orange Mound, Florida

In addition to a mortuary mound, mortuary behavior and beliefs are in evidence here. Orange Mound is a Mount Taylor and Orange periods mortuary mound in the upper St. Johns River. It was 14 ft high (4.3 m), was crescent shaped, and oriented north-south. The top 4.5 ft (1.4 m) of the mound seemed to be midden with numerous hearths, animal bones, and fiber-tempered pottery. Next came a shell and brown sand layer with one extended body on its left side with its head to the southwest. Nearby was a bone bundle on top of a skull. Below this layer was a pure white sand, under which was a layer of mixed shell and brown sand. At 8 ft (2.4 m) deep a burial area was encountered and below that more "midden" (Aten 1999:176).

See *color, mound—shell, trash/midden*

Port au Choix-3, Newfoundland

This island mortuary site is the type site of the Maritime Archaic manifestation. All ages and both sexes were present among the 93 individuals buried in Locus 2 who had been grouped into three clusters. Every grave was marked with a low pile of large stones, sprinkled with red ocher powder, and staged with offerings. Flexure on the side was the only position for articulated adults, but children were extended. Bundle burials, double burials, mass burials, a missing head, a possible adultery killing, and two dog burials were also recorded. No cremations were observed. Only one burial did not have grave goods, and one grave was a mass burial of at least nine people. Similar to the interpretation favored elsewhere in this guide, Tuck believed that "These deviations might reflect the treatment accorded individuals whose death was in some way extraordinary such as death by accident; drowning, for example" (1976:96). Gould, an associated mortuary camp, was found just opposite the island on the mainland in the view shed of the burial ground (Renouf and Bell 2011).

Among the grave goods were stone woodworking tools, bayonets, points, bird and sea mammal effigies and pendants, antler harpoons and daggers, and bone needles, combs, pendants, and pebbles. Nearly every burial had either bird bone or bird or egg imagery included. Quartz pebble concentrations suggest that bags of items were interred with many individuals. At least one individual was buried in a cape adorned with seashells and another individual in a cape of Great Auk bills (Tuck 1976).

In addition to copious amounts of red ocher, some graves contained copious numbers of specific artifacts. For example, one grave had 13 white stones, one had 100+ white pebbles, one had 50+ amethysts, and one had considerable mica (Tuck 1976). An example of numerous but different grave goods can be seen in Bu2, from Locus 4. Bones of this infant, lightly sprinkled with red ocher, were fragmented and lying on top of the following grave goods, also showing red ocher: a large, barbed harpoon point, a two-piece foreshaft, a stone ax, a caribou antler gouge, many fragments of ground-edge beaver incisors, bird long bones, the bill of a loon, two antler tines, a section of broad caribou antler, several limestone pebbles, and pieces of birchbark (Tuck 1976:23–24). Could this be the deposit of offerings and paraphernalia used in a hunting ritual?

BuC35A, a male at least 45 yo, was buried with 49 beaver incisors and had the greatest dietary intake of terrestrial food (caribou and beaver) among the 29 bodies tested for stable isotopes. He also had a cape of 200+ Great Auk bills (flightless birds but good divers) and the only projectile point found in any grave. Was this man a religious specialist?

Tuck (1976:50) wondered about the lack of bone-working and stone-working tools in the graves and offered that the religious beliefs did not include these activities in the afterlife. Instead, woodworking, fishing, and paddling seemed to have been anticipated activities of the souls based on the amulets and tools included. Fish bones and copper were rarely found in graves.

A recent study of the three subdivisions of the Locus 2 cemetery at Port au Choix-3 combined DNA, carbon and nitrogen stable isotopes, radiocarbon dates, and mortuary attributes for an investigation of the significance of the three spatial subdivisions of burials (Jelsma 2006). The 93 skeletons in 95 graves in Locus 2 were found as Cluster A 18 burials, Cluster B 30 burials, and Cluster C 47 burials. Nine new AMS dates with reservoir corrections bracketed burial activities between 2600 and 2100 B.C.

Mortuary decisions that could not be explained by the relative age of each cluster were (1) the significantly male-biased sex ratio in Cluster C, (2) the deeper and larger pits of Cluster C, (3) the goose and Great Auk association with Cluster C, (4) the exclusive presence of shark and otter tooth beads, bird skull, and gull bills in Cluster A, (5) the significantly higher nitrogen values of Cluster B bodies, and (6) the greater presence of terrestrial foods in the diets of Cluster C individuals.

Mitochondrial DNA results also indicated that these three clusters of burials in Locus 2 were not genetically distinct. These individuals had 20 different mitochondrial lineages that might mean that women had married into a patrilocal community from a wide region. The lack of genetically related clusters of individuals means a corporate group is not present. Jelsma concluded, therefore, that status differences held by men were expressed in the three clusters. These statuses were men with little hunting experience (Cluster B, with high sea mammal diets), experienced hunters (Cluster C, with a broad diet of terrestrial and marine foods), and primarily fishers, including many women buried with fishing gear (Cluster A) (Jelsma 2006:93–94).

See *bird, burial—posture, cairn, first-kill rite, island, ocher, ritual specialist/priest, sacrifice—infant and child*

Poverty Point, Louisiana

Gibson builds the case that Poverty Point was built on a selected spot on the raised shore of Lake Macon, a lake that later drained suddenly as a result of an undated flood of the Mississippi River (2010:36). The subsistence base was aquatic plants and fish, dug and caught with imported plummet stone and chert hoe stone and, equally important, in a location that provided an unbroken view of the heavens.

Gibson explains the genesis of this site as follows: "The Tamoroha appeared instantaneously, as archaeological reckoning goes, shortly before 3700 cal B.P. They seem to have materialized out of local loess and bayou water, stirred with the hyperbole of their mastery of heavenly cycles and celebration of their own venerable birth . . . the natural world they were engaging was *a watery one*" (2010:35).

Sassaman offers that the people of Claiborne, Mississippi, supplied soapstone and many of the design elements seen at Poverty Point, including the idea of arcs, mounds behind arcs, and residences on ridges. From Macon Ridge came mound surveying knowledge, and from up the Mississippi River came cherts, galena, and copper, all coalescing in northeastern Louisiana around 3400 B.P. (Sassaman 2010a:65). Other sites now included in Poverty Point culture are spread out over 1,800 km^2. The Poverty Point interaction sphere took in literally most of the eastern United States.

Mound construction at Poverty Point proper spanned 400 years, from 3800 to 3200 B.P., with abandonment of the center by 3000 B.P. Hallmarks of Poverty Point are the elaborate earthworks constructions including six nested elliptical half rings, a conical mound, two flat-top mounds, and one flat-topped platform possibly capped by a low dome (Gibson 1994:170), nearly 765,000 m^3 of mounded earth. These arcs and mounds were arranged so as to create a plaza that is 600 m (14 acres or 5.6 hectares) wide (Sassaman 2010a:57).

Clark found that all major axial alignments at the site (1) pass through much older Middle Archaic Lower Jackson mound (2004:212n4), (2) used triangulation (10 nested equilateral triangles incorporate all of the Poverty Point site), and (3) used the Standard Measurement Unit (1.66 x 52 or 86.63 m). The 3-month-long construction sequence of Mound A began by filling a depression with colored silts (Sassaman 2010a:65). This T-shaped earthwork is 60 ft (18.3 m) high and measures almost 640 ft (195 m) in both directions.

"The west sector of the rings was a sacred precinct because it had a disproportionate number of finished, hard stone lapidary objects, which we assumed belonged to civic and religious personages. Unfinished lapidary items were concentrated in the south sector of the rings" (Gibson 1998:19). The embankments, each about 6 ft (1.8 m) high and 60–100 ft (18.3– 30.4 m) wide, form an immense semicircle some 4,000 ft (1,219 m) in diameter. These embankments supported an unknown number of pole frame houses.

The C-shaped arcuate rings opening to the east at Poverty Point are likened by Gibson (1998:23) to Gulf peoples' homage to the sun. Gibson also mentions that the open-ended arc allowed evil to leave the area. Sweeping and untying spaces such as a house lot, a village, a field, and even units of time (e.g., the Voladores) were done in Mesoamerican cultures for exactly the same benefit. A water body at the opening prevented evil spirits from entering the arc as did a barrier of ashes (Hall 1976:360–363). The water barrier at Poverty Point was provided either by a creek that passed by both ends of the C or by Lake Macon.

The extensive midden present is the main reason for arguing that the place had a secular residential function as well as the obvious ceremonial one. The midden at Poverty Point "is obvious by the tons and tons of trash they left. At the site, dark midden underlies the elevated rings and it formed on top of the finished rings and along their lower edges. Dark midden incorporates abundant domestic remains—charcoal, chipped and groundstone tools and residue from tool making, fire-cracked gravel, angular pieces of sandstone and other rocks and minerals, loess cooking balls, and many other artifacts. Sometimes densities in the dark middens reach an artifact per cubic centimeter. . . . fire pits, earth ovens, postmolds, and remnants of other stationary facilities occur both underneath and on temporary building-module surfaces within the rings" (Gibson 1998:21).

The debris in the midden underlying the rings is comprised of finished tools and unbroken and unreworked bifacial tools, and that in the fill of the rings is predominantly expediently produced flakes and blades. "The amount of chipped-stone tool debris is staggering" (Carr and Stewart 2004:130), with the exotic stone estimated by Gibson (1998) to be 70 metric tons. Other minerals present are "copper, galena, hematite, magnetite, and a remarkable amount of soapstone" (Carr and Stewart 2004:130), even though the nearest toolstone source is 60 km away. However, this imported material "was often geared toward the production of mundane items. . . . [When] coupled with the ubiquitous baked-clay objects, hearths, pits, and midden accumulation, the inventory of material related to subsistence technology clearly shows that Poverty Point was a place of residence" (Kidder and Sassaman 2009:680).

Poverty Point is the key site in the trade in steatite. Steatite, whether for mundane use or not, was found in "a pit containing more than 2,200 fragments of steatite vessels in an oval pit 2.5 m long by 2 m wide and 60 cm deep, with a burned bottom. It was located west of mounds A and E" (Clark 2004:212n5).

Clearly Poverty Point was not a vacant ceremonial center. Perhaps all of the exotic materials mean that it was a center to which pilgrims may have come at different times throughout the year (sensu Jackson 1991). Sassaman believes that the spatial relationships between Poverty Point and the other contemporary sites within its sphere constituted a cosmogram (2010a). A community's place within that cosmogram may have been dictated by when in the calendar it made a pilgrimage to the center. A relevant model is the pilgrimage pattern followed by villages surrounding the ceremonial center at Chalma, Mexico, that has been enacted for centuries and continues today. Each village has its set time each year to make the trip. "It follows that Poverty Point was foremost a shared belief system, organized at a corporate level for public works and ritual but underwritten by an ethos of egalitarianism. Certainly, the symbolism of the earthworks and associated charms and fetishes points to a complex worldview of supernatural forces and spirits" (Kidder and Sassaman 2009:681).

The abandonment of the center at Poverty Point has been attributed to a flood that caused an abrupt shift in the river channel near the site (Kidder and Sassaman 2009:681). No Poverty Point burials have been found. The arcs opening to the east, the lack of burials, the lack of red ocher, and the lack of marine shell all suggest that activities at Poverty Point had a birth, new life focus rather than death/fertilization focus.

See *ashes, astronomy, bird, C-shaped site layout, cardinal direction, Claiborne, earthwork, geometry, measurement, mound—dirt, number, pilgrimage, soapstone/steatite, stone, trash/midden*

Rattler's Bight, Labrador

This habitation site is interesting for a number of reasons, including the evidence of two Maritime Archaic mortuary clusters at the edge of the housing area. While the longhouses in this region show remarkable uniformity in tool kits, these bundle burials, in two clusters, were marked by tremendous variation in grave goods. Although all graves are now cenotaphs, it was clear that bones had been wrapped in skin and bark. One human burial also contained a dog burial. Fires burned at the graves but did not burn the bones or the goods. Killing of slate points, celts, and gouges was inconsistently practiced. Burial pits were up to a meter deep with slabs placed atop some burials. "Size of burial superstructure correlated closely with the number and diversity of grave goods, and graves without rock fill tended to have smaller tool caches than graves with large, complex rock constructions" (Fitzhugh 2006:60).

Ground slate items, soapstone plummets, copper items, stemmed points, rows of small quartz pebbles, iron pyrites, walrus tusk celts, folded layers of sewn birch bark, mica, and copious quantities of red ocher were frequently deposited in the nine burial pits. One burial contained 52 stone, mineral, pebble, tusk, and copper items and another had 68 items (whale ribs, beaver incisors, and walrus tusk) with 21 refits made.

Fitzhugh (2006) thought that the two burial clusters were sequential in use and indicative of changes in burial customs. The smaller and younger of the two clusters (consisting of only two conjoined graves with a bed of red ocher) differed from the other in that it contained southern stone types, an inverted walrus skull, charred faunal remains, and pebbles.

See *ashes, breakage, dog with human burial rite, Nulliak Mounds, Port au Choix-3, ocher, pebble, projectile point*

Read, Kentucky

Dates for this bluff-top shell-bearing site are late in the SOV shell mounding phenomenon (Claassen 2010:Table 2.1). Read is outstanding for the number of dog burials present—65—none associated with a specific human. This site alone accounts for one-fifth of all known Archaic dog burials yet Milner and Jefferies (1998) consider activities here to have been quite mundane. Furthermore, the fact that people were willing to haul shells to the top of bluff suggests that Read was founded not as a village location but for some other purpose, presumably for the dog sacrifice rite.

There were also 247 human burials. Among the humans was one interment with an extra skull; another had an extra skull and long bones. One infant had a possible Milky Way belt. Thirty percent of the people had grave goods with an exceptionally high average number of items, 3.1 (Claassen 2010:231).

See *bluff, dog, dog sacrifice rite, mortuary camp, skull, trophy part decommissioning rite*

Reigh, Wisconsin

The Reigh Old Copper cemetery had several disposal modes, although not cremations, and appears to have been the scene of a hunt god rite. Both utilitarian and ornamental grave goods were included in graves (Pleger 1998:39). A single radiocarbon date of 1710+/-250 bc has been obtained.

The most interesting mortuary event is seen in Feature 6. "The upper layer consisted of a mass of secondary human bone from at least three individuals. Beneath this layer, a second deposit contained the remains of five individuals: an infant, a child, and two adults centered around an adult male" (Pleger 1998:39). The adult male was adorned with a featherlike copper headdress that consisted of 23 sheets of copper hammered around a strip of hide. "The copper sheets were 30 to 48 mm long, 7 to 11 mm wide, and 1 to 2 mm thick, and their aggregate weight was 65g" (Pleger 1998:38).

This feature is charged with various components of ritual quite distinct from those of "typical burials." While Pleger sees in the feature an aggrandizer and his kin, I propose a hunt rite marking a new year or world renewal rite because of the deer headdress, age distribution, and quincunx arrangement. This rite would have entailed the ritual killing of at least the four encircling bodies, perhaps coinciding with the natural death of the central figure, or perhaps he was also sacrificed. This five-body rite seems to be a curious mixture of a hunt god rite and the four-age rite.

See *copper, four-age rite, hunt god rite, mask/headdress, number, ocher*

Riverton, Illinois

The Riverton site in the floodplain on the west bank of the Wabash River appears to have been a Late Archaic site where several rituals were conducted, some of which included burial of corpses or cremations.

Area X, in particular, yielded 10 yellow baked-clay "floors" and 3 associated burials (Figure 15) that account for most of the ritually significant objects recovered: 41 manos, 4 tooth pendants (wolf canine, human incisor, 2 mink canines), 40+ pearl beads, 13 bone beads, a cloudblower pipe (blackened inside), 8+ flutes (3 from features), 2 turtle shell rattles, spilled red ocher powder, a sizable red ocher preparation area (Feature 32), several cup-and-pin game pieces and counterpieces, 2 gar mandibles, 2 shell paint cups, a crinoid stem, several copper tools, strike-a-lites, and numerous other items of antler, bone, and chert (Winters 1969). Area X was clearly a ritual area and provides the best evidence that baked-clay floors were associated with ritualizing in the Archaic. Perhaps these baked-clay features indicate the loci of shrines and their associated ritual paraphernalia. If so, then the 5 complete and rectangular floors indicate shrines of 68–260 ft^2 (6.32–24.16 m^2) in size.

Bu1, a flexed inhumation of a subadult with a cache of 41 items, red ocher on the upper body, and yellow ocher on the legs, had a possible embedded

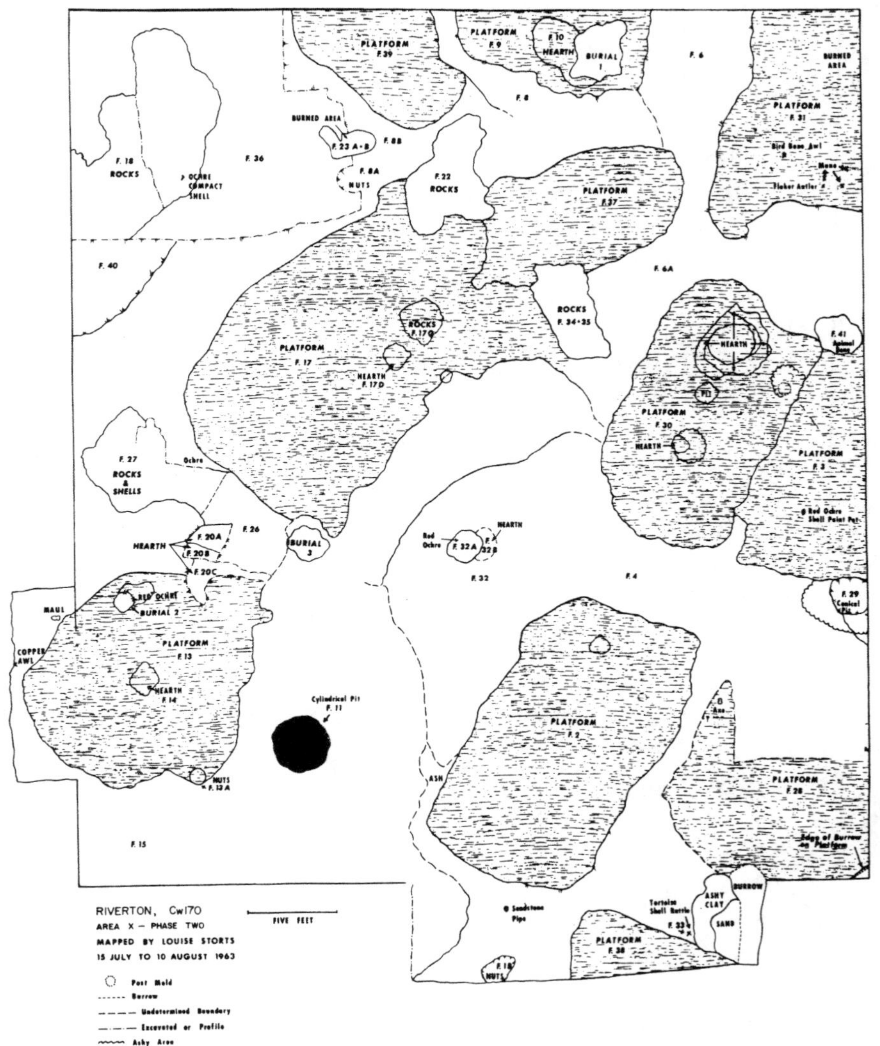

15. Plan of baked-clay floors, Riverton site. (Reprinted from Winters 1969:Figure 18, with permission from the Illinois State Museum.)

point in the rib cage. This pit and that of Bu2 cut through clay floors. Bu2, a flesh cremation done elsewhere, with copious quantities of red ocher over the bones, was associated with a Merom point, also possibly embedded, a bird claw, and a knife fragment. Bu3, a flexed burial of an older man, was found between two baked-clay surfaces. One infant burial was covered in red ocher and found outside Area X. Fragments of a skull were found south of Area X, and fragments of an ocher-stained infant were found southeast of Area X.

Other probable ritual features are the 7 large clay and sand-lined basins, 5 ft (1.5 m) in diameter with evidence of burning and posts. Several of these posts were 10–12 inches (0.25–0.30 m) in diameter and were possibly ritual poles/posts.

Several small midden deposits look like world renewal offerings. For instance, Feature 18 contained more than 200 bones of 19 taxa. The artifacts included were two cut antler sections, two splinter awls, and one triangular chert blade, leaf-shaped blade, blade fragment, shell paint cup, shuttle, canine pendant, and Riverton point fragment. These items may have been used in the accompanying ritual in which the animals were deposited. The species represent creatures from the Lower World, This World, and the Upper World.

Feature 22 had 32 large mammal bones; the bones of 2 fish, 5 bird, 3 deer, 1 porcupine, 1 opossum, 1 raccoon, and 2 snake; and 2 snapping turtle bones (Winters 1969:101), none of them burned although the feature was found amid burned sandstone and a fired-clay surface. Feature 11, called a "storage pit," had several layers of soil over a plug of yellow clay that covered 13 large mammal bones, as well as bones of 5 other creatures, 1 Robeson point, and 1 cut section of antler. Below these items was more clay, then 12 bones of at least 4 species, possibly indicating a world renewal offering.

See *baked-clay surface, music, paint/powder, ocher, offering, pearl, pipe, pole/post, rattle, shrine, world renewal rite*

Rodgers Shelter, Missouri

This shelter is in the Pomme de Terre valley of the Ozarks and, what is more significant, near several artesian springs and a Pleistocene bone bed. There were numerous elements uncovered during excavation that suggest Rodgers was a ritual shelter in Archaic times. The record of rites begins with a Dalton-aged feature that contained most of the skeleton of a trumpeter swan (Kay 1982), a bird associated with Historic rituals.

A world renewal bone offering was found in this shelter, Feature 8233, in the Middle Archaic Horizon 8 (Kay 1982). The variety of animals' bones included—a human humerus and tibia, a bison tooth, a large bird bone, a terrapin shell fragment, cottontail parts, squirrel parts (humerus, calcanium, and radius fragments), and a pharyngeal fragment of a drumfish—as well as one finely flaked point expressed the concepts of bone soul and renewal. Six inches away sat a hematite processing slab (Feature 8242). A second pit feature contained the pelvis and sacrum of a deer, one bison phalanx, rabbit parts (teeth, ulna, and radius), a terrapin shell, a turkey ulna and coracoids, a canis premolar, and a squirrel radius that also can be interpreted as a world renewal offering. In these ritual acts a high diversity of species but low numbers of individuals were used.

A different renewal focus may be indicated by a feature filled with bivalves and aquatic gastropods found in the Late Archaic horizon. A dog sacrifice rite of some nature is signaled by the burial of a dog.

Several minerals were present in the shelter and were apparently prepared for use there. The hematite quantity was the most remarkable here of any of the Middle Archaic ritual shelters or caves. In Middle Archaic Horizon 7 there were two hematite grinding areas with large quantities of powdered hematite, hematite-stained grinding slabs, pieces of ground hematite, and adjacent hearths. Kay points out that the suite of items supports the "idea that chunks of hematite were purposely fired both to enhance the color and make the hematite softer" (1982:571). Did most red ocher used in caching and burial in eastern North America have prior ritualized processing?

Three possible structures were identified by Kay (1982) in the Horizon 7 levels inside Rodgers Shelter, further adding to the impression that it was ritual space during the Archaic. Structures 1 and 2 were rings of rock 5 ft (1.5 m) in diameter. Structure 2's outline incorporated 3 pieces of hematite, 1 hammerstone, 5 cores, 2 biface preforms, 3 projectile points, 1 scraper, 4 utilized flakes, 1 tooth, and 1 piece of galena. Structure 3, which was 6.7 ft (2.04 m) in diameter, enclosed 2 groundstone fragments, 5 cores, 1 biface preform, and 1 projectile point. Both Ahler and McMillan (1976) and Kay (1982) allowed that these might be Middle Archaic ceremonial structures inside Rodgers Shelter.

Three flexed burials were also uncovered. Bu1 was an adolescent with grave goods, Bu2 a woman on the left side with no grave goods, and Bu3, no age or sex, with grave goods. An engraved dolomite plaque was in the general area and at the depth of Bu1 and Bu2 (Kay 1983:62). Bu1 and Bu3 had points associated with bones.

See *dog sacrifice rite, Graham Cave, ocher, offering, paint/powder, Pomme de Terre River, projectile point, rockshelter, shell, world renewal rite*

Rosenberger, Kentucky

This is a shell-free, open-air Late Archaic burial ground on a narrow ridge paralleling the Ohio River. C14 dates procured by the author in 2012 for two nondescript features are 3862+/-34 and 4085+/-28 B.P.

Rosenberger has no cremations but numerous examples of secondary interments and six extended burials, four of which are oriented northward. Eight individuals had red ocher staining and 62 individuals had grave goods among the 231 Archaic burials (Driskell 1979:759–762). Few subadults had grave goods (Driskell 1979:774). The deepest burials at Rosenberger are four double interments and a single infant. One of these double burials appears to be a childbirth death pair, but the extended position of the "mother" suggests something different about this death episode. Elsewhere among the burials are four four-age rites, a possible adultery killing (Feature 108) with a large faunal collection, a possible ritual specialist (Feature 239) with a large faunal collection, and a dog burial.

Rosenberger has four four-age rites, three Archaic and one Woodland in age (Feature 362). Details on the Archaic four-age rites are as follows. Feature 1 had two children, a flexed mature man, and a young adult. A flake, a biface, a core, and a hollow tine were included, possibly symbolizing the flintknapping skill. Feature 97 contained an extended young woman, an extended mature man, a flexed mature man, and a fetus. Seven artifacts were included: cut antler, a fishhook, modified flake, a core, and three Archaic points (Wade and two McWhinney). Feature 206 held the skeletons of a mature man with head to the northwest, a mature adult, a young adult, an infant, and four artifacts: two bifaces and two pestles (Driskell 1979:781).

One blade cache was associated with a burial. It consisted of 41 blades in two groups placed perpendicular to each other. Another cache contained 12 cores (one weighing at least 700 g), four bifaces, and four modified flakes, all multiples of the number 4. Eight individuals had bannerstones, two had a grooved ax, one had drills, one had a drilled canine, two had net weights, and two had turtle shell. One of the most common grave inclusions was a lithic core. The burial ground matrix and most features are "littered" with flakes.

There are two features at Rosenberger that suggest poles. These "irregularly shaped pits," Driskell says, "contained deep, conical depressions in the bottoms of elongate irregularly shaped pits." Neither potential pole is in the midst of burials but rather to the edge, one a part of a small cluster of pit features. One pit's dimensions are 90 to 100 cm long with depths of 26–45 cm (Driskell 1979:775).

Shell-free burial grounds like Rosenberger lack the large feasts indicated by piles of naiad shells (as well as marine shell objects), suggesting more sequestered burial activities and rites.

See *adultery killing, burial—group, burial—posture, cache—blade, dog sacrifice rite, four-age rite, number, pole/post*

Russell Cave, Alabama

There is a pair of openings here, an east-facing rockshelter, where all excavation has occurred, and an adjacent cave through which runs a stream for two miles (see photo in Claassen 2012c). Numerous elements of the archaeological record from Russell Cave's rockshelter suggest ritual activities.

This cave was the site of both human and dog burial. Among the six burials found during the National Park Service excavations (Griffin 1974) were two infants, one child, one adolescent, and two adults (possibly one woman and one man and potentially comprising one four-age rite). The deepest burial was an infant 20–24 months old found between rocks, facedown, head to the south and returned the oldest date at the site, 8500+/-320 rcy. The posture and location suggest a sacrifice. Four other skeletons were found in the Middle Archaic layer F. One burial was covered with limestone slabs and had two large points and a stone pestle. Two older adults, one sexed as female, were flexed on the back with extraordinary abrasion and attrition of all the teeth (Griffin 1974:69). The adolescent was present as a bundle burial and included legs, pieces of arms, clavicles, ribs, and vertebrae.

The Archaic levels had other interesting features. Postholes for a lightweight frame of some sort and a basket with charred seeds were found. Slightly below the weighted skeleton was a small dog. "Its tomb was better built, with a stone base and slab sides to protect the body . . . a broken stone blade had been buried with this one" (Miller 1956:556). Bear bones were found in all levels and reportedly two bear long bones were hollowed out for lamps (Miller 1958:432). Ground hematite and split bone awls were concentrated in Early Archaic levels (among them only four small mammal awls). A deer mandible with three drill holes was found in the deepest level, suggesting a mask. Twenty different types of bifaces were found in that level as well.

Overall, 45 to 60 percent of the Archaic points retrieved in the National Park Service excavations were broken (n = 119). Rushes, cane fibers, and bone needles suggest weaving and sewing in the shelter. "Some pits had floors lined with rough limestone blocks, while others were of hard-packed earth" (Miller 1958:431). Atlatl hooks were found in Archaic levels.

Over 30,000 pieces of bone were recovered, representing at least 66 species and suggestive of an Archaic bone shrine function for the shelter at some point. Small terrestrial mammals were represented in greater or equal proportions to deer in both Early and Middle Archaic levels (Goldman-Finn 1994:219). Larger mammals and birds dominate the species list, but deer were uncommon. Black bear was present in all layers except the later Middle Archaic. Porcupine occurs here quite south of its modern range. Thirteen species of birds were recovered: passenger pigeons, loons, teal, wood duck, red-tailed and red-shouldered hawks, barred owl, and red-bellied woodpecker, many with Historic ritual or status associations. At least 20 turkeys and 155 gray squirrels were retrieved from one layer, suggesting a specific ceremony, a bone shrine, or a feast. Amphibians and reptiles were numerous as well, and at least 12 fish species were present, drum and catfish being the most common. Partial skeletons (e.g., heads of birds and hindquarters of deer) were common (Griffin 1974).

The bone debris from these early levels at Russell Cave suggests that this place was used repeatedly during the Archaic for rites related to renewal. The deposit of a human infant as the deepest burial in this cave also suggests a ritual sacrifice related to fertility, continuation, and renewal, as well as an acknowledgment of a reciprocal alliance with the entities responsible for earth renewal. Given the abundance of squirrels deposited, the question arises as to whether one of these spirits was later referenced by the Chickasaw as Squirrel King.

Finally, layer D, which appears to be comprised of sediments brought into the cave (Hack 1974; Miller 1956:555), was used to seal the Archaic material, yet rituals continued at the cave, as indicated by the numerous broken five-gallon capacity ceramic vessels. Griffin (1974:104) surmised that the time spent in the cave each trip was very short or involved very few people, a perspective in keeping with a ritual cave. Winter use was favored by Griffin. I propose that the rituals conducted in the rockshelter, and probably at the creek (a disappearing creek), at the associated sinkholes, and at a waterfall located upriver were directed at spirits residing in those places.

See *bear, bird, bone shrine, cave, dog, feasting, four-age rite, sacrifice—infant and child, sinkhole, turkey, waterfall, world renewal rite*

Salts Cave, Kentucky

The entrance to Salts Cave is at the bottom of a large sink that is wetted by water dripping from the rock face. The soot inside the entrance is sufficient enough to evoke the impression of a "dirty" cave (Watson 1969:12). Inside the cave are three levels of passages, called Upper Salts, Middle Salts, and Lower Salts, with large rooms, narrow passages, and canyons, where artifacts and feces were recovered. Charred cane bundles, used for lighting, were collected from the valley below the ridge. Two uncorrected dates, including one from the deepest passageway, indicate late Late Archaic activities (Watson 1969:70).

In a passage leading from the entrance chamber an excavation unit revealed six prepared floors of alternating layers of ash and fill with a hearth located in ash layer 5 (Watson 1969:21). Footprints of at least four people were found in Indian Avenue of Lower Salts (Watson 1969:25), and footprints found in the connected Crystal Cave suggest a fifth individual. A desiccated body of a young boy, who apparently died from a blow to the chest, might be an initiate or apprentice to a cave priest.

Early Woodland evidence of gypsum and mirabilite mining was found in all levels of Salts Cave. Undated parts of at least 44 people were found in the vestibule mixed with other animal remains. Several skulls and lower jaws of young children as well as adult bones were found in crevices between the stones, covered by ashes with fires on top of the ash layer. These bones sorted into 3 fetuses, 4 infants, 6 children, 4 adolescents, and 23 adults (8 female and 6 male). Many of these fragmentary remains suggest trophy parts and possibly decommissioning rites involving burning, as well as infant/child sacrifices.

See *ashes, cave mineral/mining, Mammoth Cave, ritual specialist/priest, sacrifice—infant and child, trophy part, trophy part decommissioning rite*

Sand Run Slough West, Iowa

This site on Lake Odessa with dates of 2685 B.C. and 2890 B.C. had components separated by fan sediments (Benn and Thompson (2009). The Archaic levels incorporated large quantities of fire-cracked rock and debitage, several structures, and numerous large (one meter in diameter) storage and roasting pits. Apparently the burial ground here was part of a habitation area.

Ten to eleven flexed or bundled burials and an isolated skull were recovered. An ossuary pit held the jumbled remains of five or more of these people. No grave goods were found, but high numbers of projectile points were recovered by collectors from an area of the burial ground (Benn and Thompson 2009:558), suggesting point offerings. Two dog burials were encountered. While this is the only known Middle Archaic cemetery in eastern Iowa, numerous bluff-top cemeteries are suspected around the mouth of the Iowa River contemporary with the Hemphill phase of Illinois.

See *dog sacrifice rite, offering, ossuary, projectile point*

Savage Cave, Kentucky

The Late Archaic Feature 6 in Savage Cave contained a point and a concentration of artifacts including "a tubular stone pipe, a bone pin, and an antler flaker, lying side by side, overlain by two incised shells. . . . One element each of big brown bat, a small bat, a frog, and a gray fox . . . were also associated" (Schenian 1988:79). "The pipe is decorated at the smaller opening by an incised chevron design. The wider opening is also decorated by an incised design, but this has been obscured by fracture lines in some areas. Both macroscopic and microscopic examination indicate that the design consists of chevrons and diagonal lines. The bone pin also is decorated with an incised chevron design, which appears to be stained with red ocher. One incised shell has a cross-hatch design along the interior rim. The second shell [and the awl tip are missing]" (Schenian 1985:19–20).

The predominance of four species in the cave—two daytime/sun species (deer and turkey) and two nighttime/moon species (raccoon and rabbit)—may reflect ritual remains.

See *amphibian, bird, bone pin, cave, design element, ocher, pipe, shell, sucking tube*

Short Cave, Kentucky

Short Cave is in the Mammoth Cave vicinity. A burial of a 45 yo woman suggests the burial of a ritual specialist in the Late Archaic. She was accompanied by a variety of faunal elements and seeds that were interpreted as ritual/medicinal items apparently contained in a fiber bag or medicine bundle (Jefferies 2008:238). Here we see that it is not the least among them, as suggested by others, but an important person buried in this cave.

See *cave, medicine bag, ritual specialist/priest*

Sloan, Arkansas

Erosion led to the discovery of Dalton artifacts in this series of sand dunes, which were professionally excavated in 1974. The site appears to have been a Dalton burial ground but none of the 28–30 skeletons has preserved (Morse 1997). From tiny bone fragments it was concluded that both juveniles and adults had been buried; 439 artifacts were found in clusters, suggesting graves and grave goods, primarily consisting of Dalton points and adzes. Minority items were scrapers, burins, hammers, lumps of red ocher, and an iron oxide nodule. Sloan constitutes the oldest burial ground in eastern North America, indicating something of Late Paleoindian beliefs and rites.

See *cemetery*

Spout Run, Virginia

This open-air site located in the Blue Ridge Mountains of Virginia consists of 15 stone features including several stone circles. Given that a circle provides vantage to every point on the horizon, it is not unexpected that one sight line would capture the solstice sunrises. However, in the case of one circle, the summer solstice sun rises over a feature known as Bears Den Rocks. Another set of rocks creates a sight line to Eagle Rock, where spring and fall equinox sunrises cross. A third set of stones points to a saddle in the mountain, where the sun rises at the winter solstice and footprint petroglyphs seem to orient the viewer (http://www.newsleader.com/article/20140511/NEWS01/305110011/1002/rss?nclick_check=1, accessed May 13, 2014). This stone circle was dated through retrieval of a jasper flake that was subjected to thermoluminescence. The result was 10.5+/-2.0 (thousands of years) (James Feathers, personal communication with the author), indicating a Paleoindian date.

In addition to the stone circles and solar alignments, shaped portable objects resembling bears and other creatures have been found on the surface. Up a slope from the circle described are stacked stone, creating an apparent altar. "The boulders, two wide and two high have been stacked and 'artificially shimmed, to try to make it as flat and level as possible'" (http://www.newsleader.com/article/20140511/NEWS01/305110011/1002/rss?nclick_check=1, accessed May 13, 2014).

See *altar, feet/footprint/track, rock formation, sun*

Stallings Island, Georgia

Burial in freshwater shell began during the Mill Branch occupation of Stallings Island, in the Savannah River, 5200–4450 B.P., in what was apparently an early expression of the Cult of the Bivalve Feast. The later immigrant Classic Stallings people waited some 250 years before moving onto the abandoned burial mound, doing so around 4200 B.P. They created a group of houses arranged in a circle around a plaza near the apex of the shell mound, filling huge pits with shell-feasting debris. The older Mill Branch shell was littered with "domestic refuse." A large number of Stallings carinated pots and bowls were discarded here as were other artifacts such as decorated bone pins. Sassaman (2006:145) links the pottery to feasting and the feasting to the mortuary activities. He estimates that the known 84 burials were part of a larger burial population of perhaps 300 individuals. Grave goods were rare.

Most of the Classic Stallings burials were made inside the plaza (all adults), and 12 more bodies were found in the house ring. Women were located in the southeastern quadrant of the plaza area, and two infants were found outside the house ring on the east and west sides. Five men were clustered in the very center of the plaza with their heads to the center, a possible hunt god rite, although Sassaman considers them to be affines symbolically adopted into the matrilocal community upon death (2006:152).

The usual body posture of plaza burials was flexed, but one seated burial was found in each quadrant of the housing circle (Sassaman 2006:148). This may be the farthest north the seated burial position is found on the Atlantic coast, a burial posture that may indicate people native to the St. Johns River (Claassen 2012d).

Stallings Island was abandoned for the second time at 3800 B.P. There was no evidence of resource depletion to explain the abandonment. Sassaman favors an explanation of a fissioning residential group, all of whom abandoned shellfishing and the Savannah River floodplain, pulled by the Poverty Point trade phenomenon westward into Georgia (2006:173).

See *bone pin, burial—posture, camp circle, Cult of the Bivalve Feast, gambling, hunt god rite, island, mound—shell, shell*

Stanfield-Worley Shelter, Alabama

This shelter is a wide-mouthed overhang opening to the southeast some seven miles south of the Tennessee River. Most of the material under the overhang derived from Archaic and earlier Dalton activities. Elements of ritual recovered here were a high number of mortars and nutting stones found inside pits, baked-clay surfaces, a tremendous number of projectile points, and human burials.

Seven of 10 pit features contained mortar stones, nutting stones, and/or anvil stones, suggesting termination rites or renewal offerings. For instance, Feature 77 had "A large, irregularly-shaped storage pit 4.2 feet in diameter. The pit was intrusive to Zone B from Zone A. It contained 3 mortars, 2 nutting stones, a flake knife, a flake scraper, a unifaced knife, a unifacial side scraper, and 2 [intrusive] Mulberry Creek Cord Marked sherds" (DeJarnette, Kurjack, and Cambron 1962:19). Feature 78 contained 2 mortars, a nutting stone, a rock, and 3 broken points. Three of the features had aquatic snails and at least 1 deer bone inside, and 1 pit with a mortar had a few pieces of turtle. Placement of mortars in pits with bits of bone or a small sample of tools could indicate offerings.

Five baked-clay surfaces were encountered in 3 shapes: circular, oval, and rectangular. These surfaces were unusually thick, 12 inches (0.30 m) or more, when compared to those found elsewhere in the Tennessee valley (Sherwood and Chapman 2005). Most of Zone B was a baked surface in contact with Zone A. This surface contained 10 points, a unifacial knife, and another tool.

Ten burials were found encircling 3 central burials (Figure 16). Morrow Mountain points and unifacial scrapers were found with 3 burials originating in Zone B and the baked floor but intruding into Zone C (DeJarnette, Kurjack, and Cambron 1962:80), indicating that all were Middle Archaic burials. An adult was flexed on the back with 2 cache blades, 4 Morrow Mountain points, 2 triangular points, a knife, and a bone atlatl hook. The pit was partially lined with rocks. Two other bodies were stacked in a single pit also lined with rocks. A drill and 4 Morrow Mountain points were with the man on the bottom. The mature man on top was flexed on his back and was the richest burial found. Around his skull had been put 7 Morrow Mountain points, 4 other points, 3 end scrapers, 4 awls, a core, a knife, an antler tine, and a pebble hammer.

Seven additional burials were contained entirely within Zone B, the Morrow Mountain zone. Three graves revealed only bone fragments. Another body was incomplete and on top of a large rock. An adult male tightly flexed on his right side was covered with rocks and given 5 points and a tine. Near the back wall an adult was intruded upon by a juvenile. A turtle shell was found in that pit. The turtle and the double burial suggest a priest and apprentice. The weighting of a body with stones suggests death occurred in a troubling way. The extremely rich male interment suggests a beloved ritual specialist or lineage founder.

Projectile points were commonly encountered. From one trench of 200 ft^2 (18.6 m^2) divided into four 12-inch (30-cm) levels came 171 points, 82 points, 79 points, and 33 points, respectively, a quantity suggesting point offerings. From the rest of the excavation, conducted inside the shelter and in two trenches outside, came another 2,375 points. The 2,500 points collected suggest a long history of honoring or appeasing these souls and the spirits inhabiting the shelter. What processes other than point offerings could possibly account for this many projectile points from less than 50 percent of the sheltered area and less than 15 percent of the talus? Hundreds of other formal tools were also found.

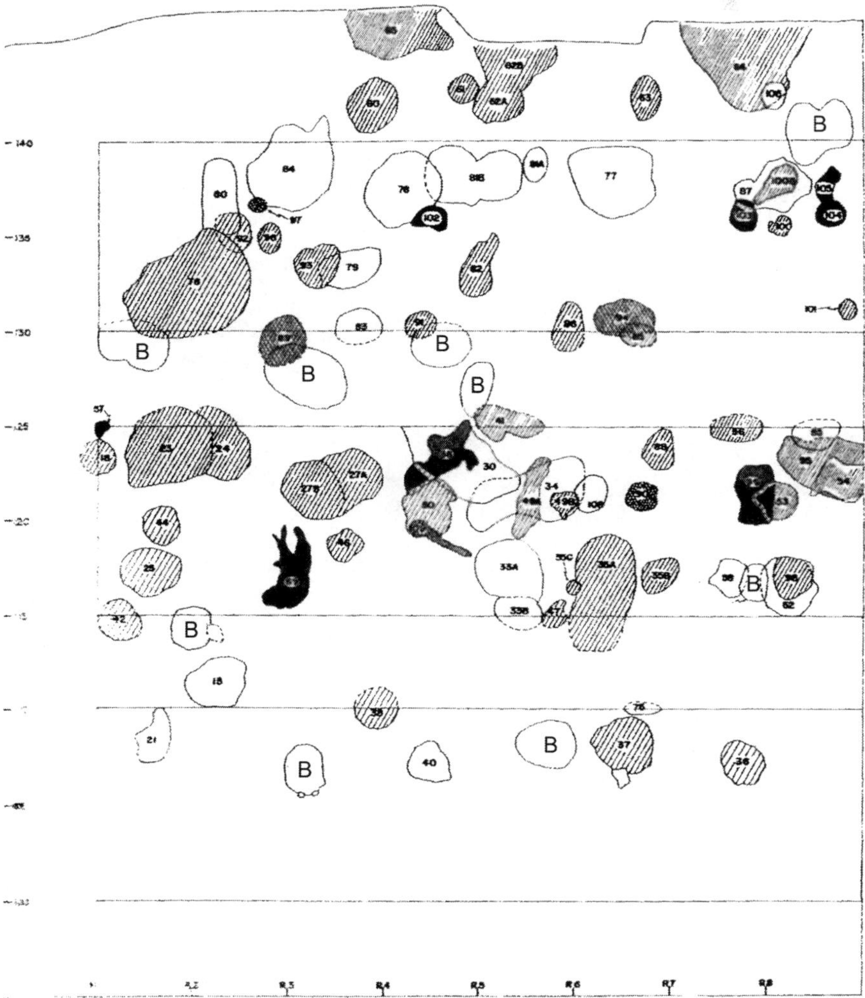

16. Plan of lower zone features in Stanfield-Worley Shelter. Note the encircling and central burials (B). (Reprinted from DeJarnette, Kurjack, and Cambron 1962:Figure 17, with permission from the Alabama Archaeological Society.)

Stanfield-Worley was a shelter where several generations of Archaic people roaming in the Tennessee valley buried at least 10 ritual specialists. They and subsequent generations left offerings to powerful souls including points and meat parts or dry bones of deer, gray squirrel, and passenger pigeon.

See *deer, Dust Cave, flintknapping, offering, projectile point, ritual specialist/ priest, Russell Cave*

Stanhope Cave, Ohio

This east-opening shelter is one of four adjacent rockshelters in one ravine with a spring less than half a mile uphill (Spurlock and Prufer 2002). The deepest stratum (Archaic in age) was a pit at the back end of the cave filled with brown sand and the disarticulated remains of at least eight people. Artifacts, including a steatite bowl rim sherd, were included. There was very little fauna or ash. One woman had been shot three times with antler points on the right side of the head (photo in Prufer and Prufer 2012:229). Two other women were represented, as was a fourth adult, three subadults (ages 5–10), and one child (ages 0–5). All individuals are incomplete and represented by dry bones. Spurlock and Prufer (2002:8) stress that the spatial capacity of this cave would have been three people. Although it was too small for habitation, it was suitable for the deposit of a possible witch's body and bone bundles. Again this is a rockshelter with special function, not one for habitation.

See *burial—bundle, ritual specialist/priest, rockshelter, trophy part, violence, witch*

3rd Unnamed Cave, Tennessee

Hearth charcoal more than a kilometer underground dates mining from 3320+/-70 to 2900+/-40 rcy. Markings in this cave (located near Icehouse Bottom site) of the same date and the Adair Glyph Cave are very similar: geometric lines, zig-zags, hatching, and cross-hatching (Faulkner 1997). Actual footprints dating to about 3,000 ya in the passageways, as well as copious flakes found along the passageway and in hundreds of piles inside the Mining Chamber, were associated with hearths and mining pits. Flint nodules were being mined from the floor sediments and from the walls in five loci. Pine and red cedar were burned in the hearths. The chert had been tested in the chambers with chalcedony hammers and removed as large, exterior flakes (http://faculty.etsu.edu/franklij/3UC_page.htm, accessed June 11, 2012). The cave setting, the markings, the act of mining, the stone, and the cedar wood are elements of ritual and belief.

See *Adair Glyph Cave, cave, cave mineral/mining, design element, flake/chip, stone*

Tick Creek Cave, Missouri

This is a rockshelter rather than a cave on the Gasconade River of Missouri filled with bones in the front half and a stream in the back half with points indicating Early Archaic through Woodland use. A 53-pound mortar was found here while dozens of portable mortars lay on the hillside above. Artifacts are depicted online (http://users.stlcc.edu/mfuller/tickcreek.html, accessed June 17, 2014).

Parmalee (1965) worked through 31,950 bones, 11,523 of which came from Archaic levels and the rest from Woodland levels. In all, he identified 36 species of mammals, 30 birds, 28 naiad species, 7 reptiles, and other taxa. There were at least 825 individual deer, 312 raccoons, 269 birds (205 turkeys, 12 passenger pigeons, but few waterfowl), 255 turtles, 88 striped skunks, 48 foxes, 31 rabbits, 28 dogs, 10 elk, 5 mountain lions, and 3 bears, among other species. A drilled alligator tooth and a single piece of *Busycon* sp. were recovered as well. Although Parmalee did not give MNIs by component, the rank order seems to be duplicated in the two components.

A rockshelter with this many bones, primarily bones of one species, deer in this case, and with 80 percent identifiable bones (thus large pieces) is a prime candidate for a bone shrine used by one or more hunters. Other offerings appear to have been the 263 bifaces. In addition there were 48 scrapers, 34 knives, 21 drills, 2 hematite axes, a gray banded slate atlatl weight, and several mortars and metates from Archaic levels. There simply are too few tools to argue for a camp function. To have so many deer in this one shrine suggests that generations of hunters returned their skeletal elements to this shrine, a persistent place as much as any mound.

It is also interesting to consider the species that were *rarely* included in this shrine or included but in numbers well below their presumed abundance in the Ozarks: badger (MNI 1), opossum (MNI 7), woodchuck (MNI 17), coyote, mink, and otter (MNI 9), beaver (MNI 14), rabbit (MNI 31), bear (MNI 3), fish, frog, and snake, as well as the water birds that could have been found along the major rivers. The picture that develops is that the remains of underground burrowing animals and the "wet" animals were dealt with differently than were the "dry" animals (with the exception of naiads), the latter found in this rockshelter shrine. Among some historic groups in the Northeast there was an aversion to mingling dog and bear bones, and the Tick Creek collection of several dogs and few bears could be signaling the same belief. The dogs do not appear to have been buried, and about 20 percent of the bones show butchering marks, suggesting meat use. One cut and polished dog rostrum, a possible mask element, was identified by Parmalee as were a small number of mammalian and bird bone tools. The wet animals may have been disposed of in the water (Harper 1999:176) rather than in this rockshelter.

See *Austin Cave, bone shrine, deer, mask/headdress, offering, projectile point, rockshelter*

Tomoka, Florida

Mound construction at this nine-mound site on the northeastern coast of Florida began sometime after 4629 B.P., late in the Mount Taylor period. Tomoka presents important modifications to earlier ritual platforms and mounds. Unlike other Mount Taylor ritual sites, it has no shell mound but instead has a coquina (marine bivalve) shell midden and nine or so Archaic sand mounds, some with burials, steeply mounded midden, or possibly midden-covered sand ridges as well as several large depressed areas. Small domes or low mounds may also exist (Piatek 1994:109). Nine bannerstones were recovered from near the center of Mound 6 in the 1800s, the oldest and largest bannerstone cache known (Harvey 2006).

The mounds range in height from 0.5–3 m and from 12–32 m in diameter. A crescent-shaped pond lies on the southeast side of Mound 6. Construction of Mound 6, the largest at 3 m x 32 m, began on top of a dark midden with a layer of yellow-brown sand, followed by very dark gray-brown sand, ending with a very thick layer of dark brown sand containing some coquina shells. Color symbolism was clearly employed in its construction.

This complex was abandoned by 4000 B.P. in favor of a location just to the north where village midden includes ceramics. Around 2880 B.P. the mound was capped with yellow sand containing human bone and interments but no pottery (Piatek 1994).

See *capping*, *color*, *mound—sand*

Turner Farm, Maine

The Turner Farm site is located on North Haven Island off the central Maine coast. This habitation, shell midden, and burial locus date between 3870 and 3480 B.P. and is recognized as an important site in the Susquehanna Tradition. These Late Archaic people collected shellfish and depended on maritime fauna and practiced both inhumation and cremation (Bourque 1995).

Three components were uncovered here. The first, lacking plummets, gouges, and other heavy equipment but having swordfish rostra and small stemmed points, dated roughly between 5200 and 5000 B.P. The second, Moorehead component had numerous bone artifacts, caches, and deer bones and was very similar to the finds at the Nevin site (Byers 1979). Unique in New England and in Moorehead components, however, were six dog burials, two with red ocher and one possibly associated with a cache. There is evidence of a substantial exploitation of shellfish by these people 4500 ya. A surprising find included three contiguous pits that contained remains of four deer: a fetus, a calf, and two adults (Spiess and Lewis 1995). Was this a four-age rite with deer?

The third, Susquehanna component had a dramatically different record of activities and concerns. These newcomers to the area favored cervids over marine taxa although shellfishing increased and they greatly neglected bone as a tool material. The dates for Susquehanna at Turner Farm are 3870 to 3480 B.P., suggesting only a very brief penetration of Maine by these southerners (Bourque 1995:167). Most significant for archaeologists, they created two cemeteries in soil that preserved the bone, giving the best picture of Susquehanna mortuary practices available for Maine.

Burials and cremains were deposited in two areas, south and north. In the southern and possibly older area, a cluster of six bodies was found interred with a seventh, a woman, off to the side. It is very interesting that these contiguous individuals were a male, a female, a subadult, a child, and an infant, with comingled remains of a newborn, a possible four-age rite grouping. Bourque reports that three of these individuals had occipital flattening. Other places where Archaic occipital flattening has been seen are at Parrish Village, Kentucky, an Archaic shell-free burial ground, and at Indian Knoll, "a site that bears numerous other resemblances to the Susquehanna tradition" (Bourque 1995:147). A four-age rite would further emphasize that similarity. Furthermore, the woman in the group was missing her mandible and the subadult had no femurs, evidence of trophy taking. The woman off to the side of the group also lacked most of her legs, and her skull had been mounded over, "visible from the surface" (Bourque 1995:151). Pits over both legless individuals revealed that the leg bones had been removed postburial. A rich, black soil lens covered most of the group, suggesting a fire had been built over them.

The only cremation in the southern burial ground was a deposit of cremains from four adults, a subadult, and animal bones, all embedded in the black, charcoal-rich matrix seen in the other grouping. Beech tree charcoal and beechnuts were part of this lens. Complete individuals had been burned, and red ocher was visible on the unburned fragments. Objects included were fragmented and burned, as were some bones of several duck-size birds, seal, deer, and a red fox maxilla.

A southern deposit consisted also of three piles of human bones with skulls and a fourth isolated skull. Analysis revealed that five individuals were included. Bone samples from each of the piles revealed that these individuals had the lowest indication of marine protein of any people tested at Turner Farm (Bourque 1995:152). Any one or all three of these deposits could qualify as a hunt god rite owing to the number of bodies, cremation, the postburial fire, and still later disturbance. Their terrestrial diet could indicate that they were captives from an interior group.

The northern burial ground consisted of numerous deposits of secondary cremations and a few skeletal inhumations, both primary and secondary, all showing extensive manipulation, previously credited only to post-Archaic mortuary programs. All inhumations had subsequently been opened and cremains added. Both dry and green bone had been cremated, isolated bones of different individuals had been mixed in some cases, some primary inhumations had been opened and bones removed, and some inhumations were secondary deposits.

The grave goods consisted of items such as mandibles or rostra of predatory mammals and turtle shell rattles with quartz pebbles (similar to those used in SOV practices), as well as gaming pieces and items both "killed" and pristine, apparently made for burial rites. The richest burial features were always secondary cremations. There is much here from which to argue ancestor recognition. Rites of recognition seem to have played out over years, if not decades.

See *ancestor, cremation, deer, dog sacrifice rite, four-age rite, gambling, hunt god rite, jaw, occipital deformation, rattle*

Twombly Landing, New Jersey

This bluff-top site is one of several oyster shell heaps along the Hudson River started during the Archaic. Shell covering approximately one-quarter acre and an associated habitation area lay on a ridge 50 ft (15.24 m) long, located 90–110 ft (27.43–33.53 m) above the Hudson. Like other Atlantic marine shell heaps, there are no burials in Twombly Landing. At the northern end of the ridge oyster shell was piled 4 ft (1.22 m) deep (Brennan 1968). The sheer quantity of shells suggests the Cult of the Bivalve Feast. Here we find rattlesnake bones and more than 600 bifaces, a number strongly suggestive of offerings. A full-grooved ax and a two-hole gorget supply further evidence of Archaic beliefs and rituals in this site's record (Claassen 1995:135).

See *bluff, Cult of the Bivalve Feast, projectile point, snake*

Vaughn, Mississippi

The final mound built at Vaughn on the Tombigbee River was 2–2.5 m high and measured 70 m east to west by 76 m north to south. It was tested with only four 1 m x 1 m squares yet revealed 8 burials (Atkinson 1974). Beginning ca. 4660 bc, low earthen mounds were constructed over flexed or semiflexed bodies. "These low earthen mounds, comprised of fill containing occupational and midden debris [?], seem to have grown by accretion until perhaps the entire basal one-half of the mound consisted solely of smaller, contiguous burial mounds. These mounds, in turn, appear to have been occupied by later Archaic peoples who left relatively scanty material evidence of their presence" (Atkinson 1974:116). Small mounds over individual burials were not the common mode of disposal elsewhere in the SOV. Late in the Archaic the mound was covered in a thick midden accumulation of shells and dirt as 300 more interments were made.

Naiads were more abundant in Zones 2 and 3 of the large inclusive mound than in Zone 1, the ceramic zone. All burials were found in the lower portion of Zone 2 or the top of Zone 3, capped with 2–4 cm of "very dark humus-like soil" (Atkinson 1974:120). All head orientations fall within a 120-degree arc north to east.

An adult male (45–50 yo), placed on his back, may have been the first burial at Vaughn. The description of this burial is of interest for its unusual treatment: "The left leg was tightly drawn alongside the torso, but the right leg was extended well back over the body, paralleling the vertebral column . . . although the skeleton lay on its back, the skull was twisted almost 180 degrees, and lay face down in the sand. With the exception of two left tarsals, the bones of both feet were absent, as were the right fibula and scapula. Strangely, all metacarpal bones of the left hand exhibited jagged breaks characteristic of bones broken during life or soon after death. The distal halves of these metacarpal bones and all phalanges were also absent" (Atkinson 1974:124). This burial was radiocarbon dated to 4660+/-95 bc and suggests a violent death. The head-twisted position may indicate the killing of a deer impersonator. Together with the partial recovery of bone from three men interred together in another locus of the mound, this may be evidence of a hunt god rite at Vaughn.

A woman 35+ yo was flexed on her left side with her head on a whelk shell ornament. Two large naiads rested between her skull and left knee. Gray soil was brought in and mounded over the area of her head. A second pit to the northwest contained the disarticulated portion of a child on top of an adult. Scattered parts of an adolescent were also found.

See *burial—posture, hunt god rite, trash/midden, violence*

Wapanucket No. 8, Massachusetts

Located on a low bluff in southeastern Massachusetts is this "complex burial site [of the Piedmont Tradition], with multiple mortuary-related features, including hearths, funeral pyres, pits, caches, an ossuary, and a presumed ceremonial structure," as well as a ramp (Pagoulatos 2009:236). Organic remains included bird, deer, and nutshells in some graves, and dry-bone secondary cremations. "The Wapanucket site possesses several 'snail-shaped' house patterns proximate to numerous cremation burials" (Pagoulatos 2009:247).

Locus 2 contained a large circular pit holding a lot of charred wood but no artifacts. Nearby were several small hearths, each equally spaced in an arc conforming to the circumference of the Locus 2 pit. The pit feature has been interpreted as a crematorium or pyre (Robbins 1969:54–55). Feature 206 (4290+/-140 B.P.) contained 11 cremation burials within a large pit associated with red ocher and numerous grave goods, including small-stemmed and Squibnocket bifaces, as well as large stone slabs that may have served as grave markers or covers. The feature was surrounded by an enclosure and a ramp leading to the entryway of the enclosure (Robbins 1969:242–243). A stick image, possibly showing a human or a thunderbird, was curious for its rarity.

See *bluff, crematory, ocher, ossuary*

Ward, Kentucky

Ward is a bluff-top shell-bearing ceremonial center on Cypress Creek. That shellfishing occurred here first on this tributary of the Green River and on a bluff top that was not easily accessible from the creek or from Green River is a surprise. WPA excavations occurred primarily in the southern hemisphere of the site area, exposing 433 burials in two clusters in the northern sector of the excavation (Pedde and Prufer 2001:64) or the center of the site. (Approximately 25 of these burials were post-Archaic.)

Cult of the Bivalve Feast elements found in this bluff-top site were turtle carapaces in many graves, 16 dog burials, and 7 dog and human burial pairs. A body of an infant and the head of a child had been covered with turtle carapaces. A carapace had been placed under each shoulder of another child (remains of a pack?), and a third carapace was placed by the left radius of this child. That body was then covered with yellow clay. Yet another child was beside an upturned carapace, itself on top of a large knife, all positioned at the child's left humerus. A needle was next to the right ulna.

According to Robert Mensforth (2001), who resexed and aged most of the Ward skeletal material, victims of violence and trophy parts were present in the burial ground. Three women were buried with one man who was missing left and right legs, had been stabbed multiple times in the back, and had a shell carved like a carapace over his face. A second group had four women, two of them headless. A third group had five men, all of whom had been murdered, flexed, and arranged in a quincunx, one with four points in the chest area (see Meindl, Mensforth, and York 2001:Figure 5). Mingled elements of eight additional bodies were found in the fill, giving a Mississippian feel to this possible hunt god rite (Hall 2000; Webb and Haag 1940:80). Elsewhere a trench or ossuary with at least 18 bodies was encountered. One of the last bodies to be added to the pile was that of a 35–40 yo man with scalping marks. Two other scalping victims were present. A human mandible was in the trench, as were a 24 yo male with the complete arm of another male; a headless male with disemboweling cuts; an adolescent male missing most cervical vertebrae whose head had stabbing cuts; and three other headless individuals, one with an embedded bone point and an unhealed penetration wound.

This bluff-top site on a first-order stream may well be the oldest Green River valley shell-bearing site. As such it might offer the oldest dog sacrifice rite, the oldest human burial with dog, and the oldest hunt god rite in the valley, as well as the oldest feast with shellfish. A huge pit (23,524 liters) contained black earth, charcoal, ashes, fire-cracked rock, considerable shell, bones, antlers, bone needles and pins, and several projectile points. Much about this site is enigmatic, and it provides intriguing elements of Middle Archaic ritual. More details can be found in works by Claassen (2010), Mensforth (2001), Meindl, Mensforth, and York (2001), and Pedde and Prufer (2001).

See *bluff, carapace, dog with human burial rite, dog sacrifice rite, hunt god rite, mound—shell, naiad, number, pack, shell, turtle, violence*

Watson Brake, Louisiana

Dirt mound construction began here in the Ouachita River valley around 5883+/-100 B.P. Ultimately 11 mounds were built and connected with ridges composed of midden and fill. One hundred and seventeen galena cubes were collected from the site, including many in a pit in Mound C (Saunders et al. 1998:73). Over 1,000 stone microdrills have been recovered along with 2 bead blanks and 3 beads, leading to the interpretation of stone bead making. However, Camaxtli, the Aztec hunt god and the probable descendant of the Archaic hunt god, was the giver of the fire drill, which is essentially the stone drill. It is possible that these microdrills were offerings in a hunt god rite.

Mound B showed three building episodes on top of an extensive Middle Archaic submound shell and earth midden (Jackson and Scott 2001:189). Stage 1 of Mound B dates to 5442 B.P. and the submound midden to 5703 B.P. A greater quantity of deer bone was found on the surface of Stage 1 of

Mound B than elsewhere, and deer plus the large proportion of bird bones in the faunal collection suggest ritual behavior such as a consecrating rite and feast. Other possible indications of ritual were the scattered bones of at least three humans in the submound stratum, an adult, a child, and an infant, hinting at an initial four-age rite.

Among the 175,000 bone fragments from eight excavation units in Mound B and its ridge were 58 taxa including those typically considered to be accidentals (mole, vole, cotton rat, rice rat, pocket gopher, toad), those commonly found (e.g., turkey, deer, fox squirrel, rabbit, 31 fish taxa), and more unusual species (eel, grouse, muskrat, mink, alligator, and several kinds of snakes). Fish provided the largest proportion of the MNI. Jackson and Scott cogently ask, "How may the assemblage recovered from Watson Brake have been affected by activities related to its probable functions as a ceremonial or ritual site? Chief among these assemblage-altering activities could have been feasts or ritually prescribed meals" (2001:192). It also seems that Mound B and the ridges may have been treated as appropriate places to which to return skeletal material, a bone shrine writ large. Particularly interesting is the return or primary discard of fish bones.

See *bone shrine, four-age rite, geometry, hunt god rite, mound—dirt, number, stone bead*

White Rocks, Ohio

The tremendous number of bones—73,000 fragments—and bone tools found in this rockshelter strongly suggests that this place was a bone shrine beginning in the Late Archaic, although it was most intensively used during the Woodland (Spurlock, Prufer, and Pigott 2006:450).

See *bone shrine, bone soul, rockshelter*

Windover, Florida

Windover is an early Middle Archaic pond cemetery in Florida in which many of the excavated bodies still have stomach contents and brain tissue. One hundred sixty-eight burials were encountered (more than 270 burials were estimated), half of whom were subadults and most of whom were flexed and put on their side into saturated, anaerobic peat. One hundred and ten skeletons were found in situ; the rest had slipped toward the deeper center of the pond and become disarticulated.

Body preparation at this site often involved wrapping in complicated fabric, at least some with hoods, and staking the bundle inside the edge of the pond or creating a teepee of branches over the body. Less often, the body wrapping was made of hide. The bodies were "tightly clustered but not superimposed" (Dickel 2002:73). "About 64% (37) of the burials had been placed with the head west of the pelvis (i.e., 270 +/-45 degrees). . . . About 48% (28) of the burials were placed with body axes oriented within the 298.5–241.5 compass arc" (Dickel 2002:77).

Most bodies had associated objects of bone and antler, and some had associated masses (ca. 1 liter) of prickly pear and grape seeds mixed with ground fish bone. Equal numbers of men and women were included in the pond and constituted 60 percent of the bodies, and they and subadults (40 percent) were evenly distributed throughout the pond. The only violent deaths documented were those of 2 men and 1 woman, all extended burials. One man had been impaled with an antler point and beheaded (Dickel 2002:76), and the richest burial recovered was that of the woman. Other rich burials at Windover were an 11 yo (Bu90) and a neonate in a bag with 22 formal artifacts including 14 bone and antler tools (Dickel 2002:94).

It is interesting that the burials in Windover Pond seem to have happened in the fall. The stomach contents and brain preservation indicate burial within 48 hours of death. If burial occurred only in the fall, and happened within two days, several issues about the burial program arise. (1) Where were the individuals who died at other times of the year? Were they put into sinkholes elsewhere in the state? (2) If flexed posture indicates transport of a body, the group utilizing this mortuary pond was no more than 1.5 days travel from Windover given the rapid burial after death. Flexed burial has been proposed for those to be transported to a burial ground, but given that all but 3 individuals were flexed, it seems that flexure was employed regardless of proximity to the burial ground. Windover burial postures provide more evidence that the extended posture was given to those who died violently.

See *burial—head direction, burial—posture, pond burial*

Part III

Annotated Beliefs and Rites

Part III presents various alphabetically ordered annotated topics related to beliefs and rituals. These topics were suggested by ethnographies and archaeologists and reflect my particular views on the topic. Cross-references are given to other relevant entries. Both data and interpretations are included. Table 1 and Figures 1–4 will aid the reader.

Adultery Killing

It is from the ethnographic record that we learn of the killing of adulterers, usually by stoning but also by strangulation (Miller and Taube 1993:86). If this situation was viewed negatively in the Archaic, then the burials of woman, man, and fetus or newborn may reflect the practice of killing adulterers who might have been discovered only upon pregnancy or childbirth. Such killings can explain several burials found in Archaic sites. Feature 108 at Rosenberger, Kentucky, contained a woman, a man, an infant, and 21 grave goods plus 96 pieces of deer, painted turtle, drumfish, and bird. Two male + female + newborn groups were found at Indian Knoll, and a possible killing may be seen at Hermitage Springs on the Cumberland River where a woman, a man, and two fetuses were buried together (site burial file, University of Louisville). A burial of a woman and a man facing each other and an infant on the man's arm at Port au Choix suggest this treatment was carried out in the Far North as well.

See *Hermitage Springs, Indian Knoll, Port au Choix-3, Rosenberger, violence*

Alligator/Crocodile

Alligator parts were found only with women at Windover, Florida, as could be predicted based on a widespread association between earth, women, water, and the caiman earth monster among Gulf societies. Alligator was among the remains at Watson Brake (Jackson and Scott 2001). One burial ceremony at Bluffton Burial (shell) Mound, also in Florida, began with a prepared shell floor, then a fire atop this shell, and then the individual laid on the coals and covered with an organic matter that might have been alligator feces. Finally, shell layers were created over the body (Sears 1960). Was this a creation ritual? One drilled alligator tooth was found in Tick Creek Cave in Missouri (Parmalee 1965:3). The caiman (*Caiman crocodilus*) with a spiny back was "a common metaphor for the mountainous earth floating upon the sea" (Miller and Taube 1993:48) dating to Olmec times (3000 B.P.) on the Gulf Coast of Mexico. There was iconographic equivalence of the caiman, the creator god Itzamna, and the spiny trunk ceiba tree, the world tree. In keeping with its role as the symbol of the ancient earth was the caiman's calendrical role in Mesoamerica as the first of the 20 day-names and the first of the 13 day-names (Miller and Taube 1993:48). Robert Hall (2006) thinks that birdstones, which typically have four feet instead of the implied two feet, were actually a composite bird and crocodilian atlatl grip or the feathered caiman (ultimately Quetzalcoatl) of Mexican belief, suggesting antiquity for the symbolism. Crocodile fossils have been found in the area of the Lenape Indians in the Delaware River valley (Mayor 2005:69–70). Powdered fossils were smoked. The Muskogee ceremonial ground has a place for the alligator clan on the south side of the square ground (Swanton 1928:251).

See *atlatl*, *turtle*, *Windover*

Altar

Altars may employ natural surfaces or projections or be human made. Two modern examples of stacked stone altars can be seen in Figures 18 and 19.

The arrangement of two pieces of roof fall in the center of Newt Kash Shelter in eastern Kentucky may have been an altar (Claassen 2011a). Between and below them was a facedown infant. Exactly the same situation was encountered in the Russell Cave rockshelter. An altar may exist among the rock arrangements in Ragged Mountain Shelter (Fowler 1971–72) and at Spout Run. Anderson, a Middle Archaic open-air shell site, had a feature consisting of "three large flat limestone slabs placed together, possibly used as a bench, table or seat" (Dowd 1989:44)—or altar? Claflin's field notes from Stallings Island (1929, p. 6, on file at the Peabody Museum, Harvard) refer to a stone altar made of four large stones and several smaller ones somewhat

17. Altar for calling rain on Mishuehue mountaintop, Guerrero, May 2011. (Photo by author.)

18. Waymarker altar on Acatlan pilgrimage, Guerrero, May 2012. (Photo by author.)

near a dog burial, both placed in clay subsoil. LeBeau (2009) gives examples of types of altars built today by the Lakota.

See *Anderson, limestone slab, mountain, Newt Kash Shelter*

Amphibian

Amphibians have significance in American beliefs as watery animals and as small animals. Ritual deposits in Savage Cave, Kentucky, at the Bullskin Creek site, Ohio, and in Mound B of Watson Brake, Louisiana, contained one or more amphibians. A salamander and a frog were found in some of the fecal specimens from Salts and Mammoth cavers, which, when considered with the other constituents, appear to be part of a cave ritualist's diet. The historical association of both caves and amphibians with rain and fertility would suggest that those cavers were rain priests.

A Woodland Period sucking tube found in the Rainy River site, Ontario, was decorated with a frog or toad. The tube may demonstrate a watery disease concept and its mode of healing (Rajnovich 1994:18). Perhaps people who died by drowning or causes classified as watery diseases (leprosy, dropsy, scabies, and gout) were those presented with the bones of, or grave goods enhanced with, amphibian or reptiles.

In Caddoan stories amphibians (and reptiles such as snakes) not only are creatures of the watery Beneath world but also were emblematic of the place from which the Caddo emerged into This World (Dowd 2011). Figures of various amphibians taken from the medicine chest of the Caddoan highest priest were used to intercede when disaster or drought was at hand. Amphibians are like newly dead humans, both of whom go through transformative life stages and both of whom are generated in the Beneath World. These creatures helped humans transition into the land of the dead (Dowd 2011:90). Their watery associations also make them suitable animal allies for Wixárika women weavers (Schaefer 2002).

See *animal other, feces, miniature, rain*

Amulet/Charm/Talisman

Bannerstones and birdstones are obvious candidates for creating a hunting charm, "A personal ornament which, because of its shape, the material from which it is made, or even just its colour, is believed to endow its wearer by magical means with certain powers or capabilities" (Andrews 1994:1). Historic references to these items abound and involve myriad substances—fossils, claws, teeth, pebbles, arrowheads, and so forth. Historic Indians often subjected a selected item to fire to release its magic powers (Mayor 2005:69).

See *bannerstone, birdstone, dream/vision, fetish, fossil*

Ancestor

Although ancestors as intercessors are said to figure prominently in the agricultural religions (Joralemon 1996) and thus not in the "shamanism" of the Paleoindian and Archaic eras, it is hard to imagine what the point would be otherwise of gathering together all the dead in one place if not for their utility as intercessors. Likewise, what would be the purpose behind collecting some skulls, a practice that began in the Middle Archaic of the SOV, if not for their relationship to the bodies of specific dead? Therefore, given burial ground creation, ancestors as a category of kin seem to have been recognized at least by Dalton times.

While all of the dead in a cemetery often are referred to as ancestors, it is more likely that only some of the dead would qualify, such as the lineage founders and their descendants. In modern state societies in Mexico, and probably in the ancient states as well, "the ancestors" is an allusion to the departed *founding members* of the community and all subsequent leaders and ritual specialists, not to all of the departed. These founding members, leaders, and ritual specialists were often placed in a "senior" cave or rockshelter, a place of honor. Even though Archaic cultures were not state-level polities, it is possible that they distinguished, by burial place, between "the ancestors" and "others." A working hypothesis should be that caves and rockshelters were the appropriate burial places for numerous categories of special deaths, including the people meriting ancestor status rather than people of "lesser value." These ancestors would be expected to intercede on behalf of the living with the earth spirits most readily contacted through the rockshelter crevice or cave portal to the Underworld into which the ancestors had been positioned.

In keeping with this idea—that ancestors were few rather than many and often were buried apart from cemetery populations—we should find elderly men and women in rockshelters and perhaps even infants of the lineage as well as possible offerings and sacrifices with them for renewal petitions. And the elderly, as well as people who died violently, are who we find in many rockshelters and caves. Burial in these remote places stands in sharp contrast to the visibility of ridge-top mounds, a criterion for "ancestor" used by

Charles and Buikstra (2002). These remote places could still be very much a part of the mental landscape of a people.

If the recent ancestors were buried in cemeteries, they may be treated with unique or a large quantity of grave goods. Or they may be those people buried in the camps rather than the bluff tops. They are probably found among the bodies with postburial head removal. Again we read that in the LIV, the elderly and very young are buried "in midden," which Charles and Buikstra (2002) see as convenient disposal of the unproductive members, but perhaps instead we see the individuals the living wanted to keep close, creating an actual foundation for the community, and these could be the Ancestors, or some segment of them. Removal to and concentration of the dead in a distant place suggest to me more of an effort to protect the living from something powerful, even onerous, such as the accidentally dead. After all, what killed so many prime-of-life individuals who are found in the ridgetop cemetery mounds? If it were accidents, then the living would surely have wanted to both distance themselves from those wandering souls and attempt to contain those dead with the weight of a dirt mound.

Ancestors as beings from a prior creation, the long dead, seem to be recognized by Middle Archaic times. These beings, the Stone People, were recognized in Clovis points, stone profile rocks, fossilized giant animals and their tracks, fossil beds, mountaintops, and sinkholes. The Stone People were addressed with offerings of cache blades.

Pauketat and Emerson (2008:82) stress that ancestors and stars are conceptually interchangeable in Mississippian society. This set is much larger in historic groups—ancestors, rain, clouds, water, thunder, fertility, and caves (most clearly in various southwestern U.S. religions)—and probably so in Mississippian and even Archaic groups.

See *ancestor worship/cult, burial—posture, cemetery, fossil, mountain, rockshelter, sinkhole, spring, Stone People*

Ancestor Worship/Cult

Much of my perspective in this volume is predicated on an assumption that eliciting the aid of ancestors, including the Stone People, the long dead, was fundamental in the beliefs and ritual practices of Archaic peoples. Removal of heads and femurs after burial likewise suggests ancestor referencing. But did this referencing constitute ancestor worship? I think not when I consider the cults of Aztecs, Maya who were marking graves of and memorializing rulers in word and architecture, and the Inca, who were mummifying and worshiping dead leaders.

Charles and Buikstra (2002:18–19) think that the creation of cemeteries constitutes the emergence of an ancestor cult for the LIV, Poverty Point region, and Maritime Archaic beginning about 6000 B.P. An ancestor cult "serves to represent the status quo, the contemporary power arrangements," and "represent[s] division and exclusivity" (Charles and Buikstra 2002:18).

But ancestor cult behavior is not as simple as the making of cemeteries as Nutini (1988) and Constance Classen (1993) make clear. It is highly likely that no other group in North America was as concerned with ancestors as were the Aztecs, yet Nutini (1988) argues that they did not practice ancestor worship because they lack lineages and unilineal descent to which such a worship would be tied and because the dead were celebrated as one step in a calendrical round of many other rituals with different concerns and not year-round.

For Mesoamerican people the category "ancestor" refers to a particular subclass of individuals, not all of the dead. Ancestors were lineage and community founders, their descendants, and important ritual specialists. These individuals were often placed in a "senior cave" or in some other locus *apart* from the general dead, and I have argued that perhaps some "ancestors" were buried in caves and rockshelters during the Archaic.

One of the most significant developments of the Archaic was the collecting of the dead into burial grounds. This practice indicates a concern with the dead but probably as helpers for the living in negotiations with the spirit realm and as offerings themselves in petitioning for the renewal of the social unit. They were buried with apparent ritual, sometimes including human and dog sacrifice, and in places where world renewal rites were held. In some cases the burial was opened later to retrieve the skull, mandible, or femurs, presumably for display, for veneration, for reburial elsewhere, and perhaps even for use as an oracle. Presumably pilgrimages were made to these places by subsequent generations and rites were conducted there because of the dead therein, expressing ideas about bone soul. Charles and Buikstra (2002) do suggest the use of the dead in earth fertility rituals that are probably more pertinent to Archaic beliefs than is the notion of an ancestor cult.

See *ancestor, bone soul, burial—secondary, cemetery, offering, rockshelter, Stone People*

Animal Other

Visions and dreams often brought an animal helper and instructor to the petitioner (Irwin 1994). In these cases the animal selected the human. Humans can also select animal allies, as is done among the Wixárika (Schaefer 2002).

For instance, Wixárika women vowing to complete themselves in weaving choose an ally from among the boa constrictor, horned toad, and beaded lizard, usually choosing the first female creature they come upon. Many archaeologists have suspected that loose faunal elements included in a grave might represent the deceased's animal other.

See *bear, beaver, bird, bobcat/lynx, caribou/elk, crane, deer, dream/vision, hawk, insect, owl, shark, snake, turkey, turtle*

Animate

Native American languages distinguish between animate and inanimate objects. Hallowell (1960:22) said the Ojibwas placed in the animate category persons, stones, shells, trees, sun/moon, thunder, and material culture like pipe and kettle. But, Hallowell explains, one Ojibwa man, after contemplating the question "Are all stones alive?" answered, "No! But *some* are." The Ojibwa example shows us that there is the *potential* for any object to be animated by a spirit who takes up residence in it or owns it. Breaking the spirit's home, or burning it, would force out the spirit rather than "release" the spirit as it is commonly expressed.

See *dream/vision, offering*

Antler

Antlers were widely recognized as symbols of chiefly status and power in historic Algonkian and Iroquoian groups (Hamell 1989; Smith 2005:115) and probably into the Middle Woodland as well given the context of antlers in Hopewell mounds and burials. Antler also seems to be signaling something related to the spirit world during the Archaic, such as a hunt god.

What may be the earliest antler headdress was found in Feature 1 (a pit of 4,050 cm^3) at the Anderson site, which contained the cremains of an adult (Bu73) as well as the burned skull and antlers of a deer. Another possible Middle Archaic antler headdress was found at Flint Creek shell mound on the Tennessee River.

Fox and Molto (1994a) warn against a facile interpretation of antler tines as flakers or punches given their use by healers in later times. Chomko (1975) examined tine polish and determined four different use-wear patterns. Antler was included in one or more burials in all of the shell sites in Alabama, all of the riverside Green River sites, and all of the seven shell-free burial grounds. Antler was not included in graves at Big Sandy, Eva's shell-bearing levels, the Middle Archaic bluff-top shell-bearing sites on the Green River, the Kentucky Air National Guard site (KYANG), or East Stubenville on the Ohio (Claassen 2010:128–129).

See *Anderson, deer, hunt god rite, mask/headdress*

Art

"The functional context of art in band societies is religious ritual; the forms of art are limited in kind, and the aim is control" (rather than to give "aesthetic pleasure") (Service 1966:77), control over the spirits. Memory making is also expressed in the "art," which is equally important. Rock markings were, in many cases, efforts to record vision elements (Rajnovich 1994).

See *design element, dream/vision, hematite, paint pot, paint/powder, rock marking*

Ashes

A striking feature of some Cumberland Plateau rockshelters is the tremendous volume of ash found in them (e.g., Funkhouser and Webb 1929). This ash was generated possibly when women in retreat in these places burned clothing, menstrual pads, and other organic items at the conclusion of their retreat period. There may well have been great fires at the time of initiation and during medicine ceremonies held in these ash caves as well as in Salts Cave, where six prepared floors of alternating layers of ash and fill were encountered.

In the Lower Rockhouse Cave of Missouri, a sterile stratum of hard-packed ashes was composed of layers of white, gray, and brown ashes "so compact that it was necessary to break it into small particles before it could be examined . . . it may represent a prepared floor, perhaps puddled with water and trampled" and up to three-feet (91 cm) thick in places (Adams 1950:29). Three burials were underneath this floor.

In addition to the rockshelter sites mentioned, some open-air sites are remarkable for their quantity of ash. Deep ashes were found at Hodges (layer) and at Lamoka Lake. Ash layers may have created a barrier to evil spirits (Hall 1976:360–363) while fire carried offerings upward.

Ash, as purified and transformed trees and fibers, may have had a medicinal use itself, one that could help explain the large quantity of missing ash given all of the Archaic cremations. The ash from the cremations may have been eaten, and, in fact, one of the fecal specimens from Salts Cave, herein attributed to a cave ritual specialist, contained charcoal. Bone soul may account for the fact that some American groups did or still do eat the ashes of the cremated human dead. Reportedly once widespread, this practice was followed until recently by the Luiseño of California and is followed today by the Yanoama of Brazil (Furst 1977:18).

See *bone soul, burning, capping, fire, paint/powder, pearl, tree*

Astronomy

Alignment symbolism was probably more important than was precision or prediction. Aligning monuments with heavenly phenomena might have been employed (1) to capture the "parallelism between the eternal movements of the heavens and the cyclical biological rhythms of life on earth," (2) to "simultaneously reference the mythical spaces of worldly creation," (3) to "average two or more orientations to commemorate a cultural event or direct a natural process toward some perceived end" (Gartner 1996:130), or (4) to correct accumulation errors (Kehoe and Kehoe 1979).

The one area where heavenly alignments have been sought and found during the Archaic era is in the Middle and Late Archaic mound sites of the Gulf Coastal Plain (Clark 2004). Lunar observations are evident in the use of a multiplier of 28 at Poverty Point for spacing constructions and solar observations in the placement of key features of Poverty Point 360 Standard Units apart.

Clark is "convinced, as [Norm Davis] argues, that planned azimuths and celestial observations for calendrical purposes (both lunar and solar) were involved in constructing mound centers. Precise dating of centers will be required to match alignments to the changing heavens" (2004:210n2). The purpose of these alignments and units continues to be debated, but the attention to the sky may have been motivated by a concern with cosmic balance.

See *ancestor, burial—head direction, C-shaped site layout, constellation, measurement, Milky Way, moon, Poverty Point, sun*

Atlatl

Koldehoff and Walthall (2009:145) believe that the atlatl was part of the tool kit possessed by the earliest immigrants into the Western Hemisphere. While the atlatl is considered primarily to be a weapon system, atlatl inclusion in burials highlights its symbolic role in the Archaic. The atlatl was found at Windover pond burial ground in Florida exclusively with males and one subadult. No atlatl parts have been recovered in Koster Middle Ar-

19. Mixcoatl/Camaxtli, the hunt god. Notice atlatl, antlers, and Milky Way stars on head. (From the Aztec Codex Borgia, p. 25.)

chaic Helton phase. There is no evidence for the atlatl system in the Maritime Archaic (Tuck 1976:84), but farther south, atlatl weights were found in the Middle Archaic of Neville Site in New Hampshire and at the Doerschuk site of North Carolina. Side-notched points have been attributed to the atlatl (Dunbar and Webb 1996:352), as have the broad spear points of Late Archaic times (Oliver 1985).

With a Nahua name meaning "water" and its use in Mexico as an aquatic bird hunting device, the atlatl is nevertheless considered to be part of land mammal hunting technology when discussed by eastern U.S. archaeologists. Notched butterfly preform weights cluster near swamps and marshes in Ohio (Bowen 1994), suggesting a marsh fauna use, as do the so-called birdstones that logically could have served as hunting charms for aquatic bird hunters. The antler hooks have also been interpreted as knitting needles (Moore 1916; Pedde and Prufer 2001:79). The weapon interpretation is of course problematic in light of the high number of subadults buried with hooks or "weights," as well as the frequent inclusion of "weights" only.

Kwas (1981) has suggested that the atlatl cross-section may have changed from round to flat and required the change from bannerstones to birdstones. The atlatl ultimately disappeared as a hunting weapon and became the pipe and flute (Hall 1997).

After reviewing the age and sex data for those buried with atlatl parts including isolated handles, weights, or hooks, William Webb (1974:333) said, "The facts revealed [41 percent with subadults, some with women]. . . . somewhat astonishing. . . . This would seem to argue that such occurrences represent true 'burial offerings' to the dead of artifacts primarily intended for the use of men. This would seem to point to some form of ceremonial ritual during which the atlatl was deposited in the grave, sometimes broken and parts either intentionally scattered, or carefully piled together, and which was accorded to a limited number of persons regardless of age or sex." I propose that this ceremony was an element in a hunt god or first-kill rite. Atlatls placed in graves possibly were included with individuals who had been sacrificed during these events, adults for the hunt god rite, infants for the first-kill rite. The god Camaxtli, closely paralleling the Cherokee Kanati in deed and pronunciation, is depicted in central Mexico holding an atlatl aloft and wearing deer antlers (Figure 19) (see the entry for "hunt god rite"). Furthermore, the stylistic move proposed by Webb (1974:330–333) from wooden atlatl to antler atlatl may have been motivated by a desire to strengthen the visual and tactile association between the hunt god and deer.

See *bannerstone, deer, first-kill rite, hunt god rite, sacrifice—adult, sacrifice—infant and child*

Atlatl Weights—see Bannerstone

Auditory Exostoses

According to the report of Mensforth (2005:466), 36.4 percent of 88 men at Carlston Annis, 51.6 percent of 254 men at Indian Knoll, 25 percent of 12 Kirkland men, 21.3 percent of 94 Barrett men, 22.6 percent of 84 Ward men, and 25 percent of the skulls at KYANG, more than a mile from the Ohio River, had exostoses (Meindl, Mensforth, and York 2001:Figure 2 is a photo of this condition). In addition to the burials at Kirkland, a shell-free burial ground, exostoses appear in individuals in three other shell-free mortuaries, Eva (Big Sandy component), Rosenberger, and Ensworth.

Both extremely cold water and hot water can bring about the formation of these exostoses if exposure is frequent enough (Lambert 2001). Mensforth (2001) attributes them to winter shellfishing by men, and Lambert (2001) suggests a sweat lodge rite centered at Indian Knoll and Carlston Annis. A contemporary Maya sodality of river keepers (Rissolo 2005) suggests the hypothesis that there was an Archaic version of river and cave water cleaners, particularly focused on the Green River. Perhaps people buried away from the Green River but with exostoses cleaned the waters of their respective rivers, pools, springs, and caves.

See *cave, rain, spring*

Awl

Awls are made by polishing the tibia, radius, ulna, fibula, splanchnic, bacula, jaw, scapula, metapodial, or spine of numerous large and small animals. The inclusion of these items useful for tattooing, basket making, leather working, eel killing, and medicine making in graves, however, cannot be written off simply as items to be used by the soul in the afterlife or as personal tool kits buried with their owners because they are, in fact, relatively speaking, rarely included in graves. For instance, although 7,338 awls were tallied from Webb's Indian Knoll excavation (Claassen 2010:Table 6.2), only 4.4 percent of the 880 burials contained an awl (Claassen 2010:Table 6.8). Considering the record from the SOV, even though all sites of the Tennessee River and Green River yielded awls from their matrix, no awls were included in the Middle Archaic Eva, Jackson Bluff, Jimtown Hill, Baker, or Kirkland sites, none was found in the Middle and Late Archaic burials at O'Neal and Ward, and none was found in the Late Archaic burials of Big Sandy, Whitesburg Bridge, or Bowles. When they were included, the percentage is highly variable, ranging from 47 percent of graves at Robinson on the Cumberland to 1 percent of graves at Kay's Landing and Chiggerville (Claassen 2010:Table 6.8). For whom was an awl an appropriate grave good? Ritchie (1932) believed that awls, arrows, and celts in graves were offerings.

Were some activities and thus a particular gender associated more with one animal species than another and the corresponding species used for the awl? The close association with weaving and Father Deer among the Wixárika suggests deer long bone awls in eastern North America were manufactured for weaving. Blunt deer ulna awls were interpreted as fish scalers at Lamoka Lake. Men alone were found with carnivore radius awls at Windover, where men and subadults also were found with "expanded head awls, small flat pointed awls, and sharpened deer tines" (Dickel 2002:86). Human bone awls might have been employed in tattooing or in witch killing. It could be then that the lack of awls made from some species or from a body part might indicate the absence of that activity at a site. Only two ulna awls (dog and deer) were found at Rabbit Mount, South Carolina, and ulna awls also were rare at Lake Spring, Bilbo, and Stallings Island, all on the Savannah River (Stoltman 1974:132), and in several ash caves of eastern Kentucky. The preliminary work by Chomko (1975) on awl use-wear needs to be continued.

See *animal other, bone pin, bone soul, textile/weaving*

Ax

Chipped-stone axes are Middle Archaic in age. Polished, full-grooved axes were present in the LIV by ca. 6000 B.C., and the three-quarter grooved form may have been present as early as 5000 B.C. (Farnsworth 1987:17). Axes apparently are not common at bluff-top cemeteries in the LIV but are common at floodplain cemeteries (Farnsworth 1987:18–19), nor are they found in the Middle Archaic bluff-top burial grounds on the Green River. Polished, full-grooved axes seem to have first appeared in Virginia during the Late Archaic (McLearen 1991:99).

See *tree*

Baked-Clay Surface

These clay surfaces are "discrete, localized red (2.5YR, 5Y) clay, cultural deposits that are often fired to a hard consistency" and often show a textile impression (Sherwood and Chapman 2005:70). Among the shell mound sites, baked-clay floors have been found in Rabbit Mount and Ed Marshall on the Savannah River, at Riverton on the Wabash, and in several Green River and more notably in Tennessee River shell heaps. Baked-clay floors have been found in several caves and rockshelters, including Stanfield-Worley, Dust, Modoc, and Russell, all in Early Archaic contexts (Sherman and Chapman 2005:78). Open-air sites with clay surfaces include East Aberdeen in Mississippi (Rafferty, Baker, and Elliott 1980:252), Icehouse Bottom, Tennessee, and the geographically close 31Sw265 in North Carolina (Kimball and Schumate 2001). At Icehouse Bottom and Dust Cave, both in the Tennessee River valley (as are Russell Cave and 31Sw265), these features were always composed of a silty clay specifically selected from alternative clays, they were located in central activity areas, and they were often superimposed.

Dust Cave has the earliest baked-clay features, beginning at 12,000 B.P. Over 160 fired-clay features were found averaging 0.67 x 0.42 m, over 100 of which associated with ash and charcoal and 29 marked by textile or net impressions (Sherwood and Chapman 2005:72). The clay chosen appears to have been derived from within the cave, then moved and used unprocessed. The hard-surface clay features were usually associated with a traditional hearth.

A clay surface at the Johnson site, Tennessee, contained Paleoindian tools dating to 11,500 rcy (Sherwood and Chapman 2005:77). The clay floor at Rabbit Mount was nearly 10 ft^2 (0.93 m^2) in area and was directly below the shell midden. At one edge it had two postholes 6 inches (15.24 cm) in diameter. At least 27 artifacts, including a hollowed antler tine, 5 Savannah River points, pitted cobble, a netsinker, and drills, were associated with this floor. The Mulberry Creek shell mound clay features were 6–10 ft (1.83–3.03 m) in diameter (Webb and DeJarnette 1942:238). The East Aberdeen, Mississippi, surface had one posthole to the side and was 20–40 cm above a circle of postholes encircling a hearth, a larger posthole, and a burial. If the burial "house" didn't constitute a shrine, the surfaced area above it with a post (?) may have enshrined the burial below.

The best evidence for baked-clay "floors" as part of ritualizing is seen in the very late Riverton, Illinois, shell-bearing site on the Wabash River. While the burial program was small, as was often the case in bluff-top shell-bearing sites, there was abundant evidence of ritual being conducted there (Winters 1969:97). Ten rectilinear and ovoid baked-clay features were found measuring 10.5 x 6.5 ft (60 ft^2 or 5.57 m^2) and even 20 x 13 ft (260 ft^2 or 24.15 m^2), similar to the size of floors at Mulberry Creek. Several of these floors overlapped and all were confined to one area of the site, suggesting a ritual zone. Several postholes were on the outside of a floor.

These features were either cooking griddles for plant foods, particularly nuts, or fish as proposed by Sherwood and Chapman (2005) and Homsey, Walker, and Hollenbach (2010) or floors to a ritual facility like a shrine or screen when postholes are present. Given their preparation, their large size, their association with fire, and in the case of Dust Cave, the use of cave clay, ritual cooking is suspected.

See *Icehouse Bottom, Riverton, Russell Cave, textile/weaving*

Bannerstone

According to Sassaman's recent summation (2010a:107–112), bannerstones do not seem to be older than 8500 ya. Three centers of their deposition are Green River shell mounds, the Northeast, and the lower Ohio River. The production of oversized bannerstones seems to center in the southern Great Lakes, coastal Massachusetts to New Jersey, and Piedmont North Carolina to central Florida. The Hardaway site in central North Carolina has perhaps the largest number of bannerstones (n = 200) found at any Archaic site. They are quite rare in the LIV except at the Middle Archaic Bullseye site (Farnsworth 1987:19). Other key Middle Archaic sites for bannerstones are Denton, Mississippi, and Neville, New Hampshire.

The Green River forms and eastern forms may share a history. "Forms diversified over the ensuing millennia, only to become less varied but more elaborate in the millennium before bannerstones disappeared altogether, ca. 3100 cal BP" (Sassaman 2010a:107). More important than form, however, may have been the context of disposal, says Sassaman. In the earliest cases in Green River sites and in New England (Stanley/Neville points), bannerstones are found (1) in graves, (2) with other parts of the atlatl, and (3) with men at least.

Bannerstones also appear in graves of several Illinois valley individuals and Middle Archaic mounds in Florida. In Florida, they appear in both non-burial and burial contexts while at Stallings Island they were never found with burials.

Kwas (1981) talks about three possible uses of bannerstones—ceremonial, ornamental, weights—while Sassaman (2010) favors the clan emblem, as does Harvey (2006). The "weighted" atlatl has many doubters, among them Harvey (2006). Many bannerstones seemingly exist without atlatl hooks in New York sites, in North Carolina, and frequently in SOV burials. At Hardaway, North Carolina, 200 stones and only one atlatl hook were found. Some bannerstones were found in graves with incomplete bore holes, with bore holes too small to fit an atlatl, forms too fragile to have withstood the rigors of hunting, or forms too heavy to have been used while throwing (Harvey 2006). If they weren't weights, the "atlatls" and "weights" in Green River graves might have been weighted spindles and knitting needles (Bowen 1994:5; Pedde and Prufer 2001).

Numerous archaeologists now see bannerstones primarily as status symbols for individuals (Sassaman 2010a), insignia of a hunting sodality (Kwas 1981), insignia of distinct bands (Curtin 2011:7; Whaley 1992), or as hunting charms. As charms, their shape usually suggests abstract birds in flight. In some places they were appropriate grave goods while in others they were not. By 3,500 ya bannerstones were replaced by "birdstones" in the Midwest (but see Hall 2006) and by 3,100 ya by two-hole gorgets in the lower Mississippi valley.

The winged shape and frequent association with burials suggest the soul's departure imagined as a butterfly or bird by many cultures. The segmented shell atlatl weights look like vertebrae, and Robert Hall (1997) has linked the atlatl to the pipe and flute, the lungs and windpipe. Hematite also was used to make bannerstones, suggesting a medicinal role. Finally, bannerstones may have had a role as a weight for a fire drill, adding to the accumulating evidence for a hunt god ritual dedicated to a figure like Camaxtli/Mixcoatl, who not only hunted with atlatl but also invented the fire drill (Figure 19).

See *amulet/charm/talisman, atlatl, fire making, hunt god rite, ocher, powder*

Bayonet

The stone bayonet seems to have evolved from a bone bayonet, and some graves in Port au Choix-3 contained bone bayonets while others held stone bayonets. Hafted slate bayonets were frequent grave inclusions there and in other coastal northeastern Archaic cultures, giving rise to the idea of a Cult of the Bayonet. Slate bayonets "are more widely distributed in Nova Scotia than in New Brunswick," and none has "been reported from Prince Edward Island" (Tuck 1976:261–262). Bayonets were thrusting weapons used against aquatic mammals and cervids while swimming (Tuck 1976:32). However, slate bayonets have the shape of swordfish rostra and are in some cases, like their predecessor bone form, etched with a triangular or zig-zag motif that has suggested to several archaeologists shark teeth (Betts, Blair, and Black 2012:635). A main prey of sharks and humans in the Maritime provinces was swordfish, so the imagery may signal a desire on the part of the fisherman to succeed like a shark in capturing swordfish.

Most bayonets have been found in graves, and in some cases they are covered with ocher (Betts, Blair, and Black 2012). According to Tuck (1976), when these items are found in infant burials, the bayonet and the infant may have comprised offerings in a hunting ritual, as is suggested for the SOV.

See *Cult of the Bayonet, offering, sacrifice—infant and child, shark, stone*

Beak/Bill

The only part of the Great Auk to appear in the burials at Port au Choix-3, Newfoundland, was the beak. Two hundred and thirty-seven Great Auk maxilla were found in eight graves, over 200 of them found in one burial. Bird bills of other species found in graves suggested caps made of bird skins or, more often, bags made from bird skins with heads attached (Tuck 1976:54, 68–69). Tuck wondered if the swan's bill found with a young woman in Port au Choix-3 signaled an Archaic form of a modern belief that a swan's bill attached to a girl's clothing would ensure the birth of a boy.

Loon beaks were found in graves at Black Earth (Illinois). Five upper beaks and four lower beaks of an unspecified bird were found in Feature 61 at Carlston Annis (Webb 1950:303).

See *bird, feet/footprint/track, jaw, teeth*

Bear

Bears clearly had some role(s) in Archaic rituals throughout the eastern United States; bear teeth were found as earrings and pendants from Elizabeth Mounds in Illinois to Port au Choix-3, Newfoundland. Lamoka Lake, New York, also had a bear canine scraped down to the pulp cavity. Might scraping have occurred in the course of deriving powder for ritual use? Fossil short-faced bear bones were collected by historic Indians to be ground into a powder that, when ingested, would increase running speed.

Bear rostral masks were found with two men in the Hind cemetery, Ontario (Ellis, Kenyon, and Spence 1990:117; Spence and Fox 1986). Prepared sections of bear crania have been found at the Terminal Archaic Williams site in Ohio. Bear cranium masks were tentatively identified in several other Ohio cemeteries (Purtill 2009:589). Two bear long bones had been hollowed out at Russell Cave, Alabama, and a bear humerus "lamp or handle" was found at Perry, Alabama (Webb and DeJarnette 1948b:46). Bear ulna awls are occasionally found.

Bear effigy pestles have been recognized at the Bent site in New York. It "may be unique as a center for bear effigy pestle manufacture and distribution" (Curtin 2011:6).

The special disposal requirements for bear recorded in historic times may have been practiced in Archaic times as well. At the Eva site in Tennessee, only bear vertebrae were encountered (Lewis and Lewis 1961:22–23), strongly suggesting that the other bear bones were taken elsewhere. One such appropriate disposal area may have been a burial ground. Ritchie (1932) reported finding two piles of 50+ bear bones at Lamoka Lake, New York.

See *animal other, bone soul, paint/powder, teeth*

Beaver

Beaver remains are most common in the Northeast. Beaver incisors (n = 54), some hafted, were included as grave goods in Locus 2 at Port au Choix-3. These items were typically ground, indicating that they had been used tools. One knife with antler handle was found buried with an infant. A few of the 118 unmodified incisors appeared in pairs and seemed to be amulets (Tuck 1976:48, 63). Two beaver front paws were also enclosed in one grave.

Ontario Iroquoians believed that beaver teeth allowed the owner to divine the future (Fox and Molto 1994b:110). Six-inch-long (15.2-cm-long) fossil teeth of the giant beaver (*Castoroides*) were collected by the Micmacs and others to dig out tree trunks for canoes (Mayor 2005:51). Two jaws came from Table Land, New Hampshire. Skeletons of beaver were common at the island bone shrines of Allumettes and Morrison sites in Quebec.

Beaver incisors were found in the Middle Archaic levels at Eva, Tennessee. Both burials at the sinkhole Lawrence site, Kentucky, had beaver tooth necklaces. Beaver mandibles were recovered from graves at Indian Knoll and Carlston Annis, Kentucky.

See *animal other, medicine bag, teeth*

Bedrock Mortar/Nutting Stone

Bedrock pocked with mortars began appearing in the Late Archaic with one or two holes in freestanding chunks of rock and dozens of holes in outcropping bedrock or rock balds. Bedrock mortars are particularly common in the Cumberland Plateau of Kentucky, Tennessee, the western side of the southern Appalachian Range (Franklin 2002; Ison 2004), and in southern Illinois (Carey, McCorvie, and Wagner 2010).

The frequent association of bedrock mortars with rock markings and rockshelters suggested to Ison (2004) that women made both the markings and the mortar holes. Many of these rockshelters have evidence that elicit the interpretation of menstrual seclusion or initiation rites. The rock markings also suggest ritualized marking and use of the immediate area. The frequent drawing of tracks or feet implies fertility concerns in these rites. The creation and even use of the bedrock mortars then would also be part of the rites conducted in these places.

There is much information available about the use and meaning of bedrock mortars among central California native women. In Historic times groups of women gathered together at multihole bedrock outcrops to conduct rites of passage for girls who had to bore a hole of suitable dimensions to demonstrate wifely qualities (Jackson 1992). Associated with this rite of fertility was the thought that mortar holes were female as are caves, springs, and pools (e.g., Parkman 1992:366). "In addition the mortar facilitates the transformation of raw food into that which is edible, this being another female character" (e.g., Parkman 1992:366). Pomo women and men visited these boulders to conduct fertility rituals/rain-calling rites that included incising the rock with lines and vulvaforms. They pounded rock to generate the sound of thunder and produce powder that they then rubbed on their bodies in order to conceive. Parkman recasts the Pomo activity of producing a mortar from one of food processing to one of ritual. "The sound produced by pounding the cupule was probably the intent of the manufacture. If such is the case, then the resultant cupule is an incidental feature of a ritual focused on producing sound and thus affecting the weather . . . when observing these boulders after rains, one is struck by the fact that various quantities of rainwater are collected in the cupule depressions. It seems likely that such water would have been utilized, and it is possible that it would have been consid-

20. Graham Cave (23Mt2) nutting stone from "general surface." (Photo courtesy of Missouri State Parks.)

ered sacred, especially if the rock (or its use) was considered sacred." These rain rocks date to at least 5000 B.C. in California (Parkman 1992:367).

It is also interesting that the burial of mortars and nutting stones was practiced in the east. For instance, Feature 111 of the Villier site near Louisville (Robinson and Smith 1979:646), a large circular pit, 40 cm deep, with charcoal and oxidized clay, contained a "large multiple pitted stone" as well as a stone bead, a worked piece of bone, and some human tooth and mandible fragments. The nearby Rosenberger burial ground had a pit with grinding stone inside as well as shale and bones of turkey, deer, and bird (Driskell 1979:777). Stanfield-Worley shelter had 10 pits 2–4 ft (0.61–1.23 m) in diameter in which large rocks had been stashed, most with depressions. Some pits had multiple rocks. Seven of the 10 pits had faunal remains, but the pits with multiple stones had fewer bone pieces than the others (DeJarnette, Kurjack, and Cambron 1962:17). Is this a version of a renewal offering where an essential tool was included?

Attention also should be drawn to exceptionally large mortars and nutting stones. These have been recorded at East Steubenville shell bluff-top site in West Virginia (Lothrop 2007), McLean in Illinois (McElrath 1986), Tick Creek bone shrine in Missouri (Parmalee 1965), Graham Cave (Figure 20), and the shell-bearing Victor Mills site in South Carolina (Sassaman 2006: 112). That at East Steubenville, West Virginia, measured 107 x 98 x 60 cm and had at least 13 pits 2–4 cm in diameter, 1–2 cm deep. Excavation around the stone "recovered large numbers of cobble tools, groundstone tools, unfinished bifaces, and flaking debris" (Lothrop 2007:538).

See *feet/footprint/track, Newt Kash Shelter, rain, Stanfield-Worley Shelter, sound*

Benton Blades

"Benton points mark the beginning of the [Late Archaic] period and are common from the Tennessee River valley westward to within a few miles of the Mississippi River bluffs. Benton blades are found as isolated bifaces and as caches. For instance, 13 caches have been documented along the Tombigbee River containing 238 blades of various shapes and sizes" (Johnson and Brookes1989). Caches of Benton blades are found both in cremations, sometimes burned, and with inhumations, in both shell- and non-shell-bearing burial grounds. Sometimes red ocher is present. Blades can be oversized, bipointed, notched, or of "normal" size with no notching. Caches have been assigned utilitarian, ceremonial, and mortuary purposes. There is a "general reduction in length corresponding to distance from source in the Benton point data, [but this reduction] does not appear in the cache material . . . suggesting that unused Bentons were selected for the caches" (Johnson and Brookes 1989:143).

The Benton record of the Harpeth River south of Nashville has been explored by Deter-Wolf (2004). At least 13 sites have yielded Benton blades, including the important Anderson and Ensworth School sites' caches. At Ensworth, most of the blades were made with Dover Flint and other flint types rather than Ft. Payne chert.

These blades and others themselves may have embodied ancestral spirits. The number of blades may encapsulate meaning as well. In this regard in numerous cases the resultant count is a prime number.

See *cache—blade, Caradoc Site, number, Stone People, Turkey-Tail blade*

Bird

Birds appear to have been very important in the rites and beliefs of the Maritime Archaic people of the Far North and to people in the lower Mississippi valley. There was "a wide array of bird-related items found in most Maritime burials, such as merganser heads carved on bone pins, natural or modified limestone concretions resembling birds, swan ulna whistles, great auk beaks, wing skeletal elements, and bones from . . . 30 different bird species," particularly the heads, wings, and feet of loons, mergansers, gulls, and other fish eaters (Renouf and Bell 2011:57). Rasmussen (1931) observed that among the Netsilik Eskimo the possession of heads, bills, and feet of gulls, who preyed on salmon, was thought to make the owner a good salmon fisher while possession of the feet of auks, guillemots, and cormorants made one a good paddler. Tuck (1976:68) consequently understood these body parts in graves at Port au Choix to represent amulets. Presumably the soul of the deceased would need these amulets to fish and paddle in the afterlife.

Bird effigies were very important in the lower Mississippi valley judging from beads, pendants, and carved designs found there. Birds in the Poverty Point sites are most often owls or owl composites, but there are also examples of songbirds, crows, nestlings, and crested, long-billed, and big-headed birds (Gibson 1998:26). Aquatic birds were found with 25 men in Windover Pond but with only two women and four subadults. Many southeastern groups considered Thunder and Lightning to be birds and woodpeckers to be guardians.

Loon beaks were found in graves at Black Earth, and five upper beaks along with four lower beaks of an unspecified bird were found in Feature 61 at Carlston Annis (Webb 1950:303).

Song, size, and feather colors made songbirds attractive. Cardinal was identified at Anderson, and a probable sparrow bone was found in feces at Salts Cave. Five songbird-sized bones were found in a cremation at Hodges, Michigan. The multicomponent (including Late Archaic) Raven Rocks shelter in southeastern Ohio yielded few artifacts but a very large faunal assemblage consisting primarily of "large numbers of small birds. It looks as if the Raven Rocks inhabitants performed some very strange practices at this site" (Prufer and Prufer 2012:232). This shelter may have been a bone shrine for song birds.

See *animal other, birdstone, crane, fossil, miniature, moon, owl*

Birdstone

Contextual differences between "birdstones" and "bannerstones" in Ohio are significant. "Unlike Notched Butterfly bannerstones, however, many Bar-type birdstones have been recovered from graves" and seem to have appeared sometime after 1500 B.C. with a radiocarbon dated burial association of 760 B.C. at 33Sa41 (Bowen 1994:13) on the lower Sandusky River. "No more than two preforms have been reported from any 100 km^2 tract. It is completed birdstones which seem to cluster" (Bowen 1994:14) in the lower Maumee and the lower Sandusky rivers. Cameron Parks (1970) pointed out that rarely is more than one birdstone found at a site. Parks offered that birdstones depicted the departing soul of the deceased, but Hall (2006) noted that most have four legs and better resemble the caiman or alligator.

See *alligator/crocodile, amulet/charm/talisman, atlatl, bannerstone, pole/post*

Bluff

Many of the bluffs of the Plains were known to be spirit homes (Irwin 1994). In addition, many of those bluffs were comprised of fossil-bearing chalk (Mayor 2005:185), ancient creatures that gave further credence to the idea that these high places were where one could find the oldest ground and the homes of Stone People. Bluffs are also often monadnocks, strange visual apparitions. Placing the dead in these locations might have facilitated an association of the dead with stars by juxtaposing their burial location with the night sky when viewed from below.

Numerous Archaic burial grounds and ritual sites were located on bluffs such as those overlooking the upper Ohio River (East Steubenville), the Wabash River (Robeson Hills, Riverton), the Mississippi River in Iowa, and the LIV (Elizabeth Mounds, Mound 1) and those along and on tributaries of the Green River. In fact, the oldest shell-bearing site in the Green River valley may be that of Ward, on a bluff top on a tributary stream, where river shells were hauled overland and then up a steep incline before being deposited. The various Green River bluff-top shell-bearing sites contain the highest number of dog burials in the valley. The dog sacrifice rite, the location, and the effort of hauling shells and human bodies up these landforms suggest that these topographic features were charged with special meaning.

See *cairn, constellation, dog sacrifice rite, mountain, Stone People*

Bobcat/Lynx

Feline parts were present in the Titterington phase (late Late Archaic) stratum at Modoc RS, Illinois, and with infants at Carlston Annis (a Kentucky shell mound). Another six jaws of lynx and a fossil tapir tooth were found in the deepest burial in Indian Knoll, a young adult, and three jaws were placed with another male, 30–35 yo. Lynx distal phalanges were interred with an infant. Lynx bones also appear in Archaic contexts at Lamoka Lake, New York, and at Morrill Point, Massachusetts. Lynx would have been a distant northern creature in any of these locations.

A bobcat hair was found in one fecal specimen from Salts Cave, Kentucky (Yarnell 1969). A perforated bobcat scapula and cut bobcat mandible were found in Riverton test units while a bobcat femur was found in a red ocher–

covered cache in Bu1 in Area X at Riverton (Winters 1969:84). Bobcat bones were found with infant Bu606 and with an extended adult member of a four-age rite at Indian Knoll. A right mandible of a bobcat was found with Bu58 at Robinson on the Cumberland River.

Throughout North and Central American cultures, nocturnal cats in general were associated with the feminine and darkness. Feline coat spots were interpreted as the starry night (Hall 2006:467) and shooting stars (Gatschet 1895). The central Mexican Codex Rios has a diagram that associates women, the left side, amphibians, feet, jaguars, and night. Jaguars are "the hungry powers of night," noted Read (1998:172). Given the spotted fawn association with infants and children, the spotted bobcat may have had the same infantile association.

See *animal other, constellation, deer, Milky Way, moon*

Bone Pin

Bone pins, presumably worn in hair or used to fasten mortuary clothing (Jefferies 2004), are remarkable for their various head styles and distribution during the Middle and Late Archaic. Design elements and head styles formed the basis of Jefferies's study of 140 Middle Archaic pins from 7 sites between the Ohio River and the Mississippi River and one site along the Ohio in Kentucky, allowing him to uncover 7 styles over a 500-km region spanning a 1,000-year period, 6000 to 5000 B.P. Very few pins, and then in unique styles, were found in only three Green River sites—Ward, Carlston Annis, and Indian Knoll—suggesting to Jefferies that very little interaction occurred between groups on opposite sides of the Ohio River. In addition, Jefferies surveyed the Atlantic Coastal Plain sites that had pins. Thousands of pins have been found in St. Johns River sites, and many of the designs resemble those found on Orange period pottery. The Savannah River sites of Bilbo and Stallings Island had dozens of pins. Pins have also been found in several Gulf Coastal Plain sites. Perhaps as a result of preservation, most of these pins have been found in shellworks although this context was less common west of the Ohio River.

Pin head types are carved into crutch-top (the most widely distributed), t-top, cruciform, fishtailed-cruciform, and double-expanded heads that seem to be specific to the southern Midwest region. Designs on pins were engraved, burned, or painted. Painted pins are widely distributed south and east of the Ohio River, and designs "usually consist of horizontal or diagonal banding or a combination of banding and curvilinear designs such as spirals or concentric circles" (Jefferies 2004:83).

Although marriage may account for the distribution of the various styles of pins in the 500-km region uncovered by Jefferies north and west of the Ohio River, this explanation seems less applicable to the concentration of pins in Savannah River and St. Johns River sites. An alternative explanation can be found in an article about stick-dice or arrow gambling by Eyman (1965) and mortuary games specifically by Ventur (1980). Frances Eyman (1965) depicts historic Indian gambling sticks remarkably similar to some carved pins and painted pins depicted by and eluded to by Jefferies. Gambling, she said, was "a ritual substitute for the hazard of real life" and notes that all games are "rituals of communication with deities" (1965:39) usually involving divination.

One possible explanation of the markings on the pins discussed by Jefferies is seen in the Mexican-derived patolli or sholiwi stick-dice game of the Zuni Bow Priest Society, a warrior society. In this game four reeds (dice) are marked with designs specific to each cardinal direction and cast over the course of a game to divine the future. Additionally, color symbolism is present as are complex calculations of odds. In a Dakota example of a stick-dice game, before a buffalo hunt, each hunter is given a stick die—painted either black for a mature man or red for a young man—marked with an identifying personal symbol that he deposits with the others before leaving camp. After the hunt a stick-dice game was played to redistribute the buffalo meat (Eyman 1965:47).

See *gambling*, *game*, *number*

Bone Shrine

These shrines were places to which animal bones were returned in thanksgiving and in recognition of bone soul (e.g., Harper 1999), evident by the Middle Archaic. Such places are often rocky in nature and characterized by extremely high numbers of bones. A bone shrine function is proposed for two rockshelters, Tick Creek Cave, Missouri (31,950 bones), and White Rocks, Ohio (73,000 bones), a shell ceremonial site at Indian Knoll, Kentucky (MNI of 1,550 deer), a shell-free burial ground in Illinois Black Earth (n = 197,000 bones), the dirt mound complex Watson Brake, Louisiana (n = 175,000 bones), an island site, Allumettes, Quebec (45,000 bones), and the sinkhole Austin Cave, Kentucky (8,693 bones). Caves do not appear to have been used as bone shrines. Although 956,000 pieces of bone were collected during excavation at Meadowcroft, they were recovered primarily from raptor pellets (Adovasio et al. 1998).

Most of these shrines seem to have been places to put a variety of species, although there was emphasis on deer at Indian Knoll and Tick Creek Cave. Both jute snail shells and animal bones are returned to separate shrines today in the Maya region (Brown 2005; Halperin et al. 2003).

See *animal other, bone soul, rockshelter, shrine, soul*

Bone Soul

The idea of bone soul is visible to archaeologists in the curation of bones and shells and in mortuary rituals. The modern Huron have a single word for both bone and soul, and the Iroquois recognized a soul residing in the bones, the enduring portion of the body (Harper 1999:51). Ravens, bison, and humans were animals attributed with bone soul in Paleoindian times judging from the formal interment or curation of their skeletons and body parts in a few caves in the western United States (e.g., Driver 1999). By Middle Archaic times, many other species were included in bone soul rites, particularly eel, beaver, deer, and squirrels. Their bones have been found in bone shrines in Missouri, Louisiana, Kentucky, Ohio, and Quebec. A Mayan bone soul rite is described by Brown (2005), and a detailed discussion of bone soul, or yolia, in Mesoamerica is offered by Furst (1995).

The use of specific species of animals in the manufacture of bone tools for particular types of crafts may also reflect bone soul thinking, as do fetishes and amulets using animals that emphasize certain desirable qualities such as good eyesight, good fishing, true aim, fecundity, and so forth. A bone of an animal provided the means to transform into that spirit animal and thus obtain its spiritual power. As suggested earlier for tool selection, "each bone had a specific task" (Betts, Blair, and Black 2012:626).

See *amulet/charm/talisman, animal other, bone shrine, fetish, Graham Cave, Rodgers Shelter, soul*

Breakage

Breakage is a tricky characteristic to interpret when seeking evidence of ritual. It is certainly true that breaking an object was a common characteristic of ritualized discard, and breakage is an important test implication for ritual deposits. However, whole, and thus usable, items also make suitable offerings. Tuck (1976:96) noted that a few utilitarian items recovered from Maritime Archaic graves at Port au Choix-3, Newfoundland, were broken, which to him meant that the spirit of the item once liberated, rather than the item, was meant to interact with the dead person. Spirits were not *trapped* inside stone, bones, and other materials and freed by breakage but rather their homes were destroyed by breaking (or burning), forcing them to seek new homes. Several bifaces in the Caradoc cache (Figure 10) demonstrate ceremonial breakage.

See *burning, decommissioning rite, offering*

Burial—Age of Deceased

Charles and Buikstra have written a number of articles in which they make note of differential treatment by age under the rubrics of "personal capability" and "social contribution" in which the lack of grave goods and the place for burial figure into an interpretation of impaired abilities, diminished social standing, and so forth (e.g., Milner, Buikstra, and Wiant 2009:124).

Several alternative explanations have been offered in Part 1. (1) Old adults were less likely to have been perceived to have died "before their time," or accidentally, so that burial practices directed toward them may be those associated with "normal" or "natural" death, not requiring exceptional attention or concern. The greater number of grave goods accorded younger individuals and their placement in mounds or other specially designated locales *away* from the living may have been required to appease the soul of the person who had died accidentally, in anger, or at the hands of peers, souls that many cultures believe wander and harm the living. (2) While among elderly individuals there were revered priests and ritual specialists, they may well have passed on their paraphernalia/bundles at their death, which would explain the lack of ceremonial or ornamental items. (3) Burial in rockshelters may be closely associated with particular individuals in the "ancestor" category such as group founders, ritual specialists, and lineage heads. None of these alternative explanations for fewer or different artifacts or lesser burial facility preparation correlates with low productivity or physical impairments. We should assume that the elderly were elders with greater "heat" or personal power, greater spiritual and practical knowledge, more animal allies, more kin, and more stories than the younger members of their group, and thus that their burial treatments do not translate easily into disregard by the living.

The high frequency of disturbed infants rather than other age groups at Indian Knoll must mean that the infant burials were either separated from the rest of the burials or marked. "Mothers often visited the graves of their children and noticed the least change in the appearance of the enshrouding earth; sometimes they identified the spot of an unmarked grave after years of absence" (Wallace and Steen 1972:94).

Burial postures for infants in the Archaic were flexed or extended on their backs. Lewis and Lewis (1961) suggested that extended burial might mark the use of the cradleboard, but if so, it was not widely adopted during the Archaic in the SOV. At Port au Choix-3 cemetery "children were more often buried with their arms extended, on their backs, and . . . their bodies were interred in a more extended position" (Jelsma 2006:89). The placement of infants facedown, between and below rocks in the center of rockshelters such as Newt Kash, Worth Creech, and Dillard Stamper Shelter 1, all in Wolfe and Menifee counties, Kentucky (e.g., Funkhouser and Webb 1930; Webb and Funkhouser 1936), Breckenridge Shelter, Arkansas, and Russell Cave, Alabama (Griffin 1974), suggest a ritual sacrifice as do infants buried with copious marine shell items (Claassen 2010, 2013a).

Newborns were more often accorded grave goods in the SOV during the Middle Archaic than they were during the Late Archaic. No other significant differences in the treatments of newborns versus infants were encountered in a recent study (Claassen 2013a).

See *altar, burial—posture, rockshelter, sacrifice—infant and child*

Burial—Childbirth Death

One way that women who died in childbirth were buried was flexed on the back. Women with fetal remains at Indian Knoll were placed on their back, a woman with newborn at Hayes was on her back, and a woman with infant at Rosenberger was extended on her back. The on-the-back position in the SOV is often associated with violent death (e.g., 40 percent of Indian Knoll and Carlston Annis burials with obvious violence are on their backs), suggesting that death in childbirth or shortly after birthing may have been equated with other types of violent death, as it was among the Aztecs. Those women became feared spirits that inhabited the western sky and crossroads at night.

See *burial—group, burial—posture, violence*

Burial—Group

Mensforth (2001:117; Mensforth 2007) confirmed that graves with multiple bodies in the SOV often had at least one skeleton showing violent death (embedded points, decapitation, limb removal). Some of these group graves may hold the victims of ritual sacrifices, such as the men thrown into a pit at the base of the Mulberry Creek shell mound and various graves with the age combination of infant, adolescent, and adult male and female, or infant, child, adolescent, and adult. Threesomes, with woman, man, and infant, could be adultery killings. Group graves are also found in most other regions of the eastern United States, and several mass graves have been referred to as ossuaries.

See *adultery killing, four-age rite, hunt god rite, ossuary, sacrifice—adult, violence*

Burial—Head Direction

Some effort has been directed toward deciphering the meaning of body orientation. Confusion has been expressed about whether the axial line of spine through the top of the head is to be recorded or the direction that the skull is facing. Given the belief among Mexican groups that the soul is drilled into the newborn through the fontanel and leaves the body via the fontanel, the alignment of greatest relevance should probably be the line passing through the top of the skull and down the spinal column rather than the facing direction.

At Windover, 64 percent of those buried had their heads pointing to 270+/-45 degrees and 48 percent had an axis pointing between 298.5 and 241.5 degrees (Dickel 2002). Over half of the bodies at another site near Windover, Harris Creek, were oriented south-southwest-west and a third were headed north-northeast-east (Aten 1999:174). There was a notable western direction for most of the Middle Archaic bodies at Elizabeth Mound 1 (Charles, Leigh, and Albertson 1988), at Black Earth (Lynch 1982:1137), particularly for males and juveniles, at Meyer, Indiana (Bader 2010/11), and at Little Salt Spring (Wentz and Gifford 2007). Ohio burial grounds had all burial directions except east (Purtill 2009:589).

The Nevin, Massachusetts shell heap shows head orientation differences between primary burials and secondary burials. Primary burials had western head orientations when recorded (4 of 9 bodies) and 11 of 17 secondary burials had northern head orientations, all of those recorded (Byers 1979:25).

Many researchers have discussed head orientation in terms of sun movement (Dickel 2002:79), but time was also reckoned in the passage of nights. "The Inuit bury their young in the direction of the rising sun, but place the aged in the opposite direction" (Smith 2010:44). The night sky was viewed by numerous cultures as the Underworld rotated into the upper position. Since the dead were also the source of new life, it may well be that Underworld time was of greater relevance to head orientation. Researchers might consider moonrise and set points, the movement of various stars, various constellations, and gender in future analyses.

See *astronomy*, *cardinal direction*, *constellation*, *moon*

Burial—Posture

Heckenberger and colleagues (1990) say burial posture variability is a hallmark of Early Archaic burial, but it is no less so later in time. For example, in the Middle Archaic levels of Mulberry Creek shell mound, flexed and extended burials were found but in the Late Archaic levels cremations, bundles, and sitting burials were made in addition to flexed (Shields 2003:83). Posture variability in burials in the Wisconsin and Kankakee-LaPorte regions was like that of the SOV: most often flexed and if not flexed, extended (Didier 1967:39). Late Archaic burials in Newfoundland had infants in both extended and flexed positions, but all adults were flexed or bundled (Tuck 1976). Flexed on left or right side are the dominant burial postures in the Early Archaic at Archaic sites in Florida and in the Middle and Late Archaic of the SOV. There is a hint of men being buried more often on their right side and women on the left side during the Middle Archaic at Anderson, Tennessee, and younger adults continuing to be so placed in Late Archaic times. Even at Port au Choix-3 during the Late Archaic, based on some sexing criteria no longer employed, "there seems to have been a slight tendency, especially in the case of adult males, to bury individuals on the left side" (Tuck 1976). Studies of the relationship between burial position and gender and age need to be performed.

Tuck believes, as do I, that burial postures reflect different circumstances surrounding the cause of death: "These deviations might reflect the treatment accorded individuals whose death was in some way extraordinary such as death by accident; drowning, for example" (Tuck 1976:96). The dominant burial mode should show us those who died in "normal" ways. Minority burial postures, then, signal some class of special death and in a few cases, such as the sitting posture, may reflect ethnicity.

Sitting burials occur occasionally in Middle Archaic contexts in the St. Johns River and may be an ethnic marker. A few sitting burials are found in Late Archaic settings at Stallings Island and in the Tennessee River and Green River shell mounds (four seated burials at Indian Knoll) and may be people originating from Florida. If so, then sitting posture may be an ethnic marker. Other sitting bodies have been encountered in Dravo Gravel and DuPont sites in southwestern Ohio (Purtill 2009:587).

It was common for Algonkian people to bury their dead in a sitting position. In life children sat in front of elders and their fathers, a position of respect (Smith 2010:42), suggesting that in death all sat before the spirits out of similar respect. Likewise, the sitting posture (Figure 21) is the iconographic means of depicting the highest-status individuals in Mesoamerica, the leaders and priests with the greatest access to and responsibility to the spirits. Sitting is also the posture for desiccated bodies revered as oracles, possibly explaining "Fawn Hoof," a corpse (priest) found sitting in Short Cave, Kentucky. The stone arrangement inside Graham Cave suggests that a centrally seated figure led councils or rites there (Figure 12). Exactly when the sitting posture appeared in the eastern United States and its distribution should be examined for possible social implications of leadership or migrations.

21. Sitting body entombed in Zaachila, Oaxaca, Mexico. (Photo by author.)

Extended burial seems to the normal position west of the Ohio-Mississippi confluence (e.g., Black Earth and surrounding sites) as well as in New York, but it is usually the posture for murder victims in the SOV. If foreigners were the victims, then it could be that extension was both an ethnic marker and a cause-of-death marker.

There are additional burial positions that suggest violent death and possibly sacrifice. These are the head- or torso-twisted body, the flexed body put in head-first, and the flexed or extended facedown burial.

I have proposed two explanations for the twisted bodies (Claassen 2010, 2012a). In light of beliefs about an earth deity turning around and a world turning upside down among the Inca when profound change is at hand (Classen 1993), the twisted and upside-down flexed bodies may be those of priests or sacrificial victims killed in a rebalancing rite mandated by extremely unusual cosmic circumstances (Claassen 2010:184). It also may be that the head- and torso-twisted men were deer impersonators killed through head twisting, emulating the killing of a sacred deer in a hunt god rite (Claassen 2012a). These burials were rare enough to attract—even demand—our attention for they may imply very specific rites. Torso-twisted bodies have been recorded at Long Branch, Mulberry Creek, Tick Island, McCain, Reigh, and Buffalo (West Virginia). Tennessee sites are Ryan, Ensworth, Penitentiary Branch, and Anderson, where the young man was completely weighted down with slabs. In perhaps what is a variation of this position, legs were pulled completely over the head of a man at Vaughn, Mississippi.

Fleshed burial positions, then, reflect several beliefs about the proper treatment of the dead. They reflect an ethnic-based idea of normal death (dying from old age or from a protracted illness or debilitation) or abnormal death (murder, a fall, lightning strike, drowning, etc.), and may also reflect the timing of death (with head alignment) and ideas about gender and age.

See *burial—age of deceased, burial—under limestone, hunt god rite, sacrifice—adult*

Burial—Secondary

Secondary burial—of selected bones, of skeletons, of cremains—was ubiquitous during the Archaic and throughout eastern North America. Dry bones were dug up or gathered up and were reinterred as well as included with cremations or themselves burned.

Secondary and bundle burial may have begun in the Middle Archaic, but both were more widely adopted in the Late Archaic. The Middle Archaic examples can be found on the St. Johns River, in the LIV, in Wisconsin, and in the Maritime Archaic burial grounds. They may be earliest during the Terminal Archaic in Wisconsin and in the Late Archaic along the Tennessee River, and in Missouri.

Trace element analysis at Harris Creek in Florida indicated that people buried as bundles had lived in the vicinity of Harris Creek and had been extensively processed whereas other burial positions showed greater geographical diversity (Tucker 2009). "The idea of keeping bundles of tightly wrapped, flexed bodies and even secondary bone bundles in storage for a time before their placement in graves calls to mind mortuary ritual structured around the general lines of spirit-keeping and spirit-release described by Hall (1997:24–31)" (Aten 1999:180).

In addition to demonstrating evidence of the ideas of spirit-keeping and spirit-release beginning late in the Middle Archaic, secondary burial was an opportunity for the living to interact with one another through the icons of the bones of the dead (e.g., Clay 2013). These collective burial programs are clearly in evidence at burial grounds such as Osceola and Williams, each with hundreds of bundle burials.

At Turner Farm "elements of the recently deceased were combined with elements of the previously deceased, stored or exhumed for inclusion in the [mortuary] ritual . . . some primary inhumations were reopened, and bones were removed . . . all other inhumations [with one possible exception] had cremation deposits incorporated into the grave fill" (Bourque 1995:163).

Bourque also pointed out that manipulation of the dead was also suspected or noted at New York Susquehanna tradition sites (Dincauze 1968:65) and at Nevin (Byers 1979:24–71). Secondary bone burials were tabulated by Webb in various SOV reports, and they are well represented elsewhere in the Ohio and Illinois River valleys. "Diachronic changes in such behavior over time in a given region should prove useful as a relative scale for measuring, if not complexity, at least the strength of 'ritual affirmation of corporate structure' (Charles and Buikstra 1983:124)" (Bourque 1995:163).

See *cremation, trophy part decommissioning rite, Turner Farm*

Burial—Under Limestone

Limestone rocks or slabs on burials were encountered in Paleoindian Horn Shelter, Texas, in Early Archaic Horizon 11 at Koster and at Godar, both in Illinois, in Middle Archaic context at Elizabeth Mound 1, and in numerous Late Archaic contexts in the Ohio River valley (Milner, Buikstra, and Wiant 2009:119). Limestone-weighted burials were less common in the SOV.

Perhaps these burials are instances of premature or accidental death. Mexican peoples have long been concerned with this type of death and work to prevent the soul of one who has died by accident from troubling the living through means such as elaborate funerals with food and gifts, pinning the soul at the place of death with a cross, and dedicating a day to the remembrance of these deaths. Weighty rocks could serve this purpose.

A variation on this theme is the covering of a domed burial mound with limestone, frequently seen in Archaic mounds of the LIV and among Maritime Archaic burials. Again we may be seeing an attempt to contain those souls and prevent their movement among the living.

See *burial—posture, limestone slab, witch*

Burning

A pervasive practice in rituals worldwide is the burning of incense as well as non-odiferous items as offerings, appealing to the spirits. Burning items is also an act of transformation and purification. Fire itself is often used to signify the initiation of new temporal cycles and renewal.

Burning bone to the point of calcination suggests a ritual practice since it moves well beyond the simple charring effected by cooking or needed for sanitation (Harper 1999:356). For example, at Campbell Hollow in the LIV, 69 percent of the bones from the Middle Archaic component were calcined and 1 percent were burned (Colburn 1985). There are at least two reasons for calcifying bone, both ritual in nature. One is for divination. Harper recounts the practice of exposing animal bones to fire in order to locate their living counterparts: "By reading the heat-induced cracks and scorching on bones, [Iroquoian] hunters interpreted these signs in reference to known geographical places and as representing various animals" (1999:160). The color of a burned bone was also useful tracking information. The Naskapi used beaver bones to find beaver and caribou for caribou, but rabbit and partridge bones could be used for all types of game. The burning of bones, particularly the scapula, pelvis, and patella, was also used to divine the answers to more esoteric questions, including the whereabouts of hostile humans.

The other reason for calcifying bone is for proper disposal of the bone soul of the animal. Harper cites numerous examples of different beliefs about which species should and should not be burned (1999:176–178). For many groups, feast foods were to be burned. The frequent encounter of calcined bone in Archaic features strongly suggests that these ideas were extant and that at least for some species (e.g., drumfish at Higgs) fire disposal was appropriate. At the Range site in the American Bottom, for instance, "The heavily calcined nature of the bone remains found in pits indicates that food was cooked directly over the pits or in the pits. This pattern of bone deposition and preservation was observed at all of the Late Archaic sites mentioned above and was an atypical pattern for bone materials recovered from pits from later components" (Fortier 1987:102).

It may well be that Spiess and Lewis (1995:343) exposed precisely this type of rite with regard to the distribution of deer bones at Turner Farm, Maine. There was a significantly different distribution of deer axial and appendicular elements. Hearths contained far more axial bones (skull, vertebra, ribs, pelvis) and pits more limb bones during the Moorehead phase. Future research will uncover greater nuance in terms of what species were and were not calcined in the past.

The association of fire with human burials is well documented. Funeral fires were maintained above or beside graves in some groups and sites (e.g., Bader 2010/11), sometimes resulting in inappropriately identified cremations (Owens 2010). In Florida there are several examples of bodies put on top of hot coals (e.g., Harris Creek). In the Cumberland River valley graves at the Ryan site and Penitentiary Branch were "capped with rock and burned," thus marking the cemetery area (Barker and Hazel 2007:5).

See *ashes*, *breakage*, *cremation*, *decommissioning rite*

Busycon sp.

From specimens with identifiable characteristics we know that individual shells of the left-handed whelk *Busycon contrarium* and fewer of a right-handed whelk *Busycon carica* moved throughout the Mississippi watershed and were utilized for various ornaments and containers during the Middle and Late Archaic. Probable *Busycon* shell items were found with 3 percent of the bodies at Windover burial pond. Unmodified shells were found only with one woman, but a cache of *Busycon* shells was found situated among a tight cluster of bodies.

Middle Archaic use of marine shell is evident at Harris Creek, Florida. "While it is tempting to imagine that the shell dipper/receptacles with scorched and broken cup bottoms may indicate ceremonialism at the mortuaries, only one of these artifacts was clearly associated with the mortuary zone. They may, however, point to other non-mortuary ceremonies performed on the summit platform" (Aten 1999:162).

North of the Ohio River marine shell objects are found mostly in the Old Copper culture (Goad 1980). Within the Southeast region, the marine shell distribution does not conform to a fall-off model of decreasing quantities as distance from the Gulf source increases (Goad 1980:6). If a site lacked a freshwater shell accumulation, it also lacked marine shell artifacts (e.g., Rosenberger, Black Earth, Kirkland, Ensworth). Nor is there enough *Busycon* shell moving around the landscape to *require* trade as the predominant movement mechanism (Claassen 2008). No Archaic marine shell redistribution centers are known. Offerings and gifts of marine shell items at the time of marriages and intercommunity rituals could account for much of the quantity and spatial distribution of these items.

Marine shell in later times was associated with beginning time, the primordial world. It was a symbol of renewal among New England groups partially for its white color (Hamell 1989). The spiral of the gastropod symbolized the spiraling world at the time of creation, gastropods were stars in the night sky (Richard Dieterle, www.hotcakencyclopedia.com/ho.JourneyToSpiritland.html, accessed September 19, 2010), and the left-opening *Busycon contrarium* encapsulated the movement of the sun and moon from right to left, the spiraling world, the cave portal to the Underworld, the womb, and the grave.

See *gastropod, Leptoxis/Anculosa, Olivella, shell, shell bead*

C-Shaped Site Layout

Construction of sacred precincts in a C-shape, made famous by the layout of the Poverty Point site, apparently began during the Late Archaic period and continued to govern site layout for ritually important earthwork centers in the Southeast until the Europeans arrived. This shape can be seen at Archaic shell rings such as Joseph Reed, Rollins, and Guana. Broken elliptical mound groupings characterize the multimound Archaic sites of the lower Mississippi valley. Shellworks along the Gulf Coast also often assume a broken ellipse or broken ring shape.

"The broken-circle (actually arcurate) plan is a recurrent theme of sacred areas, ritual activities, and dance movements of peoples linked linguistically to ancient Gulf or proto-Gulf language speakers" (Gibson 1998:23). Poverty Point's concentric arcs of dirt open to the east, the direction of the rising sun that Gulf tribes recognized as the prime cosmic being. "The opening in the rings gave a clear view of the awakening sun each day during its solstice-to-solstice journey along the horizon; such sighting paths were used in historic times by holy men to awaken the sun and summon its blessings (LePetit in Swanton 1911:174)" (Gibson 1998:23).

But east is the direction from which one would await the rising moon as well. One possible model for such a formal pattern is the crescent moon. Since most such C-shaped sites also incorporate a river that completes a D shape, and the others often have a shell ridge that forms the D, perhaps that D was the target design rather than the C. Either shape encloses a space that could be viewed as a portal. The river and ponds of borrow pits would situate the portal in the Underworld, with implications for the moon and the night sky.

We also find frequent use of the C-shape by Mesoamerican groups to signify the cave portal to the Underworld. Ascent from this Otherworld realm by an important political personage was illustrated by seating the individual inside the arc, the same illusion as would be created when a priest was working inside the arcuate space of southeastern earthworks.

See *cardinal direction*, *constellation*, *moon*, *Poverty Point*, *shellworks*, *sun*

Cache—Blade

Three functions of blade caches are recognized by archaeologists: for burial, for sacred purposes, and for storage. While the "sacred purposes" have not been specified, caches of blades found in isolated places on the landscape may have been offerings to particularly old deities and spirits, the Stone People of the earliest creation.

Paleoindian caches are rare in the eastern United States but increase dramatically in the Archaic. Many of these caches have been found in localities that suggest propitiation of an Earth Spirit—in rocky outcrops, in elevated places, at springs. Where hypertropic blades or groups of them are placed in only a few burials in a burial ground, perhaps there was some connection between the individual and an earth deity/spirit (a flintknapper, cave specialist, etc.) or perhaps someone who died in a particular way. When many people in a mortuary area are buried with hypertropic blades or caches of bifaces, this might indicate a collection of kin who claim some particular relationship to the Stone People.

Oversized Daltons were occasionally burned with the human body (never broken), a situation seen both before and after the Dalton period. Susquehanna Tradition caches were much more common in New England sites than to the south and, like Daltons and Bentons, were found burned, unburned, broken, and whole. Like the Midwest cache blades, they were also found used (Sassaman 2010a:99–105). Sassaman observed that "the manufacture and caching of either hypertrophic forms or large numbers of preforms is something that happened routinely in only limited locations for limited periods of time. The trend over time is for decreased biface size but increased numbers of cache blades. All of the northern traditions involved at least occasional destruction of points" (2010a:104–105).

The Neralich cache consisted of two blades of white Burlington chert, removed from a small pit in the Olive Branch site, in southern Illinois. "The bifaces were enveloped in red-tinged soil suggesting that they may have been wrapped in ochre-painted robes, matting, or some other sort of pliable covering, the absence of human bone, calcined or otherwise, indicates that the bifaces are not grave offerings. A more likely explanation for this spectacular pair of blades is that they are sculptures representing ancestral men and women. . . . the very early Archaic folk who resided at the Olive Branch site," noted Mike Gramly (www.lithiccastinglab.com/gallery-pages/olivebranchnotchedpointspage1.htm, accessed March 30, 2011).

It also seems that there is unexplored symbolism imparted by the number of blades in caches. For instance, there were 2 blades in the Neralich cache at Olive Branch, 4 blades in a cache at Maple Creek, Ohio (Vickery 2008:21), 6 in another cache at Olive Branch, and 29 lithics in a cache in Oklahoma (Calf Creek), all suggestive of cosmic phenomena. It is curious that several caches have prime numbers of blades, such as the 41 blades in a cache at Rosenberger, 47 blades in a cache at McCullough Run, and so forth. In a short summary of Clovis caches, Deller and Ellis said, "It is becoming increasingly difficult to see these Clovis [caches] as utilitarian caches since we would expect most to be retrieved" (2001:280).

See *Benton blades, Caradoc Site, Grandstaff and Davis Cache, number, stone, Stone People*

Cache—Debitage

Watson (2005:519) lists caches of flakes and blanks at Ward and at Chiggerville in the Green River valley. Debitage caches are infrequent, but at site 9Wr4 in Georgia several debitage caches are clearly ritual in origin. There were three caches of debitage in three postmolds outlining a structure. Each cache contained flakes of a single type of stone different from the other two caches. Each cache contained metavolcanic "reduction debris, manufacturing failures," and, in one case, two complete Savannah River bifaces (Ledbetter 1995:177). A fourth cache of quartz was found outside but adjacent to the structure, a possible consecration or commissioning rite.

Flakes had reference to children in Aztec society (Furst 1995:175), and I propose that the same link between fertility and flakes existed in the deep past of eastern Archaic societies. Although not caches per se, extensive workshop areas or springs with hundreds of thousands of flakes may be the equivalent of flake caches.

See *commissioning rite for a place, flake/chip, flintknapping, lithic workshop*

Cache—Groundstone

Most caches were probably offerings, and the caches of pestles, hammers, and manos may have been offerings made by women. These caches of heavy groundstone items are fairly common in the Green River valley. Watson (2005:518) provides the following inventory of heavy tool caches from 8 Green River sites: 14 from Read, 13 from Barrett, 13 from Ward, 10 from Carlston Annis, 7 from Butterfield, 5 from Indian Knoll, 1 from Chiggerville, and 4 from Kirkland. Later caches were often found on the eastern side of mounds, but spatial information for these caches is buried in the field notes. A cache of 10 manos was found in the ritual area of Riverton, at the corner of a baked-clay surface (Winters 1969:98).

The Keenan bead cache contained 449 unmodified pebbles, preforms, and bead blanks (Connaway 1981). Caches of bannerstones and bannerstones with stone beads were found on the St. Johns River in Mount Taylor times in combinations that suggested communal mortuaries (Randall 2015).

Harvey (2006) points out the rarity of more than two bannerstones, calling them caches; when three are found in a burial, this indicates an extremely important person. These caches have been found at Bullseye, Crib Mound, and Tomoka.

See *bannerstone, cache—blade, cache—other, offering, world renewal rite*

Cache—Other

Utilitarian caches may have included meat caches and caches of quartz quarrying tools for steatite seams (e.g., Oaklawn cemetery steatite quarry; Fowler 1971–72:10), but they, too, could have been offerings. The caches of mixed items are most frequently considered to be stored equipment, such as the Hawkins Cache in Arkansas with Dalton points, adzes, abrader, chisel, end scraper, and backed blade (Morse 1971). Caches of broken tools have also been found (e.g., Crowfield site).

See *Barrington Oaks, cache—blade, cache—debitage, cache—groundstone, Crowfield, offering*

Cairn

Three sites of stacked rock features have been reported on Arkansas bluff tops overlooking the White River (House 1965), each with artifacts related to Middle Archaic activities (chips, knives, points [only Archaic points], metates) and each with an expansive view of the river below. A series of stacked rock features in Tennessee has attracted archaeologists' attention as well, although dating them is problematic (Deter-Wolf and Hockersmith 2007). These cairns did not seem to cover bodies.

Archaic cairns are more commonly associated with the surface of graves. Mortuary cairns occur in the LIV at places such as Etley (Wiant, Farnsworth, and Hajic 2009:265). Short cairns comprised of large stones marked every grave at Port au Choix-3. Farther north, cairns also marked Archaic graves at Nulliak Mounds, Labrador.

From the western United States comes evidence that individuals seeking cures carried a stone to a medicine stack and added it as an offering. Western ritual specialists and children on vision quests built cairns, and groups built cairns for rituals (Whitley et al. 1999:234). Cairns and altars are often the same facility (Figure 17) (LeBeau 2009).

See *altar, rock formation, stone*

Camp Circle

Circular living seems to have characterized Archaic community life in several regions. Circles of pits were found at Range, Missouri Pacific #2, Dyroff-Levin, and Go-Kart North in Illinois (Fortier 1987:49). Circular community plans were also found in Archaic sites of the Savannah River (Sassaman

2006, 2010a) and obviously in the shell rings of the Atlantic coast. Historic Indian groups that set up camp circles attached much complementary cosmic significance to the north and south halves and the east and west halves, significance that is potentially recoverable if it held during the Archaic. Russo (2004) and Curtin (2011) have discussed or investigated social inequalities associated with circular living. "This pattern probably is associated with the River phase of the Late Archaic period [Vosburg site, New York], about 1800–2000 B.C., based upon projectile point type-frequencies from the various surface collections. The distribution of chert flakes forms a broad, ring-like area of elevated artifact density surrounding a low to very low density central area. The ring appears to contain a series of small, high density artifact concentrations" (Curtin 2011:5).

See *duality*, *geometry*

Cannel Coal

Beads made from cannel coal are primarily, although infrequently, found in burials of the Green River shell mounds. They also have been found at Anderson in Tennessee, in Ohio cemeteries such as DuPont, and in James Creek in West Virginia. The black color, origin in veins, and crayon characteristics no doubt conditioned the ritualized application of coal.

See *color*, *paint/powder*

Canoe

Canoes in Florida are typically found in springs or at the margins of ponds and typically as isolated finds. At least 37 of the dated canoes from Newnans Lake were found to be Archaic products, and the oldest canoe in Florida, from De Leon Springs, was made 7,000 ya (Wheeler et al. 2003). The information about the finding of canoes in springs suggests, just as it would for humans found in this context, a burial rite for canoes at an auspicious place.

Capping

Numerous shell mounds of the Green River were capped with a shell-free soil that had been transported to these sites (Stein 2005). While the artifact content was clearly derived from the activities of the prior shell gatherers, shell disappeared entirely from these sites. Capping with sand, shell, or muck was part of apparent termination rites on earlier shell-bearing mounds in Florida. Capping was a finishing act. "Capping," says Sassaman (2010a:72), was "signaling the ecological 'death' of a place of dwelling" even when its use continued.

Cardinal Direction

Gibson (1998:25) sees in the six sets of concentric arcs at Poverty Point the Gulf-Muskogean cosmic division of This World into the four cardinal directions and directions up and down. Given the pan-American numerology suggested by Clark (2004), it is possible that the Mesoamerican association of certain numbers/days with each cardinal direction was employed during the Archaic in the eastern Woodlands. Burial head-spine orientations may constitute the strongest evidence of an awareness of the cardinal and the intercardinal directions in Middle Archaic times.

East was the direction of the sunrise, the birthplace of day, light, and warmth. It was also the direction to which Algonkians sought Nanabojou, bringer of life and giver of the Midewiwin medicine society (Rajnovich 1994:136). There are numerous reasons to propose that east was specifically associated with birth, beginning, and daytime in Archaic cultures of the eastern United States, such as the lack of freshwater shell burial sites in the SOV located on any segment of an eastward-flowing river, the rare occurrences of Archaic adult burials pointing in an easterly direction, and the location of shell burial grounds west of the Atlantic Ocean, never on its shores. The direction east, then, was not associated with death during the Archaic. The arcs of Poverty Point opened to the east.

Conversely, *west* (and southwest) is frequently associated with death based on head-pointing direction and the location of shell burial grounds west of the Appalachians and the high number of shell burial mounds found on western-flowing segments of river. West is also often the direction from which rain arrives in the eastern United States, leading to a conflation of the dead and rain bringing. Ball courts, situated conceptually in the Underworld, were established in the west (and south) in ceremonial centers in Mexico. Three mounds at Poverty Point, including the largest one, were situated in the western portion of this ceremonial center. The Gulf-Muskogean peoples believe the souls of the dead can be found in the west (Gibson 1998:25). The southwestern association with death and the place of the Underworld ball game is echoed by Caddoan speakers who believe that the spirit world resides in the west, southwest, or south sky. They associate death with the winter sun that rises and sets in the south (Kay and Sabo 2006:33).

The east-west directional axis is the one most prevalent in North American groups (DeBoer 2005:67). The important and persistent difference between east and west symbolism is that west, associated with the Underworld and fertility, is primarily associated with *conception*. The east, associated with This World and the daily birth of the sun, is primarily associated with *birth*. Conception takes place in the Underworld and through the dead while birth takes place in This World.

Gibson invokes Gulf-Muskogean cosmology to offer that *north* was the direction of witchcraft and social disharmony for historic groups (Gibson 1998:25). Nevertheless, a high percentage of shell burial mounds were located on north-flowing rivers (St. Johns, western Tennessee River, Green River). The Gulf-Muskogean peoples believed benevolent spirits/winds came from the *south* (Gibson 1998:25). The Muskogee seat alligator, turkey, and Támi clans in the south of the campground have women enter the square grounds from the southeast corner and take medicine in that corner and locate the ball ground to the southwest of the campgrounds (Lankford 2004:209).

Lawson described eight directional points used by Indians in the Carolinas that were named for various characteristics of winds. The northwest was the cold wind, the northeast the wet wind, and the south, the warm wind (Lawson [1860] 1960:213). Colors were also associated with each cardinal direction (DeBoer 2005; Gartner 1996:145). These directions were referred to in either clockwise or counterclockwise sequence. As specified by DeBoer (2005:75), cultures living above 35° latitude perceived the directions to circle in a clockwise direction while those below that line favored them in a counterclockwise sequence.

See *astronomy, burial—head direction, center, constellation, moon, number, rain*

Caribou/Elk

Unmodified caribou bones and teeth—a rib, a dew claw, five styliform bones, two phalanxes, and five sets of incisors—were found as grave goods in the Port au Choix-3, Newfoundland, burial ground, as were three caribou antler combs (Tuck 1976:64). The nearly exclusive appearance of caribou bone and antler in the unmodified bone remains at Port au Choix-3 led Tuck (1976:50) to suggest that the modern Naskapi and Montagnais belief that all caribou bone had to be used rather than wasted was characteristic of Archaic peoples in this region. He further interpreted the incisor sets as amulets.

Elk teeth and their cloven hooves were associated with women's fertility by Plains tribes (Sundstrom 2004). Therefore, the elk ribs associated with two women in Elizabeth Mounds seems significant while deer appear to be absent from this Illinois RV bluff-top mortuary (Leigh and Morey 1988:281). Elk bones were also found in the vestibule of Salts Cave, a ritual place, and bones of at least 10 elk were placed in the Tick Creek Cave hunting shrine in Missouri. Elk bone awls were found at Lamoka Lake, New York, and one piece of elk antler came from the midden at McCain, Indiana, and from a single grave at Indian Knoll, Bu774. The Black Earth site had a possible priest burial with an elk antler cup.

See *animal other, antler, deer, feet/footprint/track*

Carolina Bay

Carolina Bays are wet depressions found from New Jersey into Florida and consistently show, in the Carolinas, Georgia, and northern Delaware at least, the greatest association with Paleoindian and Early Archaic activities (Brooks, Taylor, and Ivester 2010:156). The Carolina Bays are northwest-southeast skewed in their outline, and dense artifacts and features are always concentrated on their eastern side. Given the Paleoindian attraction to sinkholes in numerous karstic zones of the eastern United States and ponds in Florida, their attraction to Carolina Bays is not surprising. No one has yet considered a ritual role for these bays, as is apparent for the Florida ponds, or that some of the material (including hematite) might be offerings from rites.

See *sinkhole*

Cave

Some caves—which are deeper than rockshelters, thus having areas of total darkness—were chosen as sites for rites in the Archaic. All of them are located in the SOV or on its border: Wyandotte, Indiana; Russell Cave and Dust Cave in Alabama; and Adair, Austin, Mammoth, Salts, Savage, and Short caves in Kentucky's central karst. Tippins (2007:40) could find no sign of usage of any of the 79 western Pennsylvania caves. Witthoft (1951:33) likewise found no "aboriginal use or knowledge of limestone caverns of Pennsylvania," and Converse (2006:20) knew of few Ohio caverns with artifactual material. Although there are Late Archaic radiocarbon dates from Mammoth and Salts caves in Kentucky, the time of greatest mining activities in these two caves was the Early Woodland.

Utilized caves were typically accessed through a sinkhole. Cave mouths and vestibules were apparently the locations for the rites most frequently held, rites that seemingly differed from those conducted in the dark zones. When midden is found it is located in the mouth or vestibule such as that in the vestibules of Salts Cave and Mammoth Cave. One interment of a young woman (undated) was reported from the vestibule of Salts Cave. Savage Cave and Salts Cave have pits filled with ritual items in their vestibule. Dust Cave has a deposit of goose humerii. Austin Cave is interesting in that a tremendous quantity of lithic debitage was found in the sinkhole off of which the cave opens (Barker 1997). A human femur with embedded Kirk point was found in a cave in Tennessee. A murdered woman was placed in Stanhope Cave, Ohio.

Faulkner (1997) and Crothers (2012) believe that caves with markings inside were scenes of rituals. Cave mouths and vestibules are symbolically the open maw of an earth monster for Mexican cultures and the limit of egress for most pilgrims. Caves were viewed as the passageway into sustenance mountains through which exited game (e.g., Cherokee story of Kanati). "The Algonkian universe was layered with Sky, Earth, Underwater and Underground being distinct worlds connected in places such as deep lakes, whirlpools, caves and crevices where a man or Manitou could travel from one realm to another" (Rajnovich 1994:35). The midden and the pit deposits often found in eastern U.S. caves therefore may have been the result of numerous rituals that deposited offerings, human trophy parts, and feasting remains. The flintknapping may have been part of a fertility rite.

Rites and activities held deep inside caves were probably conducted by specialists including apprentices, rather than by pilgrims. The activities deep in these caves documented so far are exploring, mining, marking, making offerings, preparing and using baked-clay floors, nut and seed processing, dog burial, and human burial. I have proposed that these activities constituted parts of rites for world renewal, rain-calling/fertility, rebalancing, and possibly ancestor burial (Claassen 2010, 2012a, 2012b, 2012c, 2012d). If salts were collected during the Archaic they would have been used for purging (Crothers 2012).

Marking ceilings, walls, and rocks inside caves was under way in the Late Archaic in a few places. Adair Glyph Cave, Kentucky, gives us the earliest look at this practice: Archaic/Early Woodland drawings largely consisting of geometric forms (zig-zags, chevrons, and cross-hatching), zoomorphic figures, random lines, stroke marks, and herpetomorphic figures. Interestingly, geometric forms like those seen in cave drawings are very similar to designs engraved on late Middle to Late Archaic bone pins (Jefferies 1997). Cave markings are currently interpreted not as "art" but as "tattooing" (Diaz-Granados 2004) and communication (Rajnovich 1994).

The activities conducted at Russell Cave proper may have been staged from the adjacent rockshelter. Excavations occurred in this rockshelter and revealed an initial Early Archaic infant sacrifice at a slab altar and subsequent human and dog burials. There is an adjacent sinkhole and a disappearing creek runs some two miles through the actual cave. These features and the rockshelter were probably part of the ritual complex. Furthermore, these caves were not isolated ritual zones but may have been part of ritual districts and visited as nodes in ritual circuits. Russell Cave is within two miles of a dramatic waterfall upstream and the shell burial mound at Whitesburg Bridge downstream. Dust Cave is within a mile of the very important Perry shell mound, and both places have human burials and dog burials. Mammoth Cave is upriver from the famous Green River shell mounds and bluff-top dog burial sites. Wyandotte Cave is within two miles of the Ohio River and 15 miles of the shell burial mounds of the Falls district. Cheek Bend Cave in central Tennessee is within 15 miles of Ervin, one of the earliest shell-bearing mortuaries. Of interest for its Pleistocene fauna, as well as human remains, it and Ervin have equally old dates, ca. 7,000 ya (Klippel and Parmalee 1982).

By the close of the Archaic caves were associated with an earth deity or spirit and a particular type of medicine. These were appropriate places to return bones and trophy parts. This deity gave not only medicine but fertility in the form of rain, stream water, and babies, and was also petitioned for balance in the cosmos with dog sacrifices (Claassen 2010). It may also be that the bodies of particular people were conserved as oracles in caves such as Short Cave. Testosterone and estradiol levels in 12 fecal specimens from Salts Cave gave positive results for male origin (Sobolik et al. 1996), suggesting that caves may have been a domain for male priests.

See *cave mineral/mining, feces, mummy, oracle, paint/powder, ritual specialist/priest, rockshelter*

Cave Mineral/Mining

Cave salts of interest to prehistoric miners were selenite, mirabilite, and gypsum. Dates from caves with mining indicate that Native Americans extracted these mineral resources as early as 1000 B.C. and probably earlier (Jefferies 2008:243). Crothers (2012) attributes some activity in mining salts to Early Woodland boys undergoing initiation.

Many caves have chert and limestone veins, red ocher, and crinoid stems that could have been of interest to ancient people as well. Indians dug red ocher "out of a deep cave in a cliff face and climbed to the mountain top to cut it into useable chunks" in northeastern Ontario (Rajnovich 1994:11).

See *cave, Mammoth Cave, ocher, paint/powder, Salts Cave*

Cemetery

A "cemetery" is an area set aside for the dead with a visible arrangement of the bodies lying therein. It served as a spatial reference point for the dead, making them ancestors according to Charles and Buikstra (2002:18). Use of the word is not without contention. Renouf and Bell do not think that the Maritime Archaic mortuary sites qualify as cemeteries and use instead the phrase "burial ground," which is "without assumptions about size, delineation or formalization and which instead focuses attention on location and landscape" (2011:45). However, many other archaeologists do use the word for various configurations of Archaic burial collections, most to simply mean a concentration of skeletons. We even have an Early Archaic "cemetery" in Arkansas and others in the Maritimes that have no bodies. Several authors have commented that as the Archaic developed, there was an increasingly prevalent practice of separating habitation and burial areas, or the creation of cemeteries.

I think that it is most useful to understand cemeteries and other concentrations of humans (not all are "cemeteries") during the Archaic as bone shrines. These bone shrines differ from those I have defined for nonhuman bone collections in (1) their preferred locations, either on knolls, on bluffs, or in shell, (2) the common act of individualizing the humans, (3) the inclusion of objects, and (4) use of fire.

Cemeteries usually have mostly flesh interments and a mixture of burial postures, but there are a number of cremation cemeteries. Late Archaic period cremation cemeteries are common in New England (Dincauze 1975) and around the Great Lakes, and they are occasionally found in the midcontinent and in the mid-Atlantic. For instance, the Late Archaic Kimberly-Clark (Tennessee) burial ground was made up of 23 cremations (Chapman and Myster 1991:39) and was isolated from any habitation area.

Charles and Buikstra (1983) see the Late Archaic phenomenon of cemeteries as a ritual affirmation of resource and land ownership. But were cemeteries "owned" as they believe, or were they far more often shared? I have proposed elsewhere that the shell mounds of the SOV were shared facilities for major rituals and not private places or villages (Claassen 2010). Bullseye in the LIV may have been shared mortuary space according to Milner, Buikstra, and Wiant (2009). Evidence suggests that at least middle period Moorehead cemeteries in the Northeast were shared among groups (Robinson 2006:356). Frontenac Island has always been viewed as a shared facility (Ritchie 1945).

See *ancestor, ancestor worship/cult, bone shrine*

Center

Center was evidently an important point in Archaic cosmology. The quincunx focused attention on the center as did hearths, altars, plazas, and poles as did the location of a sacred site situated between two mountain ranges. In Mexican cultures the center was associated with the color of jade, or green, and the number five. Among the Q'eqche of the Andes, the center is not only a point but also a line where two halves come together and is thus an auspicious place for ceremonies (Classen 1993).

See *cardinal direction, plaza, pole/post*

Charnel House

Charnel houses "were designed to shelter both the dead and associated mortuary processing activities. Specific space was allocated to burials and a crematory basin was located inside [Hopewell charnel houses]" (Brown 1979:212). Charnel houses have been posited for Illinois ridge-top mounds and Harris Creek shell mound in Florida, but in both cases the evidence has been reinterpreted to exclude charnel houses. There are as yet no convincing charnel houses dated to the Archaic.

Chenopodium/Helianthus/Iva annua/Phalaris caroliniana

A possible ritualistic or medicinal use for *Chenopodium* is suggested by the stashing of caches of these seeds in the same rockshelters that also indicate use as birthing and menstrual retreat locations (Claassen 2011a). *Chenopodium* was also found in 67 percent of the Mammoth Cave fecal specimens and 87 percent of those from Salts Cave, usually co-occurring with sunflower, sumpweed, and hickory nut shell, possibly derived from priests conducting ritualized activities inside Mammoth and Salts caves (Claassen 2012b, 2012c). If so, then these seeds would have been part of ritual diets.

A ritual recipe of wild chenopod, sumpweed, sunflower, and/or a nut species may be indicated from the frequent co-occurrence of these taxa at places such as Ozark Bluff shelters, Dust Cave, Modoc, Ash Cave in Ohio. They were mixed with cedar wood charcoal and a mass of faunal remains at Higgs, Tennessee. *Chenopodium* also shows up in a cremation at Hodges, Michigan. The presence of Iva and *Chenopodium* seeds in several menstrual retreat shelters in the Cumberland and Ozark plateaus suggests that there was a connection between retreating or women's medicine and these seeds.

An intriguing article by Schoenwetter (2001) suggests that maygrass seeds

(*P. caroliniana*) were fermented with a fruit additive to produce maygrass beer. Beer drinking was possibly part of visionary quests.

See *Mammoth Cave, Newt Kash Shelter, Salts Cave*

Claw

Claws of bears and some birds were used as ornaments and grave goods during the Archaic. What their symbolism might have been is hinted at by the Cheyenne belief about the crescent moon, a shape that claws, bison horns, ungulate hooves, and footprints share. The moon provides light that keeps darkness and death at bay, say the Cheyenne, and natural arcuate shapes convey this protection (Nagy 1994).

See *feet/footprint/track, moon, sandal/slipper*

Cliff

Cliffs, as edges and as rock, were spiritually charged places where the manitous lived. "The places where these realms meet, such as the base of a lakeside cliff where sky, earth, water and underground touch, were the 'home[s] of the manitous'" (Rajnovich 1994:35). They were often chosen for painting. "Interpretations of the rock paintings should begin with the cliff faces themselves because the mountain itself is especially sacred, not just the rock art" (Rajnovich 1994:65). Some rock faces are streaked with red and black stripes, as are seen around Newt Kash Shelter and elsewhere (Figure 22). Striping on human faces was symbolically significant in historic times and may call forth images of Camaxtli/Mixcoatl (e.g., Hall 1997).

See *color, hunt god rite, mountain, rock formation*

Color

In native societies today colors carry a tremendous amount of symbolism, and anyone who has viewed blade caches, such as that in the Robinson site's Bu58, surely is convinced of the importance of color in the symbolic behavior of people of the past. Giles (2010) talks about the role of color in creating mnemonic devices. DeBoer (2005) explores the geographical and ethnolinguistic correlations of a basic color set consisting of white, black, red, and yellow, most often found in this clockwise sequence. In Mixtec and Aztec codices stone objects are frequently striped in four colors: blue, red, yellow, and white. The Osage origin story has a priest receiving ceremonial

22. Offering placed before a red-and-black-streaked cliff face, Acatlan pilgrimage trail, May 1, 2012. (Photo by author.)

knives in the colors blue, red, and yellow (Alice Kehoe, personal communication with the author, December 2012).

A brief study of Limestone County, Alabama, fluted point colors (Cole 2006:49–53) assumed that if two sites had at least two points of the same color that there were travel connections between those two sites. The site with the most pairings (n = 4) for both the Clovis and the Cumberland point samples was Big Sandy, Alabama, a small, deep, sinkhole rim site, reinforcing the idea that some sinkholes attracted visitation and point offerings.

Aquamarine is the color of the primordial sea and mountain lakes and is thus associated with the center, sky, water, and beginning time (Miller and Taube 1993:65, 102). The Green River in Kentucky has been called the greenest-colored river in the east (Stein 2005:20). A green river associated with Mammoth Cave may explain the concentration of Archaic ritual shell mounds and hilltop shell sites found on its banks. The green of native copper was intimately bound to the appearance of underwater monsters in the Northeast, and sky blue–green (aquamarine) meant life and social states of being (Hamell 1983).

Black is associated with night, the Underworld, and antisocial states. Black dime-sized flints were part of witchcraft charms among the Iroquois (Fox 1993). Black animals, black stone, and charcoal each had its role in Archaic symbolism.

White implied renewal as well as purification. For renewal Archaic people manipulated shells, bones, Burlington chert, Haldimand County (Ontario) stone, white sand in Mount Taylor mounds, white, clean, shell strata for building and capping, and even white quartz pebbles in (rain) rattles.

For all of the color red's abundance in the Archaic record of eastern North America, in the form of red ocher, we remain baffled about its meaning. Was it "blood" that made the pipestone red or the "sun" as the Plains tribes believed? Red probably bundled both meanings as blood was the primary offering to the sun in Mexico. Red ocher has been found on cache blades, bison skulls, infant skeletons, adult skeletons, and medicine bundle contents, in cremation pits, as chunks, and as paint/powder. Red ocher, red cedar, and some red stones represented "long life, wellbeing . . . and success, particularly in the conceptually related activities of hunting and fishing, warfare, and courtship" in northeastern groups (Hamell 1983:25). Red was the color of antisocial states of being. There is evidence that red ocher was associated with the hunt god.

In late Historic times men and some social groups (e.g., high-ranking moieties) were associated with the sun, day, up, and things bright, shiny, and reflective. In those situations we can expect that yellow, silver, white, and bright coloration were symbolic of those social groups (Hamell 1983; Mester 1989). In many other American cultures those colors contrasted with dark, terrestrial elements and the lower moiety (Mester 1989:162). North and west directions were most often black, south and east directions most often red (DeBoer 2005). DeBoer (2005:86) found no support for the idea that nature suggested predominant color/direction pairs.

The color of a stone in particular was obviously important, but even the interior color of naiad shells when fresh may have figured in their selection for inclusion in bundles, bags, graves, pits, and caches. Banding, spotting, and graduated hues were also important visual elements in stones and pebbles collected for offerings and medicine bags.

The construction of Horr's Island Mound A gives evidence of the importance of the colors white, light and dark tan, gray, and black, all expressed in sand mixed with varying amounts of charcoal (Russo 1994b). In Mount Taylor mortuary mounds of Florida we find "layers of dark material (swamp muck) over either white sand or clean shell [that] perhaps symbolized the cycle of life and death . . . it stands to reason that the contrastive layers of unburned and burned shell in Mount Taylor ridges held similar symbolic import, even outside of mortuary contents" (Sassaman 2010a:74). Builders of Tomoka Mound 6 used contrasting layers of yellow and gray sand to build their largest mound.

See *capping, cardinal direction, center, hunt god rite, nut, paint/powder, Tomoka*

Comb

Three graves at Port au Choix-3 contained caribou antler combs, two of which had bird images. One was recovered from the chest of an adolescent, a second was among the bones of a multiple burial, and the third comb might have been worn or carried on a thong around the wrist of the body (Tuck 1976:58). Tuck thought that these three combs had magic qualities. Sedna, Arctic goddess of the water animals, released animals into the ocean by combing them out of her hair.

Combing the hair was often taboo during certain times such as when mourning and while menstruating. Hair was associated with the sense of touch, which was often part of the "fasting" regimen (abstaining from touch), and with the soul known as tonali among Nahuas and Caribbean peoples. Combs were used to prepare the dead and were associated with the west and the color black by the Q'eqche Maya. Since possessing the hair of someone was one way of capturing one's tonali, combs, as hair-collecting devices, could be expected among a ritual specialist's equipment. The adolescent at Port au Choix-3 with a comb may have been an apprentice.

Commissioning Rite for a Place

In a number of sites the deepest burial was that of a woman with grave goods or a violently killed man with grave goods. I suggested several years ago (Claassen 2010:122–124) that these burials were part of commissioning or dedication rites for planned places of ritual import. Just as women were killed and placed in post pits before ceremonial posts were erected in the Cahokia area (Skousen 2012), it seems that women were often used in the Archaic for dedication rites. A young woman was found buried in the vestibule of Mammoth Cave and subsequently covered by the mixed cremains of numerous animals and humans (Robbins 1974:146). Women's bodies were the deepest burials at Big Sandy, Kay's Landing, O'Neal, Read, and Carlston Annis and both the richest and deepest burial at Robinson on the Cumberland River.

A possible consecrating rite or commissioning rite attended the erection of a building at Georgia site 9Wr4. Each of four corner pits was filled with stone of a different lithology.

Simultaneous commissioning and decommissioning rites were held at many of the mound sites, particularly evident at shell mounds. Old surfaces were buried by new surfaces, often in very visible ways such as with contrasting dirt and shell.

See *cache—debitage, capping, Cult of the Bivalve Feast, decommissioning rite*

Constellation

Lankford (2004) attributes the historic Underwater Panther that has a red crystal eye to the constellation Scorpio and its star Antares, the Orion belt stars to the hand constellation, and the Milky Way to the westward path of the souls. The *Leptoxis* belts found on four men in Elizabeth Mounds and numerous infants in Indian Knoll could have been Milky Way belts given that shells were conceptually stars in the night sky for the Aztecs. Surely this night sky feature was important to people even well before the Archaic. Pauketat and Emerson (2008:82) stress that ancestors and stars are conceptually interchangeable in Mississippian society.

See *ancestor, astronomy, bluff, bobcat/lynx, burial—head direction, cardinal direction, color, Milky Way, ritual calendar*

Container

Hearths, houses, mounds, bounded space, bodies, vessels, pipes, stone, wood, shells—any container could have been used in an act of transformation via heating, adding, fermenting, grinding, and so forth. Containers and other concavities—uteruses, skulls, mouths, mortar holes, graves, *Busycon* shells, caves, fireboards—were part of fertility symbolism. Large cupped shells could hold the spirit of the deceased and purify it (Ceci 1989), and mortar holes caught rainwater, so necessary to life and thus symbolizing fertility.

See *bedrock mortar/nutting stone, pottery, rain*

Copper

Lake Superior copper was in use as early as 7,000 ya. Labrador and Newfoundland copper may have been used as early as 6,000 ya in the far northeastern United States (Levine 1996:172). However, copper was found in but a single Archaic grave at Port au Choix-3, in a medicine bag (Tuck 1976:64). Archaic copper use, most readily referenced as the Old Copper complex of the Great Lakes regions, was primarily in the form of "heavy" tools, knives, and projectile points. Copper harpoons were in use on the north shore of Lake Superior by 4000 B.C. (Pleger 1998:44). By 1000 B.C., however, these heavy tools were fading from use and were replaced by lighter copper ornaments, particularly beads (Pleger 1998). Copper beads were found in Horizon 6 at Koster (3900 to 2800 B.C.).

Mary Anne Levine's study (1996) of Late Archaic copper items from sites east of Lake Superior to Vermont found that the copper used was extremely pure judging from both the presence and concentrations of trace elements. From the geological sources available at that time, the Late Archaic pieces she sampled most often sourced to Michipicoten Island and occasionally sourced to Cap D'Or, Nova Scotia, and Centennial, Michigan, although other sources are suspected based on purity (1996:172).

"The copper artifacts of the Late Archaic include rat-tail points, knives, awls, celts, adzes, and fish hooks and such ornaments as rings, beads, rectangular gorgets, crescents, and tubes" (Goad 1980:3). They are found predominantly in Wisconsin and Michigan where the source of native copper can be attributed to the Keweenaw Peninsula and the Menominee River/Green Bay area of Wisconsin, but occasionally they are found in Late Archaic contexts in Canada, Illinois, Indiana, Kentucky, and Tennessee. More than 20,000 copper artifacts are known for Archaic Old Copper and (Early Woodland) Glacial Kame and Red Ochre cultures, but fewer than 50 copper artifacts have been found in the Southeast (Goad 1980:5). Furthermore, south of the Ohio River utilitarian copper items are rare and symbolic items predominate, the opposite of the situation in the heartland.

Metals, including copper, were understood to be the excrement of the gods in Mesoamerica (Read 1998:136), and Harper (1999:26) has assembled numerous examples of many historic Woodland peoples who "believed that certain minerals were derived from manitous." Among Caddoans, pieces of defeated water monsters were seen in copper pieces (Dowd 2011). The Ojibwas believed copper would bring good luck and that the tail of an Underwater Panther turned to copper when cut off (Harper 1999:36). Copper nuggets were frequently carried by people in the Lake Superior area, inherited through men and imbued with wonderful powers.

See *alligator/crocodile, cave mineral/mining, fossil, galena, mica, obsidian, ocher, paint/powder*

Cosmology

Cosmology is the "[c]ulturally specific ideational beliefs about the universe and their philosophical underpinnings" (Williamson and Farrer 1992, cited in Brown 1997:470). "All attempts to create cosmos may be said to have two things in common, regardless of the level of their creators' ability to sense and measure the great Cosmos—their goal of providing a sense of transcendence and the power to use it, and their inability to describe it or symbolize it adequately" (Lankford 2004:207).

The Archaic cosmology of at least those groups west of the Appalachian Mountains probably consisted of a layered Above World and a layered Below World or Underworld, knowledge of the life of the spirits inhabiting each layer and their adversarial relationships, and the ways and means of accessing them. The cosmology would also impart information about the creation of the cosmos, earlier and subsequent creations, the origin and nature of the various beings in the cosmos, and the reasons for phenomena in This World.

The two different ancestries identified by Sassaman (2010a) also brought two different cosmologies into contact. Ancestry I, the resident eastern group in the midcontinent primarily located north of the Ohio River and on the Gulf Coastal Plain, seems to have recognized an earlier creation in stone beings and practiced releasing the souls of some people through cremation. They first mounded dirt, expressing a renewal belief in soil, and, in the Gulf area, evidently used astrologically derived templates for ceremonial life. They intentionally created monumental architecture. Winged animal imagery was important.

Ancestry II, with a focus in the SOV, believed there were four world quarters, with caves and springs as access points, linked women's procreative and creative powers, at least in textiles and fiber work, and sought renewal of humans through cave offerings and burial of some humans in shell-bearing sites, if not directly in shell, and through rites of human sacrifice. Feasting was extremely important in their ritualizing both in the SOV and on the Atlantic coast where Ancestry II populations turned to ceramic containers to enhance their feasts. Ritual specialists existed and dogs were important guides for the dead in the SOV proper.

The Maritime Archaic people expressed a different cosmological reality, one referencing the ocean in many ways and the sun, if that was the meaning of red ocher. Bird imagery was important, particularly that of auks, and "eggs." Symbolic items were first produced in bone but were eventually replaced with copies in stone. Grave goods were selected with regard to tasks to be completed in the afterlife (Tuck 1976, 1984). Rock cairns and low mounds were used on some occasions to mark burials.

See *animal other, cardinal direction, center, color, constellation, moon, ritual calendar, sacrifice—adult, soul, sun, world renewal rite*

Crane, Goose, Swan

Given the documented significance of the color white and the wings of white aquatic birds in Historic times, it is advisable to note the occurrence of these bones in Archaic contexts. Middle Archaic contexts may be the oldest occurrences of these white birds. Middle Archaic features at Campbell Hollow (LIV) had snow goose and Canada goose. Goose, swan, and crane bones occurred at the Middle Archaic Anderson, Tennessee, site.

The right humerus of a swan (*Cygnus* sp.) was found as a flute in a burial at the Middle Archaic Oconto cemetery in Wisconsin and was associated with two pieces of hematite (Pleger 1998:86). The nearby Reigh site had two burials with swan bones (Baerreis, Daifuku, and Lundsted 1954:18–19, 26). Some Maritime Archaic burials at Port au Choix-3 and elsewhere had swan and goose radii and ulnae whistles (Tuck 1976:69).

The Archaic levels at Modoc had goose (*Branta canadensis*) bones. Stratum 8 E also had sandhill crane bones. The Late Archaic components at Tennessee's Eva and Bailey sites and the vestibule of Mammoth Cave had goose and crane bones mixed with dozens of other species, including humans, in Late Archaic or Early Woodland context. Lamoka Lake had bones of Canada goose, whistling swan, and great blue heron (Ritchie 1932:115). The bill of a swan occurred in a woman's grave at Port au Choix-3. The eight flutes recovered at Riverton seem to have been made with crane leg bones (Winters 1969:71).

These birds had symbolic roles at least by the Middle Archaic, and their bones were used as flutes by then. As suggested by Tuck (1976), swan bills may have been used to petition a spirit for a male child in the Archaic as they were in Historic times. The significance of swans in Mississippian times has been discussed by Kelly and Kelly (2007).

See *bird, color, music*

Cremation

Burning a human corpse was practiced at least by the late Paleoindian era in Wisconsin at the Renier site (Mason and Irwin 1960). This, the oldest in situ cremation in the east, occurred on a sand ridge and had various burned-stone grave goods. Cremation was practiced at the Early Archaic Slade Site in the Chesapeake Bay (Egloff and McAvoy 1990:70) and in New England around 8300 B.P. at Annasnappet Pond, Massachusetts. Curiously, cremation may have been abandoned by 8000 B.P. around the Gulf of Maine (Robinson 2006:351). There were two cremations at Icehouse Bottom in Kirk Corner

Notched and bifurcate levels. A Middle Archaic male cremation at Anderson in central Tennessee strongly suggests that a leader or hunt god impersonator was cremated judging from the antlers included. Cremation was in use at 6000 B.P. in Louisiana at Monte Sano mounds. Surprisingly, cremations are not found among the thousands of burials on the Green River.

Thanks to the analysis of Amanda Owens, details about the cremations found in the Tennessee River shell mounds are available. Of the 2,000+ burials from seven (Alabama) sites, only 42 individuals were cremated: 3 children, 2 juveniles, 6 young adults, and 10 older adults (21 not aged). Eleven individuals with degenerative arthritis and osteoarthritis suggest that older individuals were most frequently the ones cremated. Sex was determined for 35 percent, revealing 10 males and 6 females (Owens 2010:54). Very little trauma was noted in these individuals.

Thirty-one of the bodies had been exposed to heat 600+ degrees Celsius, and 5 more bodies had been intentionally burned at lower temperatures, 2 of those at ca. 440 degrees Celsius. Eight had been accidently burned. Thirty-three of the bodies were burned in the flesh while at least 4 were burned as dry bones. Twelve bodies had burned crania as the only burned bones, and 6 individuals (including 4 of 11 cremations from Little Bear Creek) were represented by burned crania alone (Owens 2010:59).

Other analyses of the cremation practices are available for New England (Barbian and Magennis 1995 for Turner Farm; Dincauze 1968 for eastern Massachusetts). Burning attained a very high level of efficiency, leading to the conclusion that "the burning took place in the open, on a pyre that was exposed to wind and weather. There was no restriction on the duration of a cremation. . . . there was no great risk of deficient oxygenation, while the remains were accessible throughout the whole process and could be pushed back into the flames . . . to ensure effective combustion" (Geijvall 1963:380–381). Speaking of cremations in Late Archaic eastern Massachusetts, Dincauze said, "all the identifiable pieces in the dry-burned category, and they are few, were definitely not human" but were antler and bird bone fragments. "The green-burned class includes all the fragments which can be identified as human, and only three which are definitely not. The latter are parts of a canine maxilla" (Dincauze 1968:40). Dincauze failed to find those pieces "which typically survive cremation intact—metacarpals, metatarsals, axis, petrous bone, heads of femuri and humeri" (Dincauze 1968:41) and concluded that at these cremation cemeteries only token human remains were bagged and buried. Additional traits of Massachusetts's cremation disposals are the mingling of dog bone and human bone.

Byers (2005) views postmortem cremation as an act of human sacrifice.

Cremation is a faster way to release the soul than is decomposition of the body. Leveillee (1999), talking about cremations and burned and broken artifacts in features at Millbury, Illinois, thinks the burning and breaking released the spirits within and allowed for the mingling of the living and the dead, which formed the basis for claiming continuity and ancestry with meaningful social identities and over key natural resources. The concepts of spirits within and spirit release from bodies are well documented in dozens of cultures.

See *ashes, burning, crematory, Millbury III, soul*

Crematory

Crematories are rarely found despite the great number of Archaic cremations. The imbalance between the two data sets may be partly the result of overenumeration of cremations when watch fires built on top of or beside burials burned the bones (Bader 2010/11). These are not true cremations.

The Hodges site in Michigan did have a crematory. Two features at Wapanucket, Massachusetts, were interpreted as crematories. Mulberry Creek shell mound on the Tennessee River had a possible Late Archaic crematory. Feature 20 was a four-foot-diameter pavement of limestone slabs with a three-inch-deep layer of black ash on top. "On and between the stones were numerous fragments of burned human bones" (Webb and DeJarnette 1942:238). The central feature in Monte Sano Bayou site Mound A (Louisiana) was "a small truncated pyramidal mound 8.5 x 6.5 x 0.45 m. It appears to have functioned as a pyre" (Saunders 1994:121). A radiocarbon date of 6220+/-40 rcy was obtained, but the bone may not be human.

See *ashes, cremation, soul*

Crevice

Crevices, rifts in the earth's surface, were believed to be openings into the Underworld or supernatural world in many American cultures. This rift concept may explain the early attraction to rockshelters.

"The placing of the quartz offerings in cracks in the rocks warrants further comment. It appears to reflect a key belief about rock art sites specifically, and large rocks in general: rocks were believed numinous; the supernatural world was thought to lie within these rocks; and cracks in the rock were conceived as the portals into the sacred realm (Whitley 1994). Among the Numic, for example, spirits were believed to reside 'inside' rocks using cracks to move in and out of the supernatural, just as these same cracks were believed to open up for the shaman, when he entered his trance and went into the sacred realm. . . . Placing the quartz rocks in cracks was akin to leaving a gift at the spirits' door" (Whitley et al. 1999:234–235). Crevice burials were made on the face of Eagle Rock by the Ottawas (Hanks 1990). Crevices in vulvaform are still revered by Paiutes as fertility shrines (McGowan 1978).

See *rock formation, rockshelter, stone*

Crinoid Stem

Crinoids are echinoderms, a folded lily-looking marine plant with a stem. Fossilized stems are found in various places including in the walls of rockshelters along the Tennessee River and in fossil beds at the Falls of the Ohio. Single crinoid beads were found at the Middle Archaic Denton lapidary site in Mississippi, at the Eva site, the Ohio River Villier (Kentucky) site, Read on the Green, and at Swan Island, Illinois. At least seven beads were found in midden and one in an Indian Knoll burial; many more were found in the shell mounds along the Tennessee River such as three bodies with one bead each in Little Bear Creek, Alabama (Webb and DeJarnette 1948a). Several stems were found in Indiana in the McCain site (Miller 1941:31). These fossilized plants may have been recognized as part of the first creation.

See *fossil, Great Flood, Stone People*

Cross

The pre-Columbian existence of the equal arm cross was documented by numerous Spanish authors (see Astor-Aguilera and Jarvenpa 2008:487fn6) as well as several authors in northern North America. "The cross, like the circle, is ancient on this continent. . . . Adena stone tablets from the Ohio Valley are carved with designs using the cross as the basic element of design organization. It is on rock paintings, for instance at Fairy Point on Lake Missinaibi, northeastern Ontario, and a site east of Sassaginnigak Lake in Manitoba" (Rajnovich 1994:134). Marquette came upon a village of Miamis, Mascoutens, and Kickapoos in the Green Bay area who had erected a cross and hung it with offerings (Harper 1999:166). In the Northeast in historic times the cross represented a count of 10 (Giles 2010:47).

The quincunx arrangement of pits in the Late Archaic Newt Kash Shelter suggests that the equal arm cross was employed by Archaic people. The four world quarters may be implied in its use, as was the case in Mississippian times. The quincunx arrangement of burns, pits, and burials, found in several Archaic settings, adds further support to the idea that the symbol was used during the Archaic. In two other examples, a cross was engraved on a whelk shell gorget found in Indian Knoll's Bu687, and several bird bone flutes found at Carlston Annis had equal arm crosses incised into the bone (Webb 1950:324).

See *cardinal direction, center, Newt Kash Shelter, number*

Crystal

One reason for the attraction to quartz crystals is surely the phenomenon of triboluminescence "easily illustrated by striking or rubbing two quartz rocks together in a dark room; the effect is also easily achieved with a number of other crystals" (Whitley et al. 1999:236). Their water-like clarity was also attractive (Hamell 1983). Crystals of all types are used to ferret out witches by concerned Iroquois (Fox 1993). Quartz crystals were used by Cherokee war priests to divine the fate of warriors. They were essential equipment in the weather control bundle of Numic (western United States) priests, particularly crystals gathered from a place where lightning had struck (Whitley et al. 1999:235).

Area D of the Lewis-Walpole site (6Ht15) was a workshop for preparing crystal quartz and quartz end scrapers, manufactured in several sizes and averaging somewhat larger than those at the Neville site (Starbuck 1980:20). Other crystals were found in a number of graves of the Maritime Archaic peoples at Locus 2, Port au Choix-3. These crystals included 2 small garnets, 51 individual quartz, 3 masses of quartz crystals, calcite, and 40+ amethysts (Tuck 1976:72).

See *color, crystal, flake/chip, fossil, galena, medicine, rock marking, stone*

Cult

A group of people who focus on a single person or principle, often associated with curing or salvation, or a group that follows an unorthodox religion constitutes a cult (Barfield 1997:92). The medicine societies and other dream-based sodalities that I have projected into Archaic life would all be cults. Cults, then, would have conducted a great deal of ritual activity for groups. "Cults were formed to gain favors of one kind or another; as an aid to such action, numerous objects were devised, such as pendants and fetishes" (Fowler 1966:34). "Cult" is the word that Sassaman (2010a:49–50) uses to talk about rituals in the Archaic and matches the conception fostered in this guide of the largest scale of Archaic spiritual practice.

At least four cults were prominent in the Archaic: Cult of the Bayonet,

Cult of the Blade, Cult of the Bivalve Feast, and Cult of the Snail Shell. All of these cults were quite widespread geographically.

See *ancestor cult, auditory exostoses, Cult of the Bayonet, Cult of the Bivalve Feast, Cult of the Blade, Cult of the Snail Shell, dream/vision, Stone People*

Cult of the Bayonet

A Cult of the Bayonet may have existed in the Moorehead phase in the Maritime provinces. This presumed cult began with bone versions of clubs that later transformed into "slate" bayonets (Tuck 1976). Betts, Blair, and Black (2012) argue that cod and swordfish were the mainstay of Late Archaic hunting and the bayonets were used to dispatch swordfish. Many bayonets, bone clubs, and foreshafts were etched with a triangular or zig-zag motif that alluded to shark teeth and thus the desire of the fisherman to be a predator like a shark.

Several ritual specialists—both men and women—of the cult can be identified, such as the man with the auk cape and the woman (Bu9) with abundant avian and bear bones, both animals good fishers themselves. Both burials were found at Port au Choix (Tuck 1984:137). Mnemonic devices employed by cult members in addition to bayonets were bills, wings, stone effigies, shark teeth (Betts, Blair, and Black 2012), and red ocher. One rite of the cult may have been a hunting rite that included the sacrifice of human infants and disposal of the body with one or more bayonets (Tuck 1976). Betts, Blair, and Black (2012) proposed the possibility of men using bayonets and sharks' teeth as amulets but then could not explain the placement of sharks' teeth with children and women. This seeming contradiction of expectations could be alleviated by allowing for women ritual specialists and child and infant sacrifices or apprentices.

See *animal other, bird, jaw, ritual specialist/priest, shark, teeth*

Cult of the Bivalve Feast

This cult was expressed with the consumption of huge quantities of oysters and freshwater naiads. The oyster version was found along the Atlantic coast in New York on the Hudson River at places such as Dogan Point and Twombly Landing (Claassen 1995) and from South Carolina southward along the Atlantic and Gulf coasts. Russo (2004) has suggested that competitive feasting occurred between groups. These feasts seem to have been the focus of social gatherings during which goods were exchanged and shellworks were enlarged. The activities of this cult may have resulted in the adoption and diffusion of pottery 4,000 to 3,500 ya.

The rites of the marine shellfish version of the Cult of the Bivalve Feast differed most noticeably from the naiad version in its lack of human burials, lack of human sacrifices, and lack of dog burials. Given that the coastal setting is cosmologically the birth locus for humanity, death themes may have been inappropriate in coastal ritual sites.

Naiad shellfish feasting took place in the SOV and the Savannah and Oconee rivers of Georgia. The flesh of naiads is unmistakably congruous with labia and is thus a fertility symbol. The paired valves are the equivalent of a cave. The main features of this cult were the rites of rebalancing and renewal that included human sacrifices (particularly the hunt god rite, the first-kill rite, and the four-age rite), human burial, dog burial, feasting with freshwater shellfish, river cleaning, and mortuary gambling. The billions of naiads remaining in the freshwater heaps would have contained millions of pearls, but no pearls have been found clearly in an Archaic context. This lack of pearls strongly suggests that part of the cult beliefs included the eating of pearls.

Feasting with naiads was well under way in Middle Archaic times on small tributaries of the Green River and larger tributaries of the Tennessee River; this had started in the Early Archaic at Eva and Big Sandy on the Tennessee River (dates obtained by Thad Bisset, personal communication with the author, April 2013). In many loci of freshwater shell-bearing sites, Paleoindian points have been discovered, perhaps implying that the cult was founded in places where the Stone People were evident or that these points were collected and then deposited as part of commissioning rituals. Sassaman (2010a) believes that the incoming Ancestry II people were the ones with the interest in shellfish. It seems to have overwhelmed a Middle Archaic little Cult of the Snail Shell in central Tennessee.

The geographical scope of the Cult of the Bivalve Feast shrank dramatically after 4000 B.P. It continued on the upper Ohio, the Wabash, and Cumberland rivers until about 3200 ya. It seems to have continued as a little cult among people utilizing the upper Tennessee River in eastern Tennessee after the Archaic and may have morphed into the rituals of people burying their dead at Hiwassee Island still later in time.

See *dog sacrifice rite, Cult of the River Keepers, Cult of the Snail Shell, naiad, pearl, sacrifice—adults, sacrifice—infant and child, shell, shellworks, Stone People*

Cult of the Blade

This cult is evident in the caching of hypertrophic blades. It began in Paleoindian times west of the Mississippi River as well as around the Great Lakes and continued through Late Archaic times north of the Ohio River primarily. Caches of blades occurred in varying numbers, often prime numbers that, no doubt, had social significance. Stone People, those of the most ancient creation (before the Great Flood), were probably depicted as blades by Archaic people, as well as recognized in found Paleoindian-made bifaces. Blade caches may have been given to the Stone People as gifts to honor them as well as to solicit favors.

See *cult, Great Flood, profile rock, stone, Stone People*

Cult of the River Keepers

This cult has been suggested in order to account for the extremely high incidence of ear canal exostoses among men at Indian Knoll and at several other SOV sites (Claassen 2010:189–192). While men engaged in shellfishing has been proposed as the explanation (Mensforth 2005), individuals with these exostoses are also found at non-shell burial grounds such as Rosenberger.

The River Keeper idea is based on the river keepers in modern Maya communities (Rissolo 2005:356). The river keeper cult members (men primarily but a few women) would have frequented the large rituals at the Green River and Ohio River sites and cleaned the river, springs, and pools in the area's caves.

A cult with sweating that required plunging into icy cold water and met so often that these bony growths occurred could also explain the localization in the SOV of auditory exostoses. Whether river keepers or sweat lodge users, the cult was clearly populated by few people outside of the Green River, making this a "little cult."

See *auditory exostoses, Green River, sweat lodge*

Cult of the Snail Shell

This cult appeared simultaneously on the middle Harpeth (Anderson, lower level) and Duck rivers in central Tennessee (Ervin and Hayes sites) and on the St. Johns River in Florida in Middle Archaic times. In all three locations, small numbers of burials were put into the heaps of gastropod shells. A variety of freshwater snails were the focus of collection in Tennessee and in Florida. The freshwater snails of the Ohio valley were also mixed with bivalves in later shell heaps.

The spiral symbolism of the gastropod shell may have been a key part of the cult lore, as may have associated imagery of the Milky Way and night sky. The Aztecs thought that the watery Underworld rotated into the sky position each night and the white shells of the sea were then visible as stars. The millions of shells piled in these sites suggest that a soup or broth rather than meat was derived from cooking them. This broth may have been medicinal in use. This cult died out in Tennessee by 4200 B.P. (Claassen 2010:15), although aquatic snails continued to constitute part of the matrix of the SOV shell mounds. Gastropod piling lasted through most of the Late Archaic in Florida. Feasting and gambling during burial rites characterized this cult.

See *cosmology, Cult of the Bivalve Feast, Ervin, gambling, gastropod, hunt god rite, Milky Way*

Decommissioning Rite

Decommissioning or termination rites were clearly part of the ritualizing practiced by Archaic peoples; this is evident in capping layers in shell mounds particularly. Shell and sand mound platforms were terminated and then renewed by creating capping layers of different colors or different substances (e.g., muck, or soil transported to the shell heap). Other decommissioning/termination rites appear to have accompanied the end of naiad mounding such as is seen in Alabama at 1Ct17 where bodies of a four-age rite were placed on top of the final shell (Webb 1939). Many bone burials appear to have been deposits of trophy parts, another proposed decommissioning rite.

Throwing bones of certain animals into a fire may have been a final act of a first-kill rite. Breakage of stone or bone mnemonic devices, cremation and burning, and burial are all elements in the act of ending or putting away a power-filled object or place.

See *breakage, burning, capping, commissioning rite for a place, trophy part decommissioning rite*

Deer

Antlers and fawns seem to have served as mnemonic devices and offerings during the Archaic, as well as mature deer. From historic groups we learn that a deer is often envisioned as the Guardian of or King of the Animals. Deer antlers have long been recognized by archaeologists as symbols of leadership, a use that can be traced into the Archaic. Shed antler burr and beam sections were included in the grave of a woman at Hayes shell midden on the Duck River, Tennessee (excavation notes on file at the McClung Museum, University of Tennessee). A complete pair of antlers was found on the bottom of a deep pit, of probable Benton affiliation, at Ensworth School site in Tennessee (Deter-Wolf et al. 2004:124), and a cremation at Anderson, Tennessee, contained antlers (Dowd 1989).

Fawns and children are associated in several ways in the Archaic record of the SOV. An infant was buried with a deer fetus at Anderson, and a fawn's lower leg and hoof were found in Newt Kash Shelter, a Late Archaic women's birthing and medicine shelter (Claassen 2011a). A drilled deer ulna and a disarticulated human infant constituted Bu6 at the Middle Archaic Hayes shell-bearing site (Tennessee). Spotted fawn hunting medicine had to be prepared and kept by a pure young Menomini girl (Fox and Molto 1994b). Toddling boys and girls were brought into the Menomini sweat lodge to aid the Sacred ones and bring hunting power to the assembled men. "Fawn" is the name of the gentle south wind that calls Spring to plant her seeds in Iroquoia (Fox and Molto 1994b:109).

The Wixárika believe adult deer are the intermediaries between priests and all of the deities as well as a required offering to Grandfather Fire and Father Sun (Schaefer 2002). In many ways, explained by Schaefer (2002:202–206), deer are feminized and symbolically hunted with weavings and looms by women.

Deer also figured prominently in some versions of the hunt god rite and the four-age rite. At Reigh, Wisconsin, a man with antlers is surrounded by four different age categories of individuals. The hunt god Camaxtli or Mixcoatl was the giver of the fire drill and heat treating and was celebrated with a deer hunt and human deer impersonators in central Mexico. He is depicted with atlatl and deer antlers (Figure 19) as in the fire god. It is possible that deer were ritually killed by neck twisting and that burials wherein the human individual's head or torso is twisted 90–180° (of which there are several examples) contain a deer impersonator. These hunt god associations would have provided a symbolic rationale for the pairing of deer tines and flintknapping in tool kits and in graves such as Features 1 and 97 at Rosenberger.

See *antler, bobcat/lynx, burial—posture, caribou/elk, constellation, feet/footprint/track, hunt god rite, mask/headdress, Rosenberger, Turner Farm*

Design Element

An exhaustive list of elements is not possible at this time. However, Archaic-aged contexts have been asserted for chevrons, diagonal lines, ovals, circles, cross-hatching, zig-zag (teeth), ladder, and quincunx. The equal-arm cross is implied by the quincunx arrangement of pits (such as in Newt Kash Shelter) or dots. Site layouts indicate a design complex including arcs, crescents, broken circles, and complete circles.

The most frequently decorated items in the Paleoindian and Archaic periods are pebbles, such as the slate pebbles found in the Piedmont of North Carolina (e.g., Hardaway and Doerschuk sites) and those at the Gault site in Texas and bone "pins" (Jefferies 2004). The 49 specimens recovered at Doerschuk site had "designs which ranged from simple crisscrossed lines that extended across and down the edges to very fine and intricate geometric designs. . . . [some] even suggest a drawing" (Coe 1964:53).

The meanings of these designs are perhaps lost to us. Zig-zags may mean lightning or snake although the two entities are interchangeable in Mesoamerican thought. Cross-hatching in Mesoamerica signifies the darkness of the Underworld. Circles and squares as houses are often used to distinguish summer and winter activities. Crescents most assuredly refer either directly or indirectly to the waxing crescent moon, a time for conception.

Animal shapes also figured in Archaic motifs. Owls and cicadas are seen in the lower Mississippi River valley stone beads. Faces are minimally implied by dots and lines in some marine shell gorgets of the SOV. In addition to these minimal design elements one should also consider cardinal direction, color, and location to be elements of design.

See *Adair Glyph Cave, bone pin, C-shaped site layout, cardinal direction, insect, pebble—engraved*

Divination

Attempts to find game and even humans by modern groups in the Northeast were made by burning bones of target species until they were calcined (Harper 1999). The same may have been done with cremated human bone and calcined bones of other species. Ritual specialists read the map of the cracks in the bones and gathered additional information from the color of the bone. Divination was probably one important purpose behind most games and gambling.

See *bone pin, burning, gambling, games*

Dog

Although dogs probably accompanied people as they moved into and through North America, their presence is hidden until the Early Archaic. Spiess and Lewis (1995:349) think they identified a dog yard at the Turner Farm site dating to the Middle Archaic because of the high number of seal bones.

Warren's investigation (2004) of dozens of Archaic dogs from SOV sites found that several of the dogs buried with humans had spinal damage commensurate with pack carrying but that most dogs formally buried did not. There are several enigmas in the archaeological record of Archaic dogs (Claassen 2010). Why are Archaic dogs buried primarily in only two shell mound sites of the SOV, Read and Perry? Why are bluff-top shell-bearing sites the most typical dog burial place? Why do dog burials typically border human burial grounds? And why do dog burial numbers drop off dramatically after 3,000 ya?

Dog burials seem to have begun in Early Archaic times but accelerated in Middle Archaic contexts. Among types of Archaic dog burials are burials or dog skulls at the bottom of pits (e.g., one at shell-free Kirkland, Kentucky), occasional humans buried with dogs, occasional double dog burials, and some headless dog burials. Like Kerber (1997), I believe that each type of burial reflects a different rite.

A disarticulated and butchered dog skeleton was found in Ashworth Shelter in western Kentucky (Phil DiBlasi, personal communication with the author, 2008) in an Early Archaic context. The butchering seems to suggest that this dog was eaten, and isolated dog bones are found among those of other animals in dozens of sites.

The fact that dog burials occur in very few places suggests that these burials are not performed by humans mourning a pet. The ritual significance of dogs associates them with women, hearth spirits, leading the dead along the Milky Way, leading ritual specialists into the afterlife, and nighttime (Cantwell 1980; James 2006; Kerber 1997; Strong 1985).

See *dog sacrifice rite, dog with human burial rite, Milky Way, rebalancing rite*

Dog Sacrifice Rite

Dog burials appear to have begun in the Early Archaic and in the LIV. The Stilwell II site on the west side of the Illinois River in Illinois had two separate human and dog burials on a house floor in a phase dated 9600 to 8800 B.P. (Wiant, Farnsworth, and Hajic 2009:242). Two late Early Archaic dog burials were found in Horizon 11 at Koster dated to 8470+/-110 B.P. (Wiant, Farnsworth, and Hajic 2009:249). Later Archaic burials in Illinois/Iowa include two dogs at Sand Run West site in eastern Iowa (Benn and Thompson 2009:524), three at Tree Row, and four at Black Earth. No dog burials have been reported in the Wabash, Savannah, or St. Johns sites or in the Atlantic and Gulf coastal saltwater shell rings (Claassen 2010:95–98, 184–187).

Dog burials were extremely rare in Maritime Archaic burial grounds, but they did occur at Turner Farm in the Moorehead phase (n = 2) and in the Susquehanna phase (n = 4), some with humans. The inclusion of bones of cervid, large bird, and sea mink in one Moorehead phase dog burial (Spiess and Lewis 1995) may indicate a hunting rite.

By the transitional period in New England and New York, dog burials are found in elaborate funerary rituals of the Orient culture. Dog bones have been found in cremations in Massachusetts and were "a significant element of the burial ritualism" (Ritchie 1959:56). At Lamoka Lake, all animal crania had been broken open with the exception of two dog skulls (Ritchie 1932:115). Five dog bones were found in a ritual deposit of walrus mandible and soft-shell clams in the Rustico Island site (Leonard 1989:16).

Kerber (1997) suggests at least three ancient ritual uses of dogs: (1) skull retention for rites of skull-only burials, (2) whole dog burial near hearths as a domestic ritual, and (3) dogs buried with humans for unknown ritual purpose. To this must be added their role in healing rites. Kerber's literature search found dogs strangled, buried alive, shot, and disposed of in Long Island sites in reused pits, in graves, in cremations, in villages, and in peripheral contexts. The dog-hearth rituals were evident to Kerber beginning in the Northeast in the Late Archaic. Strong (1985:36) also saw Archaic dog burials to be part of home and hearth rituals.

Archaic dog rites typically manifest as the burial of a complete dog, often with no cause of death indicated and typically apart from a human. Such a rite was conducted at least 466 times, 419 of those occurring in the SOV shell heaps and 50 percent of them coming from eight sites in the Green River valley (Claassen 2010), the indisputable center of dog sacrifice rites during the Archaic where dog burials typically frame the human burial area.

Two SOV sites stand out for having 31 percent of all dog burials, Read (n = 65) on the Green River, a bluff-top site, and the multicomponent Perry shell mound (n = 75) on the north bank of the Tennessee River in Alabama. Other major dog sacrifice rite locations were four riverside sites: Eva during the Three-Mile phase (n = 15), Carlston Annis (n = 29), Ward (n = 27), and Indian Knoll (n = 21). Within the Green River valley, bluff-top shell-bearing sites had 55 percent of the dogs, while riverside shell heaps had 38 percent and shell-free mortuaries had 7 percent. The central Tennessee River has yielded at least 15 dog burials, 36 burials are known from the western Tennessee River, and 33 are known from tributaries of the Tennessee. There were at least 18 dog burials from the Falls of the Ohio area with the Bluegrass site having 11. Four dog burials were recovered from Dust Cave.

In an analysis of 25 variables in SOV sites (Claassen 2010), the most statistically significant difference found was between sites with 14 or more dog burials and those with no dog burials. Among the high dog sacrifice rite sites, there was an increased number and density of human burials, quantity of grave goods, proportion of graves with marine shell, number of atlatls, heavy items, points, bifaces, and bifaces, and number of groundstone items per non-infant. Dog burials, much more than human burials, serve to distinguish the sites of the SOV.

Most of these dog burials may reflect dog sacrifices—for group rebalancing rites associated with handling the dead or in a rite similar to that of the historic Winnebago clan ceremonial for Disease Giver. White dogs were hung and offered to this spirit during a large rite for eleven spirits. Other possibilities have been suggested (see Blick 2010; Cantwell 1980; Claassen 2010; James 2006; Kerber 1997; Strong 1985).

See *dog, dog with human burial rite, Read*

Dog with Human Burial Rite

Burial of dogs with humans is quite rare, occurring only 67 times in the SOV and then in the Green, Tennessee, and Cumberland river sites primarily and only once in a shell-free burial ground in the SOV. Warren's (2004) analysis indicates that many of the dogs interred *with* humans were pack animals that had lived hard lives but that very few of the *isolated* dogs had been pack dogs. This means then that since none of the 65 dogs at Read was buried with humans, few if any of them were probably pack dogs.

This paucity of dogs interred with humans is further evidence that the beloved pet is not at the root of the 460+ dog burials. Only 30 of the 212 dogs buried in the Green River sites were buried with humans, 25 of the 150 Tennessee River dogs, 2 of the 18 Ohio River dogs, and only 1 of the 19 dogs found in shell-free mortuaries of the SOV (Claassen 2010:Appendix). Few of the dogs buried with humans were buried with adults, the potential traders. For instance, the two dog-human combinations at the Barrett shell-bearing site on the Green River were buried with a young adult and an adolescent. The infrequency of dog-human burials suggested to Voegelin (1944) and Strong (1985) that clan membership, cause of death, age, or sex explained the combination. I, too, think that a special and rare circumstance determined burial with a dog, perhaps a priest-dog pairing such as that at Mulberry Creek (Alabama) shell mound, a Middle Archaic man with two dogs (Shields 2003).

Dogs have been found under the head of adults, on top of the head of a woman, under the feet of a man, at the feet of an adolescent and adult, and beside a human. The Mulberry Creek shell mound dogs were buried most frequently with sitting burials or with extended burials. At Indian Knoll, dogs were placed with three women, two men, and three children (recent sexing). Two of the ten people were buried facedown, a probable sign of violent death. One child was buried with two dogs. Strong (1985:33) reported that Frontenac Island dogs were buried in association with adult males. An Old Copper Culture burial in Michigan had two very old dogs buried with an adult male. Grave goods included copper and bifaces (Prahl 1967). A grave at Port au Choix contained the skeletons of a woman, a man, and an infant, a possible adultery killing, and above them were buried two large, flexed dogs, one killed by a blow to the head (Kerber 1997:82).

The Cherokee performed rebalancing rites for a person or a household for which they killed a dog, but they also believed that dogs specifically protect, guard, and guide priests (James 2006). The grave goods accorded some adult humans with dog burials give a strong impression that several held the role of ritual specialist such as a man in Mulberry Creek shell mound with two dogs.

See *dog, dog sacrifice rite, rebalancing rite, ritual specialist/priest*

Dream/Vision

Visions were probably the primary source of Archaic ritual content, vestments, artifacts, and change in ritual. It is highly likely that most Archaic people sought visions or were visited by visions/dreams at least once in their lives.

Today, people who become ritual specialists among the Nahuas of Puebla, Mexico (Huber 1990), and the Wixárika of northern Mexico (Schaefer 2002) often begin learning after surviving a serious illness during which they have a vision. Another way of moving into healing specialties is via frequent dreaming and collecting multiple animal others (Irwin 1994). But Irwin shows us that any individual young or old could seek or be surprised by a vision, and most understood that to ignore the message of the vision created great peril for them.

Any visionary could have received instruction that led to particularistic, private rituals, a life as a doctor, or the founding of a secret medicine society (a cult) with its own criteria for and levels of membership and esoterica. Vision medicine would have created a tremendous amount of variability in the archaeological record for curing could have been achieved with a seed, a pebble, a song, bark figures, and so forth. Recalling a vision and remembering the details and the instruction were achieved through collecting the things seen into a bundle or making marks on rocks. Whitley and coauthors (Whitley et al. 1999:232) and Rajnovich (1994) believe that the motivation for rock marking is and was to record visions and to communicate with the spirits with which one was allied.

See *animal other, cult, medicine, ritual specialist/priest, rock marking*

Drumfish

This denizen of deep water may well have been recognized as an ancient form of fish, specifically, a Stone Person. Its pebbly pharyngeal teeth filled a carapace rattle at Eva and another at Barrett, Kentucky. If the rattle sound was meant to simulate thunder then it seems that we can deduce from these rattles an Archaic belief that Thunder came from the Underworld, as seen in the use of the Underworld elements of stone and fish. We may also be seeing evidence of a belief that the pebbly teeth of drumfish were stone and dated to an earlier creation.

A perforated drumfish operculum was included in a cache at McCullough's Run, Indiana (Cochran, Knight, and Bush 1997). A drumfish was calcined in a possible ritual feature at Higgs, Tennessee (e.g., McCollough and Faulkner 1973). At the Rosenberger burial ground drumfish parts were found in a rich burial of three people and in a possible renewal offering (Driskell 1979). Segments of drumfish tooth plates were common in the shell heaps of the Green and Tennessee rivers.

See *fish*, *fossil*, *Great Flood*, *rattle*, *sound*, *Stone People*

Duality

Dualities are pervasive in modern beliefs of native peoples and no doubt were part of the cosmology of Archaic people as well. Day/night is suggested by alternating bands of white sand or shell with charcoal-enhanced shell or soil in Florida mortuary mounds and by day and night animals used in tandem in world renewal offerings. Sun/moon may be present in site and body alignments. Water/land is suggested for copper and stone use in the same artifact forms and in complementary use or disposal of water and land animal species such as seen at Tick Creek Cave. Bone/stone may be behind the burning of bone items but not stone items in Moorehead cremations (Sassaman 2010a:119) and in the transition from bone to stone forms of bayonets in the Far North. Birth/death and east/west seem to be visible in the lack of burial in eastward-flowing segments of any interior river, but they are present in shell heaps on westward- and northward-flowing rivers before 4,000 ya (Claassen 2010).

Paired sites such as the Archaic shell heaps across from one another in sections of the Tennessee River or Green River (Claassen 2010) suggest some form of duality. Neighboring sites with opposite conditions such as the situation between St. Catherines and McQueens shell rings in South Carolina or the U-shaped ring sites Cedarland and Claiborne in Mississippi *demonstrate* dualities (Saunders 2014:45). In the latter situation, for instance, Cedarland had marine shell, clay hearths, no pottery, no steatite caches, no effigy jasper beads, bipolar flaking, and no Jaketown perforators, and Claiborne had the opposite of each situation, including only brackish water mollusks.

Dualities were apparent in social organization, as has been argued for the shell rings of the Atlantic coast (Russo 2004), particularly those taking a U-shape. The two arms or two shell ridges facilitated the social ranking in competitive feasting between two groups. Curtin (2011:4) wondered whether the Vosburg site houses were arranged in a circle with an internal division, suggesting unequal halves. Moieties have been posited for Poverty Point (Sassaman 2010a:359).

See *camp circle, cosmology, moon, sun*

Earthquake

Thomas and colleagues (2004:125) propose that a Late Archaic mound was built over an earthquake fissure at the Burket site in Missouri. "It is probable that populations also gathered ritually to cover the openings created by earthquake events. The occurrence of mound construction over earthquake activity has been documented elsewhere in the Cairo Lowlands at Towosahgy (23Mi2), where Mound A was placed over a seismic event dated to A.D. 400" (Thomas, Campbell, and Morehead 2004:125).

See *crevice, sound*

Earthwork

Earthwork creation—dirt ridges, platforms, and mounds—seems to have begun in the Middle Archaic on the Gulf Coastal Plain and in the lower Mississippi valley. Clusters of mounds also occurred in Illinois, Missouri, and Iowa.

The first flurry of earthwork creation in the lower Mississippi valley was concentrated between 5500 and 5000 B.P. over the Tensas, Ouachita, and Tertiary Uplands of Louisiana and Mississippi. The largest site, with 11 mounds, is Watson Brake, Louisiana. Several of these mounds cover features that themselves suggest shrines, such as the 10 m x 10 m structure found underlying Monte Sano mound. Saunders (2010) documents an abrupt drop-off in mound site use at 4700 B.P. although not a total cessation. He favors megaflooding 5000 to 4600 B.P. for the explanation.

The second period of earthwork construction in the lower Mississippi valley surrounds the activities at Poverty Point and its environs. In addition to the mounds and arcs constructed at Poverty Point proper, 11 other places saw mound and ridge construction. Other places in Louisiana had no more than two mounds and seven had one mound (Saunders 2010). Two sites in Mississippi, Savory with eight and Jaketown with seven mounds, are the largest. The largest mound at Savory was 30 m at the base x 1.5 m high. Again, a collapse is seen at around 3000 B.P. (although mound use did not completely disappear on the Gulf plain), and megaflooding is favored as the explanation by Kidder (2010) and by Saunders (2010). Gibson (1994:178) thinks that while other Archaic-aged mounds could have been built by small groups working for a relatively short time, it took a lot of people to accomplish the construction at Poverty Point. The grouping of and design of earthworks at Poverty Point have been heralded as expressions of "root metaphors . . . namely that its earthworks were something of an historical atlas, symbolic of the places, events, and forces of its genesis" (Sassaman 2005:337).

See *mound—dirt, Poverty Point, shellworks, Watson Brake*

East—see Cardinal Direction

Feasting

Feasting, as an element of ritual and political life, has gained central importance in studies of Archaic life (e.g., Claassen 2010:149–155; Jackson and Scott 2001; Russo 2004; Saunders 2004; Thompson and Andrus 2011). Various scholars have suggested a number of useful criteria for identifying feasting.

Abundant deer and bear remains mixed with artifacts at Lamoka Lake were attributed to feasting by Ritchie (1932:113, 115). Earlier still was a case of feasting at Harris Creek, Florida. The black zone of layer 3—a deposit of "midden refuse"—was interpreted by Aten (1999:180) as a surface for a feast held for the dead. Of the seven platform surfaces making up Harris Creek mound, only this one had any significant amount of excavation. Perhaps more food was offered than was consumed here, and perhaps the black zone was artificially enhanced with charcoal to achieve the dark color.

Feature 17, a large silo at Stallings Island, had several distinct layers of clam, charcoal, nutshell, and fishbone. Some of the fish were of exceptional size as were clams in other pits. "Related to these are smaller features with enormous quantities of fish bone, like Feature 10. . . . When we add . . . a large number of carinated vessels and human interments, the pit fill unique to this site appears even more significant . . . it seems reasonable as well to suggest that feasting was directly associated with mortuary activities" (Sassaman 2006:145).

A final example of feasting is offered from five late Late Archaic pits at the County Home Site in Ohio. Pit volumes ranged from 0.35 m^3 to 0.421 m^3 (Heyman, Abrams, and Freter 2005:76). The pits contained charcoal, coal, fire-cracked rock, chert, groundstone, clay pellets, calcined and noncalcined bird, mammal, fish bone, and wood, leading the authors to posit that stones had been placed inside or against meat packets that were then coated in clay slurry and baked in these pits.

Much ritual is anticipated by feasting evidence. Furthermore, feasting may have dictated and circumscribed the adoption and diffusion of pottery and built the shell rings of the Atlantic and Gulf coasts (Saunders 2004) and shell mounds of the SOV. Feasting may be responsible for the midden typically found directly under the early dirt mounds in Louisiana and scattered about the Poverty Point rings. Feasting with shellfish characterized two of the Archaic cults.

See *baked-clay surface, container, Cult of the Bivalve Feast, earthwork, shellworks*

Feature Diversity Index (FDI)

Published by Peter Pagoulatos (2009) for burial grounds in the northeastern states, the FDI is used to evaluate the variety of features, in his case: "pits without human bone, pits with incinerated human bone, caches without human bone, caches with incinerated human bone, hearths, inhumations, ossuaries, pyres, ramps, and structures. The FDI ranges from 1 to 10. Each site receives a count based on the number of different feature types present" (2009:233).

See *grave good, mortuary offering index*

Feces

Ritual diets and purging are commonly prescribed before performing, competing, traveling, and, of course, administering medicine, and thus fecal contents in samples recovered from caves, rockshelters, and shell-bearing sites (e.g., deep in Eva) may well represent ritual diets and not habitual diets. It is probable that one purged before arriving at a particularly auspicious place or feature in a cave. Fecal samples were encountered in all parts of Mammoth Cave and Salts Cave but may have clustered in the area just before arriving at Mummy Valley, the location of a desiccated boy. In the 100 fecal specimens examined by Yarnell (5 of which were dated to the period 1000–300 bc uncorrected), the following constituents and taxa were noted: 4 cultivars, 13 wild plants, 3 mammals, fishes, 2 insects, mites, snails, 1 bird, and 1 amphibian. "Charcoal, rootlets, grass, small stems, pollen, sand, rock powder and fine organic debris" (Yarnell 1969:41) and spruce pollen from at least 150 miles to the east were also identified.

The animal remains found in the feces are all candidates for symbolic consumption given that they are small (mice, sparrow), aquatic (salamander, small fish, fish scales), or with known mythic import (bobcat, grasshopper, beetle). Fruits encountered in the specimens were blackberry/raspberry, strawberries, and grapes, suggesting a June meal. The floral material was apparently ingested uncooked, although microscopic examination of five Salts specimens found some roasted seeds of chenopodium, squash, marshelder, and sunflower (Yarnell 1969:45).

Kay Read (1998:136) tells us that for the Aztecs, excrement signified fertility. Even the gods had excrement: precious stones and metals were often described as excrement of various celestial entities. Gold was the powerful yellow excrement produced by the sun, perhaps the purest of bowel movements. Earth's rain was urine and also likened to gold. Mica and lead were both excrement of the moon. A small stone that was used for medicinal purposes was considered Lightning's excrement; it was called the powerful excrement of rainstorm. It grew bigger with time. Edible algae was either excrement of rocks or excrement of water.

See *alligator/crocodile, ashes, cave mineral/mining, copper, galena, hematite, mica, ocher*

Feet/Footprint/Track

Tuck (1976:70), citing Rasmussen (1931:276), attributed the presence of the feet of auks, guillemots, and cormorants in Port au Choix-3 Newfoundland graves to amulets. A pair of beaver forepaws was found in one Maritime Archaic burial and perhaps can be explained in similar fashion.

A turkey foot was found in a fecal specimen inside Salts Cave (Watson 1974b:234). A complete bobcat foot and complete mink foot were recovered from two child burials, both with shell and stone beads at Carlston Annis (Webb 1950:304), artifacts and animals that suggest a fertility rite. Indian Knoll infant Bu857 was buried with lynx foot bones. At Indian Knoll the 1,551 deer were primarily represented by foot bones. These could be the remains of hides received as gifts during feasting or indicate a use of deer feet in human fertility or renewal rites at Indian Knoll. A beautifully executed pair of feet was engraved next to a mortar hole on a piece of roof fall in Cave Fork Hill Cliff, Lee County, Kentucky, although their age is unknown (Funkhouser and Webb 1929:Figure 37).

Feet are in contact with the earth and the Underworld and convey fertility symbolism in Andean cultures (Classen 1993) and in Mesoamerica. In the case of the ungulates in the Ohio valley and in the Plains, the split hoof was likened to women's genitalia in historic cultures (Hall 1997; Sundstrom 2004) and to the crescent moon (Nagy 1994). Numerous boulders have vulvaforms in the Plains and eastern United States, again associating the crescent moon and the footprint of ungulates. Sassaman (2005:359) has also invoked a symbolic link between feet and immaturity when talking about the possible body symbolism of the nested rings of Poverty Point: "the body (head to outside, feet to inside, with head symbolic of maturity, feet symbolic of immaturity)." The use of foot bones in divination games (cup-in-pin, astragalus dice) strengthens the association of future/fertility with feet.

Where footprints of various creatures are juxtaposed with mortar holes pecked into rock, it is likely that fertility is being solicited. While bird footprints may be more directly linked to the Little People or the bird helps of Old Woman, throughout Mesoamerican cultures Little People or tlaloques/chaneques were keepers of game and assistants to the rain deity—both roles linked to fertility. Not only feet but footwear could also convey this fertility symbolism, thus explaining the presence of sandals and slippers in caves and shelters (Claassen 2013b, 2013c). Sandals would have been used as offerings to Underworld earth spirits residing in caves when a group was seeking fertility and continuation.

"Fossilized footprints of mammals and dinosaurs, known to the Iroquois as uki prints ('uki' meaning 'sky powers,' such as thunder and lightning), also drew intense interest. Near Jamestown, New York, for example, the Onondagas brought offerings to a set of foot and handprints impressed on a rocky ledge, believed to have curative powers" (Mayor 2005:46). The footprints of tridactyl dinosaurs have been found replicated in rock markings near Syracuse, as have extinct bird and mammal tracks in Pennsylvania. The thousands of real tridactyl prints in the Connecticut River valley were also copied on granitic rocks as petroglyphs and are found across southern New England (Mayor 2005:48–49). In these cases footprints recall the distant past, but it is the ancestors and the Stone People who give fertility to living humans.

See *ancestor, bedrock mortar/nutting stone, cave, fossil, rain, rockshelter, rock marking, sacrifice—infant and child, sandal/slipper, shrine*

Femur

Human femurs were particularly imbued with significance in late pre-Columbian times in Mexican cultures. A femur was brandished as a sign of descent from an important male ancestor. Because a human femur might signify an important ancestor, the presence of a human femur in features and as isolated bones in caves, springs, sinks, and even burials should be noted.

Among the few pieces of unidentifiable calcined bone below Mound B at Poverty Point was a burned femur (Gibson 1994:177). Modified human femurs have been found in Salts Cave and at Carlston Annis. Human femurs were abundant in the collection from Little Salt Spring, Florida (although preservation or collector behavior may explain this). A femur with an embedded Kirk point was found in an unspecified cave in central Tennessee (Hodge and Berryman 2008). At Turner Farm, Maine, two pits intruded two inhumations over the femur area and the femurs were missing in both cases (Bourque 1995:150–151).

See *bone soul, head removal, human bone artifact, jaw, Little Salt Spring, skull, teeth, trophy part, Turner Farm*

Fetish

Hodge explained "fetish" as an object possessing consciousness, volition, and immortal life that could achieve ends magically. A fetish is a spirit house or, as Hodge explained, a spirit entombed (Hodge 1907:456–457). These portable, often attachable objects may present themselves to the carrier through a dream, a vision, a thought, or an action. They may be loaned, inherited, or bought. "In return [for blessings] the fetish requires from its owner worship in the form of prayer, sacrifice, feasts, or protection . . . the fetish which loses its repute as a promoter of welfare gradually becomes useless and may degenerate into a sacred object—a charm, an amulet, or a talisman—and finally into a mere ornament" (Hodge 1907:457). Hodge says that "fetish" is the appropriate word for most articles found in the medicine bag (1907: 457).

Multiple styles of zoomorphic beads have been found within single Middle Archaic burials, suggesting fetishes (Connaway 1977:126). Chapman (1975: 156) thinks that some of the well-worked hematite pieces from Rose Island in eastern Tennessee "may have functioned as fetishes, valued for their relative density." Several small, engraved stones that seem to come from Archaic contexts in New England are shown in work by Fowler (1966:44) and interpreted by him as fetishes.

See *amulet/charm/talisman, dream/vision, fossil, offering*

Figurine

Figurines are surprisingly rare in eastern North America. They have been found at Claiborne, an Archaic shell ring of Poverty Point affiliation (Webb 1971:110). A possible limb from a clay figurine and a head from a second figurine were found at Doherty, Missouri, a Late Archaic site (2600–1600 bc). The head had a nose, ear tabs, and forehead cleft with an estimated width of 20 mm and thickness of 9 mm. "Poverty Point figurines are similar to this in the cleft in the forehead, similar noses, and in being modeled of untempered clay" (Deel 1985:73). Fired and unfired clay figurines first appear in the Late Archaic (pre-1700 B.C.) in Mexico as well (Clark and Colman 2008:95).

See *feet/footprint/track, fetish, human, rock marking*

Fire

Fires were transformative agents, changing wood or bone into smoke and ash. In some settings the intent was to drive out the spirit inside the bone or wood; in others the motivation for fire may have been the creation of smoke to carry a message, to create a screen, to create a good smell, to clean a space, or to renew a unit of time. Cleaning and renewal of time may explain the fires burned on the summits of the first three mound stages of Mound B at Poverty Point (Kidder, Ortmann, and Allen 2004:111).

Burning a fire for a period after burial seems to have been a consistent element in mortuary ritualizing. Bader (2010/11) has identified numerous smudge pit/burial pairings at the Meyer site in Indiana. Many "cremations" during the Archaic in the SOV appear to have been burials in round pits upon which fires were built, inadvertently charring and in some cases calcifying the bones (Webb and DeJarnette 1948b). Aten also identified the occasional use of mortuary fires but under, rather than over, the burial. "Rarely (i.e., only in eight of the small grave pits—four each in Mortuaries A and B), a fire was made in the grave pit and the flexed body placed over the flames or hot coals. In a least two instances, some bones were scorched or lightly burned, and in nearly all, there was some cementation of bones, sand, and shell . . . they probably were more likely to be symbolic sterilizations of the grave and/or body after a preliminary storage and decomposition phase" (Aten 1999:163). A fuller picture of a mortuary fire is visible in Nevin Shell heap's Bu2 (Byers 1979:40): "A platform of till, somewhat higher on the edges . . . was laid over the basal humus to make a trough-like bed . . . a fire was lighted over the southern part of the platform and burned before the ochre was spread over the [platform and the infant interred]."

See *burning, fire making*

Fire Making

Fire could be produced using pyrite and a striker or the fire drill. Eight graves in Port au Choix-3 contained lumps of iron pyrites, some altered to limonite, that may have been part of firemaking kits. In support of this interpretation, Tuck reports that at Port au Choix there is only one example of a drilled hole but eight graves had pyrite lumps (Tuck 1976:78), both facts suggesting that people of the Maritime Archaic did not use the fire drill, stone drill, or spindle but rather used strike-a-lights. Strike-a-lights have also been found in Susquehanna sites and iron pyrites in Nevin Shell Mound in Maine (Byers 1979:25). The Hodges site in Michigan reportedly had a firemaking kit also of the strike-a-light type. The evidence consisted of pieces of limonite and "triangular scrapers" in a pit (Binford 1963). A strike-a-light kit was suggested at the Riverton site in Illinois as well.

Use of the fire drill rather than strike-a-lights is implied by the presence of the stone drill in the SOV and Gulf Coast. In addition to the technological implications of drills, drilling (fire drill, stone drill) and spinning (drop spindle) carry symbolism of sexuality (see Schaefer 2002) and beginning time when the world was spinning. These beliefs seem to be absent in the Maritime Archaic and Susquehanna cultures given the lack of drill technology but possibly were present elsewhere in the eastern Woodlands where drills were used to make stone and shell beads. It is possible that the atlatl and fire drill were conceptually equivalent given that both the fire drill and atlatl were later associated with the Aztec god of the hunt, Mixcoatl/Camaxtli, who gave the fire drill to humans.

See *fire, hunt god rite*

First-Kill Rite

First-kill rites were probably observed for both the first animal kill of a boy's life and for an entire social group before, during, and after the first hunt of a particularly important seasonal animal (walrus, seal, caribou, deer, duck). Tuck (1976) believed a rite celebrating the first kill of the season by the people using Port au Choix burial ground included infant sacrifice. One infant was accompanied by numerous items of weaponry including 75 percent of the bone points recovered as well as bayonets, a harpoon, daggers, and a knife.

A similar first-kill rite could be preserved in the burial of infants, children, and juveniles with atlatls at Indian Knoll and Bluegrass. Indian Knoll had 24 subadults buried with one or more parts of atlatls, and other SOV sites had just one or two such burials.

See *atlatl, hunt god rite, Indian Knoll, Port au Choix-3, sacrifice—infant and child*

Fish

Fish and eels are obviously dwellers in the Underworld realm. Catfish and bass were found in the excavations in Salts Cave, and fish scales were found in some fecal specimens (Duffield 1974:130), most likely left by cave specialists. Four fish species were found in a single ritual feature at Higgs (Tennessee) shell-bearing site. Fish bones were the second most frequent remains in the island hunting shrines of Morrison and Allumettes, Quebec.

See *bayonet, drumfish, ritual specialist/priest, tattooing, teeth*

Flake/Chip

Numerous chert chips as well as small pieces of slate, shale, agate, and rhyolite were included as grave goods in Maritime Archaic burials. Tuck (1976) did not hesitate to call these chips grave goods, which are often assumed to be accidental inclusions in graves elsewhere.

A hint at the symbolism that flakes might convey can be found in Nahuatl texts. The flaking of siliceous stone was understood as a reproductive act, as seen in the Aztec practice of referring to children as "the chips," "the flakes" (Furst 1995:175). Aztecs believed that a female deity gave birth to flint, hurled it to earth (as lightning), and from it sprang 1,600 terrestrial gods (Miller and Taube 1993:88). Cherokee speak of a woman monster who exploded into chips that became arrowheads, a story that could also be interpreted to imply children and to equate chips and projectile points with fertility, babies, and descendants.

The possible Archaic belief that chips and flakes could be used as fertility petitions cast new light on sites with hundreds of thousands of flakes—like 9Wr4 in Georgia (Ledbetter 1995), the extensive debitage in the bottom of the sinkhole of Austin Cave (Barker 1997), or in the Ft. Payne lithic workshops underlying the shell mounds along the Tennessee River, each with a layer thick with flakes (Webb and DeJarnette 1942). These extremely high numbers of flakes give rise to the idea of lithic shrines, similar to bone or hunting shrines. Either lithic or bone offerings then would constitute offerings at fertility shrines.

See *Austin Cave, flintknapping, projectile point, shrine, stone*

Flintknapping

To work stone, through quarrying, flaking, or drilling, or even breaking off speleothems, was to be in close contact with spirits and ancient knowledge, to perform an act that was spiritually charged. This sacredness derives from both the source of the technology—deities—as well as the properties of the stones—the sparking when struck, or piezoelectricity (Whitley et al. 1999), shininess, color—and the methods of working stone, particularly drilling, a sexual metaphor, or hitting with antler billet, a possible reference to the hunt god. Consider the following quotes:

> The people painted pictographs in the quest for many medicines, one of which was surely flint. . . . Medicine songs praise the powers in the stone and some of the rock art was probably done in respect for the gathering of this prized medicine. Some even portray the stone points themselves, and other[s] depict the ancient spears and bows-and-arrows. (Rajnovich 1994:145)

> The [Blackfoot] man known as Rain Cloud had a vision in which he was instructed to find a piece of flint, put it in a fire, select a sliver of stone and work it with a stick. [He produced a unilateral unifacial knife.] The visionary source of this technique is accepted by the community and, as a consequence, imbues stoneworking and flint tools with a sacred quality and origin. (Irwin 1994:192)

> Tawi-skala (Flint) was very loud and greatly feared. His . . . terrible arrows dealt death when the darts of the lightning came down into the valley. . . . Rabbit drove a stake into him to pin him down. In an instant the air was filled with flying stones and flashes of fire. Tawiskala [Cherokee] had broken up into a shower of small pointed bits of flint that filled the valley. . . . These were the first arrow-heads. (Bailey 1975:100)

A similar story was told by the Aztecs. A female deity gave birth to flint, hurled it to earth (as lightning), and from it sprang 1,600 terrestrial gods (Miller and Taube 1993:88). The Aztec god of the hunt, Mixcoatl, gave the fire drill to humans. Algonkians believed that "Nanabojou was the first stone-tool maker and all later flint-knappers copied him" (Rajnovich 1994:145). Flintknapping then was heavily embedded with images and thoughts of long ago time, as were the objects produced with flint.

See *ancestor, flake/chip, hunt god rite, point reuse, projectile point, stone, Stone People*

Fossil

Among the fossil localities with Paleoindian and Archaic artifacts are those of Big Bone Lick, Kentucky; Afton Springs, Oklahoma; and Cutler Fossil Site and Little Salt Spring, in Florida. It may be no coincidence that one of the heaviest concentrations of fossil beds in the east is that near the Falls of the Ohio, the scene of a dozen or more shell-bearing burial sites in auspicious places

Crinoid stems may have been harvested from rockshelter walls in the Tennessee valley. Fossil sharks' teeth have been traded from Mount Taylor shell sites and collected on the Atlantic coast. Petrified wood was recovered from many sites including Dameron Rockshelter, Kentucky. Extinct Tapir teeth and a Calamites fossil plant stem were recovered at Indian Knoll and extinct peccary bones in the deepest level of Russell Cave, Alabama (Webb 1974:313).

Father Hennepin "observed the Dakotas making offerings at St. Anthony Falls (on the Mississippi River between Minneapolis and St. Paul)" to Oanktayhee, said to be a gigantic buffalo living there. "In 1874, mammoth teeth and tusks were recovered from St. Anthony Falls" (Mayor 2005:233). Are these remembered animals or stories explaining discoveries? Mayor considers all of the stories to be tales related to the finding of fossils that natives throughout the continent recognized as ancestors and used in powdered form as powerful medicine (2005:29).

Fossil bone doctors, using powdered fossils, were once common among the Pawnee (Mayor 2005:169). One of the benefits of this fossil powder medicine, particularly the powder of a leg bone from the extinct short-faced bear (*Arctoduys simus*), was great running speed (Mayor 2005:45). Some doctors used fossils for evil stinging power (Mayor 2005:246–249). Baculites and cylindrical cephalopods that today appear as crazed crystalline cylinders up to the length of a forearm were used as amulets (Mayor 2005:217). Absarokee visionaries could identify the gender of a sacred stone—a fossil ammonite or baculite—by its shape (Irwin 1994:224). Ivory from fossil mammoths was collected by historic Indians and traded from the Inuit southward into the St. Lawrence valley (Mayor 2005:8–9).

See *amulet/charm/talisman, cave mineral/mining, crinoid stem, fetish, Great Flood, Little Salt Spring, medicine, paint/powder, petrified wood, Stone People*

Four-Age Rite

Four, five, or six people of four different ages were buried together in several sites, often including two adults (a man and a woman) and two more individuals from two of the other age categories: infant, child, and adolescent. Many native groups associate different cardinal directions with different life stages (e.g., in Museum of the American Indian dioramas), suggesting that the four-age rite was conducted at or as a new year ceremonial. A variation of this rite appears to have been conducted in a few cases as a deer hunt rite as well, with four individuals or individuals of four different ages positioned around a central man with deer antlers.

This rite seems to have begun in Early Archaic times given the evidence in the Jerger Site on the White River in Indiana (Schmidt et al. 2008:233). Feature 3 contained the cremations of a newborn, a child, a young adult, and an old adult and five burned *Olivella* sp. beads. It is this cremation that suggests that at least here, the four-age rite was part of a new fire rite.

Rosenberger, on the Ohio River, had three four-age rites in Archaic contexts. One of these groups had a fetus, an adolescent, an adult male body (both extended), and a flexed mature male. A second foursome labeled Feature 1 included two children, one adolescent, and one mature male. The third four-age rite had an infant, an adolescent, and two adults, one of them male (all aging and sexing needs to be redone). The nearby Black Earth burial ground had one probable four-age rite, Bu225. These four bodies were basically stacked. A Late Archaic version of the rite is found at Reigh, Wisconsin, where four people of different ages were emplaced surrounding a central male with headdress. This deposit is covered with a mass of bones from at least three other bodies (Pleger 1998:39).

Four-age rites also seem to have occurred at Turner Farm in Maine, raising the question as to whether there are other examples in other Susquehanna burial grounds. Feature 7, Feature 9, and Feature 12 all contained the cremains of four or five individuals, each in a different age category. Some bones had been burned when fresh, but most were calcined as dry bones. Red ocher was present. Feature 12 consisted of a fetus, a newborn, a child, and two adults, all incomplete skeletons. The child was burned in the flesh (Barbian and Magennis 1995). At Turner Farm, then, it seems that a four-age rite was conducted with previously dead individuals at or near the time of the death of one of the individuals. Quite curiously, three associated features at Turner Farm contained the remains of four *deer*—a fetus, a calf, and two adults (Spiess and Lewis 1995:342). How many other such associations of faunal remains lie undetected?

It is also possible to find four-age rites where the individuals were not put into the same grave and may not have been buried at the same time yet the concept remains important. From Short Cave, Kentucky, came four desiccated bodies including the female "Fawn Hoof," who was a probable ritual specialist, an infant, an adolescent, and a second female, although the adults need to be reexamined for sex assignment (Watson 1969:67). The shell mound 1Ct17 had five bodies placed on *top* of the shell heap, each one a different age and in a different burial posture that may have constituted a four-age decommissioning rite. Furthermore, the only bodies found *within* the shell matrix at 1Ct17 were four bodies sorting into an adult, an adolescent, a child, and an infant, again each in a different posture, highly suggestive of another four-age rite even though the burials were not contained in a single grave (Webb 1939). The six bodies excavated in Russell Cave, although in separate places, are suggestive of one four-age rite given that they were an old adult, a younger adult, an adolescent, a child, and two infants (Griffin 1974:63).

These differently aged individuals probably constituted part of a world renewal ceremony. Alice Kehoe (personal communication with the author, December 2012; Kehoe 2007) pointed out the close resemblance of some of these age-graded groupings to the historic Osage war ritual killings. That rite included the killing and interment of "first the young male adolescent, then the maiden, then the man of military honors, then the woman who has borne children."

See *Cult of the Bivalve Feast, first-kill rite, hunt god rite, Rosenberger, Russell Cave, sacrifice—adult, sacrifice—infant and child*

Galena

Galena from the upper Meramec River valley was present at local sites such as Rodgers Shelter and Modoc and as far away as the mouth of the Mississippi River during the Early Archaic (Walthall 1981). In the Missouri area the galena occurs on the surface, in soft clay, and in creek beds. Its co-occurrence with red ocher nuggets, powder, and stained grinding slabs in both shelters suggests an interest in galena as a powder, although it did not become part of burial ceremonialism until the Late Archaic (Walthall 1981:5).

In the Late Archaic and Early Woodland periods the main sources of galena were the upper Mississippi valley, the Potosi deposit of southeastern Missouri, central Missouri, and an Ontario/New York source. "It does not appear that galena from either Central Missouri or Ontario/New York was exchanged outside the territories surrounding these deposits during this time" (Walthall 1981:37). The Potosi galena and upper Mississippi valley galena were among those pieces found at Poverty Point, demonstrating "north-south cultural contact along the Mississippi River" (Walthall 1981:37). Upper Mississippi valley galena was also found in Ontario.

Over time local galena was substituted for exotic ores in several regions. Galena stones have historic uses as charms, and galena powder was the source for gray or silver paint used on the faces of dancers and priests.

See *cave mineral/mining, feces, hematite, mica, ocher, paint/powder*

Gambling

Fowler (1966:62) interprets some Late Archaic steatite bits as gaming pieces, and Winters offers the same for several cut bone pieces from Riverton. Tallies were identified by Winters (1969) at Riverton and Swan Island. Bone dice were found in burial features and in habitation context at Turner Farm, Maine (Bourque 1995). The bone pins of the Midwest and Southeast may be stick-dice.

Gambling results were often interpreted as a measure of one's personal relationship with the spirits or that of a group's favor before a spirit. Gambling and games were divination mechanisms as well (e.g., Eyman 1965; Vennum 1994; Ventur 1980). Bourque (1995:163), referring to bone dice in a mortuary feature at Turner Farm, and Ventur (1980) talk about gambling and games as part of mortuary ritual among groups in the Northeast and Southeast. Most significant for archaeologists, DeBoer (2001) believes that the wagering of ornaments and other personal possessions may have been the major means through which such objects and styles moved across the landscape. It could well be that the spread of pottery from the Atlantic coastal shellworks westward and northward was the result of gambling. Vennum (1994) documents the willingness of Historic native villages and individual stickball players to impoverish themselves in wagers and rapidly seek a rematch if they lost. Even wives and children were wagered. Ballgames were viewed as contests between priests with priests (and doctors) losing favor in their communities if they failed to secure success for the contestants (patients) they represented.

Other evidence of gambling in the Archaic may be in the sites of the lower Ohio valley where decorated bone pins are found (Jefferies 1997). Eyman (1965) documents and depicts historic stick-dice and the games that used them, and DeBoer (2001) adds that this was a women's game. The resemblance between the illustrated stick-dice and the decorated bone pins of the Archaic is quite striking. Jefferies mentions that some of the "pins" are perforated for suspension, which may mean that some individuals derived pleasure from flaunting their winnings. He also mentions that a few of the "pins" are found in graves, suggesting that this was a mortuary gambling game.

See *bone pin, divination, game, number*

Game

Games were not simply entertainment but serious measures of cosmic relationships and future events. "Every Cherokee game preceded a ritual or was part of a rite" (Eyman 1965:43–44).

Evidence for several historic games has been recovered from Archaic contexts. The cup-in-pin games, dart/arrow casting, stick-dice, and other dice gambling games are among them. The cup-and-pin game of modern Algonkian-, Athapascan-, and Siouan-speaking peoples seems to have been played in Archaic times at Riverton and Swan Island, Illinois, as well as in Green River and northern Alabama shell mounds. Its identification is based on the removal of the proximal end of several deer phalanges that are graduated in size and fit one inside the other (Winters 1969:83). At Eva the game may have been played with the antler and foramen magnum of deer (Lewis and Lewis 1961:100–101). Eva also yielded telescoping wing and femur bones, suggesting the cup-and-pin game (Lewis and Lewis 1961:84, 85). DeBoer (2001) suggests that the common association of ornaments with women such as is seen at Bluegrass and Frontenac Island burial grounds was due to women's playing of dice games for which they wagered ornaments.

Dart casting (where one flips a dart at a target) and stick- or dart dice (used for divination, redistribution) may be seen in the bone pins found in Midwest and southern coastal sites. "The names and shapes of pieces in Indian stick-dice games, and the context of archaeological specimens, indicate that dice games are older than the bow and that games originated when the spear-thrower and javelin were the most advanced hunting tools. Early dice were portions of a dart or light spear; the original arrow-casting game was played with such darts and the spear thrower" (Eyman 1965:43). Given that bone stick-dice seem to have evolved into dart and arrow (cane) dice and were left in graves, the points of darts may have been used as dice and also left in graves. Ventur (1980:86) cites examples of dice in later stone box graves of central Tennessee made with astragalus bones of deer. This association of feet with the future, via divination, strengthens other claims for foot-fertility associations.

Games of different types were favored by men and women in the Historic record. Games of dexterity, such as cup-and-pin, hoop-and-pole, ball games, races, and archery, were played by men in Historic times (DeBoer 2001:217). Dice games were the most common among women and required very complex calculations of odds (DeBoer 2001; Eyman 1965). "Well over 100 dice games alone are recorded, distributed from the Atlantic seaboard to the Pacific coast and from the subarctic . . . to northern Mexico" (DeBoer 2001:217). Two-sided dice were the norm and employed materials such as beaver teeth, canes, plumstones, nutshells, persimmon seeds, stones, shells, and sherds. They could be tossed in a bowl and used in multiples of six or eight. Moieties were often represented in the contest. Stick-dice often were used as foursomes.

See *divination, feet/footprint/track, gambling, gorget, oracle, point reuse, projectile point*

Gastropod

Various aquatic snails were made into beads and had other uses beginning in Paleoindian times. The beads recovered in a 9,700 ya double grave of a probable ritual specialist at Horn Shelter, Texas, included several Olive shells and 80 *Neritina reclivata*. Burned *Olivella* sp. beads were found in a group burial at Jerger, Indiana (Schmidt et al. 2008), and may have symbolized the stars of the night sky. *Leptoxis* beads, ubiquitous in many Tennessee, Green, and Harpeth river burials, have been dated to 6600 rcy at Modoc RS and to 6100 rcy at Ervin in Tennessee in a cremation (Hofman 1986). *Leptoxis* are native to the Tennessee River but are rare in Tennessee River shell mounds. *Marginella* shell beads were present in Archaic context at Krill Cave, Ohio, and at Lamoka Lake, New York.

Members of the *Busycon* genus, the marine whelk, seem to have been used for spiritual items first during the late Middle Archaic. Cut whelk shell was found in the same dated cremation at Ervin with the *Leptoxis* beads. A directly dated piece of *Busycon* comes from the Ward site, 4180+/-150 (dated by the author in May 2011). Milky Way belts and rebosos made up of hundreds of *Busycon* beads or *Leptoxis* beads have been found at sites like Indian Knoll, and a *Leptoxis* shroud seems to have covered a single young adult at 40My105 (Moore 1991:43).

Several archaeologists have pointed out that the distinguishing characteristic of *Busycon contrarium* is that it is the only whelk that spirals, or grows, to the left, counterclockwise. This contrary species served perfectly for the ritually important counterclockwise spiraling motion associated with the daily path of the sun and moon and their passage into the Underworld, as well as the spiraling earth in the beginning time. Living in the Underworld as gastropods do, some groups, such as the Winnebago, likened gastropods to the stars in the night sky (Radin 1970), indicating that the Underworld rotated into the upper position at night.

Unmodified gastropod shells (*Pleurocera, Lithasia, Elimia,* and *Leptoxis*) piled in midden comprise the matrix for mortuary activities in central Tennessee during the Middle Archaic at the Ervin (8153–6300 B.P.) and Hayes (6995–4697 B.P.) sites on the Duck River. On the St. Johns River in Florida *Viviparus georgianus* and *Pomacea paludos* were mounded and seem to reflect a Cult of the Snail Shell.

See *Busycon, Cult of the Snail Shell, Ervin, Harris Creek, Leptoxis/Anculosa, Olivella, shell, shell bead, St. Johns River*

Geometry

Clark (2004:170) argues that the equilateral triangle was the basic layout model for Archaic mound centers (Figure 23), including Middle Archaic Watson Brake and the late Poverty Point site (see also Sassaman 2010a:54). The legs of the triangle used multiples of the Standard Macro-Unit of 86.63 m (Clark 2004).

Any circle is composed of six equilateral triangles. "In many cases, the curve or arc of a circle delimits outer edges of mounds whereas the sides of inscribed triangles pass through the mound's center points" (Clark 2004:195). Clark discovered that all of the early mound sites were preplanned according to simple geometry and arithmetic, and Sassaman and Heckenberger (2004) found that Watson Brake, Caney, Frenchman's Bend, and later Poverty Point "subscribe to the same geometric and proportional regularities and to a common Archaic measurement system" (Sassaman 2010a:56) found by Clark (2004).

The arc and circle were prominent spatial models for Middle and Late Archaic sites along the Gulf and Atlantic coasts. Circular house rings with central plazas have been identified at Mims Point and Stallings Island on the Savannah River and in the numerous shell rings of the South Carolina–Florida coast (Sassaman 2006:98–99). The Oxeye Ring may be the earliest example of community living in the round, even though it is the only known Mount Taylor culture ring (Russo 2010:153). Life there began 3000 B.C. (Sanger 2010:206). There may have been a circular shrine at Jaketown and at Robeson Hills (see Winters 1969:92, 97).

Archaic use of the rectangle appears in large burial pits holding multiple bodies, in rectangular structures such as that at the base of Monte Sano, in rectangular platforms, and in rectangular gorgets. When oriented with the

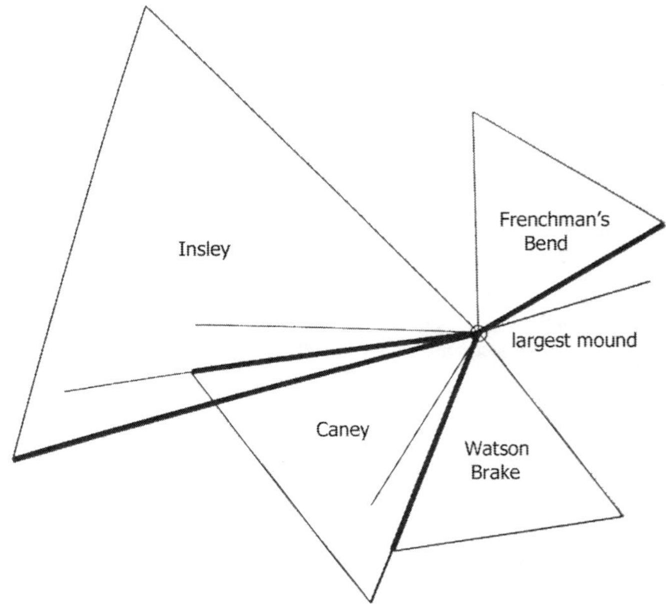

23. "Archaic mound complexes georeferenced to largest mound and baselines (top) to show scalar differences, as well as to largest mound and azimuth (bottom) to show integration. Note: baselines (a') are emboldened." (Reprinted from Clark 2004:Figure 11.5, with permission from the University of Alabama Press.)

long axis north-south, the corners mark the intercardinal points, points of summer and winter solstice sunrise and sunset, and create a bounded This World. The quincunx, a form of rectangle, is present in pit arrangements (e.g., Newt Kash Shelter; Claassen 2010) and in a few group burials with five individuals. There is as yet no evidence that an Archaic ritual site was centered in a quadrilateral space with natural features marking the corners or midpoints such as has been found now at the Middle Woodland Biltmore Mound in North Carolina, but I suspect that evidence exists (Kimball and Johnson 2012).

See *astronomy, C-shaped site layout, cardinal direction, constellation, cross, measurement, Poverty Point*

Gorget

In New England gorgets appear in the Middle Archaic and increase in frequency, lithological variety, and shape variety through the Late Archaic. The oldest ones may be made of soapstone/steatite (Fowler 1966:38). In the lower

Mississippi valley bannerstones gave way to two-hole stone gorgets about 1200 B.C. and they in turn gave way to boatstones ca. 600 B.C. (Kwas 1981:156).

Charles Peabody and W. Moorehead (1906:60–61) found that gorgets could have functioned as buzzers, puzzles, gambling tallies, or gaming pieces or as thunderstones, badges, totems, magic tablets, amulets, and bullroarers if they were ceremonial in nature, or as shuttles, netting sticks, and mesh gauges if they were utilitarian objects. They concluded (1906:71) that there were multiple uses for stone gorgets but that shell gorgets were unique and deserving of separate analysis. Robert Hall (1997) favored the bullroarer function for sandal-sole gorgets.

Binford reasoned stone and shell gorgets were a mark of some rank or status. "The relatively infrequent occurrence of gorgets in assemblages argues against their function solely as ornaments of personal adornment or as amulets, articles which generally have a relatively high frequency of occurrence within any given population. It was suggested that gorgets function as a material accompaniment of a system of ranking, being available only to those occupying certain defined positions within the system and subsequently deriving 'ritual value' from their history of ownership" (Binford 1963:143). He went on to posit that "gorgets extant at any one time were probably known individually in terms of their ownership history . . . gorgets may have been given away or destroyed . . . and repaired items may have been of greater social significance because of the particular history of the events leading to breakage, distribution of parts, and the eventual acquisition of two or more parts by a given individual" (Binford 1963:144). The evidence he offered was the rarity of gorgets per site, multiple gorgets in a grave, the frequent presence of fragmented gorgets, and the association of gorgets with other ritual items such as birdstones, tubular pipes, and quartz crystals.

See *amulet/charm/talisman*, *bannerstone*, *gambling*, *game*, *shell*, *stone*

Grave Good

Rolingson (1967) was the first to note that Green River Archaic shell mounds each typically had a single outstanding burial from the perspective of the number of grave goods. In several cases, this individual had died violently and/or was the deepest burial (Claassen 2010:105, 122–124). Interestingly, both the average number of goods and the percentage of people with goods serve to statistically distinguish the large SOV riverside shell heaps from shell-free sites and bluff-top sites. Both statistics also distinguish the sites with no dog sacrifices from the sites with 13+ dog sacrifices, and the sites on tributaries versus sites on rivers (Claassen 2010:105).

What the number of goods signified about social life has been debated by archaeologists, but typically the discussion revolves around achieved status (for an adult) or acquired status (for an infant). Rarely have the circumstances surrounding the death been considered as an explanation for the presence or absence of goods or their number (but see Claassen 2010; Tuck 1976). Grave goods are offerings, made to one of the souls of the deceased or to any spirits that might be implicated in the person's death. If the individual had been sacrificed or had died violently, in anger, by lightning strike, by drowning, by accident, or from one of several specific health conditions, offerings may have been made to the spirits responsible and to the spirit that the newly departed soul would soon serve. Other useful ways of accounting for the differences in grave goods in Archaic settings involve clan or cult membership, medicine bags, ritual specialists with their paraphernalia, and clothing and hair attachments.

See *burial—posture, mortuary offering index, offering, ritual specialist/priest*

Great Flood

Numerous cultures in the eastern Woodlands speak of a great flood long ago. They are probably referring to the inundation of landscapes in the Late Pleistocene-Early Holocene as sea levels, lake levels, and sinkhole water levels rose, drowning valleys and flooding game drives, canyons, cave entrances, and significant landscapes. The Stone People including fossil animals were those who lived on the ancient landscape and constituted an earlier, pre-flood creation. They were recognized in fossil bone beds in swamps and bogs and in Clovis points.

See *ancestor, Cult of the Blade, fossil, projectile point, sinkhole, spring, Stone People*

Green River, Kentucky

It is the Green River itself that seems to have been the attraction for the Middle and Late Archaic people who accumulated the great shell mounds, bluff-top shell sites, and shell-free burial grounds stretching along a 100-mile segment of this watershed. They also used the caves and rockshelters and made mortars and rock markings in that valley and along several tributaries. There are two aspects of the river in particular to which one can attribute this attention: the green color of the river and its association with Mammoth Cave.

The name of the river derives from historic observations of its green color (Stein 2005:20). Green or turquoise was the color associated with the beginning of the world; Mesoamerican groups associated it with the center (Miller and Taube 1993:65). Similarly, for the Lakota, green signifies "down," or Underworld, the origin of life.

The water of the Green River brought gifts from the Underworld (mollusks, shells, fish, water), which may have been conceptually located in Mammoth Cave, and the river was purified by its passage through the Underworld. Paleoindian projectiles are evident in most Archaic Green River sites, suggesting that another draw to the river was the auspicious presence of the Stone People. Asphaltum, bitumen, and coal were also gifts from the Underworld available along the river's course.

The earliest encampment of shellfishers in this watershed occurred on a tributary, Cyprus Creek. Shells were carried to the top of a bluff known to us as the Ward site and were probably collected not in Cyprus Creek but in the more distant Green River. Another Cyprus Creek location, the Kirkland site, was a shell-free burial ground.

In keeping with the idea that the Green River-Mammoth Cave area may have been symbolically the center of the world for some Archaic peoples is the site of Indian Knoll located along the river. Only Poverty Point exceeds Indian Knoll in indications of Archaic ritual. The burial ground has dozens of examples of ritual killings, ritual specialists, and four-age and hunt god rites. The tremendous number of men with auditory exostoses indicates some version of water rites. The tremendous numbers of deer found at Indian Knoll suggest hunt god rites and feasts that were associated. I consider Indian Knoll to be the preeminent shrine for an Archaic hunt god.

See *Cult of the Bivalve Feast, dog sacrifice rite, first-kill rite, four-age rite, hunt god rite, Indian Knoll, mound—shell*

Hawk

Hawks are surprisingly rare in Archaic sites of eastern North America. *Buteo lineatus* occurred in the "sterile" Stratum 8 at Modoc with a wide array of other unusual birds, and *Circus cyaneus* hawks were found in Late Archaic levels at Modoc (Ahler et al. 1992:59). A red-tailed hawk was identified at the Bullskin Creek site in Ohio. The Paleoindian people who buried the man in Horn Shelter 2, Texas, placed a Swainson's hawk talon in his mouth and four unperforated claws of a Swainson's hawk near his neck.

See *bird, Horn Shelter 2*

Headdress—See Mask/Headdress

Head Removal

Based on a lack of cut marks and the presence of atlas and axis vertebrae, it appears that postburial removal of skulls was practiced by some late Middle Archaic and early Late Archaic peoples in southern Illinois and in the SOV. Examples can be seen at Carrier Mills (Bu162), where an artifact was substituted for the cranium (Bassett 1982:1094), and at Widow's Creek, Alabama, where a shell was substituted for a cranium. Postburial head removal indicates a differential burial program during the Archaic that some scholars (Ahler et al. 1992:132) see as the development of social ranking but Tuck (1976:14) attributes to grief.

Living individuals were also decapitated, apparently for trophy skulls. Twenty-four decapitations have been identified for Tennessee River shell sites and 36 for the Green River sites. Several headless bodies were found at Lamoka Lake, New York, as well as a few cases in other places (Claassen 2010). Isolated crania were not uncommon in Archaic burial grounds such as in Wisconsin's Old Copper cemeteries (Pleger 1998), Frontenac Island, New York, and Windover, Florida (Windover burial database on file at the Florida State University).

See *bone soul, decommissioning rite, skull, trophy part*

Headwater

Highland boggy areas with seeps and springs characterize headwater areas in the Appalachian and Ozark mountains. These natural features are candidates for ritualizing staging areas. There have been many sites discovered in these headwaters areas assigned a presumed habitation or bivouac function, such as sites in Watauga and Ashe counties in North Carolina (Ayers 1976) and Peaks of Otter, Virginia (Griffin and Reeves 1968). Fifty-six Paleoindian and Archaic points were found at Peaks of Otter as well as scrapers, flake tools, blades, cores, and numerous hearths. All three LeCroy points were associated with one deep hearth. The Morrow Mountain points were found in pits. Curiously, post-Archaic material was rare at Peaks of Otter. The excavators could surmise no subsistence reason for the arduous climb up to this locality, a problem expressed by Wilkins (1978) as well for high-elevation sites in West Virginia. The reason for the presence of artifacts may have been offerings left in a headwater setting.

See *bluff, mountain, offering, rain, spring*

Hematite

Hematite in its solid form was used to make a number of different types of tools. Hematite was fashioned into plummets, "rubstones," pestles, birdstones, and weights, as well as ground to powder. It derived its symbolic uses from its color as well as from its frequent natural occurrence with fossil beds.

"Facetted, baked hematite occurs abundantly in some Early Archaic period occupation sites from Connecticut to Quebec" and in burial sites (Robinson 2006:345–346). The Early Archaic bifurcate zone at Bacon Bend, Rose Island, and Icehouse Bottom sites in eastern Tennessee had abundant faceted and unfaceted pieces of reddish-brown hematite (Chapman 1981:72). Hematite processing stations were evident in both Horizon 8 and Horizon 7 at Rodgers Shelter, Missouri, with copious amounts of powder, chunks, numerous stained grinding stones, and hearths for heating (Kay 1982).

See *cave mineral/mining, galena, ocher, paint/powder*

Human

Fowler (1966:42, Figure 6) depicts a human face pendant of steatite—presumably of Late Archaic affiliation—from Narragansett Bay that looks quite like a false face of millennia later given its crooked mouth and nose. Another human image is pecked on a stone that covered an Archaic cist (Fowler 1966:44) (Figure 24). A stick image recovered from Wapanucket 6 site (Massachusetts) may show a human or a thunderbird (Fowler 1966:44). Armless anthropomorphs appeared in three graves at Port au Choix-3. "These objects may have been purely decorative or may have represented a spiritual being who assisted an individual in manipulation of the spiritual or real world" (Tuck 1976:59).

The human body was surely a prototype for much of the understanding and order of the Archaic world as it was for later Mississippians (Knight 1989). "It appears very possible that the human body and mounds operated as intertwined microcosms in the Southeast," writes Giles (2010:202). Elements of the body such as head, heart, hand, and feet and their left/right, down/up positions and symmetry and liquids of the body were probably symbolically loaded (e.g., Hall 1997). Multiples of the distance from sternum to fingertip were used in laying out sites such as Watson Brake and Poverty Point (Clark 2004; Sassaman and Heckenberger 2004). Observations on life cycle, skin, hair, and body heat would have generated rules of social behavior and empirical information that was likened to the changing seasons, medicine, and

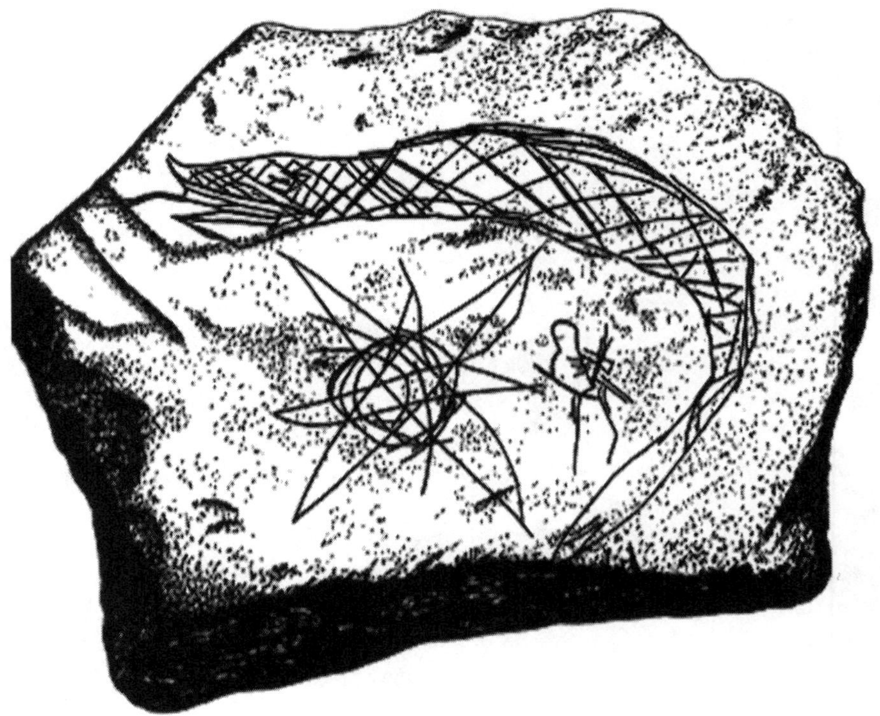

24. Archaic-aged image from Titicut site of a canoe caught in a wind. The canoe capsized and drowned the paddler. This wind was possibly created by the Underwater snake. (Reprinted from Fowler 1966:Figure 7, with permission from the Massachusetts Archaeological Society.)

the deities. Even the arcs of Poverty Point may have been laid out with reference to the human body (Sassaman 2005:359).

See *feet/footprint/track*, *femur*, *figurine*, *head removal*, *human bone artifact*

Human Bone Artifact

From the vestibule of Salts Cave, 100 cmbs and deeper, came "a fragment of bone awl fashioned from the shaft region of an adult human tibia," a proximal end of a human ulnar shaft awl, a human tibia awl, and a human fibula awl. An incised radial shaft and polished femoral shaft were also recovered from the Salts Cave vestibule (Robbins 1974:146–157). It is possible that trophy parts were decommissioned in this vestibule.

The greatest number of human bone artifacts are reported from Carlston Annis shell mound on the Green River (Morse 1967:348; Watson 2005:554), including a skull vessel. Skull vessels or skull gorgets have also been found at Anderson, Tennessee, Belle Gade, Florida (Dowd 1989:139), and Mulberry Creek shell mound in Late Archaic context (Shields 2003:83). Drilled human teeth were encountered at the Ward site, at Little Bear Creek, at Bluff Creek, and at the Dravo Gravel site (Vickery 2008:14), all SOV sites. Examples can also be found in Port au Choix-3. A human bone artifact was also included among the grave goods of an extended infant (Bu2) at the Nevin, Maine, shell heap (Byers 1979:38).

What would mandate the use of human bone awl? Killing a witch or performing witchcraft (both said to involve bone splinters [Fox 1993]) or tattooing a ritual leader are all possibilities. Skullcap bowls and cranium pendants would seem to relate to sacrificial rites.

See *awl, femur, human, jaw, scalping, skull, tattooing*

Hunt God Rite

Robert Hall (2000) raised the probability that the group burial of four extended men in the Mississippian Dickson Mounds cemetery mound and the four extended men with no heads, hands, or feet under Mound 72 at Cahokia had been sacrificed in the performance of a calendrical rite that could be understood by reference to the historic central Mexican god Camaxtli/Mixcoatl and Busk/Green Corn ceremonials of several southeastern groups. What Hall did not present was information that connected the Camaxtli rite to a much older hunter-gatherer Chichimec hunt rite involving several deity impersonators and deer killings (Broda 1998). He did mention that John Witthoft (1949:84–85) "attributed the Busk to a derivation from earlier hunting ceremonialism, especially that related to 'the first seasonal usage of each major food animal'" (Hall 2000:245).

Of relevance to a possible Archaic hunt god rite are several elements of the historic rites and beliefs. Mixcoatl (Figure 19) was not only the god of the hunt but also the god of the Milky Way, the god of the heavens and stars, the inventor of the fire drill, and the first to use flint to kindle fire (Miller and Taube 1993:115). Hall (2000) as well as Broda (1998) also mention an association with Venus and a rite that occurred at eight-year intervals honoring Camaxtli, an interval corresponding to five complete Venus cycles. In this two-day rite warriors and rulers dressed like Camaxtli went to a particular hill where they beat the grasses and killed all of the animals flushed out (Broda 1998:104–106), but they particularly sought deer whose heads they cut off and returned to Tenochtitlan. One image of Camaxtli (e.g., Miller and Taube 1993:115) shows him with atlatl raised, a black eye mask, and a candy-cane-striped red face and arms. Broda relates that before the god impersonators were killed in this monthlong (November) observation, "four captives were sacrificed who were bound and *slain as if they were deer*" (1998:105, emphasis added), and Hall writes that the Mixcoatl/Camaxtli rite was associated with a new fire and the sacrifice of four men and in some cases a fifth man or, more often, a woman. The fifth individual may often have been killed and buried later than were the first four people. He further stresses the significance of the number five. Wixárika today talk of the hunt god as having five male deer deities and five female deer deities (who transformed into dogs) all living in the four cardinal directions and sacred center (Schaefer 2002:203).

"Reenactments of events from the time of creation were a way of renewing the present by making contact with the vitality of that earlier era. Thus, the New Fire ceremony performed annually in Camaxtli's honor made use of the firesticks included among Camaxtli's sacred relics, preserved from the time of creation when as Mixcoatl he drilled fire for the first hearth" (Hall 2000:250). In the United States this rite is mirrored not only in elements of the Green Corn ceremony but also in the Venus-related Morning Star captive girl sacrifice by the Skiri Pawnee (Hall 1997; Hall 2000:247). Hall further demonstrated how the sound of "Camaxtli" could be transformed to the Cherokee first hunter named "Kanati" (Hall 2000).

Archaic evidence for a hunt god rite is quite strong and takes us to the Middle Archaic where group burials of four or five men have been uncovered at Elizabeth Mounds, Mulberry Creek, Ward (see Meindl, Mensforth, and York 2001:Figure 5 for an example), and Parrish. Those rites at Elizabeth and Mulberry were quite possibly the initial burials at both places, suggesting both a consecrating act and the founding of a ceremonial center.

The five-body deposit made before the erection of Mound 1 at Elizabeth Mounds in the LIV is remarkable for the hundreds of gastropod shell beads included as bracelets and belts worn by four of the men (see Albertson and Charles 1988:Figure 4.4). These belts implicate a Milky Way association as gastropods were likened to the stars in the night sky by at least the Winnebago (Radin 1970). As in the Mississippian rites at Dickson Mounds and Cahokia, these five men were laid side by side in an extended position, a position most indicative of violent death. Mulberry shell mound on the Tennessee River also has a deep burial of five extended men, four tossed into the grave and the fifth to the side with head twisted. Were deer ritually killed by twisting their heads and deer impersonators killed similarly? Another Middle Archaic rite could be that at Ward (Bu173–176), where one of the four men had been scalped, highly analogous to the skinning of a deer. Parrish had one rite with four adults, two stained with red ocher.

Moving to probable or known Late Archaic contexts, there are three graves at Indian Knoll with foursomes, extended bodies, Milky Way belts, and a headless man. The bone of one of these men returned a radiocarbon date of 5467–4983 B.P. at 2 standard deviations (Herrmann 2002). It may be here at Indian Knoll that the mnemonic device of the atlatl is interjected into the ceremony—an antler deer hunting device—for which Indian Knoll is so famous. Carlston Annis had one four-man grave with several individuals dying violently (Mensforth 2001:117). Barrett had two four-man burials, one of which, judging from the photo, used the flexed bodies to form a square (Webb and Haag 1947:13, Figure 4B).

There are other burials in the eastern United States with deer antler but apparently without the associated burials. Was the inclusion of atlatl with an extended, headdressed man wearing a Milky Way belt—the case in Ward's Bu1—a version of the ceremony or was just the cremation of a man with antler (atlatl?)—Anderson's cremations Bu53 and Bu73—representative? Conversely the Early Archaic Feature 6 at Reigh had five individuals with the center figure wearing a headdress, but each person was a different age (Pleger 1998). Did some cultures perform the hunt god rite with five individuals of four ages rather than the four-man combination?

It may have been this very rite that explains the large ceremonials and feasting evident in the SOV although there is as yet no evidence of it at most of the shell mounds in the region. Its geographical reach is interesting with the earliest occurrences of the rite at Elizabeth Mounds, Parrish, Ward, and Mulberry Creek. It was possibly held even at Turner Farm in Maine. If this rite happened at eight-year intervals and only at one place each cycle, then the minimum of 18 rites identified (Claassen 2012d) suggests a cult lasting at least 144 years with a focus on deer hunting, Venus, and the Milky Way. Antler billets for flintknapping would be a direct link to the hunt god. Woodland and Mississippian examples indicate its continued significance throughout the history of the central Mississippi valley.

The implications of this rite are significant for the light potentially shed on SOV beliefs and ritualizing. Could "atlatl" weights—bannerstones—actually be fire-drill weights? (Are Archaic atlatls hypertropic fire drills?) Are the atlatls with children signifying hunting ritual sacrifices? Is red ocher the mark of a sacrificial victim? Is the head-twisted, beheaded, or scalped individual a deer impersonator killed in this rite? Were the places where this rite occurred ceremonial centers rather than villages? Are the flint workshops in the lower levels of several Alabama shell mounds produced by a rite associated with the hunt god? Is the substitution of wooden atlatls by antler atlatls indicative of the blossoming of this cult? Is heat treating stone related to this hunt god who has parallels with the fire god in Mexico? Is the substitution of bone points by chert points a reflection of widespread belief about the hunt god (Webb and DeJarnette 1948a:48)? Was Indian Knoll, with at least 700 individual deer, the preeminent hunt god shrine?

See *bannerstone, dog with human burial rite, first-kill rite, flake/chip, four-age rite, Indian Knoll, lithic workshop*

Hunting Charm

"Beson," or hunting charms, were made by Onondaga or Lenape old men using roots, herbs, and seeds, some of which were purgatives for the client. These charms made the hunter invisible, were rubbed on arrows and bows to make these weapons accurate, and were placed in animal tracks to shorten the encounter time (Harper 1999:79).

Atlatl "weights," "bannerstones," "birdstones," and "boatstones" elicit the interpretation of hunting charms. Birdstones, when two-legged, strongly suggest bird quarry. In fact, the atlatl was the implement used in bird hunting on lakes in highland Mexico and the name means "water," in short, a waterfowl hunting implement. Kwas (1981) thought that different hunting cults were suggested by the geographical and temporal style zones for bannerstones. Given that so many of these "weights" occurred without any evidence of atlatls, it could be that cult membership was expressed with this item.

Betts and colleagues (2012:626–627) point out that mnemonic devices can also be the teeth, bones, claw, skull, bill, beak, scale, or nail of animal predators and of prey that then allow their possessor to enter the mind of that predator or prey and possibly cause a desired outcome: the hunting charm.

See *amulet/charm/talisman, atlatl, bannerstone, hunt god rite*

Insect

Insects were apparently part of the ritual specialist's or cave miner's diet; beetle and grasshopper parts were found in feces from Salts Cave (Yarnell 1969). Grasshopper/cicadas/locusts are well documented in Middle and Late Archaic (7000 to 4000 B.P.) northern Louisiana red stone beads (Crawford 2003), probably revered for their natural thunderous sound and their heightened activity before rainfall (Blitz 1993).

In the Sioux creation myth, the first creatures were insects and reptiles, no doubt based on the abundant fossil forms of both in their area (Mayor 2005). Surely the association of maggots and flies with corpses and rotting organic material as well as the "butterfly" impression left on the back of a supine corpse (Furst 1995) led to the use of winged insects in death and soul symbolism. In northern Guerrero, Mexico, today, the insect din is quite loud in May about which the people say, "They are calling rain."

See *fossil, locust, miniature, sound*

Island

For many hunter-gatherers, islands were favored burial locations. Oconto and Morrison's Island (Wisconsin) Old Copper complex cemeteries were on islands. Two of three known Maritime Archaic burial grounds were/are located on islands. Turner Farm in Maine is on an island as was Frontenac Island, a shared burial ground in the Finger Lakes of New York. Stallings Island was an important mortuary site in South Carolina, and Indian Knoll was an island during the flooding of the Green River. Tick Island in the St. Johns River of Florida had not only a Middle Archaic mortuary mound (at Harris Creek site) but also a St. Johns mortuary mound (Tick Island site proper). In other cases, islands were sites for hunting shrines and craft production. Allumettes and Morrison islands in Quebec were probable hunting shrines. Bannerstone production was conducted on Mount Johnson Island in the Susquehanna River (Sassaman 2010a:109). Gilman Falls Island was a stone rod manufacturing site in the Early and Middle Archaic. Rose Island in Tennessee was a site of tremendous quantities of red ocher in the Early Archaic (Chapman 1975:155, 156).

Islands offer in miniature an illustration of creation and the position of humans and their realm in the cosmos. Fox and Salzer (1999) brilliantly argue that Frontenac Island was believed to be the place to which the first human fell—a small island that then spread out to become the earth island, This World. Numerous islands are today sacred places for native peoples (Milne 1994).

See *bluff, cosmology, crevice, mountain, ocher, shrine*

Jaw

"A few cut carnivore jaws have been discovered at Indian Knoll and the Terminal Archaic Hind site in Ontario [and increased in numbers in Middle Woodland times]. . . . while such objects indicate a continuity of beliefs for lengthy periods, their specific meanings and uses no doubt changed over many generations and were not identical in all places" (Milner, Buikstra, and Wiant 2009:127).

The inclusion of jaws in burials was not widespread in the eastern United States but instead seems to be concentrated in the SOV. Webb (1950) believed that the only part of an animal skin bag that would be present in the archaeological record was a jaw if the head had been left on. The significance of a walrus mandible found in a ritual deposit on Rustico Island clearly is unexplained by the medicine bag scenario (Leonard 1989:16). If jaws in a grave signify a medicine bag, then medicine bags were not widely buried even in the SOV. Hayes, Bluegrass, and Anderson—all with Middle Archaic components—had the highest percentage of graves with jaws, 17, 7.3, and 6.8 percent, respectively. All other sites ranged between 3.4 and 0.7 percent of graves, with Indian Knoll at 1.4 percent (Claassen 2010). Human burials at Indian Knoll and Carlston Annis included "groundhog, rabbit, weasel, wolf, bobcat, and deer jaws, and incisors of beaver and groundhog" (Crothers 2005:309). "Cut upper and lower carnivore jaws similar to those used by Middle Woodland groups indicate that some rituals that were widespread later in time had antecedents in the Archaic period" (Milner, Buikstra, and Wiant 2009:127). The skeletal jaw was used by Mayans in glyphs to signify a lord of the night or god of the Underworld. Jaws of any animal could have been used to signify the same in northern North America. Of the species with jaws found at Indian Knoll and Carlston Annis, only the deer does not burrow or den in rock crevices or hollow trees, abodes of Underworld spirits.

See *human bone artifact, medicine bag, sacrifice—infant and child*

Leptoxis / Anculosa

Leptoxis snails are native to and very abundant in the Tennessee River, the probable origin point for the species, and were the only freshwater snails to have been used for beads in the eastern United States. They are occasionally found in shell sites in Alabama and on the Savannah River and in shell-free sites in Illinois.

The oldest dated context for *Leptoxis* beads—6340+/-90 rcy—is in Mound 1 Bu32 at Elizabeth Mounds in the LIV, a burial of five individuals. *Leptoxis* bead belts had been wrapped around the waists of four of the five individuals, and *Leptoxis* bead bracelets had been placed around the left wrists of three of the individuals (Albertson and Charles 1988). Since *Leptoxis* are not native in the Illinois or Mississippi River (Clark 1987), these shells had been gathered elsewhere. A cremation feature at the Ervin site on the Duck River in Tennessee with 90 *Leptoxis* beads and two disk whelk beads has been dated to 6160 rcy (Hofman 1985:3). Another interesting Archaic burial with *Lep-*

toxis beads came from Tennessee site 40My105, also associated with Benton blades, where "a mantle of anculosa shells covered the entire burial" (Moore 1991:43). Webb depicts a "reboso" of *Leptoxis* beads over a child at Indian Knoll, Bu610 (Webb 1974:Figure 21D).

Leptoxis shell beads postdated the use of the exotic marine *Olivella* snail beads. It seems that the creation of shell belts and rebosos was impossible with *Olivella* shells given that we have no examples of large numbers of Olivellas. Were *Leptoxis* snails a "cheaper alternative," providing the portable symbol of the Cult of the Snail Shell or a hunt god cult? Were the belts of white *Leptoxis* beads on four men at Elizabeth or several infants at Indian Knoll symbolizing the Milky Way, and the wearers then spirit impersonators or offerings to spirits, such as the hunt god? In Aztec depictions the hunt god wore the Milky Way on his head. Could these Middle Archaic Milky Way belts have morphed ultimately into historic wampum belts?

See *Busycon, Cult of the Snail Shell, gastropod, hunt god rite, Milky Way, Olivella, sacrifice—infant and child, shell, shell bead*

Limestone Slab

Uses for limestone slabs other than burial can be seen at the Truman Road site in central Missouri where five slabs were found. The largest slab, at the base of the midden, measured 190 cm in diameter and 50 cm thick. It "appears to have been placed upright, possibly marking some celestial event" (Harl 2009:389). A crematory floor at Mulberry Creek, Alabama, was made with limestone slabs.

The heating properties of limestone have been offered as the reason for its use in ovens and, by extension, crematories. Limestone can contain fossils and slabs should be examined for them.

See *altar, burial—under limestone, fossil*

Lithic Workshop

The Tennessee River shell heaps of Little Bear Creek, Perry, and O'Neal share a stratigraphically early layer of dense Ft. Payne chert debris above which shell accumulation noticeably increases (Webb and DeJarnette 1948a:16, 19). These layers are referred to as lithic workshops. At Little Bear Creek Feature 4 was an area 14 ft (4.27 m) in diameter, 3–12 inches (7.62–30.48 cm) deep in percussion flakes. Near the center was a very large, round, pitted anvil stone.

Another workshop was found at the shell-free Pen Point Site, South Carolina, with Morrow Mountain/Allendale point affiliations. Feature 14 was a few square meters in size, with clusters of hammers and a "discrete deposit of over 25,000 flakes, scores of biface preform fragments, and 14 narrow stemmed points [appearing] completely undisturbed from the time they were left there long ago . . . over 200 finished products were made and transported away from this single event of flintknapping" (Sassaman 2006:39).

Another dense lithic workshop was found outside the Mount Taylor–aged shell heap of Lake Monroe Outlet (Scudder 2001). The Early Archaic James Farnsley site (12Hr520) in southern Indiana has several Kirk Corner Notched lithic workshops that yielded 2,200 points, 10,000 stone tools, and very high densities of debitage (Stafford and Cantin 2009:292).

Such intensive knapping and then abandonment of the flakes and debitage may have been part of a rite where both the by-products and the products were destined for offering such as in a fertility rite. In many California and New Mexico rites conducted for rain today (see Parkman 1992), stone concussing is used to mimic the sound of thunder and call the rain. During flintknapping both thunder (sound) and lightning (sparks) can be produced and would suggest a nighttime rite orchestrated by one or more rain or weather control specialists who would also be flintknappers.

See *flake/chip, flintknapping, projectile point, stone*

Little People

Many groups have accounts of the actions and whereabouts of the homes of forest-dwelling dwarfs. The Mistissini Cree think that the Memequash (Little People) once lived in Gitchi Manitou Ouitch-chouap, a quartz cave near the summit of La Colline Blanche. From there they paddled stone canoes, raiding fishing nets and painting boulders (Milne 1994:30). The Plains Cree say the Little People make flint arrowheads and live in sandy riverbanks and in the sandhills. They are courted by humans as spirit guides who can grant powers (Milne 1994:190). The Iroquois Dark Dance and feast, held at the beginning of the fall hunting season, was conducted by the Dwarf Society to propitiate animal spirits and the Little People, both of whom attended the festivities (Harper 1999:159). Little People, the tlaloque, were the helpers of Tlaloc, the rain god.

Did a dwarf burial at the base of an Archaic shell mound on the Tennessee River (Craig 1959) mean that Archaic people believed in the Little People? Living dwarfs were one manifestation of Little People kept by the Nahua kings. Mississippians left foot petroglyphs in the Ozarks invoking the Little People (Diaz-Granados and Duncan 2005). Miniature items (points, adzes, etc.) and animals found in Archaic settings may further indicate a belief in Little People.

See *feet/footprint/track, miniature, rain*

Locust

Locusts, grasshoppers, and cicadas are known to have been of significance to Archaic peoples in Arkansas, Louisiana, south Mississippi, and north Alabama based on the production of stone beads in their shape 7000 to 4000 B.P. (Crawford 2003). These beads are usually made of red jasper but occasionally black chert, crystal quartz, brown chert, or green stone was used. The beads vary greatly in size, general appearance, and execution (Webb 1971:113). Blitz (1993) says they are one of the earliest representational symbols in the eastern Woodlands. He believes that the distribution of stone locust beads parallels the distribution of the Archaic earthen mounds. The Denton site in Yazoo Basin of Mississippi (Connaway 1977) has the greatest number of these beads (n = 23).

For Webb (1971), the significance of these insects is found in their sound. It is not inconceivable that people caught and manipulated locusts and cicadas to induce their sound at a desired time. In Mexico, the rainy season is heralded by the din of locusts in May, and people still rely on their sound to predict the coming rain. The choice of stone as the raw material to create beads in the shape of this insect may suggest that the locust was from the first creation, one of the Stone People, as the Sioux believe.

See *Great Flood, insect, miniature, rain, sound, Stone People*

Mammoth/Mastodon

Mammoth and mastodon bone and ivory were worked when fresh by Paleoindians and collected from bone beds by much later peoples who knew these giants to have been creatures of a primordial era (Mayor 2005), even the first creation. Pilgrimages of Iroquois to Big Bone Lick have been recorded for the purpose of making medicine (Mayor 2005:29). The fact that so many of these bones are found in springs, sinkholes, marshes, bogs, and stream beds clearly situates them underwater, in the Underworld and long ago.

See *fossil, Great Flood, stone, Stone People*

Mask/Headdress

The earliest probable antler headdress in the Southeast was found at Anderson in central Tennessee in a cremation of Middle Archaic age with an unsexed adult. A skull piece with antlers, attached to the wearer with five holes, was found at Flint River, Alabama, in Late Archaic context (Webb 1948:Figure 33). At Reigh, Wisconsin, a central male in a quincunx had deer antlers. Wolf and bear cranium masks were tentatively identified in Ohio cemeteries, probably the seven animal masks in north-central Ohio referred to by Purtill (2009:589). Aten (1999:153) lists possible antler headgear from Bu51 at Harris Creek, Florida, and a probable dog rostrum mask was found in Tick Creek shell mound.

Cut animal rostra are found in SOV shell mounds and may be masks. Unusual among them are gar rostra included in two burials from Indian Knoll (Crothers 2005:309). Giles (2010:103–104) provides an accounting of Archaic masks/headdresses.

See *antler, deer, fish, hunt god rite*

Measurement

"The ancients had available, and actually used, simple devices for measuring and establishing mound orientations, sizes, and positions, such as measuring cords, wooden stakes, sight lines, measured paces, plumb-bobs, orientation posts, and so forth. . . . Middle and Late Archaic inhabitants of North and South America shared a common measurement system and logic" (Clark 2004:163).

John Clark has identified a Standard Unit (SU) of 1.66 m, the span from fingertip to fingertip when arms are outstretched and a multiple of that basic unit, the Standard Macro-Unit (SMU) of 86.63 m (2004:164). The SMU and other multiples of the SU were used as the distance between dirt mounds, and as legs of triangles used in site planning on the Gulf Coast at Caney Mounds, Louisiana; Watson Brake, Louisiana; Poverty Point, Louisiana; Cedarland, Mississippi; and Claiborne, Mississippi, in addition to sites on the southern shore of the Gulf of Mexico. Other archaeologists have found 3.34 m (2 x 1.66 m), 83 cm (1.66/3), and 43 m (86/2) (Clark 2004:191) to underlie site layouts and multiples of radii 3.6 km in length to explain the distribution of sites across a landscape (Sassaman and Heckenberger 2004).

See *astronomy, geometry, number*

Medicine

"Medicine" means "something like 'mystery' and 'power' and included not only the activities of curing with tonics from plants and minerals, but also the receipt of powers from the manitous for healing, hunting and battle. The most important step in the practice of medicine was communication between the practitioners and the manitous, for without their powers the medicine wouldn't work. The rock paintings tell of the Indians' [successful] struggles for the powerful medicine" (Rajnovich 1994:10–11).

Medicinal ingredients included minerals, powders, plants, animal parts, feathers, smoke, heat, and songs of gathering, mixing, and administering. Healers sometimes traveled great distances to obtain knowledge of these items as well as the ingredient itself (Rajnovich 1994:29n40). The best plant medicines were to be found in high altitudes (mountaintops) such as Grandfather Mountain in western North Carolina.

Bone doctors appear to have been present among Archaic peoples. "The high frequency of well aligned, well healed fractures indicate the people of Windover had some knowledge of treatment of injuries and provided care and attention to those sustaining skeletal fractures" (Smith 2003:ix).

See *feces*, *fossil*, *medicine bag*, *Newt Kash Shelter*, *ocher*, *paint/powder*, *ritual specialist/priest*

Medicine Bag

"The 'medicine-bag' then, is a mystery-bag, and its meaning and importance necessary to be understood, as it may be said to be the key to Indian life and Indian character. These bags are constructed of the skins of animals, of birds, or of reptiles, and ornamented and preserved in a thousand different ways" (Catlin quoted in Webb 1950:336). Catlin goes on to specify that these bags are sealed and seldom opened and that men of the Plains carried them, beginning as young teenagers to gather their elements. Catlin observed bags made from otter, beaver, muskrat, weasel, raccoon, polecat, snake, frog, toad, bat, mouse, mole, hawk, eagle, magpie, sparrow, and wolf. Like trophy body parts, if an enemy's medicine bag could be stolen, it, too, was a trophy. Medicine bags were buried in some cultures and the place regularly visited with devotions.

Webb offers several test implications for identifying medicine bags after they have decayed; these include rarity in burials, being found with men only, and being found with bones of the face and perhaps paws of large animals. He then identified eleven burials at Indian Knoll (including three infants) as having medicine bags based on animal rostra and foot bones (particularly mustelids and bobcat) found in association with the skeleton (Webb 1950:336–343). Four infants and young children also appear to have been the recipients of medicine bags at Carlston Annis (Webb 1950:340). Those medicine bags were made of or contained bones of bobcat, mink, dog, and marten. Atlatl parts and shell beads were often associated with the animal parts. The possible contents of a medicine bag from the Maritime Archaic culture is found in Bu35a of Locus 2 at Port au Choix-3. Found together were a banded gray quartzite side-notched point, quartz cobbles and pebbles, a calcite crystal, and the maxilla of a red fox (Tuck 1976:33). Fox and Molto's (1994b) review of historic medicine bags found that often no more than 25 percent of the included items were durables.

See *crystal, mask/headdress, medicine*

Menstrual Retreat

Rockshelter menstrual retreats seem to appear during the Late Archaic in the Ozarks and Cumberland Plateau (Claassen 2011a). The characteristics of rockshelter retreats in eastern Kentucky, such as Newt Kash Shelter, include the remains of shell spoons, copious nut debris, medicinal plants, fiber and fabric, mortar holes, and often rock markings. Historic records about menstruating women in the Southeast (Galloway 1997) specify that women were removed from the nexus of community life (possibly rockshelters), used special utensils (possibly shell spoons), and ate little meat.

What women did while retreating is not specified in the historic accounts. However, it seems that fiber gathering and preparation, grinding nuts, nut oil production, bathing, and marking rocks with fertility symbols were some of the activities in the Cumberland and in the Ozark plateaus (Claassen 2011a). Many shelters have associated boulder mortar holes. In southern Illinois "approximately half [of the bedrock mortar holes] are located within or adjacent to sandstone rock shelters, either on large breakaway boulders or relatively horizontal stone ledges within the shelter" (Carey, McCorvie, and Wagner 2010:1), and many of these seem to be Late Archaic or Terminal Archaic in age. "Coy et al. (1997:153) [have] noted that bedrock mortar hole sites almost always contain either animal track or human hand or foot motifs. In his study of mortar hole sites in central Kentucky, White (1980) reports that at half of the sites where hominy holes and petroglyphs were found together, they were located on the same rock face and did not intrude upon one another, suggesting that the two creations belonged together and dated to approximately the same time period" (Carey, McCorvie, and Wagner 2010:9). Ison (2004) believed that the evidence indicated that women who used the mortars also made the rock markings. Rock markings form two clusters in Kentucky, in the Appalachian region, and in the Green River valley and are probably fertility symbols.

It is curious that caches of domesticated seeds have been found in several of these shelters, as though women's food and medicine needs are the impetus behind their presence. There is also indication that at least at Newt Kash Shelter a medicine society may have met inside (a quincunx of pits, a two-stone altar and infant sacrifice, a set of small postholes [sweat hut?], and rock fall seating arranged at the drip line) that employed eagle symbolism (abundant nests in rock face above shelter).

In addition to rockshelters, women may have built freestanding structures for menstrual and birthing purposes. Harl (2009:392) offers the menstrual hut as a function for a small (two-meter diameter) posthole pattern to the east of houses and separated from the other buildings by a row of posts at 23Sl619, a Labras Lake phase site. "This structure had a conical pit near its center, which contained various lenses of burned soil and charcoal. Ash was scattered around the top of this pit suggesting that it had been repeatedly cleaned out." Menstrual function was considered by Smith (1976) for keyhole structures in Pennsylvania but rejected in favor of sweat lodges.

Since menstrual retreating seems to reflect matrilineal social organization (Galloway 1997:50–51), the appearance during the Late Archaic of rockshelter retreats suggests that matrilineal societies (1) had just developed the concept of retreating, (2) had just begun to associate menstruation and rock crevices, or (3) had moved into these hilly areas at this time after using some other kind of space for retreating in their prior homeland.

See *bedrock mortar/nutting stone, feet/footprint/track, Newt Kash Shelter, rockshelter, shell*

Mica

Mica was extensively used in the Rattler's Bight period (Fitzhugh 2006). Speaking of Maritime Archaic burials, Tuck said, "Biotite mica, found in varying quantities in four burials[,] may have also served a magical as well as decorative purpose" (Tuck 1976:72). The majority of that mica was found in one burial. Mica beads were found in a rockshelter in western Pennsylvania.

Menomini and Delaware believed mica chips were the scales of the Horned Serpent and other horned hairy snakes and kept chips in medicine bags. When they wished for rain, the Delaware exposed these "scales" and "rain medicine," believing the simple sight of mica would incite the thunderbeings to call up thunderclouds (Harper 1999:36). Mica and lead were both considered to be excrement of the moon in Mexican cultures (Read 1998:136).

See *copper, medicine bag, rain, snake*

Milky Way

If one accepts that white gastropods could be conceptualized as the white stars in the night sky when the Underworld rotated into the upper position nightly, as do the Winnebago (Richard Dieterle, www.hotcakencyclopedia

.com/ho.JourneyToSpiritland.html, accessed April 14, 2010; Radin 1970), then one could perhaps accept the idea that a large cluster of white gastropod shells could evoke the image of the night sky, and specifically the Milky Way band. Here I refer to the shell bead belts, or rebosos, constituted of 200 to 700 *Busycon* or *Leptoxis* beads that made up the burial accoutrements of several Archaic bodies.

Gastropod shell belts were found in a Middle Archaic ritual burial at Elizabeth. Most other belts occurred in later contexts and are found only in the SOV. Six subadults in Indian Knoll were wrapped in shell bead rebosos (Webb 1974:Figure 21b, c, d, f) and 10 adults, including three women, wore Milky Way belts to their graves. At Barrett, a woman and a subadult double burial had between them 4,700 disc shell beads and 504 *Leptoxis* beads "at the pelvis" as well as other grave goods, and both bodies were interred in abnormal positions. Two other children and one adolescent at Barret had 200+ shell beads "arranged as though sewed on a garment" at the pelvis (Webb and Haag 1947:17). People so dressed appear to have been sacrificed.

The Aztec god of the Milky Way was Mixcoatl (Figure 19) with an avatar, Camaxtli, god of the hunt. The Milky Way is indicated on his head, running under the antlers and from forehead to raised arm. The Aztecs also believed Mixcoatl was the inventor of the fire drill and the first heating stone, thus associating hunt, fire, drill, flintknapping, and Milky Way. Mixcoatl slew deer but also had five male deer and five female deer helpers and was celebrated with reference to the cardinal directions.

Another probable Archaic referent to the Milky Way comes from the burial of dogs at the feet of some humans and at the borders of some burial grounds (e.g., Read, Carlston Annis). The Cherokee believed the dog created the Milky Way by spilling corn meal and lead the dead—particularly priests—across this starry road and then over the Great Rift of the Milky Way to the land of the dead (Hall 1997; James 2006).

See *astronomy, constellation, dog, hunt god rite, gastropod, Leptoxis/Anculosa, moon, shell bead*

Miniature

Gartner (1996:142) reported that "As the plan view of the [Pawnee] earth lodge becomes smaller in scale the concepts represented become more divine." This increase in divinity is related to the concept of perspective: the farther away something is, the smaller it is. This relationship holds for time as well as for space. For this reason, small and infant animals were appropriate offerings including dwarfs and insects for they reminded one of the long ago and the first creation. They were also the scale of the Little People, helpers to various deities and symbolic of new life, fertility. In North America, miniatures were also associated with witchcraft, possibly again referring the viewer to the ancient spirits.

Small size is also equated with long-ago time in Mesoamerica (Pohl 1983), as well as with Little People, helpers of the gods, particularly Tlaloc, the rain god. Small size, as the state of being for these ancient spirits, was recognized with offerings of miniature lithics, infant animals (humans included), or small animals, the "comensuals" of zooarchaeologists, including songbirds (Claassen 2012c).

With this perspective (that miniatures constituted offerings to spirits), several accounts of miniature artifacts should be noted. For instance, miniature barbed harpoons, barbed bone points, chipped-stone points, square celts (e.g., 7 cm), and small Clear Fork gouges are "strongly associated" with the Titterington/Sedalia phase in the American Bottom and are sometimes made with hematite (McElrath et al. 2009:346). Miniature hematite celts in southeastern Ohio began in the Archaic and continued into Woodland times (Purtill 2009:574).

A miniature marine shell celt and adze/gouge were associated with Bu125 in Harris Creek, Florida (Aten 1999:153, Table 5). "The celt is 66 mm long by about 20 mm in diameter. The more pointed end has a bit angle of approximately 68°. . . . This adze/gouge is only about 70% of the length/width of the full-size tools. . . . and the bit angle is about 65°" (Aten 1999:161).

Ellis (1994) argues that the six miniature points and single miniature scraper found at the early Paleoindian Parkhill, Ontario, site were ideotechnic in use. A miniature fluted point was among points found at the Crowfield Site in Ontario.

"On the Chickahominy River in Virginia, there's a site that has produced on the order of 20 of these 'shrunk in the dryer' projectile points, Morrow Mountain and Savannah River types, all made of exotic materials, basically made of some form of what appears to be heat-treated jasper. . . . they're perfect tiny representations of the real thing. . . . these little things are on the order of 1.5" [3.8 cm] long, but perfectly proportioned. I've looked at literally tens of thousands of projectile points across VA and have only seen them [in quantity] from this site, although I seem to remember 1's or 2's from other sites in VA" (Arch-L post by Lyle Browning, RPA, November 8, 2011).

See *Little People, projectile point, witch*

Monument

Monuments are "structures that are grand or large in *scale* and/or in *quality*" (Thompson and Andrus 2011:319), expressing equally grand sentiment. Monumental scale was achieved during the Late Archaic as seen in the shellworks of the southern Gulf Coast of Florida, in the mounds and arcs at Poverty Point, and in a number of the shell mounds on the Tennessee and Green rivers. Two Archaic mounds are larger than all mounds known in the United States except for Monks Mound at Cahokia: Middle Archaic Mound A at Horr's Island, Florida, and Late Archaic Mound A at Poverty Point. Fig Island Mound 1 is also quite large. Using the formula cubic meters of a mound/1,000, monumentality was calculated for numerous shell mounds and dirt mounds of the Archaic and later periods (Blitz and Livingood 2004; Claassen 2010:89). The results indicated that a number of Archaic mounds are larger than many Hopewell and Mississippian mounds (Claassen 2010:89).

Cemeteries and shell rings have also been called "monuments." Certainly the idea that cemeteries collect and make visible the ancestors and mark off traditional lands reifies their roles as monuments even when their size does not. Shell rings, with no burials, are monuments not to the dead but to the living and the grand feasts held at them.

See *mound, Poverty Point, shellworks*

Moon

Lunar alignments and lunar cycle counters are proposed for post-Archaic sites but rarely suggested for Archaic sites other than those in the Poverty Point culture. "[W]e might reasonably expect to find lunar, planetary, or even stellar counts in some of these [Archaic] mound arrangements or in mound dimensions" (Clark 2004:201). Lunar import to Poverty Point and other Archaic mound centers has been suggested by Clark, given his discovery of distances in plazas and between mounds amounting to 260 standard units (Clark 2004:201). The 260-day calendar was a key element in the lives and rituals of later Mesoamerican cultures, a number that probably corresponds to the human gestation period.

The Cincinnati Tablet of Hopewell age has been interpreted as an owl image with a count of 13 lunar months (Romain 1991), giving us additional reason to suspect that Archaic peoples also divided time into 13 lunar months. The historic Winnebago used a calendar stick with two lunar years marked into 12 months of 28–32 nights (Marshack 1985) and three moon phases. According to McCluskey's report (1977), rituals were timed by counting days from a solar observation (marked on the Winnebago stick with a dot) to the next lunar phase, a full or crescent moon. The Winnebago and the Hopi add an extra month every three years to bring this lunar year into alignment with the solar year, as did the Olmec 3,000 years earlier (Marshack 1985:42).

Lunar reference during the Archaic was probably conveyed through things feminine, as well as with rabbits (a fertility symbol and image seen in the moon), nocturnal animals, and things of crescent shape. Nagy (1994:27) says that for the Cheyenne, the light of the moon provided safety and pushed away death and darkness so that things crescent shaped such as claws, bison horns, cloven hooves, and hoofprints provided protection to the bearer, particularly against violent death. Menstrual retreating was certainly reckoned through moon phases, and travel distances may have been calculated as the number of moons or nights passed during travel.

See *feet/footprint/track*, *measurement*, *number*, *owl*, *ritual calendar*, *sandal/slipper*

Mortuary Camp

Williams mortuary and its associated Sidecut crematory site, on opposite sides of the Maumee River, and the Gould site near Port au Choix (Renouf and Bell 2011) are two mortuary camps that have been verified. Encampments located near and even beside burial grounds for preparing the dead and for mourners have been identified in numerous cases and suspected in rockshelters and sinkholes in central and northern Ohio (Purtill 2009:590). Perhaps bluff-top sites such as Jackson Bluff and Jimtown Hill on the Green River were mortuary camps (Claassen 2010:139).

Mortuary Offering Index

This index was created by Peter Pagoulatos (2009) with categories of grave goods germane to the northeastern United States. The 25 major artifact classes included abrading stones, adzes, amulets, axes, bannerstones, blades, celts, choppers, cores, drills, gouges, graphite, hammerstones, hematite, knives, pendants, plummets, preforms, projectile points, red ocher, scrapers, sharpening stones, steatite containers, strike-a-lights, and whetstones. "The MOI is calculated by adding up the total number of different artifact classes from a particular site (mortuary) assemblage and dividing this sum total by the total number of categories (25) . . . the MOI ranges from 0 to 1" (Pagoulatos 2009:233).

See *Feature Diversity Index*, *grave good*

Mound

One of the most striking developments in the ritualizing of the Middle Archaic is the move to build mounds, many actually quite low to the ground but broad at the base and others quite tall. "Mound building as a monumental practice is a substantial change from practices of earlier times. Mounds are not only an indication of the capacity to move dirt or to mobilize labor but they are also a social and conceptual statement by the builders that they are capable of re-creating the landscape to suit their needs and to fulfill their vision of how the physical and symbolic world should be constructed" (Kidder and Sassaman 2009:675).

Mounds of shell and sand were associated with shell rings in some sites (Horr's Island, Fig Island), built of dirt in the lower Mississippi valley, constructed of dirt in Missouri and Illinois on ridge tops, and constructed in the SOV and St. Johns River of dirt and shells gradually through feasts held during large public rituals. Some mounds included burials (St. Johns, SOV), some mounds were built for burial (Illinois), and some mounds had no apparent relation to mortuary programs (lower Mississippi valley, Atlantic coast). Sassaman offers that mounding by Mount Taylor peoples (St. Johns) was the logical inversion of pond burial (2010a:77). Several of these mounds have a size that qualifies them as monuments by anyone's definition, and all of them were monuments in that they memorialized events. Both flat-topped and conical mounds appear at Poverty Point, and both mound shapes were achieved during the history of its Mound B (Kidder, Ortmann, and Allen 2004:111).

"Throughout their history, very distinct cycles of use and construction have been identified that can be likened to that of death, burial, and renewal" (Brown 1997:475). At Watson Brake, Monte Sano, Frenchman's Bend, and probably Nolan as well as many northeastern Florida sites, mound stages were erected over occupation surfaces or, as at Frenchman's Bend and Monte Sano, over buildings. The mounds were then capped (Kidder and Sassaman 2009:675). "The activity of building mounds and the symbolic significance of the materials selected were of great importance" (Van Nest et al. 2001). Some scholars have argued that feasting was the prime time to mobilize the labor needed to enlarge mounds (e.g., Giles 2010:160; Saunders 2004).

Southeastern peoples associated mounds with "the underworld, birth, fertility, death, burial, the placation of spirits, emergence, purification, and supernatural protection" (Knight 1989:425), as well as "cosmic navels, 'earth mothers,' and/or places where various 'persons' were reincarnated. This suggests that mounds operated as part of a sacrificial economy through which the dead were both distanced and purified, while allowing important names, prerogatives, and positions to be recycled through mourning/adoption rituals" (Giles 2010:199).

Muskogeans understood mounds to be earth mothers (Knight 1989; Swanton 1931:37). This concept is essentially that of Mesoamerican peoples who understood mountains and their replicas to be sustenance mountains, providers of all that humans needed, and houses near people for earth spirits (e.g., Bassie-Sweet 1996). Knight (1989) relates that even the dirt used to build the mound was often considered sacred particularly if it came from plazas where ceremonies had infused the earth with power, a belief that Gibson (2000) is comfortable extending to the beginning of mound building in the Middle Archaic. Regardless of their meaning, their distance from one another within at least the Poverty Point culture was formulaic (Sassaman and Heckenberger 2004).

See *measurement, monument, mound—boulder, mound—dirt, mound—sand, mound—shell*

Mound—Boulder

Boulder mounds are found in the Labrador Maritime Archaic as early as 8000 B.P. The mounds usually cover a pit, at the bottom of which was placed a body or bone bundle, red ocher and artifacts with more red ocher, more boulders, and other grave goods in the fill (Fitzhugh 2006:57–62). Given that these pits rarely contain bone, neither the social aspects of human society nor the symbolic aspects of fauna in the decision to use a boulder mound are known. Boulder mounds appear to have been reserved for the burial of people with community-wide importance. They typically occur in groups of two or as isolated mounds.

The L'Anse Amour boulder mound covered an adolescent and several grave goods such as "square-based lanceolate points, a single-spurred toggling harpoon, and crescent-shaped toggle handle" and returned a date of 7500 B.P. (Fitzhugh 2006:57). Other equally old boulder mounds are Brador and Ballybrack. Boulder mounds continued to be built on rare occasions until the close of the Maritime Archaic at 3500 B.P.

See *burial—under limestone, mound, Ballybrack Mound*

Mound—Dirt

Archaic dirt burial mounds are present on knolls along ridgelines in Illinois, along the Pomme de Terre River in Missouri, and along the Ohio in eastern Iowa. Dirt mounds lacking burials were built earlier in the lower Mississippi valley. "Excavations in the lower Illinois Valley have indicated that many Archaic and Late Woodland cemeteries were placed in naturally occurring knolls without the addition of substantial amounts of soil to the ridge. It is the bulbous nature of the cemetery and its blufftop location, rather than the artificial accumulation of earth, that seem to be the important variables" (Charles, Buikstra, and Leigh 1988:19).

Dirt mounds in Missouri and the adjacent LIV began in the late Middle Archaic Helton phase (6000 to 5000 B.P.). Hobart Bridge Mound, Missouri, was built after the placement of a bone bundle and a cache of 25 Afton points. The Hemphill site (Illinois) burials are described as "primary burials placed on surface, covered with earth and limestone slabs; on bluff; possibly 2 mounds" (Charles and Buikstra 1983:127). The later Titterington phase Etley site was "two 'mounds' on the bluff crest, 8 or 9 groups of 3–6 burials; primary interments" (Charles and Buikstra 1983:128). The single Archaic mound at Elizabeth was comprised of burial pits dug into a knoll that were covered with redeposited dirt to a depth of 40 cm. This small mound, 10 ft x 8 ft (3.05 m x 2.45 m) in size, is typical of earthworks in this area—under 1.5 m in height and built up with dirt and limestone.

See *capping*, *cemetery*, *earthwork*, *mound*

Mound—Sand

Sand mounding and exotics appear simultaneously late in the Mount Taylor culture on the St. Johns River of Florida. The three earliest sand mound mortuaries—Bluffton Burial Mound, Silver Glenn Spring, and Thornhill Lake—date between 5,900 and 5,300 ya (Randall and Tucker 2012:223). Mounding seems to be the outcome of earlier use of sand to cap burials in shell mortuary mounds like Harris Creek.

See *capping*, *earthwork*, *mound*

Mound—Shell

Radiocarbon dates from the SOV freshwater shell mounds indicate that they grew in size over hundreds of years (see date ranges in Claassen 2010:Table 2.1). The gradual accumulation of shells occurred during regional feasts associated with mortuary activities and perhaps with additional mounding efforts at the time of the gathering. It is possible that there was also at work an idea of creating an earth island using a different Underworld substance, shell.

Horr's Island, Florida, has one of the oldest and biggest shell mounds, Mound A, composed of sand and marine shell, with only incidental burial. Harris Island, Florida, is another of the early shell platforms that grew into a sizable mound but with significant burial activity. Freshwater shell accumulations started in the SOV at Anderson, Eva, Mulberry Creek, Ward, and Hermitage Springs in Middle Archaic times and quickly ended at Anderson in the Middle Archaic (Claassen 2010:45).

See *gastropod*, *mound*, *naiad*, *shell*, *shellworks*

Mountain

It is from the Cherokee and the Nahuas of the Rio Balsas valley in Guerrero, Mexico (Goode Eschelman 1996), that we get a good idea of the significance of high places. The Nahuas say that in the beginning the earth was a flat island, but with the actions of various deities the land became sculpted. The oldest earth and deities are to be found at the top of mountains and at the bottom of valleys and sinkholes. An echo of this idea is found in the Cherokee story of the eagle that tired as it flew over the new, flat, muddy earth such that its wings dipped low and cut the Appalachian Mountains and valleys (Mooney 1900).

At least three other stories support the idea that the deities and first people did important things on the top of mountains. An unnamed Iroquois or Wyandot chief related a story in 1766 about five creations. "After the third creation, . . . the Great Spirit put up two Great Buffalo in a mountain near Big Bone Lick, Kentucky, to have at the ready should the need arise" (Mayor 2005:24). In a Shawnee version, a single wounded bull ascended the mountain source of the Monongahela River (Mayor 2005:65). The last of a race of giant bears that ate humans was killed on a mountaintop along the Hudson River (Mayor 2005:36). "Stories from Saskatchewan, Manitoba and Ontario speak of a mountain as the home of the powerful Medicine Manitou. . . . Inside the mountain were all the medicines derived from minerals" (Rajnovich 1994:65).

Today when the Eastern Band Cherokee initiate someone, the initiates and the ritual leader ascend a mountain in the Asheville area, referred to as "going up the mountain." Mounds and sacred mountains were conceptually conflated by the Cherokee (Knight 1989:424). Plants collected from mountains were said to have the greatest efficacy (Todd 2010:83–84), and elevations above 2,500 ft (762 m) also have the most recorded marked rocks in South Carolina (Charles 2010:13).

Modern rural Mexicans and Nahuas of central Mexico still make annual pilgrimages to (modest) mountaintops each May 1–17 (Figure 25). While they venerate the highest volcanic peaks as well, they rarely visit the shrines on them but rather select much closer mountains to their home with views of the volcanoes. This lower mountain, more easily climbed and closer to the tribute community, could be viewed as an "altar" mountain (see Scully 1989 for this concept among Puebloans). Broda (1998:79) believes that mountain veneration and the rain-calling rites and shrines on them are concepts more than 3,000 years old in Mexico.

Wilkins summarized the location of mountain sites in West Virginia as

25. Rain-calling shrine on the peak of Mishuehue Mountain (center), near San Agustin Oapan, Guerrero, Mexico, May 2011. (Photo by author.)

"on tops of isolated knobs, flat portions of level ridgelines, bearwallows, and saddles. The pattern is diverse rather than concentrated around any one particular topographic locality" (1978:36). Griffin and Reeves (1968) may have identified a mountain shrine at Peaks of Otter, Virginia. High mountain peaks that we might assume were venerated in the Archaic would be among those that were so viewed in historic times, such as Mount Katahdin, Maine; Mount Monadnock, New Hampshire; Spruce Mountain, West Virginia; Grandfather Mountain, North Carolina; and Stone Mountain, Georgia. Mount Logan overlooks the Scioto River, which, with its abundance of raptoral birds, is a likely Archaic mountain of importance.

See *altar, cairn, cliff, hawk, shrine*

Mummy

While no "mummies" in the sense of a chemically prepared body have been found in the eastern United States, Archaic age has been attributed to several dried bodies found in caves. Given the high probability that caves were used in rituals and were themselves recognized as spirit-filled places and portals to the Underworld, it is possible that some of these "mummified" or desiccated bodies were cave ritual specialists or oracles.

"Lost John" with mining equipment was found partially crushed under a boulder in Mammoth Cave. He was possibly a ritual specialist at work in the bowels of the cave at the time of the accident (Watson 1969:67). "Little Al" of Salts Cave appears to be a nine-year-old boy with missing left humerus, left hand, and both feet (typical trophy parts). It is possible that he was killed while serving as an apprentice to a cave ritual specialist or that he was sacrificed for a ritual that was conducted in the cave, probably during the Early Woodland.

From Short Cave, located south of Mammoth Cave, came four desiccated bodies including an infant, an adolescent male, the female "Fawn Hoof," and another female (Watson 1969:67), a possible four-age rite collection. Fawn Hoof was found sitting in a stone-lined and roofed chamber, probably indicating a post-Archaic age. Her sitting posture and placement in a prepared "tomb" suggest an oracle. The male, named "Scudder's Mummy," may have been sitting or lying flexed on the left side when found. This boy was wrapped in deerskin and had a fractured occipital bone (Robbins 1974:145).

See *ancestor, burial—posture, oracle, ritual specialist/priest*

Music

Music was a framing device for Archaic ideology. It is both a cultural resource and a cultural product that is useful in spreading ideology. It can create a sense of self and of collectivity through rhythms, lyrics, and group participation. Music is memorized and reviewed, and used in subsequent rituals, creating a sense of group and history among those who know the words and tune. Songs were also probably important gifts of visions and in some cases would have been at the core of new cults (Irwin 1994).

Archaic ways of making music included the human voice, rattles, flutes, panpipes, and rasps and may have included drums with stretched hide, water drums, hitting stalactites inside caves, and plucking stretched gut. Evoking thunder through sound for rain-calling rites was probably achieved by striking bedrock mortars, drumming, exploding rocks, and stimulating captive cicadas.

The best data on actual instruments are available for rattles and flutes. Winters (1969:70–74) examined stylistic and musical differences among flutes from Late Archaic locations of Lamoka, Frontenac, Barrett, Carlston Annis, Read, Indian Knoll, and Robinson Hills, eight or more from Riverton, and from Oakview Landing, Cherry, and Kay's Landing on the Tennessee River in Tennessee. Three whistles made of goose ulnae and four flutes also made with large bird bones (one swan radius, two swan ulnae, one eagle ulna) were recovered in Port au Choix-3 burials. Winters suggested that flutes appeared in the midcontinent between 3000 and 2000 B.C.

"The songs were absolutely necessary because they gave the medicine its power to act: music was the link to the spirit world, so the songs, drums, rattles and tinkling cones of the medicine men and women were sacred items, considered animate in the Ojibway language and treated with the utmost respect" (Rajnovich 1994:23).

See *dream/vision, crane, rain, rattle, sound*

Naiad

Naiads, freshwater mollusks, appear in ritual contexts in Paleoindian pits in Dust Cave and in several Middle Archaic contexts: a woman's burial on the Savannah River, individual valves in numerous graves on the Ohio in Indiana, in shell heaps in riverside burial sites in Florida and Tennessee, and in bluff-top shell-bearing sites in Kentucky. It is interesting that burials occurred only in freshwater shell heaps, not in marine shell heaps, implying that marine shells and naiads had different symbolic roles during the Archaic. Naiads seem to have the symbolism of death, renewal, and west, given that most shell mounds are on westward-flowing river segments (Claassen 2010).

The inclusion of naiad valves in graves appears to have been part of the mortuary practice of people utilizing burial grounds along the Ohio River and its tributaries. Most of the graves at Meyer, Indiana, had at least one valve included as did a number of graves at Black Earth. Both of these burial grounds had a shell-free matrix. Anne Bader (2010/11) believes that these valves were used to dig the grave, a conclusion supported by the semantic equivalence of grave, womb, cave, container, and shell among Pacific coast groups and in Mexico (Claassen 2008).

See *Cult of the Bivalve Feast, gastropod, shell, shell scoop/spoon*

North—see Cardinal Direction

Number

Clark (2004:197) argues for a base 20 numerical system underlying Poverty Point and a Standard Unit (SU) of 1.66 m when laying out all early mound sites based on the fingers of the human hand. Multiplying the SU by 4, 13, 20, and 52, one often finds multiples/distances of 364, 360, 260, 52, 28, 13, 7, 5, and 4 SMU when positioning mounds, all numbers important in later North American thought and Mesoamerican calendrics, strongly suggesting that Archaic numerology served astronomical purposes. "With an SU of 3.333 m [2 x 1.66 m], central Poverty Point is 364 units long and 260 units wide . . . these same measured intervals are basic to the structure of both Caney Mounds and Watson Brake. These are calendar counts and sacred numbers in Mesoamerica. . . . Distance as number, and number as ritual count, provide some insight into the significance of early Southeast architecture and enclosed spaces" (Clark 2004:199–200).

In a related discussion, Clark points out that Mesoamericanists have been stumped by the start of the Mayan long count at August 13, 3114 B.C., well before the start of monumental architecture in Mesoamerica (Clark 2004: 210n2). Instead, this date could be marking an event that occurred in the northern Gulf Coastal Plain, when dirt mound building began.

The base 20 system is again suggested by the numbers 260 and 360 and the post-Archaic Hopewell tablet with 13 tally marks that Romain (1991) argues is a lunar tally. The 260-day calendar in Mexican cultures was divided into 13 months of 20 days and the 360-day calendar into 13 months of 28 days, the last 5 days removed from the count. There are, of course, numerous blade caches that reference the various important numbers as well as blade caches that use prime numbers of blades.

Given the evidence for the 20-day month during the Archaic, it is possible also that during the Archaic every fifth number was associated with a direction as it was in later times in Mexico. If so, east would be related to the numbers 1, 5, 9, 13, and 17; north with 2, 6, 10, 14, and 18; west with 3, 7, 11, 15, and 19; and south with 4, 8, 12, 16, and 20. Just as the SU was doubled, tripled, and so forth, it is possible that these numbers could continue, such that 41, for instance, would fall in the east set. One application of such a numerology might have been head orientation of burials.

Modern Lakota numerology is based on the concept of "four by four" that dictates the number of stones in stacked stone features including offering sites. This four by four concept results in the employment of numbers of items or paces through space in the quantities 4, 7, 16, 32, 8, 14, 32, and 64 and their multiplication by 1 or 2 (LeBeau 2009). LeBeau instructs archaeologists to count the number of stones in stone features or the number of paces between features to see if they represent these special numbers.

The number 4 is found to be important in the Archaic as well. The four-age rite reifies this number and is documented in a later entry. Four projectile points with a skeleton suggest that ritual killings like the historic Morning Star sacrifice occurred in the Archaic with assailants attacking from the four cardinal directions.

Giles (2010) has addressed the role of mnemonic devices in numerical systems and in memory making and the need for archaeologists to consider these devices. Perhaps Archaic people used khipu-like knotted cords, carved sticks, and numerous other devices, which may also have employed color in their message. Clark (2004) posits that standardized lengths of rope were used to lay out Poverty Point mounds, arcs, and even sites.

See *astronomy, cardinal direction, four-age rite, hunt god rite, measurement, Poverty Point, sacrifice—adult*

Nut

Nuts were not only for eating. Their shells and hulls produce yellow, orange, and brown dyes. Walnut husks produce the darkest brown of the nuts; hickory and pecan husks produce lighter shades (http://www.practicalprimitive.com/skillofthemonth/blackwalnutdye.html, accessed February 1, 2010). Butternut husks can yield brown and orange colors. Nut shells will also produce dyes. Rinsing in lye (ash) is often called for to create other colors. The nuts, other plant parts, and lye call up images of the "ash caves" of eastern Kentucky (Funkhouser and Webb 1929) and Newt Kash Shelter.

Nut meats can also be boiled for oil. Nut oils were most frequently used in historic times for hair and body (Battle 1922). Women oiled their bodies and hair when bathing at the completion of seclusion periods and after a healing session. Newborns were also oiled. It is probable that when a high-cost nut such as a walnut is more ubiquitous or found in greater quantities than a low-cost nut that dye or oil was the motivation behind their use. Nuts are commonly associated with baked-clay surfaces, which may have been parching surfaces usually found in caves (Sherwood and Chapman 2005:71). For instance, ritual pits contained nuts at Millbury III, Massachusetts. Nut shells and meats have been found in gut areas and loose in burials (e.g., some Wapanucket No. 8, Massachusetts, burials), suggesting an unsuccessful Archaic cure, last meal, or food for the soul placed in the mouth of the corpse or beside the body.

See *color, menstrual retreat, textile/weaving, tree*

Obsidian

Two pieces of western U.S. obsidian have been found in probable Late Archaic sites in Tennessee (Norton 2008). One flake from a Big Sandy River site was sourced to southwest Nevada. A point from a site on the Harpeth River, sourced to Napa Valley, California, was "nearly identical to the Excelsior type that dates from around 2000 B.C. to approximately A.D. 50 [giving] support for the [idea of] trade of completed projectile points from California" (Norton 2008:125). Black points and translucent flakes were desired for their color and crystal-like properties.

See *color*, *crystal*

Occipital Deformation

This characteristic is generally assumed to indicate high social status among later people but may signal something else when it occurs on an Archaic individual. Two people in one group burial—a possible four-age rite—at Turner Farm in Maine had occipital flattening as did a third burial at that site (Bourque 1995). Two individuals at Parrish Village, Kentucky, had "occipital deformation" (Webb 1951). The same was reported from Indian Knoll (Webb 1974). Several individuals at Berryhill, Ohio, had cranial deformation (Purtill 2009:589). All cases of this flattening seem to have been Late Archaic in age.

See *skull*

Ocher

Ocher (the spelling adopted here when the colorant is meant) is a clay that is colored by 20 to 70 percent hematite and was typically ground to produce powder. A number of fossil bone beds in North America are associated with natural ocher deposits, such as those of Missouri (Mayor 2005:216). Ochre was quarried in numerous places including southeastern Ohio in the Unglaciated Plateau (Purtill 2009:574), in north-central North Carolina hills (Lederer [1672] 1958), and in Ontario. A red ocher mine was found in northeastern Ontario "where Indians carved the mineral out of a deep cave in a cliff face and climbed to the mountain top to cut it into useable chunks" (Rajnovich 1994:11). The red or yellow color is enhanced when the powder is mixed with grease or oil or when heated.

The association of natural hematite with Stone People (fossils) may explain the ritual importance of ocher. There are few Paleoindian examples of the use of red ocher in eastern North America, but there was an explosion in the use of hematite in worked and unworked pieces during the Early Archaic. Rose Island in eastern Tennessee had 3,792 pieces of unmodified hematite and 152 worked pieces (with sources within a 24-square-mile area of the site), but only 2 pieces, both modified, were recovered in Late Archaic contexts there (Chapman 1975:55, 156). Hematite was abundant in other Early Archaic Bifurcate assemblages in the Little Tennessee River valley and at St. Albans in West Virginia. "Of the early sites in North America, Rose Island and the St. Albans site appear to stand out with their large samples of ferromagnesian minerals" (Chapman 1975:157). Campbell Hollow (Illinois) Early Archaic levels had 2.28 g/m^3 of ocher (Odell 1985:41). Red ocher was used in the LeCroy horizon at Ward's Point on Staten Island (Chapman 1975:156).

Ocher nodule processing stations have been found in cave sites such as Graham Cave and Rodgers Shelter (Missouri) and Krill Cave (Ohio). Its prevalence in burials of the Maritime Archaic of the Far North was encapsulated in a prior name of Red Paint People. In the cremation cemeteries of eastern Massachusetts, the use of red ocher seems to have increased through time. "The normal position for red ocher when it is present is below the black fill, directly on the subsoil floor of the pit. . . . several sources of red ocher contributed to the various graves" (Dincauze 1968:65).

Ocher in sites is found as hematite lumps, as faceted crayons, and as a powder in shell or turtle cups. Ocher may have been used in hide processing, either as a dye or as a more active ingredient in the tanning process (Anderson and Hanson 1988; Odell 1985). There are historic examples of the use of ocher as medicine (Rajnovich 1994:85). One aspect of medicine was a sun association, particularly for warriors. Individuals covered in ocher powder may have been sacrificed to the sun or to the stars or died in ways that implicated a sun rite (Irwin 1994:216). The use of ocher on bodies contained in hunt god rites further indicates that it is associated with people buried as part of specific rites.

See *color, cosmology, hematite, paint/powder, sacrifice—adult, sacrifice—infant and child*

Offering

Offerings are items used by humans to lure deity or spirit from their homes and to petition for future blessings. They are also used to strike a bargain between humans and spirit and for thanksgiving. Smells, tastes, sounds, fire, and prayers are among the intangible offerings used (Figure 16, 18), while tangibles include meat, whole small animals, fruits, flowers, blood, footwear, minerals, and stones (Figures 7, 10, 18, 22, 26, 27). Sacred bundles filled with offerings are carried to each rain-calling location visited by today's pilgrims from San Andres de la Cal, Morelos, Mexico (Figure 27). Offerings for the rain spirit are placed on altars in all Guerrero rain-calling rites (Figure 17) and hung in trees at Acatlan, Guerrero, so that the vulture messenger can transport the offering to the deity.

26. Man carrying an offering of turkey and tamales to be placed on an altar at the Acatlan rain-calling, Guerrero, Mexico, May 1, 2012. (Photo by author.)

Offerings have been suggested as the source of the variety of stone types found at Poverty Point (Carr and Stewart 2004) and of various items found in SOV shell mound matrix and burials (Claassen 2010). The great number of projectile points and flakes found at some sites seem to have been left as offerings, as do many of the caches and inclusions of ocher. Ritchie (1932) concurs with this interpretation. Certainly on some occasions exotics came to be deposited in the archaeological record as offerings carried by pilgrims and left at pilgrimage centers/shrines including burial grounds. These materials could have been fetched, traded for, or procured from locals near the shrine at the time of visitation.

Offerings that were comprised of spent, broken, or burned tools, flakes, and even plaza sweepings might seem incongruous with things spiritual, but as Irwin (1994) tells us, humans envisioned deities and spirits to live lives like those of humans. They had families, including errant children, they needed to eat, they liked music and color and other things that humans liked, they had homes, and so forth. And while the deities gave many useful and delight-

27. Sacred bundles being cleansed before they are carried to springs and caves of San Andres de la Cal, Morelos, Mexico, May 17, 2013. (Photo by author.)

ful things to humans for their use, they needed humans to return them if they themselves were to enjoy them and, more important, to measure the extent of human gratitude. Complete offerings were made but were unnecessary, however, and faunal offerings often employed only a segment of an animal (and probably some of its blood).

See *cache*, *cache—blade*, *cache—groundstone*, *flake/chip*, *grave good*, *miniature*, *mortuary offering index*, *point reuse*, *projectile point*, *sacrifice—adult*, *sacrifice—animal*, *sacrifice—infant and child*

Olivella sp.

Olivella, a marine snail, first appears in Early Archaic context in a double burial at Horn Shelter, Texas, and shortly thereafter in a four-age rite at Jerger, Indiana (Schmidt et al. 2008). There five shells had been burned, apparently during a cremation. For reasons associated with the cardinal directions, a hunt god with Venus cycle connections, and Milky Way residence, I offer that *Olivella* shells were specifically used when a reference to Venus or some other element of the night sky was intended. Milky Way belts and bracelets,

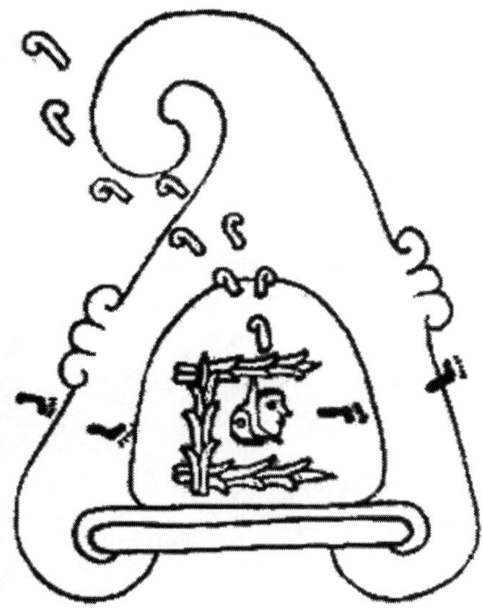

28. Oracle head placed inside a cave in a mountain consulted by the hunter-gatherer Chichimecas. (Codex Boturini.)

however, were never made with *Olivella* shells. In the case of the Jerger feature, five of these shells were included, a symbolically important number.

See *Busycon, center, gastropod, Leptoxis/Anculosa, Milky Way, shell bead*

Oracle

In numerous places in Mesoamerica and Alaska (see Hrdlicka 1941) dried bodies of adults were placed in caves and rockshelters to be consulted. The Cora of Mexico replaced the oracles' bodies housed in a temple with a more recently dead body of an "ancestor" (Coyle 1998:519) when it was necessary to do so owing to decay, a possible explanation for the bodies found in rockshelters in the eastern United States. The Aztecs frequently depicted oracles as isolated human heads situated in caves or temples (Figure 28).

There is an intriguing passage on this subject by John Lederer, traveling through North Carolina in 1669, that reads as follows: "The Indians now seated in these parts [are] a people driven by an enemy from the Northwest, and invited to site down here by an Oracle [more than] 400 years since" ([1672] 1958:11). Two possible oracles may be found in Short Cave, Warren County, Kentucky, near Mammoth Cave. One woman, called "Fawn Hoof," was found "sitting in a stone-box grave . . . arrayed in several finely fashioned skin burial garments and accompanied by a variety of grave goods" (Robbins 1974:144).

Robbins (1974:145) offers information about other late prehistoric dried bodies in Tennessee caves: "Mummies in both areas were wrapped in deer-skins and accompanied with grave goods. However, the Tennessee mummies differed in that some were disarticulated at the hips before being wrapped or dressed. Following the wrapping, they were placed upright in woven baskets." This latter treatment is highly suggestive of a role as oracle and that oracles were consulted during Woodland times if not much earlier. Head removal during the Archaic suggests the possibility that heads were used in an oracular way as well as indicating ancestor status of that deceased person. Placing bodies or skulls in caves to be consulted could have gone on for millennia.

Humans were not the only oracles. Various birds were said to foretell events by historic peoples, and divination with plum stones, pebbles, and so forth served much of the same purpose.

See *ancestor, bird, cave, divination, head removal, mummy, skull*

Ossuary

Ossuaries, or mass graves, do appear in the Archaic but typically as a large pit feature in a burial ground otherwise made up of individual interments. Ossuaries have been noted in pits at O'Neal shell mound, Alabama, with 15+ bodies (Lubsen 2004:161), Barrett, Kentucky, with 40+ bodies (Webb and Haag 1947), at Stanhope Cave, Ohio, with 8+ people (Spurlock and Prufer 2002), at Klunk Mound 7 with 40+ bodies (Perino 1961), and in Wapanucket No. 8, Massachusetts, with 11 bodies (Robbins 1969:13). The Late Archaic Lewis Central School site ossuary in southwestern Iowa contained 23 individuals, 18 of whom were adults (Anderson 1978), and the bluff-top Sand Run West site in Iowa had an ossuary with five or more people (Benn and Thompson 2009).

In the possible Mississippian hunt god rites there are numerous additional bodies placed over the central fivesome or nearby (Hall 2000). Several of these Archaic ossuaries are near or over possible Archaic hunt god rites, suggesting a reason for this rare type of burial.

See *hunt god rite*

Owl

Owl imagery is found on some lower Mississippi valley beads. Their details indicate great horned, screech, and barred owl species. All of the fat bellied owl (or possibly parakeet) pendants are made of red jasper and appear to be the products of a single artisan or a single workshop (Webb 1971:112). In addition to realistic owls, there are "owl monsters with deer antlers, owl-

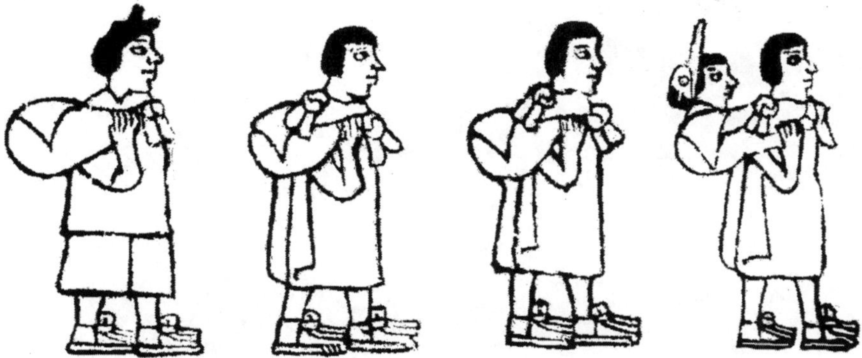

29. Four priests (three men, one woman) who led the hunter-gatherer Chichimecas from Atzlan, wearing sacred packs. (Codex Boturini.)

masked and costumed performers or shamans, and owl-human hybrids" (Gibson 1998:26).

The Iroquois thought witches assumed the shape of owls (Fox 1993), as did some southeastern peoples (Swanton 1931:198–199), screech owls particularly (Gibson 1998:26). The sight and sound of owls were omens (Gibson 2000:191). Owls, as night creatures and frequent dwellers of caves, evoke thoughts of the Underworld and death and suggest night, moon, and messenger to Underworld spirits. Owl pendants may have been amulets or fetishes.

Great Horned Owl parts were found at Reigh in Wisconsin with an extended burial that also had a swan bone tube. Great Horned Owl was among the remains at Lamoka Lake, New York, and at Bullskin Creek, Ohio.

See *bird, crane, moon, witch*

Pack

Sacred packs and sacred bundles (Figure 27) existed throughout North America in historic groups such as the Algonkians and the Aztecs (Figure 29). Some depictions of packs show that they were carried high on the back of leaders, priests, and culture heroes and contained sacred items including deities/oracles, idols, and bundled corpses. The concept of the sacred pack is visible in early Mississippian times as seen in the Birger stone figurine, a kneeling woman who is tilling the earth/snake and wearing a backpack from which extend gourds on a vine.

Evidence of packs may exist as faunal, floral, or stone items associated with the shoulders or back of a burial such as the Middle Woodland burial described by Fox and Molto (1994b). Were packs present in the Archaic?

30. Soft rock or "Holy Earth" that is eaten by pilgrims to Chalma, Morelos, Mexico. (Photo by author.)

There may be evidence of a pack on the back of a child at Ward, Kentucky, whose shoulders rest upon two turtle shells. It certainly seems that if the tightly flexed bodies and bone bundles were transported to burial grounds, rockshelters, and caves, they would have been carried in a backpack of some sort or as a bundle.

See *container, oracle*

Paint/Powder

Powdered stone of various lithologies was probably very important in Archaic rituals as paint and medicine. Medicinal uses of stone powder and marking rocks and bodies with paint still continue today among Native peoples of North America.

Archaic possibilities of paint and powder production can be seen in New England. Six hundred ninety grams of pyrolucite, similar to graphite and used as a pigment, were found in a 100 ft^2 (9.29 m^2) area of the Paleoindian

Debert site in Nova Scotia and as worked nodules at Bull Brook in Massachusetts (MacDonald 1968:107). Faceted hematite chunks may have also been the result of powder production. Stone powder was at least occasionally prepared inside a cave, particularly hematite (Rodgers, Graham Cave), or derived from gypsum found in caves (Mammoth Cave) (Crothers 2012) and from limestone, possibly meant for ingestion as medicine. Paint pots are one form of natural iron that was ground into powder.

The "defacement" of Olmec colossal heads may be the result of "harvesting" the power of these stones (Graham 1989:234, cited in Clark and Colman 2008:98). The Olmec example is not unlike the powder produced by pecking bedrock mortars that is consumed and still is used in rain-calling and conception rites in California (Parkman 1992). Eating rock continues to be an important part of pilgrimages to Chalma, Mexico (Figure 30). Powder from bones, particularly fossil bones, is still used to treat bone problems (Mayor 2005:198). In Mexico in June 2012 I participated in a medicinal clay hunt; when clay was found it was ground, wetted, and tasted to test its qualities. Such clay is eventually made into a paste and used in poultices.

See *art, ashes, bedrock mortar/nutting stone, cave mineral/mining, fossil, medicine, ocher, paint pot, pearl, rock marking*

Paint Pot

Geode-like concretions from which iron pigment was extracted are called paint pots. "These objects are iron concretions rich in hematite. . . . generally small with concavities ranging from 2 to 5 cm in diameters and measuring as deep as 3 cm. Some of these objects could have been used as containers" (Ledbetter 1995:152). As the hematite was ground out of the stone, the paint pot walls were thinned. Other paint containers were naiad shells; at Bluegrass, Kentucky, such shells were found with women only.

See *cave mineral/mining, paint/powder*

Pearl

Pearls, as shiny, iridescent, roundish items found in Underworld creatures (naiads), were valued by historic northeastern and Carolinian cultures and by Hopewell and Early Woodland Adena people, but they are rarely found in Archaic contexts. A small number of pearls do appear in a few late Late Archaic burials (Kampsville phase) in the lower Illinois River valley at Pete Klunk Mound 7 along with beads made of shell, copper, pipestone, and calcite, plummets, and bone tools (Wiant, Farnsworth, and Hajic 2009:268); they appear in a handful of other sites.

Their absence in the Archaic is an intriguing problem. Pearls, round as well as misshapen or "baroque," are abundant in freshwater mollusks of the eastern United States. There should have been a few million pearls in the billions of bivalves deposited in the more than 300 Archaic freshwater shell mounds. (For a historic account of pearling in eastern U.S. rivers, see Claassen 1994.) The lack of Archaic pearls suggest three possibilities: (1) pearls were eaten as medicine (a popular practice in China); (2) pearls do not preserve for more than about 2,000 years (explaining their abundance in Adena and Hopewell contexts); or (3) pearls were curated by lineages or clans. I suspect that along with rock powder and possibly clay and ashes, pearls were eaten medicinally during the Archaic and Early Woodland.

See *ashes*, *medicine*, *paint/powder*

Pebble

Timberlake ([1765] 1995:73–75) noted that the Cherokee collected beautiful stones for use in rituals. "Many of the smaller specimens are made from pebbles of nearly the desired shape, but in the case of the larger ones, stones with distinctive markings or with attractive colorings were often selected and worked into shape" (Fowler 1966:51). Shaped pebbles were found in a burial of the Lamar, Oklahoma, site.

Round white pebbles averaging one centimeter or less in diameter in numbers from one to 100+ occurred with 22 individuals in the Port au Choix cemetery. These pure white pebbles were not locally available on the beach and were not battered as they would have been if used inside rattles (Tuck 1976:71). Since many of the pebbles were clustered, they may have been deposited in bags. Others were found in rows, suggesting adherence to an animal skin via a sticky substance. A pit at the adjacent Gould mortuary camp also contained these pebbles. Tuck comments on the contrast these pebbles made with the red ocher and on the birth, life, and rebirth symbolism of the color white (1976:71). Other white pebbles in rows were found at Rattler's Bight cemetery in Labrador.

Egg-shaped stones, heart-shaped pebbles, black pebbles, and so forth were collected by visionaries, priests, and others in eastern North America (Irwin 1994). Some stones were drilled, some were engraved or scratched, some were painted, and many were put into bundles. Two stones in a medicine bundle could reproduce, and stones could hear and speak in visions and in sweat lodges (Irwin 1994). Stone, in the shape and size of pebbles, was placed with the cremains of individuals in central Mexico, the lithology reflecting the worth of the person (Furst 1995). Pebbles are occasionally recorded with Archaic burials.

See *pebble—drilled, pebble—engraved, stone*

Pebble—Drilled

Biconically drilled pebbles of greenish-gray, red, and reddish-brown coloration show up in plowzone and Middle Archaic midden in the Denton site in Mississippi (Connaway 1977:76–79). Four pebbles were completely perforated and 11 had drilled craters, but perforating may not have been the goal. Many of the craters are not centered on the stone as would be anticipated if a pendant function was intended. Dozens more ground but undrilled pendants were also recovered. The colors involved and the material, stone, suggest a symbolism to be decoded.

See *pebble, pebble—engraved, stone*

Pebble—Engraved

Engraved pebbles seem to be a phenomenon of the Atlantic states starting with Paleoindian activities. They may have been more common than we realize given their often small size. The Paleoindian-era West Athens Hill site (New York) yielded a pebble with a ladder-like design scratched into the surface and other lines on the other face (Funk 1973:29–30). Other incised pebbles were found at the Paleoindian Gault Site in Texas.

Early and Middle Archaic engraved pebbles have been found in the central Virginia and North Carolina Piedmont. An inscribed green slate piece was found at the Middle Archaic Slade site (Virginia) on the Nottoway River (Egloff and McAvoy 1990:72). Forty-six engraved pebbles were recovered on the surface of the Hardaway site (Coe 1964) and five in excavation. Engraved slate fragments were also found, 213 on the surface and 16 in excavation. The 49 specimens recovered at Doerschuk site (North Carolina) had "designs which ranged from simple crisscrossed lines that extended across and down the edges to very fine and intricate geometric designs. . . . [some] even suggest a drawing. . . . This practice of cutting designs on slate is not widespread in the Piedmont, and, therefore, it is surprising to find specimens of this type occurring in six separate zones of occupation" (Coe 1964:53).

See *art, design element, pebble, pebble—drilled, stone*

Petrified Wood

Heddon site in extreme western Kentucky had petrified wood, as did the Buffalo site in West Virginia (Broyles 1976). Petrified wood was used in fluted points at the Richmond site and the Petrified Wood Site, both in Virginia. All the artifacts of petrified wood found in the latter site appear to have been struck from the same core (Dent 1995:111, 127). Wood turned to rock would have been understood as evidence of an ancient creation, infused with power.

See *fossil, Stone People*

Petroform

Petroforms are comprised of cobbles moved into place to attain the shape of something recognizable to the viewer. Rock Eagle in central Georgia and various animal and human forms in Whiteshell Provincial Park, Manitoba, are examples of petroforms (both pictured in Milne 1994). There are no known Archaic petroforms, but most are undated. Milne (1994:58) cites a 5,000-year-old date for Rock Eagle in central Georgia and relates that the Cherokee say their ancestors found the Rock Eagle petroform when they arrived in the area. It is made entirely of quartz boulders not available in the vicinity. Understanding petroforms must include consideration of the symbolic roles of stone, cobbles, and the resulting shape.

See *cairn, rock formation, rock marking*

Pilgrimage

A pilgrimage is "a multiday large-scale (by local standards) ceremonial event, often annual in occurrence, . . . enacted out of devotion with varied motives, consisting of nonlocal circulation by numerous individuals, to and from what may be considered socioreligious space" (Astor-Aguilera and Jarvenpa 2008:485). Furthermore, a vow to participate in one or more actions that temporarily change behavior is common (e.g., abstention from sex, alcohol, or certain foods or walking barefoot) (Figure 31). These criteria separate the tourist from the pilgrim. Numerous native North American pilgrimages have been documented such as the male initiation trips by the Paiute (Klasky 2009/10) and Zuni, the Creek male group of pilgrims to the origin caves in Arkansas (Gatschet 1884:187), mixed-age and sex-group pilgrimages to mounds in Virginia (Dunham 1994:1–4), and Iroquois to Big Bone Lick (Mayor 2005:29).

31. Tiger fighters (young men) pray before one shrine in their multiday circuit of shrines (including wells), May 1, 2012, Acatlan, Guerrero, Mexico. (Photo by author.)

Pilgrimages to Archaic shell heaps, caves (Claassen 2010), and Poverty Point (Gibson 1998) have been suggested. Some Archaic ritual specialists may have directed or followed a circuit of shrine visitations over the course of a solar or stellar cycle. Initiates may have made pilgrimages to places important in a group's history.

I suspect that pilgrims did much to move goods around the eastern Woodlands during the early Archaic. Procurement of various toolstone types, for instance, could have been embedded in pilgrimage treks and quarrying could have been a ritual act.

See *oracle, pilgrimage center, ritual, ritual calendar, shrine*

Pilgrimage Center

A pilgrimage center's "defining characteristic is the attraction of devotees from a large, often multiethnic and/or multinational catchment area. Pilgrims travel to a pilgrimage center in order to carry out religious devotions; they are not resident at the shrine.... the pilgrimage center is noteworthy for its ability to draw a transient population of worshippers from across a social political, economic, cultural and spatial spectrum and, in so doing, to synthesize critical social and cultural elements from wider patterns of belief and practice in a region or regions" (Silverman 1994:2–3).

Pilgrimage centers (and their shrines) may have been far more common during the Archaic than we realize because they were largely natural places—Hot Springs, Arkansas; Muscle Shoals, Alabama; various islands in the Great Lakes and St. Lawrence valley; various springs in central Florida; waterfalls in the Catskills and Appalachians; caves in Kentucky; chert sources in the St. Lawrence valley; places along the sea coast; and even certain trees, mountaintops, and rock formations—whose markings have not preserved in ways that are archaeologically detectable.

However, Archaic people did mark pilgrimage centers sometimes in ways that archaeologists can see. Shoals were centers, visible as shell burial mounds on the Tennessee, on the Ohio, and on the Savannah. Poverty Point may have been a pilgrimage center and the other or older mound sites part of a pilgrimage circuit. The cemeteries of the Far North may have been pilgrimage centers.

See *pilgrimage, ritual, shrine*

Pipe

Pipes transform plants into smoke and odor. The oldest tobacco in the New World is dated to 1800 B.C. in Peru (Rafferty 2001); thus tobacco was not the substance smoked in Archaic pipes, if smoking was occurring at all. It is probable that many Archaic "pipes" had a non-smoking function such as sucking bad airs out of a sick person. Sucking tubes, used by healers, are suspected at Bullseye and Riverton.

However, smoking, or burning material in a pipe bowl, did begin in the Late Archaic. "Numerous smoking pipes have been recovered from Late Archaic Period burial contexts. . . . indicating that smoking in ritual contexts clearly has Late Archaic roots along with the rest of the Early Woodland mortuary phenomena" (Rafferty 2001:14). One of the earliest known smoking pipes was recovered at the Eva Site, Tennessee, from a component dated to approximately 2000 B.C. (Lewis and Lewis 1961:66, Figure 2.2), although this date may be too recent (Thad Bisset, personal communication with the author, June 30, 2014). Webb and Baby (1957:22) noted that " 'prototype' tubular smoking pipes were recovered from Late Archaic shell mound sites in Alabama and Kentucky." Possible smoking pipes were found in two caves, Mammoths/Salts and Savage, and in Titterington phase burial grounds, all probable ritual settings. Actual tubular pipes appeared in Terminal Archaic times (ca. 1500 B.C.); two examples were found in Prairie Lake culture sites (Farnsworth 1987:18). At the shell-bearing bluff-top Riverton site two cloudblower pipes were found with charred material on the interior (Winters 1969).

Pipes were manufactured at Late Archaic steatite quarries like Oaklawn Cemetery of Rhode Island (Fowler 1971–72:10) and the chlorite quarry of Stafford Springs, Connecticut (Fowler 1966:45). Presumably pipes, the act of smoking a pipe, and smoking tobacco diffused west to east.

See *burning, fire, sucking tube*

Plaza

Sassaman and Heckenberger (2004:230) speak of plazas as power centers in a village and containers of power, in that the structures surrounding the plaza enclose the plaza. But the plaza also embodies social hierarchies, separating public from private, men from women, chiefs from non-chiefs, sacred from profane, even culture from nature. "In this respect, human movement through the landscape may have recapitulated and amplified spatial metaphors for hierarchy manifest at particular sites, lending a multiscalar, fractal quality to the symbolism and ritual of Archaic monumentality" (2004:231). The answer to why the plaza center developed in the Archaic (e.g., Horr's Island, Florida) is to be sought among social processes. Inomata (2006) investigated Maya plazas and suggested that plaza size and nature may be clues to social structure.

See *cardinal direction, center, quincunx*

Plummet

Plummets are found in both mortuary and midden contexts, whole and broken, but are restricted in geographical occurrence: the Poverty Point area, the lower Midwest, and the Northeast (Sassaman 2010a:113). Shell plummets are found in the Florida shell mortuaries of Mount Taylor culture. They are extremely rare in Iowa and the Far North and are unknown north of the Lakes Region in New Brunswick (Tuck 1976:263). "After ca. 3800 cal BP, plummets become a mainstay of importation in the Poverty Point sphere of influence and, shortly later (after ca. 3450 cal BP) in the terminal Archaic of the lower Illinois River valley and the American Bottom" (Sassaman 2010a:115).

Plummets were found in five graves of a Maritime Archaic cemetery. One was found on the chest of a woman and the other in the torso cavity of a small child (Tuck 1976:60). In the Archaic mound beneath Klunk Mound 7, when sexing was possible, all were found with males. Five plummets lay on the chest of one man, one on the femurs of another, and one under the skull of a third. Plummets were found at Jaketown (Mississippi) with and without pottery and at Poverty Point (Louisiana). "Most of the southern plummets are made from hematite" and were "incised or had multiple grooves cut around the stem. Specimens with cross-hatched decorations are noted most frequently" (Perino 1961:56). Incising on plummets is extremely rare on LIV specimens.

As Sassaman discusses (2010a:112–117), fish net weights, fish line weights, bird net weights, and perhaps bolas are the common uses ascribed to plummets, but use in spinning is possible as well. The significant use of bird symbolism in the Northeast and in the Deep South might favor plummets as part of bird hunting technology, but the association of plummets with fishing was highlighted by Gibson (2000:146). Fishing use was made explicit by Perino, who noted an association between plummet find spots and bodies of water: "they have been recovered in numbers from drainage ditches cut through ancient lake beds in the Illinois River bottoms and have been dredged from the Illinois and Mississippi Rivers" (1961:43). He also added that in some burials plummets are found in the company of fishhooks made from shell or copper. While some plummets might be fetishes or amulets, the majority of plummets, Perino believed, could have been line and net weights for use in fishing or netting waterfowl.

Yet another use for plummets may be connected to medicine and was first suggested by Perino (1961:43). Two-thirds of the Illinois River valley plummets are made from hematite, the source of red ocher. Perino observed that sometimes when they occur in village sites there are also "numbers of irregularly shaped hematite rubstones," some grooved, and most of which could have yielded red powder or a finished plummet. The next most popular stone material for plummets was limestone, from which a white powder could be derived. In addition to having a weighting function, perhaps plummets were "powder blanks" available to scratch for powder when needed.

See *amulet, fetish, hematite, ocher, paint/powder*

Point Reuse

Curation of older points has frequently been remarked upon by archaeologists. Amick (1985:30) specifies "a pattern of systematic procurement and reuse of Early Archaic tools by Middle Archaic peoples" in central Tennessee. Also speaking of Tennessee, Broster and Norton (1996:291) observed, "Some 108 Late Paleoindian and 51 fluted points were found on later multicomponent prehistoric sites. These items probably represent the later use of Paleoindian points by Archaic and Mississippian peoples." The Godar site had "Dalton, Agate Basin, and Hardin points which like the early points found under Gibson Mound 1, indicate that earlier 'found' points were added to the mortuary goods" of Archaic burials (Cook 1976:96). Ahler et al. (1992:12) suggested scavenging of older points and their deposition at Modoc as an explanation for the presence of Dalton points as well. An unfluted Paleoindian point found at the Archaic Vosburg site in New York had been reworked into a scraper.

"The people painted pictographs in the quest for many medicines, one of which was surely flint. . . . Highly valued stone, formerly flaked or ground into tools for hunting and war, was a medicine of great antiquity. . . . Some [pictographs] depict the ancient spears and bows-and-arrows" (Rajnovich 1994:145). Older points had symbolic association with earlier creations and probably with the Stone People. Given this belief, to what extent might "multicomponent" sites actually be single component with point collecting?

See *offering*, *projectile point*, *Stone People*

Pole/Post

Poles mimic the human trunk and numerous other natural linear forms. Historic accounts describe posts as symbols of chiefly authority, symbols of tribal unity (Hall 1989:270; Hall 1997:107), as the center of the world and world trees, as social persons (Skousen 2012), and as markers for burials and boundaries (Bader 2010/11:38). Posts are best known in Woodland and Mississippian settings (Skousen 2012), but posts have been suggested in at least one Paleoindian case (Ellis 1994) and a few Archaic sites.

A "shaman's pole" was suspected at the Paleoindian Jones-Miller site in Colorado (Ellis 1994:263). Stakes were abundant in the pond mortuary of Windover, where the large stakes "may have been visible markers of burial zones" in the pond perimeter (Doran 2002:19) or mortuary poles. Similar tall stakes were uncovered at Bay West and Little Salt Spring (Wentz and Gifford 2007:334). "Next to [one woman] were post molds thought to be from effigy poles or from a shelter erected over the body" (Wentz and Gifford 2007:334). Athens (2000) suggested that the two men buried at the sinkhole rim in the Lawrence site were marked with a pole, and Bader (2010/11) proposed the same for some burials at the Meyer site (Indiana).

Other potential marker post or ceremonial poles are proposed at two Kentucky sites—Rosenberger (Driskell 1979:775) and Hedden (McGraw and Huser 1995). Fortier (1987:41) describes a class of pit features with internal posts at Range as well as Missouri Pacific #2 site, both in Illinois. Purtill (2009:584) writes that nonstructural posts in pits have been found at several Archaic sites in Ohio and interpreted as windbreaks or drying racks. Aten (1999:173) implies surface marking of the burial area at Harris Creek, Florida, and Barker and Hazel (2007:3) claim that the cemetery area at the Ryan site in Tennessee had been marked. Kidder, Ortmann, and Allen (2004: 111) suggest that a large hole near the top and center of Mound B, floor 3, of Poverty Point held a pole.

Eighteenth-century Cree buried the deceased in single round-shaped graves several feet deep and then put an upright painted sapling in the center of each grave, pine if a woman, cedar if a man. "Some woodland groups such as the Ojibway, Delaware and Menomini erected burial posts at the grave with pictographs of the deceased's ancestral totem painted in an upside-down position, representing the individual's death" (Harper 1999:54–55). Poles and crosses hung with offerings were erected by Great Lakes groups. "[Dreamers] also raised banners on medicine poles, resembling flags, to act as charms and to let others know in pride, that the owner received powers" (Rajnovich 1994:25).

See *bannerstone*, *cross*, *tree*

Pomme de Terre River, Missouri

Once known as the Big Bone River, the Pomme de Terre River of the Missouri Ozarks has a rich fossil fauna at Koch Springs, part of a geologic feature that includes Phillips Spring, a find-spot of early domesticated seeds, and Rodgers Shelter, where Early Archaic rituals were conducted. It is probably more than coincidence that this river would have Pleistocene fossils, a ritual cave, several springs with domestic seeds, Table Rock (a balanced planar stone that was the scene of thanks-offerings by historic Indians [Mayor 2005:201, 205]), precocious Archaic dirt mounds, and the only fiber-tempered pottery in the larger region. Perhaps the knowledge that the Stone People could be contacted in this area explains this probable Archaic ritual district.

See *fossil*, *Green River*, *mammoth/mastodon*, *Rodgers Shelter*, *St. Johns River*, *Stone People*

Pond Burial

Placing bodies in the water of ponds or in flooded sinkholes in Florida began in Paleoindian times and ended in the Middle Archaic (Randall 2005:17). It was concentrated in south Florida (Doran 2002:3). Windover, in Brevard County, is the most famous of the wet mortuaries with over 170 bodies emplaced between 8200 and 6900 rcy in little more than 30 cm of standing water and a red-brown peat (Doran 2002:21). The presence of brain tissue indicates that burial in this pond took place within the first 48 hours of death (Doran 2002:22). Pond burials are strikingly like fossil bone beds in the eastern Woodlands, which are typically under shallow water in boggy areas.

See *fossil, sinkhole, spring, Stone People, Windover*

Pottery

Pottery was used by some Late Archaic people beginning in shell-ring and shell-midden contexts along the southern Atlantic. There are three aspects of pottery containers that are of symbolic and ritual import: clay and the mixing of clay and fire, the concave shape, and their role in feasting.

Clay, in powder form or a sticky mass, has medicinal uses such as healing ulcerous sores, easing menstrual cramps, clearing acne, soothing bee stings, and so forth (Petra Salgado of Taxco, Mexico, interview by the author, June 2012). As a substance that can be transformed by fire it elicits wonder. "Women made pots of material they derived from the earth and used them to transform their harvested plants into food. To some extent, the relationship is also a reflection of vessels' roles in ritual" (Smith 2005:131).

Several Mexican and southwestern U.S. groups believe that Clay People existed in a former creation. This association of clay and creation, augmenting the transformative properties of firing and cooking, is easily transferred onto the clay jar, which is an enclosed, dark, uterine-like cavity from which one takes sustenance. Wonderly (2002) reports a strong symbolic association between clay pots (and later copper kettles), fertility, the earth, and death and dying, as does Smith (2005). "Vessels were closely related to death, the earth, and graves, as well as the suite of rituals associated with burial. Huron interment rites were referred to as the 'kettle,' and if a scheduled (re)burial was postponed, people said the kettle was 'overturned.' They were frequently employed as analogies to group interaction; when there was conflict between villages, the kettle was divided. When it was resolved, the kettle was reunited. Finally, references to vessels played roles in the descriptions of geographical features, such as depressions beneath waterfalls" (Smith 2005:141).

Accumulating evidence suggests that the first adoption of pottery in the South Carolina to Florida region was a response to growing demands for serving vessels, not cooking vessels (Sassaman 2004; Saunders 2004). The earliest known pottery in the eastern United States are the Stallings Island punctuated, flat-bottomed serving vessels found on the lower Savannah River in Late Archaic shell-bearing sites such as Rabbit Mount. The context of discovery and the form and decoration strongly suggest that this earliest pottery was adopted in a feasting context for serving foods and possibly given as gifts. Five hundred years later cooking vessels appear in shell-bearing sites to the north and south on the Atlantic coast. Fiber-tempered pottery left the Atlantic coast to travel along the Gulf of Mexico coast and the Tennessee River valley by 3700 B.P. (predating stone bowls), quickly reaching Missouri (Kidder and Sassaman 2009:683).

The association of large and even decorative vessels with feasts is borne out by historic records. "The ethnographic evidence suggests that Iroquoian people believed large cooking vessels were necessary for ritual feasting. This need seems to be more symbolic than pragmatic, since they were apparently unwilling to conduct a feast by substituting several small pots for a single large one. The Huron's comment about the French king making the largest kettles lends support to this hypothesis in that it suggests Iroquoians equated large vessels with social importance in general" (Smith 2005:142).

See *cave*, *container*

Profile Rock

Stone People, such as Flint, a character in northeastern U.S. stories, were the first people on earth (Irwin 1994:223). A Paiute legend referring to Bryce Canyon geology explains that the vertical erosional features were the first people, "Legend People, turned to stone wearing their face paint" (Milne 1994:120). "Among Chichimec groups . . . their ancestors were descended from giant rocks or became rocks when they died" (Correa 2000:446). There may be no evidence for Archaic veneration of "rock faces," or human face profiles such as are found at Pipestone Quarry in Minnesota or Grandfather Mountain, North Carolina, but archaeologists should suspect that such existed.

See *bluff*, *rock formation*, *stone*, *Stone People*

Projectile Point

Rajnovich (1994:157), speaking of the Algonkians of the Canadian Shield, wrote, "Stone points must not only be measured, weighed and photographed, they must also be understood, for their significance in the symbology of the people was immense. The arrow and dart combined the feathers from birds for flight, the shaft from trees for strength and the tooth of Wolf copied in stone for skill in the hunt." The Winnebago also "considered a stone naturally sharpened in any way to be sacred and offered tobacco for it" (Rajnovich 1994:150). Selig (2010) has made this same point with a dissertation filled with examples of the ritual use of projectile points by southwestern groups and other North American groups that did not shoot game but used points they found in rituals.

If point styles were governed by target prey, as suggested by O'Brien (1998), then perhaps the types of points found in graves, in pits, in caches, and in deposits are indicating something about a specific animal. Furthermore, there is mounting evidence that points with and without attached shafts were often used as offerings. This evidence comes from arrows left in caves in historic times (Sundstrom 1996, 2000), arrows shot into cliff crevasses in historic times and for 2,000 years in the Upper Peninsula at Spider Cave (Rajnovich 1994:51), and points used in rituals in the Southwest (Selig 2010). The Winnebago never manufactured points; they used scavenged points for hunting (Selig 2010:67). These found points were highly valued and revered by Algonkian people, constituting a "medicine of great antiquity" (Rajnovich 1994:145). Rock art praised this medicine, sometimes depicting the points and weapons themselves.

The extremely high number of points found at some sites and the prevalence of points as grave goods strongly suggest a symbolism for the stone point such as ancestor spirit or Stone People or even a home for the deceased's soul. Consider, for instance, the 9,424 points discarded (surely they weren't lost) at and excavated from 60 percent of Indian Knoll, the 6,707 points found in excavation blocks 3 and 4 at Perry, Alabama, and the 4,500 Dalton points and tools removed from Olive Branch, Illinois. Not only were these points left at these sites, they were not scavenged by later people. The quantities of points strongly suggest the points were offerings, a point made by Ritchie (1932:113) as well at Lamoka Lake. Using points as offerings was practiced by Paleoindians primarily in caches and by Middle Archaic peoples with caches and as individual points at cave sites, in "midden," and with burials. In the SOV, projectile points were the most frequently deposited grave good, included in up to 25 percent of the graves (Claassen 2010:Table 6.8) at both shell mounds and shell-free burial grounds. Most of the points may have been offered by their makers, while a minority may have been scavenged from nonritual locations.

See *flintknapping, offering, point reuse, Stone People, trash/midden*

Pyrite—see Fire Making

Quarry(ing)

Quarries were not simply extractive places and quarrying not simply one of a number of tasks to be accomplished in the busy lives of ancient people. Stones are the bones and veins of the living earth (Sandstrom 1991:238). Quarrying rock and fossil outcrops and veins, and removing speleothems, crinoids, cherts, and salts from inside caves and rockshelters were hurtful acts that needed to be marked with prayers and reciprocity/exchange. Old stone tools often found at quarries might be such offerings. Based on historic accounts, we should assume that quarries for important stone types were shared resources and may well have constituted "safe space," places where animosities were suspended, as documented in Milne (1994) for Pipestone National Monument.

The sounds generated by pounding rocks may have been equated to thunder and the calling of rain. "Rain rocks" were used by the Klamath and Shasta people who pounded boulders making pits in the process, to call rain. "In fact, among the Kashaya Pomo, women grinding acorns in their mortars took special precautions to prevent unwanted rain," doing "their grinding beneath specially-prepared shelters . . . and the Shasta covered their rain rocks" (Parkman 1992:367).

See *flintknapping, fossil, rain, sound, stone, Stone People*

Quartz—see Crystal

Raccoon

Raccoons, as dark-colored, nocturnal animals, may have been interchangeable symbols with women, moon, and other night creatures. The inclusion of a raccoon baculum with an infant's skeleton at Bluff Creek, Alabama, would seem to document fecundity symbolism. The raccoon was important enough to have been included 312 times in the Tick Creek, Missouri, bone shrine. It may be significant that its black eye mask duplicates that of the hunt god Mixcoatl/Camaxtli.

See *hunt god rite, moon, Tick Creek Cave*

Rain

The hunting/gathering people of the western United States have conducted rain-making, rain-calling, and weather control rites for millennia (Broda 1998; Parkman 1992) and provide models for understanding Archaic rites and beliefs in the eastern Woodlands. Among Nahuatl-speaking people and others in Mexico and the Southwest, rain, fog, snow, and hail are forms of celestial water associated with the cardinal directions, and Above World deities and spirits must be propitiated when rain is lacking. Today Jesus/Quetzalcoatl/Tlaloc is petitioned in annual May ceremonies from mountaintops and from sinkholes, caves, and springs in central Mexico with prayer and food offerings.

In Historic times scalps, flint-scalping knives, flintknapping, and arrows (they fly like lightning) were used to symbolize and call storms and rain (see Krupp 1997:254). Pounding bedrock was done to create a thunderous sound to call rain (Parkman 1992). These same holes filled with water after each rain. Shooting an arrow into the sky was one way of calling rain used by the Apache (see *Sacred Rain Arrow* sculpture by Apache artist Alan Houser). Also useful for calling rain were children's tears and blood (e.g., Broda 1998), shaking rattles, drumming, stimulating cicadas (all four of which mimic the sound of thunder), and killing frogs and snakes (Smith 1995:138). In the eastern United States the eternal clashes between the beings of the Upper World and the Lower World explained storms and even lightning strikes on trees (Dowd 2011:89; Lankford 2007).

Given the ancient and modern association of caves with rain, lightning, and fog/mist, the ritual specialists working in caves during the Archaic and the offerings of animals, human bodies, and trophy parts found in caves suggest that caves were rain-calling places. Bedrock mortars found throughout the Cumberland Plateau may also have been rain-calling facilities as well as food-processing equipment.

See *bedrock mortar/nutting stone, insect, music, rattle*

Rattle

"The distinctive 'Indian Knoll' type of [carapace] rattle, as defined by Howard Winters (1967:75) is characterized by large (12–14mm) diameter perforations in the center of the carapace and plastron" (Fox 2007:5). Other types of rattles also existed at Indian Knoll and elsewhere. Fox reported that in historic times different rites required different species' carapaces.

In addition to the rattles found in Green River shell heaps, rattles were also found on the Ohio River at Railway Museum and Rosenberger, on the Tennessee River at Eva and Kay's Landing, and on the Wabash River at Riverton. Eighteen of these rattles were buried with adults, eight with children and five with infants. Four adults and one infant had multiple rattles and one of those adults, at Kay's Landing, had five rattles (Fox 2007:6). In one case of an Eva burial rattle, the rattling sound was provided by 9 pieces of "gravel" and 25 pharyngeal teeth of drumfish while 3 quartz pebbles and 20 drumfish teeth filled another rattle in Bu328, from Barrett. A rattle from Kay's Landing returned a date of 5301–4966 B.P. (William Fox, personal communication with the author, November 23, 2007).

Outside the SOV there are only a handful of additional examples of this rattle. Three New York Archaic sites had turtle shell rattles: Lamoka Lake,

Frontenac Island, and Hanna Farm. Bourque (1995) reports carapace rattles with quartz pebbles from mortuary features at Turner Farm, Maine. This very limited distribution of carapace rattles suggests either the range of a specific dance or rite with Indian Knoll at its center or that other populations used unhafted rattles (thus no perforation) and did not include them in their mortuary programs (Fox 2007).

Fox (2004b:53; 2007) equates box turtle shell rattles to birth/rebirth/fecundity for it was upon Turtle's back the earth was supported. Furthermore, the rattle sound mimics thunder. Box turtle shell rattles seem to have carried this symbolism since Archaic times in upper New York. Curiously, turtle shell rattles disappear from use north of the Ohio River with the end of the Archaic and reappear only in the Northeast in Middle Woodland times (Fox 2007). Among historic southeastern Indians, turtle shell rattles were commonly worn by women (Swanton 1946:252).

See *music, sound, turtle*

Rebalancing Rite

Contemporary native peoples often express concern with balance, balance between the Upper and Lower worlds, balance of humans with other-than-humans, and so forth. Human sacrifice was employed to affect balance in Contact-period Mexico, and dog sacrifice has been employed by Cherokee to restore balance. Balance is restored through proper medicine/practice, possibly including dog sacrifices for individual or community rebalancing rites (Claassen 2010; James 2006). I propose that most of the dogs buried in the Green River and Tennessee River shell mounds had been killed in dozens of individual rebalancing rites, perhaps related to cleansing corpse handlers.

See *dog, dog sacrifice rite, dog with human burial rite, sacrifice—adult, world renewal rite*

Reversal

Giles (2010:216) discusses rites of reversal among Hopewell peoples that may well have occurred in Archaic ritualizing. Dosing a ritual fire with water is one such rite. Building up a shell mound and then capping it with dirt (e.g., Carlston Annis) would be another example, a termination rite. Many such acts were then themselves reversed in an act of renewal—a new fire was built directly above the old, new burials were put above old burials, crushed shell layers succeeded whole shell layers, and so forth. Reversal could also include unwinding then winding, untying and tying. Wixárika speak of the tying up/winding up of a life during living and the untying/unwinding of death. Ritual acts may have been sequenced in clockwise or counterclockwise movements. Several authors have proposed that the Left Handed Whelk, the only whelk that grows in a counterclockwise direction, was so prevalent in Archaic contexts because of this contrariness.

See *Busycon, capping, cardinal direction, color*

Ritual

A ritual is a repeated action following a covert formula with desired outcomes. The focus of this guide is on rituals meant to (1) inform, through content, meaning, and representation by use of symbols, and (2) communicate (Lohse 2007:4) with spirits, primarily, and people, secondarily. Because rituals are performed by individual agents, the rituals that are meant for group observation and practice "must have both a convincing continuity with remembered rites and a convincing coherence with community life" (Bell 1997:203).

The formal properties of rituals are repetition, acting, stylization, order, evocative presentational style/staging, and a collective dimension (Moore and Myerhoff 1977:7). To study ritual, Marcus (1999:70–71) proposed looking at content, locus, and performance. Rituals use symbols that can be material (artifacts) or performative and even built space and landscapes (Robb 1998). Many of the artifacts and arrangements are mnemonic devices such as discussed by Giles (2010). "[W]e are now in a position to regard ritual as a process which creates a regime of truth and a recognition that the origin of that truth lies beyond the immediate world. This is a different perception from that which expects ritual to reflect some pre-existing belief or creed" (Rakita and Buikstra 2008:11).

See *cosmology, hunt god rite, ritual calendar, ritual specialist/priest, world renewal rite*

Ritual Calendar

At least two calendars may have been followed by Archaic peoples, the 260-night (possibly gestation) calendar and the 365-day calendar. Certainly each calendar had rituals associated with the passage of major units of time, such as are marked by the two equinoxes and two solstice phases of the moon and the appearance and disappearance of planets and constellations. Even noncalendrical rites would probably have been scheduled according to some calendrical information. For instance, private rites associated with hearth and with menstruation may have been performed monthly on a lunar cycle. The movement of stars, constellations, and planets also may have elicited specific rites. Marshack (1985) indicates that rituals were often timed to occur on the new or full moon following a solstice event.

For hunter-gatherers 8,000 to 4,000 ya in the southeastern United States the proposed ritual calendar is:

February, March—The equinox may have signaled the New Year, March 21. The Mexican New Year began around March 15. The Iroquois New Year was marked in early February. Maple sap rites followed in March. The Pawnee new year began in March. The four-age rite may have occurred at this time.
March, April, May—rain-calling/fertility rites
May—SOV cave-petitioning rites (indicated by pollen in feces)
June—summer solstice rites around June 21
September, October, November—Cult of the River Keeper rites (SOV), Cult of the Snail Shell rites, due to low water levels in rivers. Cult of the Feast surrounding October 21 equinox, nut harvests, hunt god rite
November—SOV cave petitioning (seeds in feces)
December—winter solstice rites

Certainly this calendar was augmented with cult rites related to the behavior of particular species or conclusions of units of time (such as a Venus cycle). Deer hunting was productive in the fall and was probably preceded by a hunt god rite. River shellfishing is easiest in the fall; the huge shell mound burial rites thus also likely occurred in the fall (Claassen 2010). Pagoulatos (2009:246) believes that the presence of nuts in some Northeast graves and the prevalence of secondary and dry bone burials indicate fall aggregation burials for Atlantic and northeastern Archaic groups. The behavior of seals suggests that December netting and early spring seal clubbing were aggregation times conducive to ritual (Renouf and Bell 2006:15). Fish seasonality also suggests a ritual calendar. The seasonality of tornadoes, of hurricanes, and of snow was probably noted with rites conducted to deflect damage and protect humans and others. Marshack (1985) gives details about the calendar priests among Siberians, Eskimos, Hopi, and Winnebagos.

See *astronomy, first-kill rite, hunt god rite, moon, number, ritual, ritual specialist/priest*

Ritual Specialist/Priest

There were probably several different types of ritual specialists in the Archaic, such as calendar, broken bone, human sacrifice, and doctoring specialists. Probable ritual specialists have been found buried in Bullskin Creek,

Ohio, and Short Cave, Kentucky; in Eva and Anderson in Tennessee; at Mulberry Creek, Alabama; at Bluffton Burial Mound, Florida; at Port au Choix, Newfoundland; and at Horn Shelter, Texas.

Eva Bu62, in the latest component, was a male 20–25 yo. He "was fully flexed and in a very small pit. Beneath the skull was the curled up skeleton of a small dog, definitely associated with the human burial. Artifacts included a splinter awl, a deer ulna awl, a turtle shell rattle, a Morrow Mountain I projectile point, a rattlesnake vertebra necklace, and an antler tine" (Lewis and Lewis 1961:118, cited by Magennis 1977). Another man in the earliest context at Mulberry Creek was placed on top of two dogs. At Bluffton Burial Mound on the St. Johns River a fire was burned, a body was put on top of the coals, it was covered with alligator feces, and it was finally capped by alternating layers of sand and shell (Sears 1960).

If we accept the proposition that activities in the dark zones of caves—exploration, mineral and chert mining, and making marks—were conducted by individuals ritually prepared to enter and conduct activities inside the earth, then much can be learned about cave ritual specialists in particular. What data there are—fecal amino acids (Sobolik et al. 1996), footprints (Watson 1969:41), and cadavers—suggest that the individuals who most often entered caves were male. A boy who apparently died accidentally in the Mammoth/Salts Cave system may have been in the cave as part of an apprenticeship. Crothers (2012) believes that Woodland-era boys were initiated into adulthood inside Mammoth Cave.

The paleofeces found in places like Mammoth Cave and Salts Cave should show us the ritual preparation diet for Early Woodland cave priests. Twenty-three paleofecal specimens collected from a point within Mammoth Cave showed the top five plant constituents (in rank order of ubiquity) to be sunflower, chenopod, hickory, sumpweed, and maygrass with sporadic additions to a meal of strawberry, grape, and *Rubus*. Charcoal flecks were the most ubiquitous element. Maygrass remains appeared independently of the other four seeds, suggesting summer cave entradas, as well as others in the fall indicated by fall seeds. A second indication of specific seasonal activities in this cave system is the negative correlation of hickory nut and maygrass (interpretation by author, data from Marquardt 1974:199), again suggesting May–June entradas and October–November entradas. From Salts Cave specimens Marquardt found high negative correlations between another early summer fruit, strawberry, and all of the fall seeds (Marquardt 1974:200). Pollen remains complemented this picture of June and fall activities in Mammoth Cave. The cave specialist's diet was also augmented by some animal protein (Watson 1974b:233).

The picture the fecal specimens present of the diet of ancient ritualists is also supplemented by the intestinal contents of the young boy found in the cave. The contents were sumpweed, marsh-elder, hickory nutshell, pre-adult insect cuticle, chenopod seeds, amaranth seeds, and carbonized material (Yarnell 1974:109). Noticeably absent from these feces was meat evidence.

Overall, the contents of these various specimens suggest *ritual* not *habitual* diet. It is interesting that the four seed species are those that have been found stored in Late Archaic and Early Woodland contexts in rockshelters, some of which (Ozarks, eastern Kentucky) suggest use as women's menstrual/birthing retreats (Claassen 2011a). Might we be glimpsing a culturally proscribed use for these plants that might not be "food" conceptually, perhaps instead being "medicine" and medicine tailored for the fertility rite to be conducted? Contributing more data to this line of thinking was the high negative correlation between animal remains and sumpweed but none of the other flora components in Mammoth Cave specimens (Marquardt 1974:199). Is this finding indicating further subdivision of rites or medicine societies?

Modern cave ritual specialists exist in central Mexico. "The graniceros, the controllers of meteorological phenomena, belong to a strictly controlled organization. In order to become a member and attend the cave ceremonies a person must have been 'called from above'—that is, designated to work on earth with the supernatural powers that manage rain, thunder, lightning, and the climate. But only those who have been struck by lightning are eligible for this important task. If they survive the baptism by lightning, they cannot deny their destiny and must join the organization" (Heyden 2005:24–25). These individuals receive training in the caves at the big volcanos in central Mexico.

Most curers and weather specialists today report that they were called to make medicine (Figure 32). According to curers in Hueyapan, Mexico, various spirits force people to assume their medical role after they appeared to them in dreams or attacked them in snake, human, or lightning-bolt form. In other Nahua communities people report that they are alerted to their calling after being struck unconscious by lightning, after being attacked by a mal aire, while taking hallucinogenic drugs (Huber 1990:163), or after surviving a serious illness (Schaefer 2002).

Given these circumstances for becoming a doctor, most archaeologists' use of the word "power" when discussing Archaic ritual leaders seems off the mark. Often the implication is that the users of the mnemonic items, the performers of these rites, are strategizing how to seize power from or maintain power over their kin and strangers. The priests and ritual directors working in the Archaic surely had extensive training in the necessary knowledge and tread often in dangerous physical and spiritual localities such as the dark zones

32. Ritual specialist, her attendant, and pilgrims praying for rain at a spring near San Andres de la Cal, Morelos, Mexico, May 17, 2013. (Photo by Marilyn Smith.)

of caves, on balanced rocks, in canoes at a cliff face, at crevices, and in the night. They *earned* the respect of their peers. They were doctors or religious specialists not because they saw opportunities to manipulate other people but because they had been gifted knowledge, a debt that could not be ignored. Interviews with modern ritual specialists in Mexico (Huber 1990; Schaefer 2002) and information extracted from ethnographies of Plains Indians priests and doctors (Irwin 1994) often indicate sincere reluctance to follow this lifeway, which is filled with spiritual trepidation and the mistrust of neighbors that might result in the murder of a "witch." Whereas priest-kings may have desired to control a social group, the part-time religious specialists of the Archaic, be they hunter-gatherers or horticulturists, should not be so "accused."

See *cave, crevice, dream/vision, ritual, ritual calendar, shaman, witch*

Rock Formation

The historic record of native beliefs is rich with examples of rock formations that were considered spirit filled because of a recognizable profile, sound

33. Rock formation at the rain-calling shrine of Tepec, village of Amayaltepec, Guerrero, Mexico, May 2, 2013. (Photo by author.)

when struck, or marvelous defiance of natural laws (Figure 33). Many of these profile rocks, standing stones, balanced rocks, natural bridges, monadnocks, and cliffs are preserved as state and national parks: Pipestone, Standing Rock, Indian Rock, Ringing Rocks, and so forth. Blade caches have been found under rock formations.

See *petroform, profile rock, stone*

Rock Marking

Rock paintings and petroglyphs of probable Archaic age have been located in caves, near rockshelters, and on bedrock in western Kentucky and the Columbia Plateau of eastern Kentucky, Tennessee, and Alabama, and among some specialists they are being referred to as "tattooing" (Diaz-Granados and Duncan 2005:128). Archaic pictographs may be recorded in a few clusters at Red Rock Ridge, Jeffers Petroglyphs site, in southwestern Minnesota (Milne 1994:44). Incised stones at Gault, Titicut, and Hardaway may be pictographs as well.

Lanteigne (1992) includes a few Archaic-aged images from Manitoba and Saskatchewan in his discussion of the formal elements of markings. He highlights seven elements of those images: depth perception, perception of movement and posture, externalization of internal organs and skeletal structure, detailed presentation of fingers, exaggeration of certain body parts to show perception of supernatural powers, the depiction of physical deformities, and the depiction of fantastical creatures. It has been argued that these northern images, as well as those in the Great Basin, were created by priests to memorialize their visions and spirit trips and to acquire and manipulate power (Rajnovich 1994:14; Whitley et al. 1999:232). For instance, among the Ojibway, there were three types of healers or medical practitioners, two of whom made rock markings (Rajnovich 1994:29). Rock markings "are the dreams of the healers who appealed for aid, and their memories of the manitous who reached out to help so long ago" (Rajnovich 1994:16). The tradition of Indian rock painting is picture *writing*, not art (Rajnovich 1994:10).

"For the Algonkian Indians, every place where rock paintings occur was special. They were the homes of the medicine manitous" (Rajnovich 1994: 10). Therefore, one reason that clusters of images differ between geographical locations was because places differed in their efficacy for contacting the specified spirit or acquiring the desired type of information (Whitley et al. 1999:233). The placement of images on lithic formations next to lakes, rivers, and waterfalls around the Great Lakes and along the Ohio, Allegheny, Monongahela, and the lower Susquehanna rivers could be evidence of beliefs in horned serpents and serpent-like monsters (Smith 2005:205).

See *Adair Glyph Cave, art, color, design element, dream/vision, feet/footprint/track, paint/powder, pebbles—engraved, tattooing, 3rd Unnamed Cave*

Rockshelter

Rockshelters can be viewed as large crevices—entry points—for people to cross into the Otherworld and as exits for earth/water/game keeper spirits. As a result, there are a number of different rites conducted by Archaic people in rockshelters although most seem to concern fertility petitioning. For instance, Archaic bone shrines in rockshelters are suggested at Tick Creek Cave, Missouri, and at White Rocks, Ohio, where an adjacent waterfall further emphasized the renewal concerns. Lithic hunting or fertility shrines in or at shelters are suggested by the tremendous quantity of flakes at Wheelabout, Ohio (Spurlock, Prufer, and Pigott 2006). Wheelabout also had two burials, an infant and a woman, making more explicit the fertility role.

Menstrual, birthing, and medicine rite shelters have recently been identified in the Ozarks, in southern Illinois, and in eastern Kentucky (Claassen 2011a). Fertility shelters—themselves the shrine—still attract offerings in Mexico (Figure 7). U.S. fertility shelters have characteristics of weaving/fiber preparation, sandals, shell spoons, seed caches, quids, few meaty species, and lots of nut debris and are often associated with petroglyphs and mortar holes. Ison (2004) identified two clusters of rock art, mortar holes, and used rockshelters in Kentucky, in the Cumberland Plateau section, and along the Green River. All of the retreat shelters appear to be Late Archaic/Early Woodland in age.

The increased use of rockshelters recorded in the Late Archaic in the Cumberland Plateau may indicate either that matrilineal groups had moved into those areas (retreating is highly correlated with matrilineality) and were now using shelters for retreat or that the idea of seclusion during menstruating and birthing evolved at that time.

Other uses for shelters include red ocher powder preparation at Rodgers Shelter, Missouri, and ocher quarrying in a shelter in Ontario (Rajnovich 1994:11). Steatite quarrying occurred in Ragged Mountain shelter, Connecticut (Fowler 1971–72).

Human burials occurred in dozens of Archaic shelters across eastern North America (many of which are called caves) beginning in the Early Archaic, as seen at Horn Shelter 2, Texas, and Ashworth, Kentucky. It is possible that when a woman or mother and baby died during retreat she (and the newborn) were buried in the shelter.

Other burials appear to have been ritual specialists (e.g., Horn Shelter, Texas, a man and a youth, and Short Cave woman). Given that rockshelters were one type of portal to the Underworld, the placement of ritual specialists in these locations, as well as the bodies of witches, facilitated their trip to the land of the spirits and may be indicating the type of medicine that they controlled. Sacrificial infants and adults (e.g., at Ashworth, Breckenridge shelter, Newt Kash Shelter, Watts Cave) also were interred in rockshelters based on burial in the extended or facedown position, weighting with stones, or missing body parts.

Burying lineage heads in rockshelters may have been practiced as well, presenting the idea that rockshelters (and caves in this case) were appropriate places to petition for the continuation of a line, similar to a bone shrine, and that lineage heads, too, became spirits. Decommissioning of trophy parts is indicated at a few shelters as are dog sacrificial rites.

Most of the rockshelters discussed here are located from the Ozarks to the southern Appalachians. Tippins (2007:52) reported little evidence of ritual (four sites with petroglyphs, three sites with objects) in shelters in western

Pennsylvania. Barber (2005:40) noted a significant increase in Early Archaic interest in rockshelters over that of Paleoindian, as well as a dropoff in Late Archaic use in western Virginia, and Purtill (2009:3) concluded that there was less interest in shelters in Ohio during the Middle Archaic. Unfortunately, Spurlock, Prufer, and Pigott (2006) and Pedde and Prufer (2006) only considered caves and shelters with three or more burials in their analysis and obviously focused on burial as the main sign of ritual.

"Lantz (1969:1) found that rockshelters located 'at the heads of valleys' were the most likely to contain evidence of prehistoric occupation . . . [and that] 'most of the shelters of any consequence are on actual trails'" (Tippins 2007:53) and were probably "owned" by a community. Because some shelters were special-use sites, comparisons of the remains from rockshelters and non-rockshelters should be perceived as contrastive sets.

See *burial—limestone, burial—posture, caves, crevice, flake/chip, ritual specialist/priest, trophy part decommissioning rite*

Sacred Landscape

Places for ritualizing are made up of those with long-term importance to groups and those with short-term importance primarily to an individual, a place that may well lose its significance upon the death or relocation of that individual (Claassen 2011b). Curtin thinks similarly: "(1) some sites and landscapes have long histories of use during the Archaic, sometimes spanning the Early, Middle and Late Archaic periods; and (2) it is likely that site and landscape histories were recognized and important to the people who used these places. Over generations, memories of these sites conditioned sequences and types of site-use" (2011:8). Mnemonic devices such as songs and maps probably served to perpetuate these memories.

Unfortunately the notion of "sacred" implies "profane," specifically a profane landscape—one devoid of spirits, one simply economical—that seems unrealistic for Archaic people. I imagine that people saw every inch of the landscape as having the potential to house a spirit and from which a spirit might manifest. Based on historic information and the archaeological record, however, certain types of natural places—springs, waterfalls, caves, sinkholes, bluffs, mountaintops, bluff edges, rock profiles, balanced rocks, fossil beds, and the like—were known to be more likely places where one might encounter spirits and then were avoided or visited specifically to petition a spirit. It was these topographic features that may have constituted something we are tempted to call a sacred landscape, to which should be added old burial grounds.

See *social memory, Stone People, trail*

Sacrifice—Adult

Throughout this work I have suggested that those who were killed by other humans represent human sacrifices for rituals rather than victims of revenge killing or "warfare." We find these sacrificial victims buried in caves, rock-shelters, shell mounds, shell-free mortuary sites, and supposed habitation sites throughout the Ohio and upper Mississippi River valleys. Looking at graves containing multiple burials with at least one person dying violently as examples of human sacrifice, men were most frequently the ones shot/stabbed, scalped, and dismembered. Women were less often killed in rites that resulted in multiple-burial deposits. Mensforth (2005) reported that women were more often scalped, rarely dismembered, and sometimes shot or stabbed.

It appears that adults were sacrificed individually, such as a male victim sought during an annual ritual deer hunt, and in groups of four or five, dubbed four-age and hunt god rites, possibly accompanied with new fire, a new year, or some other calendrical event. In a surprising number of cases, the deepest and/or richest burial in an SOV Archaic site was the victim of violence, suggesting that a consecrating ritual was conducted at a location prior to its becoming a ritual center (Claassen 2010).

The killing of witches, possibly seen in the Stanhope cave killing, and even the Horn Shelter deaths, may also have been part of a rebalancing rite. Cremation of a body may have been viewed as a sacrificial rite.

It is clear that victims who were possibly captives from other social groups were killed by having their necks or torsos twisted, by scalping, shooting, or stabbing, or by possibly bleeding to death through trophy-part taking. It is also apparent upon close scrutiny of burial descriptions that one of the ritualized ways of dying was to be shot by four arrows. There are several examples of this. Lamoka Lake had a double burial with one young man who had four points in or on vertebrae and a severed head, hands, and left foot. He was weighted down with five slabs. The bluff-top Ward site had a grouping of five murdered men, flexed and arranged in a quincunx. One man had four points in the chest area (see Meindl, Mensforth, and York 2001:Figure 5). These and other examples call forth images of the Morning Star sacrifice, where a girl was shot by four priests standing in the cardinal directions. Hall (1997) has linked this rite to the Mississippian version of a hunt god rite.

See *four-age rite, hunt god rite, number, rebalancing rite, sacrifice—infant and child*

Sacrifice—Animal

The most obvious examples of animal sacrifices are those buried in their entirety. Paleoindian raven burials (Driver 1999) in caves of the northwestern United States presage later eastern auk sacrifices in Maritime Archaic practice. Most if not all of the 400+ dog burials recovered in Archaic contexts seem to constitute sacrifices. In some cases the dog lacks its head; in some cases the skull has been bashed in. There was most of a turkey found on the surface in a passage inside Salts Cave, and five perfect turkey skeletons were found in Big Ash "Cave" of eastern Kentucky. "Near the center of the shelter on the sandstone floor a large boulder some ten feet [three meters] long had fallen before the deposit of ash. On this boulder were found five complete skeletons of wild turkey. All parts of these skeletons were in natural anatomical position and the skeletons appeared to have been placed side by side and covered with ashes" (Funkhouser and Webb 1929:76–77).

The characteristics of animal sacrifices have been specified on several occasions (Claassen 2010, 2012b, 2012c). Faunal offerings often used whole small animals and infant animals, but for larger animals, only left sides, heads, wings, or forequarters might be offered in Mesoamerican contexts, either burned or unburned. In addition to burials of animals, meat and blood offerings may have been carried into caves.

See *dog sacrifice rite, dog with human burial rite, offering, rebalancing rite, sacrifice—adult, sacrifice—infant and child*

Sacrifice—Infant and Child

Infants have been found facedown and a few inches under limestone slabs in Russell Cave's Early Archaic stratum and in probable Late Archaic context at New Kash Hollow, Kentucky. Another case was found in Breckenridge Shelter, Missouri. "The major part of an infant burial was found in a crevice between large rock slabs in the west end of the shelter. The skull and some of the other bones were missing [but were] originally to the west" (Wood [1962] 2000:58). The rockshelter context and the placement between two rocks, facedown and head missing, suggest a rite conducted inside rockshelters that involved infant sacrifice.

At Port au Choix several graves of newborns and infants suggested to Tuck ritual sacrifice, probably for a spring first-kill ceremony based on the hunting gear included with the skeleton. Bu26 in Locus 2 was a newborn whose grave contained 75 percent of the bone points from Port au Choix, five duplicate points in slate, three slate bayonets, a triple barbed harpoon, a foreshaft, four bone daggers, a slate knife, a beaver incisor knife with antler handle, seven beaver incisors, a whetstone, two merganser effigy pins, and a merganser bill. This infant was extended with head to the west (Tuck 1976:145). A second newborn was found on top of a pile of tools and weapons (Tuck 1976:17).

The burial of infants, children, and juveniles with atlatls was probably another version of a hunting rite, perhaps a first-kill rite based on an Aztec hunt god who carried an atlatl (Figure 19). Webb (1950:330) uncovered five adolescents, three children, and eight infants buried with atlatls at Indian Knoll; Moore's excavations at the same location uncovered another seven children and 32 adults with atlatls. Subadults accounted for 42 percent of all burials with parts of atlatls.

Many people have remarked on the inclusion of marine shell beads with infants in Archaic burials. Shells have symbolic association with the Underworld, fertility, and the stars and I believe that shells with infants may signify a ritual sacrifice of the infant—a first-kill rite, a rain-calling rite, a hunt god rite, even a rebalancing rite. In Mesoamerica, children up to 10 years of age were sacrificed to Tlaloc, the rain god (Miller and Taube 1993:153). Two infants and two children were wrapped in *Leptoxis* or marine shell bead rebosos at Indian Knoll (photos in Webb 1974:169; modern aging by Kelley 1980). Similar wraps covered children at Chiggerville (Bu61), Carlston Annis (Bu229), and elsewhere in the SOV.

A mixture of infant human bone with that of one or more animals suggests an earth renewal ceremony. The most striking representation of an infant in a possible earth renewal/fertility deposit might be that found at Bluff Creek. This infant was buried with an ulna awl, shell beads, an ospenis of a carnivore, and an ospenis of a raccoon. Anderson's Bu72 was a human infant mixed with a deer fetus, also highly suggestive of a sacrificial rite for renewal. Perry's (Alabama) Bu50 was an extended child with 10 bone pendants made from leg bones of *Chelydra* sp., a turtle, a common representative of the earth. Several infant and child burials at Big Sandy, Alabama, were buried with animal parts.

There are numerous other potential cases of infant and child sacrifices in Archaic burial grounds throughout the east (Claassen 2013a), including the infants found in four-age rites. Those infants are characterized by one or more of the following traits: shell bead rebosos, excessive number of grave goods, other marine shell items, or red ocher. For example, child Bu121 at Read, Kentucky, had red ocher, points, beads, and a rattle (Webb 1950:Figure 3D). The only infant found at the Fennel site (Alabama), on a tributary of the Tennessee River, had a mussel valve filled with red ocher. The use of ocher again raises the suggestion of its association with sacrificial victims. Most uncommon was the Kay's Landing, Tennessee, burial that had a group burial of two infants and two children (Bu33, 34, 35, 36) with extensive red ocher, the only shell items found at the site, stone beads, perforated carnivore canines, and missing hands, feet, and skulls.

See *first-kill rite, grave good, Milky Way, ocher, offering, sacrifice—adult, shell, world renewal rite*

Sandal/Slipper

Eighty slipper specimens were found in Mammoth Cave and Salts Cave (Watson 1969:38), and more have been recovered from Arnold Research Cave in Missouri (Kuttruff, DeHart, and O'Brien 1998). Other examples of 1–3 sandals could be mustered, but sandals are much more commonly found in caves in the western United States, some over 9,000 years old.

Feet are in contact with the Underworld, the place of fertility and the future in Incan thought (Classen 1993). Buffalo hooves and hoofprints on Cheyenne shields are linked to the protective light given by the crescent moon (Nagy 1994), itself a locus of fertility in native thought. Feet and fertility are again linked in southeastern Indian ideas about rabbits' feet, suggesting that sandals, as footwear, were symbols of fertility in the eastern United States. In Mexico today pilgrims and supplicants leave items related to babies, particularly shoes and socks, at fertility shrines (Figures 7, 35), and finding a baby shoe is considered a good omen for pregnancy.

That sandals are occasionally found in both caves and rockshelters throughout the United States and Mexico suggests *not* that caves are good places for preserving sandals that would otherwise be found everywhere but that some caves and rockshelters were recognized portals to spirit homes where offerings for fertility should be left (Claassen 2013b). Textiles constitute offerings for Wixárika women and families and these are carried to the rockshelter or cave home of deities.

See *Arnold Research Cave, cave, feet/footprint/track, moon*

Scalping

Evidence of scalping, which usually was lethal, has been found on eight men and women among 201 skulls in Tennessee, Kentucky, and Ohio Archaic sites (Mensforth 2005). Two females of six Archaic burials in Watts Cave, Kentucky, were scalped. Five men from three Green River sites appear to have been scalped. One male also lacked forearms (Mensforth 2005). A different study found that one subadult at Long Branch, Alabama, showed scalping marks (Lubsen 2004:150). One victim was a possible deer impersonator in a hunt god rite, suggesting an equivalence of scalp and hide. Indeed, the scalp, hair, and skull share many spiritual aspects (Furst 1995).

See *comb, hunt god rite, skull, soul*

Shaman

The word "shaman" refers to an individual who uses dance, a mind-altering substance, and a hand-held drum while wearing an animal skin shirt with jingling adornments and has extensive training in trance induction and movement between cosmic realms to effect a life renewal hunting ritual, to divine, and to heal. This occupation is usually a family profession. "Shamanism" appears to have increased in geographical extent over the last millennium and particularly the past 300 years and does not appear to represent a remnant practice from a primal developmental stage in the history of religion according to Kehoe (2000). Shamanism thus defined may or may not have existed in Paleoindian and Archaic times, and if it did, it may well have been present in some but not all cultures.

Since the term is derived from subarctic cultural practices and requires the traits listed, according to Kehoe (2000), it is not used in this guide, although Betts, Blair, and Black (2012), Brown (2006), and Furst (1995) are comfortable with it. "Priest" and "ritual specialist" are more inclusive terms as well as more accurate. Evidence of trance and transformation could be argued from the presence of hallucinogens in pipes and from pipes that are designed to face the user rather than face outward.

See *pipe, ritual specialist/priest*

Shark

Sharks are most visible in the archaeological record in the Maritime provinces and in the form of teeth. All of the shark teeth catalogued in Betts, Blair, and Black (2012) are from 3 species in one family, out of 7 possible families and 19 possible species. The 2 living species are the mako and great white. The oldest tooth (3980–3630 B.P.) was that of a great white covered with ocher and associated with 6 celts and 9 slate bayonets in a grave at Cow Point. One of the bayonets had incised triangles that have been interpreted as a shark tooth motif (Betts, Blair, and Black 2012:630). Five fossil Megalodon teeth were found in Nova Scotia at the Liverpool site in an Archaic ritual context with a bayonet and projectile point. The nearest known source is the Calvert formation in the Chesapeake Bay (Betts, Blair, and Black 2012:631).

Both humans and sharks prey on swordfish and cod, the mainstays of the Late Archaic diet in the Maritimes, argue Betts and colleagues (2012). Individuals involved in acquiring these animals presumably wore or carried shark teeth and bayonets/foreshafts/clubs with teeth designs in order to hunt like a shark, to have the perspective of a shark (Betts, Blair, and Black 2012). Both humans and sharks are top predators, and both shared the same environment and food, making sharks a source of knowledge and a worthy animal for human emulation (Betts, Blair, and Black 2012). Presumably this logic would hold for the six males and subadults at Windover with a shark's tooth but possibly not the woman (Windover burial database, Florida State Museum).

See *Cult of the Bayonet*, *fossil*, *teeth*

Shell

Shells, being in and from the Underworld, have a pan-American symbolic role in renewal (Claassen 2008). As with all things from the Underworld, they were associated with nighttime, water, fertility, women, and so forth. Perhaps what is most significant is that in many species the soft tissue look like labia, and in a few species (e.g., *Strombus gigas*) there is a visible penis.

Shells of freshwater bivalves and gastropods seem to have acquired renewal symbolism by early Middle Archaic times. Renewal import is seen in the use of clustered freshwater shells as a burial context in the mid-south, Florida, and Georgia; in strata of whole, clean shells capping mounds; in basal deposits containing shells below mounds; in feasting with shellfish; in using a bivalve to dig a grave; and in shell spoons used by menstruating women. Naiad shell is so prevalent in Middle and Late Archaic renewal practices that a Cult of the Bivalve Feast may be suggested and seems to have been specifically focused on shell as a burial medium.

The earliest marine shell use may be the two beads—including one Lettered Olive shell—found with a burial in Horn Shelter, Texas, in Paleoindian context. Subsequent marine shell use included shell ornaments in burials, small shell burial mounds in the Far North, feasting food in the Hudson River valley (Claassen 1995), the shell heaps of the SOV and Florida, and shell rings along the Atlantic and Gulf (e.g., Russo 2004). Alternating layers of white shell and dark muck, burned shell, or midden were important construction elements in Archaic shell-bearing sites in Florida, possibly symbolizing the day-night duality.

Other indications of the symbolic role of shells can be seen in the SOV. Individual marine gastropods have been found containing the remains of an infant (Hermitage Springs Bu308 infant), supporting an infant (Bu811 at Indian Knoll), covering burials (Perry, Alabama, Bu237), inside of graves as digging implements (Meyer, Kentucky), and as paint pots (Bluegrass, Kentucky). A marine shell was placed over the face of Ward's Bu175, a man 23 yo. The skull of Bu24 at site 1Lu86 was resting in a large bivalve (Webb 1939). A conch replaced a skull in Widow's Creek, Alabama (Warren 1975). A conch shell sat in the center of cremated remains and contained the calcined skull fragments of Bu166 at Bluff Creek (Alabama), again suggesting "ancestor" or "renewal" or invoking a deity. Iroquois thought that a shell could purify a soul (Ceci 1989).

See *Busycon, Cult of the Bivalve Feast, Cult of the Snail Shell, fossil, gastropod, Milky Way, naiad, reversal, shell bead, shell scoop/spoon, skull*

Shell Bead

There are four aspects of shell beads that impart meaning: their size (small), their spiral growth, their color (white), and the raw material. Beads have been discussed as metaphors for "village edge," for "berry" (Hamell 1983), and for tears and mucus (Hall 1997), as well as having medicinal qualities in their whiteness (Hamell 1989). Shell beads in historic and modern accounts have been used to adopt and to create kin reborn through shell shooting and gifting of necklaces (Hall 1997). In the mortuary setting they had a restorative role in ritual from both their berry form and their color that effected transformation in the state of being of the deceased. Hamell (1983) maintains that white shell beads have had this symbolism in the Northeast for 6,000 years.

The earliest shell beads found in the eastern United States appear to be marine *Olivella* sp. gastropods in the 9,700 ya Horn Shelter, Texas, double burial. Five *Olivella* shells were found in Early Archaic context at Jerger, Indiana, in a four-age rite. Four marine snail *Marginella* beads at Modoc came from Stratum 12 with an 8,000-year-old date (Ahler et al. 1992:6). Beads using the locally available *Leptoxis* snail were in use by 6000 ya. Shell beads of both marine (most probably *Busycon contrarium*, with a few *Marginella, Olivella, Oliva*, and *Dentalia* sp.) and freshwater (*Leptoxis* sp.) taxa were frequent grave goods in SOV shell mounds but are rare elsewhere in the midcontinent except at Elizabeth Mounds in the LIV. As a rule of thumb in the SOV, if a site lacked freshwater shells in the matrix, it also lacked marine shell artifacts.

Shell beads were also deposited in sites of the St. Johns and Savannah rivers and in Newfoundland. Rows of *Thais* shell beads were found on clothing, bags and pouches, perhaps bands of hide, and probably the hair of at least 25 individuals at Locus 2, Port au Choix-3.

Beads of *Leptoxis* and *Busycon* were sewn together in long rebosos or belts and as bracelets in Illinois and Kentucky. They have been found around the waists of four men and wrists of three of them in a single feature at Elizabeth Mounds, Illinois, a candidate for a hunt god rite, and around the waists of at least ten adults at Indian Knoll. They were also sewn together into rebosos of different lengths for two infants and two children at Indian Knoll, candidates for hunting or rain sacrifices. These vestments may relate to the Milky Way and the starry night sky.

Necklaces of numerous shell beads and cases of one to five shell beads are also found in Archaic burials. Beads cut from *Busycon* shell walls were made into the shapes of small, medium, and large discs. Flintstone-like wheels, tubes, and medium-sized barrels and pieces of the columella (author's research). Curiously, in shell heaps that were supposed to be extensively disturbed by aboriginal digging, shell beads are rarely found outside of burial context.

See *Busycon, gastropod, Leptoxis/Anculosa, Milky Way, Olivella, shell*

Shell Ring

Rings and arcs of oyster shells occur along the coast from South Carolina to Mississippi, recently having been recognized in the Ten Thousand Islands of southern Florida (Schwadron 2010). Ring size increases as one moves southward along the Atlantic (Russo 2004:55, 64). The largest ring in South Carolina (Fig Island) is 77 m across while the largest at Rollins, in Florida, is 200 m across.

Many rings and arcs are now known to have had multiple smaller arcs and rings connected with ramps and ridges of oyster shell, and the height of stacked shells is highly variable at any one ring. These complex sites are better referred to as "shellworks" than "shell rings" since "of the 22 South Carolina and Georgia shell rings mapped or sketched sufficiently, only seven approach anything close to a closed circle; eight are open or C-shaped; one is a closed oval; two are figure eights; one is U-shaped; and three are 'rings' whose shapes defy easy description" (Russo 2004:31). The Rollins shell ring of Florida has 13 attached smaller rings (Russo 2010).

The interior of many rings and arcs is typically featureless. However, at St.

Catherine's Shell Ring, Georgia, 49 features, 36 of which were large, empty post pits, were found inside the ring. The estimated 500 postholes in that interior were thought to derive from substantial structures (Sanger and Thomas 2010:58). Shell-filled pits found under the St. Catherine's Ring suggest that activities had been conducted in a circular arrangement before the shell ring accumulated. Shell-filled pits were also found below the ring shell at Sapelo Island Ring (Thompson and Andrus 2011).

Although believed to be habitation sites, shell rings are also thought to be places where aggrandizing individuals and groups hosted competitive feasts with a rival community, the ring remaining to memorialize the event(s) (Russo 2010:156–157; Saunders 2004). These feasts were not mortuary feasts because no skeletons have been found. Russo has argued that the co-occurrence of high-quality artifacts in thicker and taller segments of shell deposits preserve evidence of a social hierarchy within both the host group and the guest group (Russo 2004). The presence of abundant oysters and a sufficient willing population to gather them demonstrated the host group's spiritual health/wealth rather than "power" (Russo 2010:157).

It is thought that most of the rings were used for only a few decades (Russo 2010:157), but the St. Catherine's ring accumulated over a 200-year period. An uncritical acceptance of all radiocarbon dates would start the ring-building phenomenon at 4700 B.P. and end the bulk of the new construction around 3600 B.P. However, it was recently demonstrated that ring construction continues into Mississippian times (Russo 2010).

See *Cult of the Bivalve Feast, mound—shell, shell, shellworks*

Shell Scoop/Spoon

Bader (2010/11) has suggested that mussel shells were used to dig out graves in western Kentucky sites and then dropped into the grave. Single valve inclusions with burials have also been noted elsewhere: at Black Earth, East Steubenville, Chiggerville, Ward, Barrett, Bowles, Indian Knoll, Big Sandy, and Widow's Creek, all in the SOV. Two graves in Vaughn, Mississippi, burial mound also contained unusually large valves that the excavator suggested were used to dig the graves (Atkinson 1974:147). Mussel valves would indeed have served this purpose well given the symbolic placement of shells in the Underworld. Although much removed in time and a continent away, the Tlingit use the same word to mean coffin, womb, and bivalve. Among the Seneca of New York, a shell could hold the soul of the dead and purify the decaying flesh, allowing for entry into the spirit world (Ceci 1989).

Based on the symbolic place for the shell in fertility, as well as that of caves and rockshelters, it is not at all surprising that naiad valve spoons are a frequent element of the material culture recovered in bluff shelters of the Ozarks, eastern Kentucky, and southern Illinois, most of which are arguably women's menstrual retreat shelters (Claassen 2011a). Unique utensils were a characteristic of menstrual huts in historic times, and it seems that shell spoons were unique utensils as far back as Late Archaic times.

See *menstrual retreat, Meyer, naiad*

Shellworks

Shellworks are "purposefully constructed features composed of primary or secondary shell refuse intentionally borrowed, piled, or arranged to form mounds, ridges, rows of mounds, rings, platforms, and depressions. . . . [in] public, domestic, and ceremonial spaces" and in some cases "canals, fishponds, water courts, public plazas, and ceremonial or residential mounds" (Schwadron 2010:123). Many of the shell rings along the Atlantic coast are actually part of shellworks, but the most elaborated shellworks are found in Charlotte Harbor and the Ten Thousand Islands sections of southwestern Florida and the Gulf Coast and began in Late Archaic times (Schwadron 2010:124). Many of the investigated sites appear to have a shell ring or arc as the earliest—Late Archaic—element and then to have been increasingly elaborated through the post-Archaic Glades period (Schwadron 2010:137).

See *Cult of the Bivalve Feast, Cult of the Snail Shell, earthwork, Horr's Island, shell, shell ring*

Shrine

A shrine is a natural or made feature where devotions are performed to a spirit or deity such as at rockshelters, cliffs, crevices, springs, trees, sinkholes, cairns, cemeteries, altars, mounds, or earthworks (Figures 7, 17, 18, 22, 33, 34).

Based on site context and structure descriptions, there were possible shrines at Bailey (Figure 8), East Aberdeen, Mississippi, Higgs (Figure 13), Riverton (Figure 15), Mulberry Creek, Lamoka Lake, Monte Sano (pre-mound), Jaketown, and 9Wr4 (Georgia). Those at Lamoka Lake were 176–208 ft^2 (16.36–19.32 m^2), that under the mound at Monte Sano 100 ft^2 (9.29 m^2), and the five complete surfaces at Riverton 68–260 ft^2 (6.34–24.15 m^2) (Winters 1969:97; Figure 15). All complete clay platforms at Riverton had one or more unprepared hearth areas, repeatedly burned, and dense midden around the platform. Bone shrines have been covered separately.

34. Cypress tree shrine in Morelos where pilgrims seeking fertility hang baggies with umbilical cords, baby shoes, baby socks, and pictures of children. (Photo by author.)

Rafferty, Baker, and Elliott (1980:255) described a circular posthole outline in a probable Archaic level of the East Aberdeen site in Mississippi: "The outer postholes formed a roughly circular shape with a large central clear space. Inside the circle were the burial, one hearth, and two postholes . . . the fact that this circular pattern [at 80 to 100 cmbs] coincided fairly well with the outlines of the [smoothed clay surface with one posthole] in the 60cm level suggests that they were associated."

The extremely high density of items in an isolated, large, semisubterranean pit surrounded by postholes (7,000+ items in Feature 30) at 9Wr4 in Georgia could be indicative of a shrine. The items included thousands of flakes and numerous hammerstones, bannerstones, drills, and soapstone pieces mostly concentrated around a large, deep hearth against the eastern wall. Four caches of flakes were found, three around the hearth, each of a different type of metavolcanic rock, and one outside the building comprised of quartz pieces (Ledbetter 1995:251). This pithouse dated 4350–4200 B.P. and had substantial posts. A second such feature (from a looter's collection) in Aiken County, South Carolina, also a large pit feature, contained hundreds of the same items (Sassaman 2006:69).

Other potential shrines can be identified. Range site's basin Feature 3975 measured 2.13 m x 1.73 m (39.6 ft^2) and was oriented northwest-southeast with 14 postmolds of ca. 6-cm diameter inside the basin. It was 50 m away from the nearest (surviving?) Archaic feature (Fortier 1987:66). A similar rectangular basin structure was uncovered at McLean, on the edge of the sinkhole at the edge of the site. Forty posts inside the basin were 9–20 cm in diameter and 5 m x 2.8 m in area (150 ft^2) and enclosed two large features and one smaller one, a possible roof support. No artifacts were found on the floor of the structure, but McElrath (1986:80) assigned it to the Emergent Mississippian component. Goddard, Pennsylvania, had a circular Archaic structure.

Rock cairns may have been shrines in the Archaic, forming either the destination shrine or waymarker shrines on pilgrimage paths like those the author observed on the 2012 rain-calling pilgrimage of Acatlan, Mexico (Figures 18, 19). There are several intriguing claims that Archaic-aged cairns exist in elevated areas of Missouri and Tennessee (e.g., House 1965).

See *bone shrine, cairn, offering*

Sinkhole

Having participated in a sinkhole rain-calling ceremony in northern Guerrero, Mexico, in 2010 (Claassen 2011c), I am convinced that some sinkholes, particularly those known to open into caves or chambers at the bottom, were spiritually charged places (Figure 14). Mountaintops and their topographical opposites, sinkholes, were where one could find the oldest earth and thus the oldest spirits. Several sinkhole springs contain the remains of stone creatures, and hundreds of sinkholes are find spots for the artifacts of people from an earlier creation (Paleoindians).

Archaeologists now recognize a strong correlation between Paleoindian sites and sinkholes in Florida and the Highland Rim in Alabama, Tennessee, and Kentucky. "The karst environment must have supported an exceptionally dense animal population" (Waselkov and Hite 1987:1). Sinkholes often filled with water, or were water traps, and supported a different flora and fauna. Sinkholes were also crevices in This World, portals to the Underworld that could open suddenly.

Currently the oldest used sinkhole in the interior United States was that of Sheriden Cave in central Ohio. The cave leads off of this sinkhole (map in Waters et al. 2009:108) and contains two bone points, one dated at 13,000 to 12,925 B.C., plus snapping turtle, peccary, and a Clovis point. The rim of a sinkhole was used for the burial of two young men at the Lawrence site, Kentucky. Grave goods were associated. The Adams site, Kentucky, had extensive lithic debris at the rim of a sinkhole. A possible shrine was found at the southeastern edge of the sinkhole upon which the McLean (Illinois) site was located (McElrath 1986). The Big Sandy site, consisting of dozens of camps and hundreds of projectile points, was on the south side of a deep sinkhole in northwest Alabama. Numerous important Archaic caves and rockshelters were entered through sinkholes. Sinkhole vestibules with remains are Savage Cave and Mammoth Cave, Kentucky; Wyandotte Cave, Indiana; Russell Cave, Alabama; and Hendricks Cave, Ohio, among others.

According to Harl (2009:385), "Late Archaic groups seem to have been particularly drawn to sinkholes in St. Louis and St. Charles counties but Hoing is the only one of these sites to have been further investigated. . . . 21 pit features clustered near the southwestern edge of the ponded sinkhole [were possible bearwallows]."

"Bearwallows" or round depressions are perhaps a cognitive variation on sinkholes found in the Appalachian Mountains. "The presence of bearwallows serves as an effective means of preserving archeological sites, which are always found in and around these circular depressions" (Wilkins 1978:17). Bearwallows vary in depth from 1 to 13 ft (30–396 cm) and in circumference from 30 ft to more than 200 ft (9.1–61 m).

See *Big Sandy, cave, crevice, James Creek, Lawrence, Little Salt Spring, mountain, projectile point, shrine*

Site Avoidance

Caves may have been places that were so powerful that they were avoided by most Archaic peoples. The lack of pottery or insignificant amounts of it at dozens of Archaic naiad shell burial grounds suggest that these places were by and large also avoided by later people. That pottery is often found atop a capping layer.

Other places may have been avoided because of bad airs associated with them. Anderson proposed that Poverty Point was intentionally avoided by post-Archaic peoples because something bad or overwhelming had happened there (2010:300n22). Lepper (2006) suggested that the subsequent avoidance of Hopewell centers and Flint Ridge flint was because of the sacredness of both: "Some tribes of the Eastern Woodlands did, indeed, regard certain sites as places to be avoided: 'Indian tradition still keeps alive the fact that these grounds have been the theatre of blood; and such is their abhorrence of scenes once enacted here, that except in a few very rare instances, they do not visit the regions near the ancient forts and burying grounds'" (Clark 1849:2: 263, cited in Lepper 2006:129).

See *capping, decommissioning rite, site reuse*

Site Reuse

Rituals and offerings make places. Places attract subsequent attention as people maneuver to either access or avoid these places where powers and spirits can be contacted, have come, and may still linger. In the case of reuse of places, it may well be that the successful record of contacting spirits in that place is part of the explanation for its reuse or continued use.

"Apparently, places of abandonment became crucial resources for reconstituting new communities, while new places and new alliances structured the outcome of future relocations" (Sassaman 2010a:78). Abandoned ceremonial centers and burial grounds might attract pilgrims or at least offerings when the location was passed en route elsewhere, as was recorded for Historic Plains Indians who passed various cave shrines while in service of the U.S. Army (Sundstrom 1996).

The span of use for the Archaic shell mounds (where more than one date is available) ranges from 607 to 1,247 years for the Wabash River sites, 670 to 3,838 years for the Green River proper sites, and 1,850 to 2,416 years for the Duck and Harpeth river sites (Claassen 2010:19–20). (It is not surprising that the widest ranges are indicated for the sites with greatest number of dates generally.) These ranges indicate from 30 to 191 generations remembering these places. But memory was even longer than that.

"Significantly, Middle Woodland/Hopewell funerary activities occurred in the same locations we described for the Archaic: bluff-top cemeteries and multicommunity gathering sites on sand ridges in the floodplains," and they were used simultaneously rather than alternately as in the Archaic, resulting in monumental burial mounds. "At sites like Elizabeth and Gibson-Klunk, the earliest Middle Woodland mounds were constructed directly on top of Archaic cemeteries" (Charles and Buikstra 2002:20). Much the same can be said for Ohio's Archaic sites. "Mound placement directly over Late Archaic mortuary pits and domestic-looking features suggests knowledge of earlier components and the deliberate association of Woodland-period burials with earlier 'ancestor' groups" (Purtill 2009:590) as well as surficial markers.

Reuse of Archaic shell ridges and burial mounds is also evident in St. Johns period site placement in Florida and in Mississippian intrusive burials into Tennessee River and Green River shell mortuaries. The latter situation indicates that these powerful Archaic places were remembered for hundreds of generations for the rites conducted at them. Curtin thinks that memories of old sites conditioned "sequences and types of site-use. This perspective allows us to assume that earlier uses conditioned and even favored later uses, in contrast to the more conventional assumption that productive sites and landscapes were not so much remembered as rediscovered in successive generations after periods of abandonment" (2011:8).

Possibly by Mississippian times these Archaic people and places occupied a space in the first creation, as Stone People. Or had they come to be seen as a second creation, a second world? Were their stones and bones scavenged to be redeposited in Mississippian rituals?

See *social memory*, *Stone People*

Skull

The painted buffalo skull found at the Cooper site, in Oklahoma, is considered to have functioned as a good luck charm, drawing the bison herd into an arroyo that resulted in a successful kill (Bement 1999:181). But why a skull?

For Uto-Aztecan speakers the skull was the seat of one of the souls known as tonali, the soul that imparted fate and vital heat. Tonali was also conveyed through likeness, name, body sluff (hair, nails, skin), clothing, and jewelry (Furst 1995). A skull of a bison would then draw other bison to it and stand as an ancestor to them just as merganser bird skulls carved on bone pins in Port au Choix graves might be expected to attract other mergansers.

A similar belief in multiple souls including one like tonali is probably behind the eastern Archaic practices associated with head removal and head keeping from both living individuals and burials. That postburial head removal was practiced in the Illinois River valley, in the SOV, and in the far Northeast is seen in the numerous examples of skeletons with no heads and missing vertebra but also no cut marks on remaining vertebrae. Retention of the skull represents the capture of the vital essence of animals and humans. This soul is probably also indicated in the curation of skulls of other animals, the honoring of head profile rocks, and the taking of scalps and pelts.

See *bone*, *head removal*, *human bone artifact*, *scalping*, *soul*, *trophy part*, *trophy part decommissioning rite*

Snake

Rattlesnakes and other snakes were accorded much symbolic significance in the southwestern United States, in Mesoamerica, and in Mississippian iconography. How far back does this important role for the snake go?

Possibly the oldest ritual use of the snake was in the grave fill of the double burial in Horn Shelter 2 (9710+/-40 B.P. from human bone), along with bird, deer, rodent, fish, and frog bones. Some Middle Archaic sites with snake bones are Black Earth (Breitburg 1982:870), Anderson, WMECO in Massachusetts (Thomas 1980), and Twombly Landing on the Hudson River (Claassen 1995:133). Rattlesnake and racers made up 4 percent of the identified bone at the Bluegrass site in Indiana on the Ohio River (Stallings 2008:181).

A few Late Archaic sites have poisonous and nonpoisonous snake bones in low numbers. Even fewer graves contained snake bones, for example, Carlston Annis's Bu239 (Crothers 2005:309), Indian Knoll's Bu708, and Bu62 at Eva, a male (priest?) apparently wearing a rattlesnake vertebra necklace (Lewis and Lewis 1961:87). An Archaic image of a snake incised on a stone lid covering an offering at the Titicut site on the Taunton River shows that snakes were conceptually associated with whirlpools or possibly hurricanes (Figure 24), although Fowler offers that the drowned man was of the snake clan (Fowler 1966:44, 51).

A rattlesnake's rattle was recovered at Newt Kash Shelter, which has been interpreted as a Late Archaic women's retreat shelter (Claassen 2011a). In historic times rattlesnakes were part of women's medicine, particularly during pregnancy, and were depicted as the earth with a female deity tilling the earth-snake in the Mississippian-aged Birger figurine.

See *medicine*

Soapstone/Steatite

Soapstone would have ritual import because of its "stoneyness," its unusual feel, and its heating properties. "Steatite occurs as early as the Middle Archaic Morrow Mountain phase, but its use as a container [and netweight] is restricted to the Late Archaic and Early Woodland" (Chapman 1981:103). The earliest use of steatite in the Savannah River valley was for hot rock cooking at 6500 B.P. (Sassaman 2006:43). "Soapstone vessel technology does not predate ca 4000 cal BP in any part of the greater Southeast" (Sassaman 2010a:133). Steatite use seems to appear after the Archaic in the Northeast (Pagoulatos 2009).

"Steatite deposits occur along much of the Atlantic Slope of eastern North America in belts [with] . . . large outcrops [in] . . . east Alabama and west Georgia, northwestern South Carolina, northwestern North Carolina, central Virginia, Washington DC area, southeastern Pennsylvania and southern New England. . . . [There is a] lack of quarries in Vermont" (Sassaman

2010a:131). "The largest local outcrops and quarries [run] from the Mason-Dixon Line's junction with the Susquehanna River to . . . Georgetown in Lancaster County, Pennsylvania" (Custer 1989:167). Occasional patches of steatite are found in the St. Johns River area and around Poverty Point (Sassaman 2010a:133). Nevertheless, the distribution of steatite vessels is much larger than the area of natural deposits and in most places followed pottery. Steatite "was the raw material of choice for the durable, heat-resistant containers of fourth millennium populations across several regions" (Sassaman 2010a:130) and directly influenced the adoption of ceramic vessels.

Ritual context for soapstone in the Deep South is seen in two caches on the Gulf Coastal Plain (Poverty Point and Claiborne), but stone bowls in mortuary context occur in the Early Woodland (Sassaman 2010a:201).

See *Claiborne, container, pottery, Poverty Point, stone*

Social Memory

It is apparent in the reuse of many Archaic sites that memorials had been created of them or that some facilities were "made to last, to be seen, and to be meaningful to groups of people transgenerationally" (Clark and Colman 2008:93). Social memory was created in dozens of ways, from trails to pits, rock markings to posts, through songs, stories, and site layouts and relationships between sites, even through distinctive vegetation attracted to camps where concentrations of chemicals such as calcium could be found.

In contrast to the idea that Indians did not know to expect previous burials in their burial grounds and would thus disturb the dead, several authors suggest the opposite. Henden (2000), for instance, reported that the memory of burial locations was very import to the Maya. A comment made by Wallace and Steen (1972:94) revealed that Seneca "mothers often visited the graves of their children and noticed the least change in the appearance of the enshrouding earth; sometimes they identified the spot of an unmarked grave after years of absence."

See *monument, sacred landscape, site reuse*

Soul

The existence of multiple souls in a being was probably one of the beliefs of the first immigrants to the New World. Where the Nahuas of northern and central Mexico distinguished three souls (Furst 1995), the Iroquois spoke of two souls, sensitive or bone soul, and a soul of the mind (Furst 1977:16). For the Nahuas, the yolia soul, centered in the heart, animates humans. It is solidified in objects like bezoars, kidney stones, heart-shaped stones, and precious gemstones and is visible departing the body as breath and winged creatures. Anger and passion, talent and endeavor are its expressions. If a person died in extreme fright or anger the yolia would stay among the living causing harm, and it is for this reason that Mexicans tack the soul of an accident victim to the (roadside) place of death with a cross. Were limestone slabs used similarly, to anchor the soul of the accidentally dead, witches, and sacrificed individuals?

The yolia of these southern groups shares much with the sensitive soul of the Iroquois. Both souls are tethered to the bones of the deceased person or animal. Both groups believe that it is from the bones, not the flesh or the semen, that new life comes. Seeds are the equivalent of bones for plants and rock is the earth's bones.

The second soul in Nahua thought is the tonali, seated in the head. It is drilled into the fetus via the fontanel, through which this soul exits during dreaming, fever, and soul loss sickness. It is the vital heat of a living being that gets stronger until midlife and then weakens with advancing age, waxes and wanes with the daily movement of the sun, and builds to dangerous levels with menstruation, pregnancy, lovesickness, and fasting (Furst 1995). It exudes from the eyes and results in several sumptuary rules regarding eye avoidance, crop avoidance, and abstention from sex before games and ceremonies, and it exudes from the body, resulting in the need for women to retreat during menstruation and pregnancy from the vulnerable ones around them including children, men, plants, and game. Weak tonalis explain the use of virgins (youths) in the service of spirits in temples and sacrifices. Building tonali heat to near dangerous levels through abstinence and sweats is the goal of specialists about to conduct a ritual, warriors and hunters about to engage another being, and players before a game. Rebuilding the tonali after a birth prompted the use of sweatbaths for mothers postdelivery.

Tonalis resided in resemblance including descendants; in scalps, skins, and bark; and in clothing and jewelry of "hot" individuals. The 260-day calendar explained the particular personality and fate of a person based on birthdate (Furst 1995), which was in evidence through the mathematics governing Poverty Point. Tonali seems to be much the same as the Iroquois soul of the mind (but confused with the yolia soul by P. Furst [1977]).

The third soul of Nahua philosophy, ihyotl, is not easily separated from the yolia and thus may be subsumed in the bone soul conception by the Iroquois and others who do not make a third division of the soul. It is easily seen, however, in wind, particularly cold breezes from the mouths of caves, dust devils, tornadoes, and hurricanes, and in smells such as putrification, flatulence, and sulfur. Auras offer another perspective on ihyotl, such as St. Elmo's fire and shimmering heat waves (Furst 1995). Fantasmas and wandering souls are sensed as sudden temperature changes, suddenly occurring odors, and inexplicable breezes. Both the ihyotl and the yolia encapsulate beliefs about the spiraling cosmos that may be expressed through the use of whole *Busycon* shells, columella shell beads, and all other gastropod beads.

Betts and colleagues (2012:624) point out that native peoples believe that all entities are capable of having souls—it is only the body, the capsule, that differs. But souls are not equally powerful and the potential for a soul is not always realized. This realization they call "perspectivism."

See *bone soul, burning, gastropod, shell, wind*

Sound

A developing investigative tool for ritual and beliefs is that of archaeoacoustics. Elements of sound and silence were created, captured, and employed in ancient ritual. Caves, rockshelters, other rock features, canyons, mountaintops, and mound/plaza sets may have been revered for the echoes produced. Sound-canceling properties of rock features also may have been important (e.g., http://www.huffingtonpost.com/2012/02/16/stonehenge-inspired-by-sound-illusion_n_1283464.html?ref=science&ncid=webmail13, accessed June 17, 2012). Ringing Rocks on the Delaware River is described as "rivers of rock"; each boulder has a unique sound when percussed. Sounds from deep within Enchanted Rock in central Texas drew specialists and pilgrims alike in the recent past (Milne 1994:80).

Mimicking the sound of thunder may have been important in fertility and rain-calling events achieved by drumming, striking turtle shells, and pounding rock mortars. Today bottle rockets serve this purpose in Mexico (Figure 35), their light recalling lightning simultaneously with the sound of thunder. Mimicking the sound of rain or flowing water was clearly evident in the pan-American use of carapace rattles and the rattles of rattlesnakes.

Various animal noises also may have been ritually important in marking the changing of the seasons or signaling oncoming rain. The hooting of owls carried death symbolism, and the calls of various birds foretold other important information.

See *bedrock mortar/nutting stone, flintknapping, locust, music, quarry(ing), stone*

Spring

Places where the earth's surface was ruptured were places one could commune with earth spirits (Figure 32). Springs could be places of revelation, such as the first appearance of the White Panther at a spring on the Huron River in Michigan. The Wyandot Land Turtle Clan made sacrifices into this

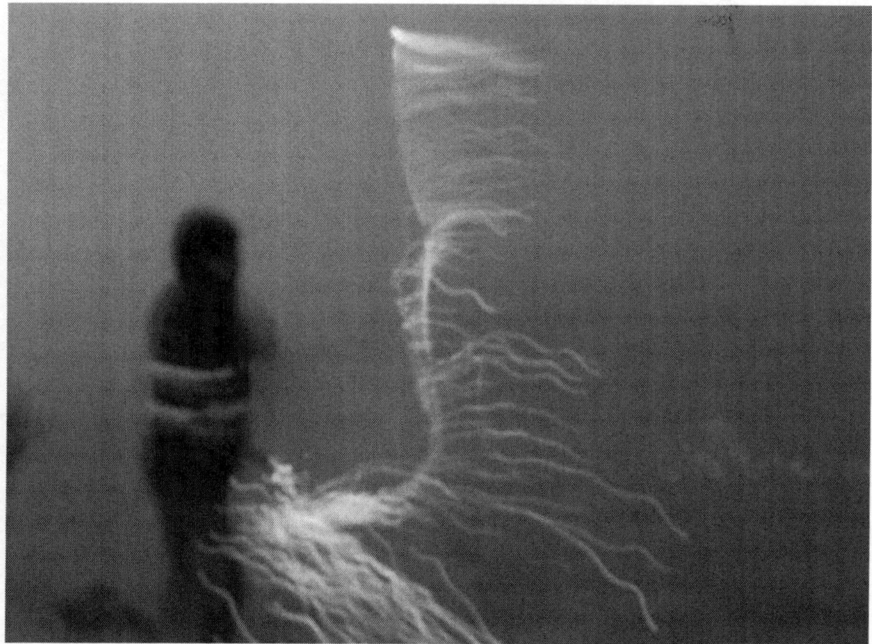

35. Pilgrim at the shrine on top of Mishuehue Mountain fires a bottle rocket over the valley below, mimicking lightning and thunder, May 1, 2011. (Photo by author.)

spring (Harper 1999:32). Hot Springs, Arkansas, was neutral territory for all native peoples (Milne 1994:69), perhaps reaching back to the Archaic. The Tunica say they originated in these springs. Novaculite is found nearby as are crystals.

Archaeological remains indicate that numerous springs did serve as shrines in the Archaic. Afton Springs, in eastern Oklahoma, contains bones of mammoth and mastodon on top of which Holmes (1903) found thousands of lithic items dating from Paleoindian through Mississippian times (Thomas 1969:5; Lee Bement, personal communication with the author, August 2011). Springs near fossil deposits with possible Archaic-aged burials include Koch Spring on the Pomme de Terre River and two springs in the Osage River valley (Kay 1983:62). Cultural material found in the excavations at Phillips Spring, Missouri, was densest closest to the spring and included deer and mussels (Chomko 1978). "Numerous springs and streamheads originate near the crests of watershed divides, and nearly 100 percent of them are surrounded by prehistoric sites, a situation like that noted . . . for South Georgia and Ft. Bragg, NC" (Brooks, Taylor, and Ivester 2010:157).

Several other springs are associated with sinkholes such as Little Salt Spring,

Florida (Figure 14). Wakulla Springs, Florida, is well-known as a spring pond with an underwater cave system where bones of extinct and modern species have accumulated along with 600+ bone points or leister prongs and stone points (Jones and Tesar 2000).

See *fossil, Pomme de Terre River, sinkhole*

St. Johns River

More than 7,000 ya people began using the landscape of the St. Johns River to express their beliefs about death and cosmology. Members of the Cult of the Snail Shell were responsible for the creation of shell mounds and shell ridges, usually located on islands where they created platforms and included some of their dead. But why the St. Johns?

The spiritual importance attending the springs that feed the river, the islands that exist(ed), the karst topography in general, and the northward-flowing water are elements in the answer. "Of the 71 springs recorded within the St. Johns basin, 59 have expression within the Middle St. Johns," and it is here that the pond burials are found. "This total includes three first-order magnitude springs (greater than 2.8 m3/s or more) at Silver Glen Spring, Alexander Spring, and Blue Spring," two of which were important ceremonial sites during Orange Period times (Asa Randall, personal communication with the author, August 2012).

See *Cult of the Snail Shell, gastropod, Green River, Harris Creek, Pomme de Terre River, spring*

Stone

The sacredness of stone has its basis in the idea that ancient spirits live inside of stone and from the association of stone with water. These spirits can be those of the Stone People, of deities, of animals, or of the living person of worth or the newly departed human. Spirit homes can be a pebble, a grouping of cobbles, a rock outcrop, a cave, a mountain, a biface, an ax, or a pestle, as well as many other forms of stone.

The stone and its resident spirit can be manipulated by dream animals, living persons, or the spirit itself and do good—such as healing, reproducing, and seeing—or do harm by destroying and killing. Because of the spirits living inside of stone, stones are known to move, hear, reproduce, sing, swallow, shoot, and behave in other anthropomorphic ways. Stones favored by a sky spirit are the sweat lodge stones, hearth stones, and the ax. It is this spirit in sweat stones who hears the comments made in the lodge (Irwin 1994:179) and who is appeased with food and drink offerings thrown into the household hearth in Nahua rituals (Sandstrom 1991:249).

Figuring prominently in Plains Indian sacred bundles, a sacred stone was "perhaps one of the oldest and most primordial religious objects among Native Americans. . . . the stone may embody a wide variety of powers according to its general form. . . . Generally, its symbolism is tied to an ancient knowledge that the earth alone possesses and that is known by the oldest members of earth, the stone people" (Irwin 1994:224). "The stones know the earth and what is happening on it at all times. A powerful shaman can send his stones after requisite knowledge because they are capable of traveling throughout the world strata" (Irwin 1994:225–226).

During the first of the four creations, say the Sioux of Crow Creek, "the age of Rock," "the Water Monsters were blasted into stone by Thunder Birds' bolts of lightning" (Mayor 2005:221). Even the Thunder Birds' bodies are now found as stone fossils, often within the same bed as their ancient nemesis the Water Monsters. "Rock, Inyan, was the origin of life, and rocks still hold the essence and record of early life on Earth" (Mayor 2005:230).

Fertility in and from stones is also derived from the drilling act to produce a hole and from the shapes of stones. Round stones are both egg-like and testicle-like, and pointy stones are penis-like. Round stones in a field bode well for a successful crop and were called eggs (Chevalier and Bain 2003:184). Stone balls were found in 13 graves at Port au Choix and inside and outside Graham Cave. Absarokee visionaries could identify the gender of a sacred stone—a fossil ammonite or baculite—by its shape (Irwin 1994:224). The baculites are cylindrical fossils with crystalline developments that occasionally resemble bison shapes. These are the Buffalo-calling stones—a gift of Weasel Woman—so sought after by Blackfeet, Cheyenne, and Sioux and occasionally found in archaeological sites of the high plains. Fertility is also implied by the stones that form the foundation of a house.

Maritime Archaic burials often contained abstractly shaped and realistically shaped small stones, concretions, and wood. Tuck (1976:71–72) cites Micmac and pre-Micmac practices of keeping such stones in houses or on the body for good luck.

Many groups believed that the life force could become hard and stony upon death (Classen 1993:30; Furst 1995:74; Irwin 1994). Rocky outcrops resembling the human face and profile, gallstones, and kidney stones provided proof for these beliefs (Furst 1995). The Aztecs believed that the animating soul, the yolia, was located in the heart. It was captured in stone as heart-shaped rocks or in a rock placed at the heart area. A rock placed with a corpse or cremation served to anchor the yolia. Unfortunately any intentional inclusion of stones and pebbles in graves has probably been overlooked frequently by archaeologists.

See *bedrock mortar/nutting stone, cairn, crevice, flake/chip, flintknapping, gorget, projectile point, soapstone, soul, sound, stone bead*

Stone Bead

Middle Archaic stone bead manufacture (debitage, tools, preforms, beads) and pebble drilling has been documented at the Denton site (Mississippi) in disc, barrel, tube, and effigy shapes including one drilled crinoid stem (Connaway 1977:79–96). Groundstone beads in Mount Taylor culture sites—Lake Monroe Outlet, Silver Glen Run, and Thornhill Lake—appear in mortuary and cache contexts (Randall 2005:22) and are quite similar to beads produced in the mid-south during the Middle Archaic (Asa Randall, personal communication with the author, August 2012).

The southern Middle Archaic beads may have diffused from a few makers across the five-state region through intermarriage (Connaway 1977:127) or resulted from the spread of a basic magical concept rather than that of objects (Webb 1971). Sassaman (2010a:122–123) points out that there was virtually no overlap between the effigy beads of the Deep South and the Benton culture, further emphasizing that Benton culture shows more affinity with the shell mound builders of the Tennessee River. Tubular stone beads did overlap with shell mounds in graves on the Green River and Tennessee River, as well as in central Tennessee, but are the only item of material culture that does. Babies of the SOV were never given more than one stone bead (Claassen 2013a).

Middle Archaic stone beads were never found in graves in Mississippi and Louisiana but were cached. "The Keenan Cache, as reported by Connaway (1981), consisted of more than 469 jasper items placed in a pit. One large effigy bead was placed on the bottom of the pit, and then long tubes were assembled in upright positions (perhaps nestled in a bag), then covered with all the other beads and buried. Although none of the items was completely finished, the cache included no lapidary tools" (Sassaman 2010a:123).

Connaway offered the following about the Middle Archaic stone bead collection from Denton, Mississippi: "at the level of social organization postulated for the group living at the Denton site, it seems very unlikely that such objects could have been created for mere ornamentation. Socio-religious connections are almost certain" (1977:126). Connaway argues for their role as either amulets or fetishes. Their rendering in stone indicates a belief that they were idols or at least amulets referencing the first creation and the Stone People.

Both zoomorphic and nonzoomorphic beads occur in the Late Archaic. They are found in both Poverty Point and non–Poverty Point loci, including Florida.

See *amulet/charm/talisman, fetish, insect, pebble, stone, Stone People*

Stone People

Irwin speaks of the belief by native peoples of today in a first creation, a world of beings turned to stone: "Generally, [stone] symbolism is tied to an ancient knowledge that the earth alone possesses and that is known by the oldest members of earth, the stone people" (1994:224). The time of the Stone People ended with the Great Flood. The people and the animals of this earlier creation were changed to stone by the deities and the world cleaned with water. This flood—the terminal Pleistocene/Early Holocene lake, river, and sea level rise—did indeed drown many important places.

Archaic beliefs and rituals about the Stone People would have been derived in three ways. First, these beliefs and rituals were captured in the stories of earlier times when places underwater in the Archaic were used by the Stone People, such as the caribou drivelines now at the bottom of Lake Huron (O'Shea and Meadows 2009) and the coastal Florida sinkholes. Second, knowledge of them was derived from their stone homes—the fluted points and other artfully chipped-stone points. Third, evidence of this people was seen in the stony remains of giant animals found in various fossil beds, as well as their stony tracks in New England, and in profile rocks. Archaic people offered groups of blades to the Stone People, sought their council at sinkhole and springs shrines where their ancient homes could be found, collected their stone homes, and deployed the points in new places. In Louisiana and Mississippi some of the Stone People were made manifest as owls and locusts in red stone and other stone beads. Red ocher, commonly found in deposits along with the fossil remains of Stone People (animals), was a sign of the stony blood.

See *Afton Springs, cache—blade, Cult of the Blade, fossil, Great Flood, Pomme de Terre River*

Stone Rod

Groundstone rods of extreme size and difficult production were a common grave inclusion in Early and Middle Archaic northeastern burials, following adzes and gouges in frequency. They are interpreted as whetstones for adzes left in the graves of boat builders. Perforated rods occurred soon after the first appearance of rods, and by 5,000 ya most rods had the form of "Penobscot" pendants, 90 percent of which were perforated (Robinson 2006:353–354). They disappeared after 5,000 ya and may have been replaced with suspended plummets.

Unused rods most often occurred in Middle Archaic burials, but a manufacturing locale has been identified at Gilman Falls Island, Maine. Since they do not appear in Late Archaic cemeteries or sites, these rods apparently lost whatever symbolism they had had and the quarry was abandoned (Sanger 2006:233–234).

See *stone*

Sucking Tube

Since tobacco did not reach North America during the Archaic, Archaic "pipes" were not used to smoke tobacco. The lack of charred material in the bowl of "pipes" at places like Anderson (Dowd 1989) suggests that many of these objects were not pipes at all but sucking tubes, used by doctors. A probable sucking tube was found at Riverton (Illinois), and three came from Perry in one subadult burial (Webb and DeJarnette 1942).

See *medicine, pipe*

Sun

In Muskogean cosmology, the sun was the most important celestial deity. Some scholars have employed this concept to explain east-facing Archaic earthworks (e.g., Gibson 1998). Red ocher may provide a reference to the sun as well. The 360-day calendar certainly refers to the sun in its daily and annual movements. There are other indications of solar orientation as well. The avoidance of "east" in siting burial grounds (no Atlantic shell site has burials and there are no SOV shell-bearing burial sites on an eastern-flowing segment of a river [Claassen 2010]) suggests that it was the direction of new life as it still is. Solstice sighting lines might explain the "aisles" separating the concentric arcs at Poverty Point into subgroups (Gibson 1998). "Some of Caney's mounds [Louisiana] are aligned with sunrise positions on the horizon during equinoxes and winter solstices but others do not" (Gibson 1994:172).

See *cardinal direction, moon, ocher, ritual calendar*

Supernatural

Should we think of the beings residing in the Upper World and Underworld as supernatural? "We shouldn't think of these events as supernatural because nothing was supernatural in the traditional Algonkian world. . . . the Algonkian manitous belonged to the same family as the people who called them 'grandfathers' and the people and manitous shared the same landscape. They could enter each other's worlds and talk to each other directly" (Rajnovich 1994:14).

See *constellation, cosmology*

Sweat Lodge

Chapman (1975:195–199) has proposed that the dense concentrations of river rock found in surface contexts in Early Archaic sites along the Little Tennessee River were sweat lodge cleanouts. At Rose Island 13 possible sweat lodge features found in the St. Albans and LeCroy levels had lengths in the range of 0.7–4.0 ft (21–121 cm) and widths in the range of 0.6–3.1 ft (18–94 cm). Sweating might also account for some of the fire-cracked rock in the Green River and Alabama shell heaps. Perhaps the auditory exostoses that appear in such high proportions of shell mound male burials are the result of sweating activities followed by plunges into the Green River, possible activities of a river keeper medicine society (Claassen 2010:191).

The sweat lodge was and is itself a ritual facility. As a cave/womb with water transformed to steam, it creates a fertility context and a small cave. Plains Indians said the rocks of the sweat lodge could hear, and Seminoles kept/keep a sweat lodge rock in a sacred bundle that permits all other sweat rocks to perform.

See *auditory exostoses, Cult of the River Keepers*

Tattooing

"Tattooing goes back to at least 6000 BP in the Western Hemisphere, and it's reasonable to assume Archaic people were . . . also decorating their bodies on a temporary and/or permanent scale using red ochre and other pigments. . . . We can identify the basic components of a tattoo tool kit based on comparative data from historic Native American groups (where tattoo kits were one of the sacred bundles) and comparative ethnologies of other tattooing cultures" (Aaron Deter-Wolf, personal communication with the author, May 2011).

Gar teeth were used in Mississippian times for tattooing and scratching (Deter-Wolf 2013). Gar mandible awls were found at the Middle Archaic Anderson site, at the Late Archaic Swan Island, Illinois, and in Area X, Riverton.

See *paint/powder, rock marking*

Teeth

Beaver teeth, skate teeth, caribou teeth, and shark teeth were curated and sometimes modified by Maritime Archaic people. Betts and colleagues (2012) give an accounting of the Late Archaic distribution of shark teeth, including fossil teeth, in the Maritimes. They posit that ancient people liked to use shark teeth as mnemonic devices and attempted to assume the characteristics of sharks when hunting swordfish and cod. The oldest shark tooth in archaeological context (3980–3630 B.P.) thus far is found at Cow Point (Betts, Blair, and Black 2012:628) in a grave and was that of a great white shark. The tooth was covered with red ocher.

Human teeth were perforated and deposited in a few SOV shell heaps and caves. Pendants of bear and dog teeth were found only in Middle Archaic context at Eva, and beaver incisors were most common in the Middle Archaic as well (Lewis and Lewis 1961:87). A pit feature at Villier, Kentucky, contained a multifaceted nutting stone and the fragments of a human jaw and teeth (Robinson and Smith 1979).

Nonhuman teeth at Windover burial pond were found with 11 percent of the bodies: 7 percent of the women, 20 percent of the males, and 5 percent of the subadults. Canid canines were found only with men while all other types of teeth were found with both women and men (Dickel 2002:88).

Teeth were slightly more ubiquitous in SOV graves than were jaws. Very early bluff-top sites on the Green River (Jackson Bluff, Jimtown Hill, and Baker) lacked teeth in graves entirely, but the Middle Archaic riverside Anderson and Hermitage Spring shell sites did have them. In fact, Hermitage Spring had the second highest percentage of graves with teeth, 3.2 percent. Five of six shell-free burial grounds had 0.1–2.0 percent of graves with teeth. The greatest use of teeth as grave goods was seen at the late Robeson Hill bluff-top site on the Wabash where 11 percent of the burials were accompanied by teeth of various animals (Claassen 2010). Stone-like drumfish teeth filled a carapace rattle at Eva.

Teeth, like other body parts, could be carried or worn and serve as mnemonic devices or charms. Betts and colleagues (2012) argue that possession of the teeth of animals (or even humans), or any other body part, allows access to the spiritual power of that animal. But we should also recall that teeth were used as dice in games. The dice function may best explain their presence in areas where other evidence of gambling is found.

See *animal other, beaver, drumfish, gambling, game, human bone artifact, jaw, shark, soul*

Textile/Weaving

The Shawnee speak of Our Grandmother, a spider, who after surviving the Great Flood rekindled a new fire, re-created people, and then began to weave (Voegelin 1944). In Mesoamerica, the act of weaving was inseparable from the act of creation and birth, and it was and is a woman's creative activity (Schaefer 2002). Berlo (1993:36) gives additional examples of the inextricable link between Cherokee women's creative and procreative abilities. Furthermore, the drop spindle is equivalent to the penis, a backstrap weaving starts in the woman's crotch and when finished is cut free like a baby, and the spinning of thread or the spinning of the spindle calls forth images of earth's creation, beginning time, winds, and so forth (Furst 1995; Schaefer 2002).

That weaving, fiber processing, and textile production were similarly associated with women in the Late Archaic is seen in the abundant bark, string, cordage, and textiles of Newt Kash Shelter, a probable menstrual retreat. While a woman was secluded she apparently processed fibers and made cordage, braided, and used textiles that were left in the rockshelter (Claassen 2011a). At other Kentucky retreat shelters basket staves were made and presumably woven into baskets (e.g., Haystack Shelter).

Textile-impressed baked-clay features allow a study of Early and Middle Archaic textiles at Icehouse Bottom (Chapman and Adovasio 1977) and place textiles directly in association with probable ritual baked-clay surfaces. Vegetal fiber was used to make large globular bags and rectangular mats, possibly used to transport the clay. A weaving-fertility complex is possibly expressed in the leaving of slippers and textiles in Salts Cave and many other caves and rockshelters.

Fabrics were important elements of the mortuary customs at Windover, Florida, and were, surprisingly, in the twinning patterns, more elaborate and labor-intensive than later examples elsewhere in the United States (Doran 2002). At Windover, textiles were created as mats and hooded shrouds enveloping some dead. In the Windover sample "woven fabric and matting were recovered from 32% of the burials" with a significantly greater occurrence with subadults (Dickel 2002:81). This woven material "ranged from coarse matting or blanket-like material to fine weave" (Dickel 2002:81).

Elsewhere textiles appear as bags holding seeds (medicine?) placed in retreat rockshelters and in burials with men and with women, as clothing for the dead, as hats, and as containers. Cordage was important for laying out distances and building structures. Furthermore, knots had meaning in historic contexts.

Awls and needles were common grave goods during the Archaic in places such as Green River shell heaps and Maritime Archaic cemeteries. In the latter their use to manufacture bark containers has been posited. All of the Port au Choix specimens "appear too small to have served as netting needles or snowshoe needles, but some fine type of weaving, probably with sinew or hair, is suggested" (Tuck 1976:43). Eight bone needles, four rounded and four flat, were found inside a bone case. Needles were common inclusions in matrix and burials at Eva but again sewing is not indicated. The needles from Eva were of various lengths, flattened, usually with sharp points, and the eye was too broad to have been pulled through skins. "The most likely function of these needles was in making nets, mats or baskets" (Lewis and Lewis 1961:81).

It is highly likely that rockshelters that contain large quantities of woven materials were specifically targeted for weaving deposits rather than being simply places with accidentally good preservation. Women weavers among the Wixárika leave miniature weavings at the cave and rockshelter homes of several spirits, including the god of the hunt, harking back to the older use of the net or snare for hunting and fishing (Schaefer 2002).

In an essay on women's art in North America, Janet Berlo (1993:32) states that myths make it clear that there were "inherent dangers in women's pursuit of art. . . . [B]oth men and women may be imperiled by women's artistry. This ambivalent message about female artists, and the cautions about the uses and abuses of their work, may take diverse forms." Cosmological concepts were inherent in weaving, in potting, in quillwork, in featherwork, and so forth and no doubt in flintknapping, boat making, and so on. All craft production gave fertile contexts for ritualizing.

See *baked-clay surface, color, nut, oracle, sandal/slipper*

Trail

"Hunter-gatherers perceive their territories . . . by monitoring the paths running between specific places" (Bradley 1994:95). This monitoring behavior is developed in greater detail by Zedeño and colleagues, who noted microgeographical movement within a homeland "including seasonal village moves, summer and winter hunts and resource gathering, and ceremonial activities such as vision quests, eagle trapping, fasts, offering placement, and replenishing of ceremonial bundles" (Zedeño, Hollenbach, and Grinnell 2009:114).

Descriptive names of places anchor memories and "trails and paths across the homeland and beyond connect people to their past and allow them to or-

36. Trail followed by mounted pilgrims to the top of Mishuehue Mountain and the rain-calling shrine there, May 1, 2011. (Photo by author.)

ganize their present and future actions. For this very reason, journeys, memories of journeys, and the actual routes followed occupy a central place in the social order. Origin and migration myths, too, incorporate landmarks and experiences that reflect the distance between the ancestors and the generation recalling the myth" (Zedeño, Hollenbach, and Grinnell 2009:129).

So where were Archaic trails? To find Archaic paths we need Archaic landscape. In New York, "an Archaic path presumably followed the ancient Catskill Path at the foot of the Kalkberg escarpment in Greene County, while another path no doubt used the Normans Kill crossing near the Vosburg site, along with the historic route north to the Mohawk valley. In addition, recorded Indian trails crossed Saratoga and Warren Counties from the Mohawk River to Lake George during colonial times, and are considered to be very ancient due to the constraints imposed by terrain" (Curtin 2011:2–). The Kaskaskia trail, running east-west from the Ohio River at Shawneetown across the Embarrass River to Kaskaskia, Illinois, on the Mississippi River, may be as old as Dalton (Koldehoff and Walthall 2004), and the Great Warrior Trail running down the Appalachians is reputedly 5,000 years old (Watson 2001:319). Wilkins (1978:36) specifies level ridgelines for Appalachian trails, which is certainly the case in mountainous Mexico today, but ascending ridgelines are used as well. In South Carolina, "the major watershed divides are oriented NW-SE, and many have modern roads running their length in the same locations as historic era roads and trails, reflecting upland travel corridors that may well go back to Paleoindian times" (Brooks, Taylor, and Ivester 2010:157).

There may have been trails that led specifically to shrines where occasional ceremonials were held (and which needed maintenance prior to a rite), as well as more numerous trails that connected frequently accessed places (Figure 36). The historic Natchez Trace connects Stanfield-Worley Shelter, Mulberry Creek shell mound, and Anderson shell mound, suggesting they were connected in the past via this path. It is on these frequently used trails that there were more opportunities for an accidental death or a manifestation of a spirit, giving rise to short-lived shrines since they would be reflecting only personal experience and histories (Claassen 2011b).

See *cairn*, *shrine*

Trash/Midden

These terms, including "debris" and "refuse," relevant to the lives of archaeologists, may not be appropriate for all of the jumbles of items found in the archaeological record. Instead of "trash" or "midden," instead of village debris at the sinkholes, the residue from Archaic council fires, hearths, sweat lodges, feasts, projectile point production, the hunt, and production of craft items was residue with a soul, residue to be tended to and cared for. Old items, chippage, and the remains of feasting were left as offerings and as potential homes for the spirits attracted to shrines, habitations, and physical features.

As explained by Cameron, trash mounds in front of Chacoan great houses had far more trash than could have been generated by the small populations resident in those pueblos. "Beginning in the Pueblo I period, formal allocation of space for trash deposition and burial of human remains in these middens became characteristic of the ancestral Pueblo" (Cameron 2002:683). Modern Puebloan people, in fact, treat mounded "trash" as part of a sacred process of renewal. "Ashes are especially important and are used in all sorts of ceremonies as protection against disease or witchcraft" (Cameron 2002:683), and trash mounds are often considered shrines.

See *ashes*, *breakage*, *burning*, *flake/chip*, *offering*, *shrine*

Tree

Trees were important beings in the cosmology of all North American people. Trees of different species were associated with the cardinal directions (e.g.,

37. Sacred ahuehuete (cypress) tree at Ocuilan, Morelos, from whose roots run gallons of water. It is a fertility shrine. (Photo by author.)

Cree, Lakota, Puebloan groups, etc.), they were metaphors for the human life cycle and descent, and some species were believed to be auspicious for fertility petitions, particularly the willow (Figures 34, 37, 38) and plum. Cree people put in the center of a grave an upright painted sapling, a pine for a woman and a cedar for a man (Harper 1999:54). The Lakota see the girl initiate as a towering tree, a source of strength (Milne 1994:42). Poles and firewood for ceremonial fires are extensions of the ritual significance of trees. Mississippian mounds were replanted with trees once the capping was finished as an act of renewal (Knight 1989:424).

Tree species and use by contemporary natives suggest older ritual uses, particularly for plum trees. A 10,590+/-500 ya hearth at Shawnee-Minisink, New Jersey, included charred seeds from hawthorn plums *Crataegus* sp. (McNett 1985:18). Wild plum mixed with calcined fish was found in a hearth in Shawnee-Minisink (Dent 2007:127) and the Early Archaic component at the Hester site in Mississippi (McGahey 1996:373). Plum wood charcoal was recovered in Salts Cave, Kentucky. Plum tree groves were preferred places to put menstrual bundles for several Plains Indian groups (LeBeau 2009; Sundstrom 2004:85). Plains women also plant plum, chokecherry, and grapes at

38. The Virgin of the Nativity Church in Tixtla, Guerrero, is planted between giant ahuehuetes, often visited as fertility shrines, suggesting why a church devoted to the pregnant Mary was sited there, May 30, 2012. (Photo by author.)

burial caves. A 1930s newspaper account mentions a Plains woman carrying cherries to a cave shrine for women (Linea Sundstrom, personal communication with the author, 2009). Finally, plum seeds served as gaming dice (DeBoer 2001).

A random selection of other species associations underscores their ritual use. Nut tree wood was used for cremation in McCullough's Run. Forty-two percent of the unmodified wood found in direct association with bodies at Windover, Florida, was ash (*Fraxinus* sp.), yet no ash was among the wood sample collected elsewhere in the pond (Dickel 2002:78). The four woods found in Milbury III cremation pits were elm, conifer, oak, and willow, three of which were identified in one feature (Leveillee 1999). The four woods may have had cardinal direction associations.

See *gambling*, *pole/post*

Trophy Part

Generally used to refer to parts of the human body, "trophy parts" could also be taken from various animals, plants, and even spirits. Returning to the human situation, parts taken as trophies were typically hands, feet, legs, arms, and heads (Mensforth 2001, 2007). In some cases, we find only a torso as a burial (two buried together at Chiggerville [Webb and Haag 1939]) or only skulls. In others, we find skeletons with no hands. While we think in terms of the anatomical part, the Aztecs spoke of "parts of the body that glisten, parts of the body that occur in strips, parts of the body that are bundled or sewn, parts of the body that are like corn" (Sahagún 1948). Buried clusters of long bones or a pair of feet, for example, is evidence that trophy parts were decommissioned in rites at burial grounds and in cave vestibules.

From Indian Knoll, Carlston Annis, and Ward come 18 skeletons showing decapitation. At least 5 of those are confirmed by cut marks on cervical vertebrae. Other trophy parts were taken from 16 additional bodies. "The 16 dismembered bodies yielded a total of 45 limb trophies, where 36 (80%) involved bilateral removal of the same limb set from a particular victim" (Mensforth 2001:118). The primary target of Archaic trophy taking was the leg severed from the hip (46.7 percent), forearms with hands (28.9 percent), complete arms (15.6 percent), and lower legs with feet (8.9 percent).

"The scalplock in particular possessed a number of desirable attributes as a trophy. . . . a final, more general property of a scalp or body part trophy relates to the fact that within the belief systems of most Native American Indians, a scalp, head, limb segment, or any other body part could be used to represent the whole victim for ritual purposes" (Mensforth 2001:112). However, it is possible that different body parts had different meanings, just as did different sides of the body and different species. Furthermore, the scalp and the head were reservoirs of tonali soul, the vital essence of a human or animal.

The decapitations and mutilations may have been part of sacrificial rites that occurred at the ceremonial/burial ground. The victim was then buried at the same burial ground used for the bodies of their captors' relatives. Studies of skeletal populations need to attempt to separate the captives or foreigners from the local population.

See *feet/footprint/track, femur, head removal, human bone artifact, jaw, scalping, soul, trophy part decommissioning rite*

Trophy Part Decommissioning Rite

People may have decommission trophy parts in a disposal rite that included burial in a cave setting, such as the vestibule of Salts Cave, Kentucky, in the Hendricks Cave sinkhole, Ohio, and in Krill Cave, as well as in a shell-bearing burial ground or in a dirt matrix open site. This practice puts the human bones on par with the animal bones returned to rockshelter bone shrines. There may be a case of this rite conducted in Krill Cave, Ohio, where two sets of lower legs were interred (Prufer 2006:361) as were a large number of hand and foot bones (Prufer and Prufer 2012:228). Parrish Village, Kentucky, had a number of burials that suggest trophy part deposits—long bones only, or long bones and skull.

Archaic peoples also buried presumed trophy parts with individuals (owners?) at the time of their burial. Human mandibles (and possibly their attached tongues) were found as grave goods with two individuals at Ward, Kentucky, a bluff-top shell-bearing burial ground, as well as at Indian Knoll. A man was buried at Ward with an additional male right arm, including the scapula and clavicle but lacking the hand, draped over the dead man's left side (Mensforth 2001:119). A skull was included with one interment at Read and a skull and long bones with another.

See *bone shrine, bone soul, cave, femur, Krill Cave, skull, trophy part*

Turkey

The bones of at least 205 turkeys were returned to the bone shrine at Tick Creek Cave in Missouri. Turkey wings and vertebrae were noticeably lacking at Carlston Annis. Turkey bones outnumbered deer bones in the ritual deposit in the vestibule of Salts Cave, and a partial turkey skeleton appeared in a passageway. Turkey bones were abundant in Russell Cave. Five complete turkey skeletons were found on top of a rock at the base of the eastern Kentucky Big Ash Cave ash layer (Funkhouser and Webb 1929:77).

The Huron believed a turkey-like spirit being controlled the rains, winds, and thunder. It is possible that a similar belief was at work in Archaic times and that the placement of turkeys in caves and rockshelters means these places were thought of as sources of rain in the Archaic.

See *awl, bird, cave, owl, rain, rockshelter, Russell Cave, wing*

Turkey-Tail Blade

The turkey-tail blades of the northern Ohio River valley discussed by Didier (1967) have now been reassigned to Early Woodland times. However, Johnson and Brookes (1989) argue that unnotched Turkey Tails are Middle Archaic in age in the mid-south based on their recovery in the Hart Site near Nashville with a Middle Archaic component and the Middle Archaic Ervin shell heap with two cremations containing Oversized Benton and Sykes points. In northern Mississippi the Late Archaic co-occurrence of Bentons and cache blades is fairly common as are Benton and notched Turkey Tails (Johnson and Brooks 1989). In the Benton phase of the Tombigbee River drainage Turkey Tails co-occur with "Cache Blades, Double Notches, Oversize Bentons, Oversize Cache Blades, regular Bentons, Tallahatta quartzite points, and sometimes ocher. There is a probable mortuary association . . . [T]he parallel with the Red Ochre complex of the Midwest is clear except that the midsouthern Turkey Tails antedate their northern counterparts by nearly 2,000 years" (Johnson and Brookes 1989:141).

If the turkey was particularly associated with rain, then non-mortuary Turkey-Tail point caches may have been for calling rain.

See *cache—blade, projectile point, rain*

Turtle

The turtle appears to be one of the oldest ritual animals. Perhaps the oldest record of turtle use is that of a now extinct land tortoise (*Geochelone crassiscutata*) in Little Salt Spring sink (Clausen et al. 1979:609). This giant tortoise had been killed with a spear/stake, burned, and cooked at what was once the rim of the sinkhole. Two other individuals of this species and two species of freshwater turtle were also found on a ledge at the sinkhole. Also noteworthy is the snapping turtle found in Sheriden Cave with a date of 10,960+/-60 B.P. (Waters et al. 2009). It is the location of these turtles that suggests their ritual use in feasting or offerings.

Turtle paraphernalia were common ritual accessories. Five box turtle carapaces were found with a probable priest in the double burial in Horn Shelter 2 dated to 9710+/-40 B.P. (from bone of the adult male), as were skull and postcranial bones. Turtle remains at Windover, both *Testudiens* and *Pseudomys*, were represented by whole carapaces and were found buried with women, subadults, and one man (Dickel 2002:87). Those carapaces may have been rattles, but the first certain rattles are the box turtle carapaces in the Late Archaic. Carapaces are ubiquitous in Archaic mortuary contexts in the SOV, particularly in Green River sites, and are usually interpreted as either rattles (when perforations or white pebbles are present) or bowls/cups (when the interior vertebrae have been scraped away).

The Ward site had other interesting uses of the turtle (Watson 2005). One infant was entirely covered with a carapace (see photo in Meindl, Mensforth, and York 2001:Figure 4), one child's skull was covered, and one adult's skull was surmounted by a whelk shell incised to look like a carapace and was drilled through the center, as would have been a carapace rattle. There were four cases of whelks incised to look like carapaces at Chiggerville and two faces probably were covered by carapaces (Watson 2005). Another child at Chiggerville had a carapace under each scapula, suggesting a backpack, and another one at its elbow. Yet another child burial employed an inverted carapace on top of a large knife at the left humerus of a child.

In Iroquois medicine societies land turtles and aquatic turtles had different roles. Aquatic turtles appear as two small, soft-shell turtle effigies made from exotic green stone with quartz inclusions at the Middle Archaic Denton Site, Yazoo valley. Other stone turtle effigies are known from Poverty Point. Neither site had rattles. The aquatic species and the green coloration of the stone, a color associated with beginning time and the "center" in Mexico, may indicate that this animal was viewed as "primordial" by at least 6,000 ya. Further supporting this symbolism is the drilled divot in the center of each turtle. Drilling stone or fire and spinning the spindle are acts associated with "beginning" and generative sex among Mexican groups. Box turtles are terrestrial and, it should be noted, particularly active after a rain.

See *pack*, *rattle*, *turtle shell rite*

Turtle Shell Rite

At the base of the bluff upon which is perched the Read site on the Green River was a "circle of large rough stones carefully laid to enclose two carapaces of terrapin at center" (Webb 1950:362). A similar ritual appears to have occurred at Eva on the Tennessee River. Feature 2, in the Three Mile shell stratum, was a prepared bed of mussel shells, four of which were arranged tulip fashion around a small terrapin shell placed top down in the center. The whole set was then covered with shells (Lewis and Lewis 1961:15).

This rite is most likely related to the creation of the Earth. For the Seneca, the Earth is the back of Turtle breaking the water where the Mother of humans landed when she fell from the Above World. William Fox (2004b) has traced this story to Middle Woodland times.

See *turtle*

Violence

Obvious interpersonal violence appears as early as Kennewick Man, in Washington, whose hip was penetrated with a point 9600 B.P. The percentage of individuals dying violently is most pronounced, however, in the shell-bearing burial grounds of the SOV. Mensforth (2001), who oversaw the reexamination of bodies from three shell-bearing sites in the Green River valley, reports scalping, dismemberment, shooting, stabbing, throat cutting, disemboweling, and cranial trauma. All of these acts were committed against male victims while females were victims primarily of stabbing, scalping, and decapitation. Most clubbings did not result in death. From northwestern Ohio comes evidence that at least one woman (Clifford Williams Site) and one man (Stratten-Wallace site) were scalped and one woman stabbed (Mensforth 2001:123).

There were far more people in the shell mounds of the SOV who were victims of violent death than there were people with obvious signs of murder. Certain burial postures when used in the SOV and related areas (Frontenac Island, Elizabeth Mounds) also were applied to individuals killed violently: extended on the back, stacked, head-first flexed, torso twisted (all members of group burials), and some flexed-on-the-back bodies. I have estimated that 16–69 percent of the bodies in these shell mounds died at the hands of others based on burial posture. There is, in fact, a statistically significant difference between the proportion of violent deaths in the shell-free burial grounds of the SOV and those in the shell mounds (Claassen 2010:132–133). Looking at Indian Knoll, for instance, where Mensforth found that 6.5 percent of the burial population died violently, I found 254 possible murder victims or 41 percent. Nevertheless, this violence was well contained, for at Indian Knoll the numbers amounted to one killing every 52 months.

Rather than for revenge or mourning warfare, people were being captured for human sacrificial rites such as the hunt god rite, four-age rite, and first-kill rite. The ballistics of the shooting deaths seem to indicate people killed at close range, possibly carried out by very specific ritual specialists. The captives may have been kept for a while and played out a role, such as "deer," their blood used in rites and some of their skulls possibly curated.

Other victims of violence appear to have been adulterous women and couples as well as their newborns (Claassen 2013a). There are graves holding an older male and younger female with a newborn, as well as graves with pregnant women with embedded points.

See *adultery killing, burial—group, sacrifice—adult, sacrifice—infant and child, scalping, trophy part*

Walrus, Whale, Dolphin, Seal

Whale-tail pendants and porpoise pendants are abundant in Late Archaic New England, often made of colorful stones. Fowler (1966:38) offered that these pendants "may have been used for personal adornment in the performance of ceremonial rites." Supporting this belief was the recovery, at the Titicut site, of a whale-tail pendant together with a Clumsy plummet of Late Archaic times in a pit containing red ocher (Fowler 1966:38). Fowler (1966:42) also depicts a steatite sperm whale pendant and steatite porpoise that he projects to be Late Archaic in age. Any of these items could have been fetishes. A whale effigy gouge, whale-tail pendant, and whale atlatl weight in a large feature at Caddy Park in Quincy, Massachusetts, are further evidence of whale-related icons and rites perhaps for Maushop (Mahlstedt and David 2002).

From Rustico Island in Prince Edward Island came a walrus mandible in a unique deposit of dozens of soft shell clam valves and five dog bones. "The mandible was laying on its side and was surrounded by a deposit of shells of *Mya arenaria*, along with pea-sized chunks of wood charcoal" (Leonard 1989:16).

Sea mammal remains in the Port au Choix-3 cemetery were limited to 18 burials and involved 97 harp seal claw cores and teeth and one killer whale tooth (Tuck 1976:61). Two stone whale effigies were also recovered there. A walrus baculum was found in a cache with 48 grooved plummets in New Brunswick, dating to 3710+/-50 B.P.

See *claw*, *jaw*, *plummet*, *stone*, *teeth*

Waterfall

The power, turbulence, volume, erosion, and sounds of waterfalls (Milne 1994:40) were important aspects that caused waterfalls to be revered. In a surprising number of cases, waterfalls cover a cave. Some Late Archaic burial grounds were located above major waterfalls around the Gulf of Maine (Robinson 2006).

Waterfalls, whirlpools, and rough water in general were evidence of the presence of the Underwater Panther for historic groups (Harper 1999:31). Father "Hennepin observed the Dakotas making offerings at St. Anthony Falls (on the Mississippi River between Minneapolis and St. Paul) to 'the great deity called Oanktayhee.' . . . said to live under the falls, and to manifest itself as a gigantic buffalo" (Mayor 2005:233). This water panther may be depicted in a scene found etched into a stone at Titicut, Connecticut (Figure 24).

An Archaic-aged bone shrine was located within four meters of a "dramatic" waterfall in Ohio. The two unique Middle Archaic freshwater gastropod burial sites in central Tennessee (Hayes and Ervin) were located near a waterfall. Seasonal waterfalls exist at or near the overhangs of several rockshelters with ritual evidence. Russell Cave, Alabama, is a little downriver from a large waterfall. Archaeologists have yet to consider waterfalls and nearby sites as ritual pairs.

See *cave*, *spring*

Wind

Winds, particularly spiraling, tornadic winds, were present at creation and are spirits capable of both goodness and evil. In Mississippian iconography, wind is seen as the looped square with hummingbird (Lankford 1987), but even more frequent are the large gastropod beads and columella pendants worn by a Hawk man engraved on shell vessels and gorgets. Embedded in the symbolism of spiraling gastropods are the spiraling cosmos and winds at the time of creation.

Nearly identical beads and pendants were worn by the Pauahtun Maya skybearers (Miller and Taube 1993:132). The cut-off top of the conch shell worn by Quetzalcoatl, a wind deity (among many other affiliations), and 9 Wind (an avatar of Quetzalcoatl) was called the "wind jewel" (Miller and Taube 1993:187). A Wind clan was/is common among Gulf groups (Swanton 1946).

It is possible that the long central whelk column pieces found in SOV shell bead inventories, with the sulcus groove clearly spiraling around the column, carried a wind meaning in the Archaic.

See *gastropod*

Witch

In many cultures witches might expect to be killed, and suspicion of witchcraft is why many individuals report that they turn away from the doctoring path or are forced to move away from their communities (Schaefer 2002). With that in mind, were the burial of the specialist and apprentice in Horn Shelter, Texas, and the woman obviously murdered in Stanhope Cave people suspected of witchcraft? At Hermitage Springs a pregnant woman had been murdered. Not only was there a fetus, but she had an antler point in her thorax and was buried on top of a child (Bu268) who was placed in an extended position. This second child may indicate that the woman had been deemed a witch and all of her offspring killed.

The high number of adult murder victims or bodies covered with limestone found in rockshelters included in this guide suggests that some of the dead may have been witches and that rockshelters were particularly good places to put their bodies. The resulting concentration of power/spirits/forces at a shelter like Stanfield-Worley subsequently elicited hundreds of years of point offerings.

Historical information has been used to identify possible witches in the Woodland period. Fox specifies the following "spiritually charged" items used in performing witchcraft: human hair, menstrual blood, white pebbles, wooden dolls, "lion clubs, arrows (sometimes tipped with conical antler points), hooks and lines which allow witches to draw back victims, plum stones and bowls, feathers which transform into roosting passenger pigeons, bone flutes, stone dogs, and pipes" (Fox 1993:21–22). Among the varied items involved in casting and countering spells, only the miniature lithic points, crystals, and odd-shaped stones could be expected to preserve in open-air sites (Fox 1993). But we might also encounter a bone-sucking or blowing tube, carved root, bone claws, and butterfly-shaped stones.

See *Horn Shelter 2, ritual specialist/priest, sacrifice—adult, Stanfield-Worley Shelter, Stanhope Cave*

World Renewal Rite

Ancient people surely understood the turning of the seasons and the repetition of sequences of constellation, sun, and moon movements to indicate significant endings and startings of units of time and growth. They apparently believed it was necessary to help or ensure that the end of one cycle would be followed by another.

A small probable world renewal rite took the form of an offering made in a pit with a small number of bones of many different species, sometimes including humans. Several deposits petitioning for world renewal were made in caves, specifically Rodgers Shelter in Missouri. There Feature 7a in Middle Archaic Horizon 8 included one finely flaked point; a human humerus and tibia; a bison tooth; a large bird bone; a carapace fragment; cottontail parts; a squirrel humerus, calcanium, and radius fragments; and a tooth of a drumfish. A second feature in Rodgers held the pelvis and sacrum of deer; one bison phalanx; rabbit teeth, ulna, and radius; a terrapin shell; a turkey ulna and coracoids; a *Canes* premolar; and a squirrel radius.

Similar bone deposits are known from both open-air and rockshelters/cave sites in the Mississippi and Ohio river valleys. It appears to me that these Archaic-aged features derive from offerings of thanksgiving/propitiation to an earth spirit with specific requests for the continuation of humans and at least seven other animals.

Bone shrines were also places of private renewal offerings used by one or a few individuals (Brown 2005). Other private renewal acts could have involved naming infants with the names of deceased kin, disposal of placenta and umbilical cords in trees, and making offerings of animals and points at sinkholes. Burning, washing, and breaking items, as well as discarding the old and replacing with the new, were other acts of renewal.

Turner (1969) opined that hunter-gatherer rituals were primarily concerned with renewal; this point also underlies the argument that the shell mounds are ritual centers (Claassen 2010). Shell was used in the renewal of souls, in the digging of burial pits, as utensils for menstruating women in retreat shelters, and, as a feast food, in the renewal of social relationships. Shells amassed made blatantly obvious the debt of people to the spirits of the Underworld, and in many cases people chose to situate their dead near or in shell deposits.

In some cases world renewal also required the hunt god rite or four-age rite. Human sacrifice and blood offerings were probably means through which renewal was affected. Blood offerings also may have come from infant humans and various animals when sacrificed, particularly deer. Capping deposits, sweeping floors and plazas, kindling new fires, eating new plant shoots, and seasonal group rites of first kill are other examples of renewal rites.

See *ashes*, *breakage*, *burning*, *capping*, *gastropod*, *hunt god rite*, *shell*

References Cited

Adams, Lee

1950 *The Table Rock Basin in Barry County, Missouri.* Memoir of the Missouri Archaeological Society, No. 1. Columbia, Missouri.

Adovasio, James, R. Fryman, A. Quinn, D. Dirkmaat, and D. Pedler

1998 The Archaic West of the Allegheny Mountains: A View from the Cross Creek Drainage, Washington County, Pennsylvania. In *The Archaic Period in Pennsylvania: Hunter-Gatherers of the Early and Middle Holocene Period*, edited by Paul Raber, Patricia Miller, and Sarah Neusius, pp. 1–28. Pennsylvania Historical and Museum Commission, Harrisburg.

Ahler, Stanley, and Bruce McMillan

1976 Material Culture at Rodgers Shelter: A Reflection of Past Human Activities. In *Prehistoric Man and His Environments: A Case Study in the Ozark Highlands*, edited by W. Wood and R. McMillan, pp. 163–199. Academic Press, New York.

Ahler, Steven, Mary Bade, Frances King, Bonnie Styles, and Paula Thorson

1992 *Later Archaic Components at Modoc Rock Shelter, Randolph County, Illinois.* Illinois State Museum Reports of Investigations, No. 48.

Albertson, Donald, and Douglas Charles

1988 Archaic Mortuary Component. In *The Archaic and Woodland Cemeteries at the Elizabeth Site in the LIV*, edited by D. Charles, S. Leigh, and J. Buikstra, pp. 29–40. Kampsville Archeological Center, Research Series Vol. 7. Center for American Archaeology, Kampsville, Illinois.

Amick, Daniel

1985 Buried Late Holocene Terrace Site Testing in the Central Duck River Basin. In *Exploring Tennessee Prehistory: A Dedication to Alfred K. Guthe*, edited by T. Whyte, C. Boyd, and B. Riggs, pp. 23–38. University of Tennessee, Department of Anthropology, Report of Investigations 42.

Anders, Ferdinand, E. R. Maarten, G. N. Jansen, and Luis García

1993 *Códice Borgia: Los templos del Cielo y de la Oscuridad: Oráculos y liturgia. Códices Mexicanos.* Vol. 5. Sociedad Estatal Quinto Centenario, Akademische Druck-und Verlagsanstalt, and Fondo de Cultura Económica, Madrid, Graz, and Mexico City.

Anderson, David

2004 Archaic Mounds and the Archaeology of Southeastern Tribal Societies. In *Signs of Power: The Rise of Cultural Complexity in the Southeast*, edited by J. Gibson and P. Carr, pp. 270–299. University of Alabama Press, Tuscaloosa.

2010 The End of the Southeastern Archaic: Regional Interaction and Archaeological Interpretation. In *Trend, Tradition, and Turmoil: What Happened to the Southeastern Archaic?*, edited by D. Thomas and M. Sanger, pp. 273–302. Anthropological Papers of the American Museum of Natural History 93.

Anderson, David, and Glenn Hanson

1988 Early Archaic Settlement in the Southeastern United States: A Case Study from the Savannah River Valley. *American Antiquity* 53:262–286.

Anderson, Duane, Michael Finnegan, John Hotopp, and Alton Fisher

1978 The Lewis School Site (13PW5): A Resolution of Ideological Conflicts at an Archaic Ossuary in Western Iowa. *Plains Anthropologist* 23(81):183–219.

Anderson, R. L., J. M. Adovasio, B. Humphrey, D. C. Hyland, J. S. Gardner, and D. G. Harding

2002 Conservation and Analysis of Textile and Related Perishable Artifacts. In *Windover: Multidisciplinary Investigations of an Early Archaic Florida Cemetery*, edited by G. Doran, 121–190. University Press of Florida, Gainesville.

Andrews, Carol

1994 *Amulets of Ancient Egypt*. University of Texas Press, Austin.

Ashmore, Wendy

2002 Decisions and Dispositions: Socializing Spatial Archaeology. *American Anthropologist* 104:1172–1183.

Astor-Aguilera, Miguel, and Robert Jarvenpa

2008 Comparing Indigenous Pilgrimages: Devotion, Identity, and Resistance in Mesoamerica and North America. *Anthropos* 103(2):483–506.

Aten, Lawrence

1999 Middle Archaic Ceremonialism at Tick Island, Florida: Ripley Bullen's 1961 Excavation at the Harris Creek Site. *Florida Anthropologist* 52(3):131–200.

Athens, William

2000 *Phase I Cultural Resources Survey and Archaeological Inventory of a 17.7 Km Long Proposed Levee Project for U.S. Fish and Wildlife Service*. Goodwin and Associates, Savannah, Georgia.

Atkinson, James

1974 Appendix A. Test Excavations at the Vaughn Mound Site. In *Archeological Survey and Test Excavations in the Upper-Central Tombigbee River Valley: Aliceville—Columbus Lock and Dam and Impoundment Areas, Alabama and Mississippi* by Mark Rucker. Department of Anthropology, Mississippi State University.

Ayers, Harvard

1976 The Occupation of Ridgetop Sites in the Blue Ridge Mountains by Savannah River Archaic Peoples. Paper presented at the Annual Meeting of the Southeastern Archaeological Conference, Tuscaloosa.

Bader, Anne
2010/2011 Evidence of Ritualized Mortuary Behavior at the Meyer Site. *Indiana Archaeology* 5(2):10–49.
Baerreis, David, Kiroshi Daifuku, and James Lundsted
1954 The Burial Complex at the Reigh Site. *Wisconsin Archeologist* 35(1):1–36.
Bailey, C.
1975 *Stories from an Indian Cave: The Cherokee Cave Builders*. Kessinger Publishing, Whitefish, Montana.
Barber, Michael
2005 Prehistoric Rockshelter Use on Virginia's Appalachian Plateaus: Settlement Patterns, Looting, and Survivability. *Archaeology of Eastern North America* 33:31–49.
Barbian, Lenore, and Ann Magennis
1995 Appendix 7. The Human Burials from the Turner Farm Site. In *Diversity and Complexity in Prehistoric Maritime Societies: A Gulf of Maine Perspective*, edited by B. Bourque, pp. 317–335. Plenum Press, New York.
Barfield, Thomas (editor)
1997 *The Dictionary of Anthropology*. Blackwell, New York.
Barker, Gary
1997 Upland Middle Archaic Adaptation in Tennessee's Western Highland Rim, a View from the Austin Cave Site. *Tennessee Anthropologist* 22(2):177–223.
Barker, Gary, and Christopher Hazel
2007 Ryan (40Rd77): A Late Middle Archaic Benton Culture Cemetery in Tennessee's Central Basin. *Journal of Alabama Archaeology* 53(1–2):1–90.
Bassett, Everett
1982 Osteological Analysis of Carrier Mills Burials. In *The Carrier Mills Archaeological Project: Human Adaptation in the Saline Valley, Illinois*, edited by Richard Jefferies and Brian Butler, pp. 1027–1114. Center for Archaeological Investigations Research Paper No. 33. Center for Archaeological Investigations Southern Illinois University, Carbondale, Illinois.
Bassie-Sweet, Karen
1996 *At the Edge of the World: Caves and Late Classic Maya World View*. University of Oklahoma Press, Norman.
Battle, H. B.
1922 Domestic Use of Oil among the Southern Aborigines. *American Anthropologist* 24:171–182.
Bauer, B. S., and C. Stanish
2001 *Ritual and Pilgrimage in the Ancient Andes*. University of Texas Press, Austin.
Bell, Carolyn
1997 *Ritual: Perspectives and Dimensions*. Oxford University Press, New York.
Bement, Lee
1999 *Bison Hunting at Cooper Site: Where Lightning Bolts Drew Thundering Herds*. University of Oklahoma Press, Norman.

Benn, David, and Joe Thompson

2009 Archaic Periods in Eastern Iowa. In *Archaic Societies: Diversity and Complexity across the Midcontinent*, edited by T. Emerson, D. McElrath, and A. Fortier, pp. 491–561. State University of New York Press, Albany.

Bentz, Charles

1988 The Late Archaic Occupation of the Bailey Site (40GL26), Giles County, Tennessee. *Tennessee Anthropological Association Newsletter* 13(5):1–20.

Bergman, Christopher, and John Doershuk

1998 An Introduction to the Early and Middle Archaic Occupations at Sandts Eddy. In *The Archaic Period in Pennsylvania: Hunter-Gatherers of the Early and Middle Holocene*, edited by P. Raber, P. Miller, and S. Neusius, pp. 45–75. Recent Research in Pennsylvania Archaeology No. 1. Pennsylvania Historical and Museum Commission, Harrisburg.

Berlo, Janet

1993 Dreaming of Double Woman: The Ambivalent Role of the Female Artist in North American Indian Mythology. *American Indian Quarterly* 17(1): 31–43.

Betts, Matthew, Susan Blair, and David Black

2012 Perspectivism, Mortuary Symbolism, and Human-Shark Relationships on the Maritime Peninsula. *American Antiquity* 77(4):621–645.

Binford, Lewis

1963 The Hodges Site: A Late Archaic Burial Station. In *Miscellaneous Studies in Typology and Classification*, compiled by A. White, L. Binford, and M. Papworth, pp. 124–148. Anthropological Papers, Museum of Anthropology, University of Michigan, No. 19. University of Michigan, Ann Arbor.

1980 Willow Smoke and Dog's Tails: Hunter-Gatherer Settlement Systems and Archaeological Site Formation. *American Antiquity* 45:4–20.

Blakeslee, Donald

2010 *Holy Ground, Healing Water: Cultural Landscapes at Waconda Lake, Kansas.* Texas A&M University Press, College Station.

Blick, Jeffrey

2010 New Radiometric Dates and Canine-Human Burial Ceremonialism at Weyanoke Old Town, 44Pg51, Virginia. *Quarterly Bulletin of the Archaeological Society of Virginia* 65(1):30–42.

Blitz, John

1993 Locust Beads and Archaic Mounds. *Mississippi Archaeology* 28(1):21–43.

Blitz, John, and Patrick Livingood

2004 Sociopolitical Implications of Mississippian Mound Volume. *American Antiquity* 69(2):291–303.

Bourque, Bruce

1995 *Diversity and Complexity in Prehistoric Maritime Societies: A Gulf of Maine Perspective.* Plenum Press, New York.

Bourque, Bruce, Steven Cox, and Robert Lewis

2006 The Archaic Period of the Merrymeeting Bay Region, South Central Maine. In *The Archaic of the Far Northeast*, edited by D. Sanger and M. Renouf, pp. 307–340. University of Maine Press, Orono.

Bowen, Jonathan

1994 *The Distributions of Five Late Archaic Time Period Artifact Types in Ohio: Notched Butterfly Bannerstones, Bar-Type Birdstones, Marine Shell, Sandal Sole Gorgets, Plummets, and Ashtabula Bifaces*. Sandusky Valley Chapter, Archaeological Society of Ohio, Upper Sandusky.

Bradley, Richard

1994 Symbols and Signposts—Understanding the Prehistoric Petroglyphs of the British Isles. In *The Ancient Mind*, edited by C. Renfrew and E. Zubrow, pp. 93–106. Cambridge University Press, Cambridge.

Brady, James

2005 The Impact of Ritual on Ancient Maya Economy. In *Stone Houses and Earth Lords*, edited by K. Prufer and J. Brady, pp. 115–134. University Press of Colorado, Boulder.

Brady, James, and Keith Prufer (editors)

2005 *In the Maw of the Earth Monster*. University of Texas Press, Austin.

Bray, Robert

1956 Culture-Complexes and Sequence at the Rice Site (23SN200), Stone County, Missouri. *Missouri Archaeologist* 18(1 and 2):47–132.

Breitburg, Emanuel

1982 Analysis of Area A Fauna. In *The Carrier Mills Archaeological Project: Human Adaptation in the Saline Valley, Illinois*, edited by Richard Jefferies and Brian Butler, pp. 863–946. Center for Archaeological Investigations Research Paper No. 33. Center for Archaeological Investigations, Southern Illinois University, Carbondale.

Brennan, Louis

1968 The Twombly Landing Site. *New York State Archaeological Association Bulletin* 42:11–27.

Broda, Johanna

1998 The Sacred Landscape of Aztec Calendar Festivals: Myth, Nature, and Society. In *Aztec Ceremonial Landscapes*, edited by David Carrasco, pp. 74–116. University Press of Colorado, Boulder.

Brookes, Samuel

2004 Cultural Complexity in the Middle Archaic of Mississippi. In *Signs of Power: The Rise of Cultural Complexity in the Southeast*, edited by J. Gibson and P. Carr, pp. 97–113. University of Alabama Press, Tuscaloosa.

Brooks, Mark, Barbara Taylor, and Andrew Ivester

2010 Carolina Bays: Time Capsules of Culture and Climate Change. *Southeastern Archaeology* 29(1):146–163.

Broster, John, and Mark Norton
1996 Recent Paleoindian Research in Tennessee. In *The Paleoindian and Early Archaic Southeast*, edited by D. Anderson and K. Sassaman, pp. 288–297. University of Alabama Press, Tuscaloosa.

Brown, James
1979 Charnel Houses and Mortuary Crypts: Disposal of the Dead in the Middle Woodland Period. In *Hopewell Archaeology: The Chilicothie Conference*, edited by David Brose and N'omi Greber, pp. 211–219. Kent State University Press, Kent, Ohio.
1997 The Archaeology of Ancient Religion in the Eastern Woodlands. *Annual Review of Anthropology* 26:465–485.
2006 The Shamanic Element in Hopewellian Period Ritual. In *Recreating Hopewell*, edited by D. Charles and J. Buikstra, pp. 475–488. University Press of Florida, Gainesville.

Brown, James, and Robert Vierra
1983 What Happened in the Middle Archaic? Introduction to the Ecological Approach to Koster Site Archaeology. In *Archaic Hunters and Gatherers in the American Midwest*, edited by J. Phillips and J. Brown, pp. 181–224. Academic Press, Orlando.

Brown, Linda
2005 Planting the Bones: Hunting Ceremonialism at Contemporary and Nineteenth-Century Shrines in the Guatemalan Highlands. *Latin American Antiquity* 16(2):131–146.

Broyles, Bettye
1976 *Late Archaic Component at the Buffalo Site (46Pu31), Putnam County, West Virginia*. Report of Archeological Investigations No. 6. West Virginia Geological and Economic Survey, Morgantown, West Virginia.

Bryant, Vaughn
1974 Pollen Analysis of Prehistoric Human Feces from Mammoth Cave. In *Archeology of the Mammoth Cave Area*, edited by P. J. Watson, pp. 203–209. Academic Press, New York.

Buikstra, Jane, and Douglas Charles
1999 Centering the Ancestors: Cemeteries, Mounds, and Sacred Landscapes of the Ancient North American Midcontinent. In *Archaeologies of Landscape: Contemporary Perspectives*, edited by W. Ashmore and A. Knapp, pp. 201–228. Blackwell, Oxford.

Byers, Douglas
1979 *The Nevin Shellheap: Burials and Observations*. Papers of the Robert S. Peabody Foundation for Archaeology No. 9. Andover, Massachusetts.

Byers, Martin
2004 *The Ohio Hopewell Episode*. University of Akron Press, Akron, Ohio.
2005 The Mortuary "Laying-In" Crypts of the Hopewell Site: Beyond the Funerary Paradigm. In *Interacting with the Dead: Perspectives on Mortuary Archae-*

ology for the New Millennium, edited by G. Rakita, J. Buikstra, L. Beck, and S. William, pp. 124–141. University of Florida Press, Gainesville.

Cameron, Catherine

2002 Sacred Earthen Architecture in the Northern Southwest: The Bluff Great House Berm. *American Antiquity* 67(4):677–696.

Cantwell, Anne

1980 Middle Woodland Dog Ceremonialism in Illinois. *Wisconsin Archeologist* 61: 480–496.

Carey, Heather, Mary McCorvie, and Mark Wagner

2010 "A Peculiar Method" of Grinding: Examples of Indian Kettles and Hominy Holes from Southern Illinois. Paper presented at the Annual Meeting of the Southeastern Archaeological Conference, Lexington.

Carr, Christopher, and Troy Case (editors)

2005 *Gathering Hopewell: Society, Ritual and Ritual Interaction*. Springer, New York.

Carr, Philip, and Jon Gibson (editors)

2004 *Signs of Power: The Rise of Cultural Complexity in the Southeast*. University of Alabama Press, Tuscaloosa.

Carr, Philip, and Lee Stewart

2004 Poverty Point Chipped-Stone Tool Raw Materials: Inferring Social and Economic Strategies. In *Signs of Power: The Rise of Cultural Complexity in the Southeast*, edited by J. Gibson and P. Carr, pp. 129–145. University of Alabama Press, Tuscaloosa.

Carrasco, David (editor)

1999 *Aztec Ceremonial Landscapes*. University of Colorado Press, Niwot.

Case, Troy, and Christopher Carr (editors)

2008 *The Scioto Hopewell and Their Neighbors: Bioarchaeological Documentation and Cultural Understanding*. Springer, New York.

Ceci, Lynn

1989 Tracing Wampum's Origins: Shell Bead Evidence from Archaeological Sites in Western and Coastal New York. In *Proceedings of the 1986 Shell Bead Conference: Selected Papers*, edited by L. Ceci, 17–24. Rochester Museum and Science Center Research Records No. 20. Rochester, New York.

Chapdelaine, Claude, and Norman Clermont

2006 Adaptation, Continuity and Change in the Middle Ottawa Valley: A View from the Morrison and Allumettes Island Late Archaic Sites. In *The Archaic of the Far Northeast*, edited by D. Sanger and M. Renouf, pp. 191–207. University of Maine Press, Orono.

Chapman, Jefferson

1975 *The Rose Island Site*. Report of Investigations No. 14. University of Tennessee, Department of Anthropology, Knoxville.

1977 *Archaic Period Research in the Lower Little Tennessee River Valley—1975: Icehouse Bottom, Harrison Branch, Thirty Acre Island, Calloway Island*. Report of Investigations No. 18. University of Tennessee, Department of Anthropology, Knoxville.

1981 *Bacon Bend and Iddins Site: The Late Archaic Period in the Lower Little Tennessee River Valley.* Report of Investigations No. 31. Tennessee Valley Authority, University of Tennessee, Department of Anthropology, Knoxville.

Chapman, Jefferson, and James Adovasio

1977 Textile and Basketry Impressions from Icehouse Bottom. *American Antiquity* 42:620–625.

Chapman, Jefferson, and Susan Myster

1991 The Kimberly-Clark Site: A Late Archaic Cremation Cemetery. In *The Archaic Period in the Mid-South*, edited by C. McNutt, pp. 35–39. Occasional Papers No. 16. Memphis State University, Memphis, Tennessee.

Charles, Douglas, and Jane Buikstra (editors)

2006 *Recreating Hopewell.* University Press of Florida, Gainesville.

Charles, Douglas, and Jane Buikstra

1983 Archaic Mortuary Behavior in the Central Mississippi Drainage: Distribution, Structure, and Behavioral Implications. In *Archaic Hunters and Gatherers in the American Midwest*, edited by J. Phillips and J. Brown, pp. 117–146. Academic Press, New York.

2002 Siting, Sighting and Citing the Dead. In *The Space and Place of Death*, edited by H. Silverman and D. Small, pp. 13–25. Archeological Papers of the American Anthropological Association No. 11.

Charles, Douglas, Jane Buikstra, and Steven Leigh

1988 Excavation Methodology. In *The Archaic and Woodland Cemeteries at the Elizabeth Site in the Lower Illinois Valley*, edited by D. Charles, S. Leigh, and J. Buikstra, pp. 18–28. Kampsville Archeological Center, Research Series Vol. 7. Center for American Archaeology, Kampsville, Illinois.

Charles, Douglas, Steven Leigh, and Donald Albertson

1988 Burial Descriptions. In *The Archaic and Woodland Cemeteries at the Elizabeth Site in the Lower Illinois Valley*, edited by D. Charles, S. Leigh, and J. Buikstra, pp. 247–274. Kampsville Archeological Center, Research Series Vol. 7. Center for American Archaeology, Kampsville, Illinois.

Charles, Tommy

2010 *Discovering South Carolina's Rock Art.* University of South Carolina Press, Columbia.

Chatters, James

2002 *Ancient Encounters: Kennewick Man and the First Americans.* Simon and Schuster, New York.

Chevalier, J., and A. Bain

2003 *The Hot and the Cold: Ills of Humans and Maize in Native Mexico.* University of Toronto Press, Toronto.

Chomko, Stephen

1975 Bone "Awls" and Utilized Antler Tines from Arnold Research Cave, 23Cy64, Missouri. *Plains Anthropologist* 20(67):27–40.

1978 Phillips Spring, 23Hi216: A Multicomponent Site in the Western Missouri Ozarks. *Plains Anthropologist* 23(81):235–255.

Claassen, Cheryl

1994 Washboards, Pigtoes, and Muckets: Historic Musseling in the Mississippi Watershed. *Historical Archaeology* 28(2):1–164.

1995 Dogan Point and Its Social Context. In *Dogan Point: A Shell Matrix Site in the Lower Hudson Valley*, edited by C. Claassen, pp. 129–142. Occasional Publications in Northeastern Anthropology No. 14. Archaeological Services, Bethlehem, Connecticut.

2008 Shell Symbolism in Pre-Columbian North America. In *Early Human Impact on Megamolluscs*, edited by Andrzej Antczak and Robert Cipriani, pp. 231–236. British Archaeological Reports 21865.

2010 *Feasting with Shellfish in the Southern Ohio Valley: Archaic Sacred Sites and Rituals*. University of Tennessee Press, Knoxville.

2011a Rock Shelters as Women's Retreats: Understanding Newt Kash. *American Antiquity* 73(4):628–641.

2011b Waning Pilgrimage Paths and Modern Roadscapes: Moving through Landscape in Northern Guerrero, Mexico. *World Archaeology* 43(3):493–503.

2011c Modern Aztec-Derived Rain Calling Ceremonies and Their Possible Applicability to Landforms and Beliefs in the Ancient Mid-South. Paper presented at the annual Mid-South Archaeological Meeting, Memphis.

2012a The Archaic Hunt God Rite. Paper presented at the Annual Meeting of the Southeastern Archaeological Conference, Baton Rouge.

2012b Cave Rituals and Ritual Caves of the Eastern United States. In *Enduring Motives: The Archaeology of Tradition and Religion in Native America*, edited by L. Sundstrom and W. DeBoer, pp. 253–263. University of Alabama Press, Tuscaloosa.

2012c Reevaluating Cave Records: The Case for Ritual Caves in the Eastern United States. In *Sacred Darkness: A Global Perspective on the Ritual Use of Caves*, edited by Holley Moyes, pp. 211–224. University of Colorado Press, Boulder.

2012d Thoughts on Burial Posture and Place for the Archaic of the Southern Ohio Valley. Paper presented at the Annual Meeting of the Society for American Archaeology, Memphis.

2013a Infanticide and Sacrifices among Archaic Babies of the Central United States. *World Archaeology* 45(2):298–313.

2013b On Sandals, Footprints, Caves and Fertility. Paper presented at the Annual Meeting of the Southeastern Archaeological Conference, Tampa.

2013c Fertility—A Place-Based Gift to Groups. In *Género y Arqueología en Mesoamérica*. Homenaje a Rosemary A. Joyce, coordinated by María J. Rodríguez-Shadow and Susan Kellogg, pp. 198–215. Centro de Estudios de Antropología de la Mujer. Las Cruces, New Mexico.

Clark, Frances

1987 Anculosa Shell Beads in Middle Woodland Exchange. Monograph Series No. 1. Research Labs of Anthropology, University of North Carolina, Chapel Hill.

Clark, J. V. H.

1849 *Onondaga or Reminiscences of Earlier and Later Times.* 2 vols. Stoddard and Babcock, Syracuse, New York.

Clark, John

2004 Surrounding the Sacred: Geometry and Design of Early Mound Groups as Meaning and Function. In *Signs of Power: The Rise of Cultural Complexity in the Southeast*, edited by J. Gibson and P. Carr, pp. 162–213. University of Alabama Press, Tuscaloosa.

Clark, John, and Arlene Colman

2008 Time Reckoning and Memorials in Mesoamerica. *Cambridge Archaeological Journal* 18(1):93–99.

2012 Structure of the Mesoamerican Universe, from Aztec to Olmec. In *Enduring Motives*, edited by L. Sundstrom and W. DeBoer, pp. 15–59. University of Alabama Press, Tuscaloosa.

Classen, Constance

1993 *Inca Cosmology and the Human Body*. University of Utah Press, Salt Lake.

Clausen, C. J., A. Cohen, Cesare Emiliani, J. Holman, and J. Stipp

1979 Little Salt Spring, Florida: A Unique Underwater Site. *Science* 203(4381): 609–614.

Clay, Berle

2013 Like a Dead Dog: Strategic Choice in the Mortuary Enterprise. In *Early and Middle Woodland Landscapes of the Southeast*, edited by A. Wright and E. Henry, pp. 56–70. Florida Museum of Natural History, Ripley Bullen Series, University Press of Florida, Gainesville.

Cochran, D., K. Knight, and L. Bush

1997 McCullough's Run (12-B-1036): A Prehistoric Cremation Cemetery, Bartholomew County, Indiana. Archaeological Resources Management Service, Ball State University, Muncie, Indiana.

Coe, Joffre

1964 The Formative Cultures of the Carolina Piedmont. *Transactions of the American Philosophical Society* 54:pt. 5. Philadelphia.

Colburn, Mona

1985 Faunal Remains from the Campbell Hollow Archaic Occupations. In *The Campbell Hollow Archaic Occupations: A Study of Intrasite Spatial Structure in the Lower Illinois Valley*, edited by C. Russell Stafford, pp. 108–120. Kampsville Archeological Center Research Series, Vol. 4. Center for American Archeology, Kampsville.

Cole, Mark

2006 Paleoindian Settlement in Limestone County, Alabama. *Journal of Alabama Archaeology* 52 (1–2):1–61.

Connaway, John

1977 *The Denton Site: A Middle Archaic Occupation in the Northern Yazoo Basin.* Mississippi Archeological Report 4, Mississippi Department of Archives and History, Jackson.

1981 The Keenan Bead Cache, Lawrence County, Mississippi. *Louisiana Archaeology* 8:59–71.

Converse, Robert

2006 The Caves and Rockshelters of Ohio in Retrospect. In *Caves and Culture, 10,000 Years of Ohio History*, edited by L. Spurlock, O. Prufer, and T. Pigott, pp. 19–26. Kent State University Press, Kent, Ohio.

Cook, Thomas

1976 *Koster: An Artifact Analysis of Two Archaic Phases in West Central Illinois*. Prehistoric Record 1. Northwestern University Archaeological Program, Evanston, Illinois.

Correa, Phyllis

2000 Otomí Rituals and Celebrations: Crosses, Ancestors, and Resurrection. *Journal of American Folklore* 113(450):436–450.

Coy, Fred, Thomas Fuller, Larry Meadows, and James Swauger

1997 *Rock Art of Kentucky*. University Press of Kentucky, Lexington.

Coyle, Philip

1998 The Customs of Our Ancestors: Cora Religious Conversion and Millennialism, 2000–1722. *Ethnohistory* 45:509–542.

Craig, A. B.

1959 A Dwarf Burial from Limestone Ct. Alabama. *Journal of Alabama Archeology* 4(1):15–17.

Crawford, Jessica

2003 Archaic Effigy Beads: A New Look at Some Old Beads. Unpublished master's thesis, Department of Anthropology, University of Mississippi, Oxford.

Crothers, George

2005 Vertebrate Fauna from the Carlston Annis Site. In *Archaeology of the Middle Green River Region, Kentucky*, edited by W. Marquardt and P. Watson, pp. 295–314. Institute of Archaeology and Paleoenvironmental Studies, Monograph 5. Florida Museum of Natural History, University of Florida, Gainesville.

2012 Early Woodland Ritual Use of Caves in Eastern North America. *American Antiquity* 77(3):524–541.

Curtin, Edward

2011 The Archaic Period in Eastern New York State. Paper presented at the Annual Meeting of the New York State Archaeological Association, Ellenville.

Custer, Jay

1989 *Prehistoric Cultures of the Delmarva Peninsula: An Archaeological Study*. University of Delaware Press, Newark.

DeBoer, Warren

2001 "Of Dice and Women": Gambling and Exchange in Native North America. *Journal of Archaeological Method and Theory* 8(3):215–268.

2005 Colours for a North American Past. *World Archaeology* 37(1):66–91.

Deel, Judith

1985 The Doherty Site (14Mm27): New Views on the Late Archaic. Unpublished master's thesis, Wichita State University, Kansas.

DeJarnette, David, Edward Kurjack, and James Cambron

1962 The Stanfield-Worley Bluff Shelter. *Journal of Alabama Archaeology* 8(1–2): 1–119.

Deller, Brian, and Christopher Ellis

1984 Crowfield: A Preliminary Report on a Probable Paleo-Indian Cremation in Southwestern Ontario. *Archaeology of Eastern North America* 12:41–71.

2001 Evidence for Late Paleo-Indian Ritual from the Caradoc Site (AfHj-104), Southwestern Ontario, Canada. *American Antiquity* 66(2):267–284.

Dent, Richard

1995 *Chesapeake Prehistory: Old Traditions, New Directions*. Plenum, New York.

2007 Seed Collecting and Fishing at the Shawnee-Minisink Paleoindian Site: Everyday Life in the Late Pleistocene. In *Foragers of the Terminal Pleistocene of North America*, edited by R. Walker and B. Driskell, pp. 116–131. University of Nebraska Press, Lincoln.

Deter-Wolf, Aaron

2004 Ensworth School Site (40Dv184) and Late Middle Archaic Benton Occupations along the Harpeth River Drainage in Middle Tennessee. Paper presented at the Annual Meeting of the Southeastern Archaeological Conference, St. Louis, Missouri.

2013 Needle in a Haystack: Examining the Archaeological Evidence for Prehistoric Tattooing. In *Drawing with Great Needles: Ancient Tattoo Traditions of North America*, edited by A. Deter-Wolf and C. Diaz-Granados, pp. 43–72. University of Texas Press, Austin.

Deter-Wolf, Aaron, and Karen Hockersmith

2007 The Indian Mountain Complex: Three Prehistoric(?) Stoneworks in Middle Tennessee. Paper presented at the Annual Meeting of the Southeastern Archaeological Conference, Knoxville.

Deter-Wolf, Aaron, Sean Norris, Marc Wampler, and Josh Tuschl

2004 *The Ensworth School Project: Archaeological Investigations at Site 40Dv184, Davidson County, Tennessee*. Report prepared for D. F. Chase, Inc., by TRC, Inc.

Devereux, Paul, and Robert Jahn

1996 Preliminary Investigations and Cognitive Considerations of the Acoustical Resonances of Selected Archaeological Sites. *Antiquity* 70:665–666.

Diaz-Granados, Carol

2004 Marking Stone, Land, Body, and Spirit: Rock Art and Mississippian Iconography. In *Hero, Hawk, and Open Hand: American Indian Art of the Ancient Midwest and South*, edited by R. Townsend, pp. 139–149. Art Institute of Chicago and Yale University Press, New Haven, Connecticut.

Diaz-Granados, Carol, and James Duncan

2005 Rock Art of the Central Mississippi River Valley. In *Discovering North American Rock Art*, edited by L. Loendorf, C. Chippendale, and D. Whitley, pp. 114–130. University of Arizona Press, Tucson.

DiBlasi, Phil

1976 A New Assessment of the Archaeological Significance of the Ashworth Site

(15Bu236). Unpublished master's thesis, Interdisciplinary Studies, University of Louisville, Kentucky.

Dickel, D. N.

2002 Analysis of Mortuary Patterns. In *Windover: Multidisciplinary Investigations of an Early Archaic Florida Cemetery*, edited by G. Doran, pp. 73–96. University Press of Florida, Gainesville.

Didier, Mary Ellen

1967 A Distributional Study of the Turkey Tail Point. *Wisconsin Archaeologist* 48(1):3–73.

Dincauze, Dena

1968 *Cremation Cemeteries in Eastern Massachusetts*. Papers of the Peabody Museum of Archaeology and Ethnology, Harvard University. Vol. 59, no. 1. Peabody Museum, Cambridge, Massachusetts.

1975 The Late Archaic Period in Southern New England. *Arctic Anthropology* 12(2):23–34.

1976 *The Neville Site: 8000 Years at Amoskeag, Manchester, New Hampshire*. Peabody Museum Monographs 4. Harvard University, Cambridge.

Doran, Glenn

2002 Introduction to Wet Sites and Windover (8Br246) Investigations. In *Windover: Multidisciplinary Investigations of an Early Archaic Florida Cemetery*, edited by G. Doran, pp. 1–38. University Press of Florida, Gainesville.

Dowd, Elsbeth

2011 Amphibian and Reptilian Imagery in Caddo Art. *Southeastern Archaeology* 30(1):79–95.

Dowd, John

1989 *The Anderson Site: Middle Archaic Adaptation in Tennessee's Central Basin*. Miscellaneous Paper 13. Tennessee Anthropological Association, Nashville.

Driskell, Boyce

1979 The Rosenberger Site (15JF18). In *Excavations at Four Archaic Sites in the Lower Ohio Valley, Jefferson County, Kentucky*, vol. II, edited by M. Collins and B. Driskell, pp. 697–803. Department of Anthropology, University of Kentucky, Lexington.

1996 Stratified Late Pleistocene and Early Holocene Deposits at Dust Cave, Northwestern Alabama. In *The Paleoindian and Early Archaic Southeast*, edited by D. Anderson and K. Sassaman, pp. 315–330. University of Alabama Press, Tuscaloosa.

Driver, Jonathan

1999 Raven Skeletons from Paleoindian Contexts, Charlie Lake Cave, British Columbia. *American Antiquity* 64(2):289–298.

Duffield, Lathel

1974 Nonhuman Vertebrate Remains from Salts Cave Vestibule. In *Archeology of the Mammoth Cave Area*, edited by P. J. Watson, pp. 123–134. Academic Press, New York.

Dunbar, James

2006 Paleoindian Archaeology. In *First Floridians and Last Mastodons: The Page-Ladson Site in the Aucilla River*, edited by S. Webb, pp. 403–435. Springer, New York.

Dunbar, James, and S. David Webb

1996 Bone and Ivory Tools from Submerged Paleoindian Sites in Florida. In *The Paleoindian and Early Archaic Southeast*, edited by D. Anderson and K. Sassaman, pp. 331–352. University of Alabama Press, Tuscaloosa.

Dunham, Gary

1994 Common Ground, Contesting Visions: The Emergence of Burial Mound Ritual in Late Prehistoric Virginia. Unpublished Ph.D. dissertation, Department of Anthropology, University of Virginia, Richmond.

Egloff, Keith, and Joseph McAvoy

1990 Chronology of Virginia's Early and Middle Archaic Periods. In *Early and Middle Archaic Research in Virginia: A Synthesis*, edited by T. Reinhart and M. Hodges, pp. 61–79. Archaeological Society of Virginia, Richmond.

Eliade, Mircea

1959 *The Sacred and the Profane*. Harcourt, Brace and World, New York.

Ellis, Christopher

1994 Miniature Early Paleo-Indian Stone Artifacts from the Parkhill, Ontario Site. *North American Archaeologist* 15(3):253–267.

Ellis, Christopher, I. T. Kenyon, and Michael Spence

1990 The Archaic. In *The Archaeology of Southern Ontario to AD 1650*, edited by C. Ellis and N. Ferris, pp. 65–124. Occasional Publication of the London Chapter, Ontario Archaeological Society 5. London, Ontario.

Eyman, Frances

1965 American Indian Gaming Arrows and Stick Dice. *Expedition* 7(4):39–47.

Fagan, Brian

2005 *Ancient North America: The Archaeology of a Continent*. 4th ed. Thames and Hudson, New York.

Farnsworth, Kenneth

1987 Part Two: Preliminary Evaluation of Bannerstones and Other Ground-Stone Artifacts from the Bullseye Site, 11-Ge-127. In *The Bullseye Site: A Floodplain Archaic Mortuary Site in the Lower Illinois River Valley*. Illinois State Museum Reports of Investigations 42:13–19.

Faulkner, Charles

1997 Four Thousand Years of Native American Cave Art in the Southern Appalachians. *Journal of Cave and Karst Studies* 59(3):148–153.

Feder, Ken

2001 Prehistoric Land Use Patterns in North-Central Connecticut: A Matter of Scale. In *Archaeology of the Appalachian Highlands*, edited by L. Sullivan and S. Prezzano, pp. 19–30. University of Tennessee Press, Knoxville.

Fitzhugh, William

2006 Settlement, Social and Ceremonial Change in the Labrador Maritime Archaic. In *The Archaic of the Far Northeast*, edited by D. Sanger and M. Renouf, pp. 47–81. University of Maine Press, Orono.

Fogelson, Raymond

1989 The Ethnohistory of Events and Nonevents. *Ethnohistory* 36:133–147.

Fortier, Andrew

1987 The Archaic Occupation. *In the Range Site: Archaic through Woodland Occupations*, assembled by J. Kelly, A. Fortier, S. Ozuk, and J. Williams, pp. 38–113. American Bottom Archaeology FAI-270 Site Reports Vol. 16. Illinois Department of Transportation, University of Illinois Press, Urbana.

Fowler, William

1966 Ceremonial and Domestic Products. *Bulletin of the Massachusetts Archeological Society* 27(3–4):33–68.

1971–1972 Ragged Mountain Shelter-Quarry. *Bulletin of the Massachusetts Archeological Society* 32(1–2):9–19.

Fox, William

1993 Owls and Orenda. *Archaeology Notes* 93(3):19–25.

2004a Horned Panthers and Erie Associates. In *A Passion for the Past: Papers in Honour of James F. Pendergast*, edited by J. Wright and J. Pilon, pp. 283–304. Mercury Series, Archaeology Paper 164. Canadian Museum of Civilization, Gatineau, Quebec.

2004b Islands of Creation, Islands of Rebirth. *The Bulletin: Journal of the New York State Archaeological Association* 120:47–57.

2007 Shaking the Earth: Turtle Shell Rattles among the Ontario Iroquois. Used with permission.

Fox, William, and Eldon Molto

1994a The Shaman of Long Point. *Ontario Archaeological Society* 57:23–44.

1994b A Special Child: The Monarch Knoll Burial. *Midcontinental Journal of Archaeology* 19(1):99–136.

Fox, William, and Robert Salzer

1999 Themes and Variations: Ideological Systems in the Great Lakes. In *Taming the Taxonomy: Toward a New Understanding of Great Lakes Archaeology*, edited by R. Williamson and C. Watts, pp. 237–263. Eastendbooks, Toronto.

Franklin, Jay

2002 The Prehistory of Fentress County, Tennessee: An Archaeological Survey. Unpublished Ph.D. dissertation, University of Tennessee, Knoxville.

Friederici, G.

1907 *Scalping in America.* Annual Report of the Smithsonian Institution, 1906. Pp. 423–438. Government Printing Office, Washington, D.C.

Fundaburk, Emma, and Mary Foreman

1957 *Sun Circles and Human Hands: The Southeastern Indians—Art and Industry.* Southern Publications, Fairhope, Alabama.

Funk, Robert

1973 The West Athens Hill Site (Cox 7). In *Aboriginal Settlement Patterns in the*

Northeast, edited by W. A. Ritchie and R. E. Funk, pp. 9–36. New York State Museum and Science Service, Memoir 20, Albany.

Funkhouser, William, and William Webb

1929 *The So-Called Ash Caves in Lee County Kentucky*. Vol. 1, no. 2:37–112. Department of Anthropology and Archaeology, University of Kentucky, Lexington.

1930 *Rock Shelters of Wolfe and Powell Counties, Kentucky*. Vol. 1, no. 4. Department of Anthropology and Archaeology, University of Kentucky, Lexington.

Furst, Jill

1995 *The Natural History of the Soul in Ancient Mexico*. Yale University Press, New Haven, Connecticut.

Furst, Peter

1977 The Roots and Continuities of Shamanism. In *Stones, Bones, and Skin: Ritual and Shamanic Art*, assembled by Artscanada, pp. 1–28. Society for Art Publications, Toronto.

Galloway, Patricia (editor)

1989 *The Southeastern Ceremonial Complex: Artifacts and Analysis.* University of Nebraska Press, Lincoln.

Galloway, Patricia

1997 Where Have All the Menstrual Huts Gone: The Invisibility of Menstrual Seclusion in the Late Prehistoric Southeast. In *Women in Prehistory: North America and Mesoamerica*, edited by C. Claassen and R. Joyce, pp. 47–64. University of Pennsylvania Press, Philadelphia.

Gartner, William C.

1996 Archaeoastronomy as Sacred Geography. *Wisconsin Archeologist* 77(3/4): 128–150.

Gatschet, Albert

1884 *A Migration Legend of the Creek Indians*. Brinton's Library of Aboriginal American Literature, No. IV. D. G. Brinton, Philadelphia.

1895 Tecumseh's Name. *American Anthropologist* 8:91–92.

Geijvall, Nils-Gustaf

1963 Cremations. In *Science in Archaeology*, edited by D. Brothwell and E. Higgs, pp. 379–390. Basic Books, New York.

Gell, Alfred

1998 *Art and Agency: An Anthropology Theory*. Clarendon, Oxford.

Gibson, Jon

1994 Before Their Time? Early Mounds in the Lower Mississippi Valley. *Southeastern Archaeology* 13(2):162–186.

1998 Broken Circles, Owl Monsters, and Black Earth Midden: Separating Sacred and Secular at Poverty Point. In *Ancient Earthen Enclosures of the Eastern Woodlands*, edited by R. Mainfort and L. Sullivan, pp. 17–30. University Press of Florida, Gainesville.

2000 *The Ancient Mounds of Poverty Point: Place of Rings*. University Press of Florida, Gainesville.

2010 "Nothing But the River's Flood": Late Archaic Diaspora or Disengagement in the Lower Mississippi Valley and Southeastern North America. In *Trend, Tradition, and Turmoil: What Happened to the Southeastern Archaic?*, edited by D. Thomas and M. Sanger, pp. 33–42. Anthropological Papers of the American Museum of Natural History 93.

Giles, Bretton

2010 The Ritual Mnemonics of Hopewell Symbols: An Analysis of Effigies and Ceremonial Regalia from Tremper, Mound City, and Hopewell. Unpublished Ph.D. dissertation, Department of Anthropology, Binghamton University, New York.

Goad, Sharon

1980 Patterns of Late Archaic Exchange. *Tennessee Anthropologist* 5(1):1–16.

Goldman-Finn, Nurit

1994 Dust Cave in Regional Context. *Journal of Alabama Archaeology* 40(1–2): 212–231.

Good Eshelman, Catharine

1996 El trabajo de los muertos en la Sierra de Guerrero. *Estudios de Cultura Nahuatl* 26:275–287.

Gould, Richard

1980 *Living Archaeology*. Cambridge University Press, Cambridge.

Graham, J.

1989 Olmec Diffusion: A Sculptural View from Pacific Guatemala. In *Regional Perspectives on the Olmec*, edited by R. Sharer and D. Grove, pp. 227–246. Cambridge University Press, Cambridge.

Gray, M.

2001 The Pilgrimage as Ritual Space. In *Holy Ground: Theoretical Issues Relating to the Landscape and Material Culture of Ritual Space Objects*, edited by A. Smith and A. Brookes, pp. 91–97. British Archaeological Reports #956. British Archaeological Reports, Oxford.

Griffin, John

1974 *Investigations in Russell Cave, Russell Cave National Monument, Alabama*. National Park Service Publications in Archaeology 13. U.S. Department of the Interior, Washington, D.C.

Griffin, John, and John Reeves

1968 A Stratified Site at Peaks of Otter, Blue Ridge Parkway. *Quarterly Bulletin Archeological Society of Virginia* 23:54–62.

Hack, John

1974 Part 2: Geology of Russell Cave. In *Investigations in Russell Cave*, by John Griffin, pp. 16–28. National Park Service Publications in Archaeology 13, U.S. Department of the Interior, Washington, D.C.

Hall, Robert

1976 Ghosts, Water Barriers, Corn, and Sacred Enclosures in the Eastern Woodlands. *American Antiquity* 41:360–364.

1979 In Search of the Ideology of the Adena-Hopewell Climax. In *Hopewell*

Archaeology: The Chillicothe Conference, edited by D. Brose and N. Greber, pp. 258–265. Kent State University Press, Kent, Ohio.

1985 Medicine Wheels, Sun Circles and the Magic of World Center Shrines. *Plains Anthropologist* 30(1985):181–193.

1989 The Cultural Background of Mississippian Symbolism. In *The Southeastern Ceremonial Complex: Artifacts and Analysis*, edited by P. Galloway, pp. 239–278. University of Nebraska Press, Lincoln.

1997 *An Archaeology of the Soul: North American Indian Belief and Ritual*. University of Illinois Press, Urbana.

2000 Sacrificed Foursomes and Green Corn Ceremonialism. In *Mounds, Modoc, and Mesoamerica: Papers in Honor of Melvin L. Fowler*, edited by S. Ahler, pp. 245–253. Illinois State Museum, Springfield.

2006 The Enigmatic Copper Cutout from Bedford Mound 8. In *Recreating Hopewell*, edited by D. Charles and J. Buikstra, pp. 466–474. University Press of Florida, Gainesville.

Hallowell, A. Irving

1960 Ojibway Ontology, Behavior, and World View. In *Culture in History: Essays in Honor of Paul Radin*, edited by S. Diamond, pp. 19–52. Columbia University Press, New York.

Halperin, Christina, Sergio Garza, Keith Prufer, and James Brady

2003 Caves and Ancient Maya Ritual Use of Jute. *Latin American Antiquity* 14: 207–219.

Hamell, George

1983 Trading in Metaphors: The Magic of Beads. In *Proceedings of the 1982 Glass Trade Bead Conference*, edited by C. Hayes, pp. 5–28. Rochester Museum and Science Center Research Records No. 16.

1989 Abstract of Life's Immortal Shell: Wampum among the Iroquois. In *Proceedings of the 1986 Shell Bead Conference: Selected Papers*, edited by L. Ceci, p. 205. Rochester Museum and Science Center Research Records No. 20.

Hanks, Christopher

1990 The Foxie Otter Site: A Multicomponent Occupation North of Lake Huron. Anthropological Papers 79. University of Michigan, Museum of Anthropology, Ann Arbor.

Harl, Joseph

2009 Archaic Period of East-Central Missouri. In *Archaic Societies: Diversity and Complexity across the Midcontinent*, edited by T. Emerson, D. McElrath, and A. Fortier, pp. 377–400. State University of New York Press, Albany.

Harper, Ross

1999 To Render the God of the Water Propitious: Hunting and Human-Animal Relations in the Northeastern Woodlands. Unpublished Ph.D. dissertation, Department of Anthropology, University of Connecticut, Storrs.

Harvey, Edward

2006 Bannerstones: An Ancient Native American Art Tradition. Electronic document, http://www.arrowheads.com/BannerstoneBannerStone.pdf, accessed August 9, 2013.

Hayden, Brian

1996 *Pithouses of Keatley Creek*. Harcourt Brace College Publishers, Fort Worth, Texas.

Heckenberger, Michael, James Petersen, and Louisa Basa

1990 Early Woodland Period Ritual Use of Personal Adornment at the Boucher Site. *Annals of Carnegie Museum* 59(3):173–217.

Henden, Julia

2000 Having and Holding: Storage, Memory, Knowledge, and Social Relations. *American Anthropologist* 103:42–53.

Herrmann, Nicholas

2002 Biological Affinities of Archaic Period Populations from West-Central Kentucky and Tennessee. Unpublished Ph.D. dissertation, University of Tennessee, Knoxville.

Heyden, Doris

2005 Rites of Passage and Other Ceremonies in Caves. In *In the Maw of the Earth Monster: Mesoamerican Ritual Cave Use*, edited by J. Brady and K. Prufer, pp. 21–34. University of Texas Press, Austin.

Heyman, Margorie, Elliot Abrams, and AnnCorinne Freter

2005 Late Archaic Community Aggregation and Feasting in the Hocking Valley. In *The Emergence of the Moundbuilders*, edited by E. Abrams and A. Freter, pp. 67–81. Ohio University Press, Athens.

Hodge, Frederick Webb

1907 *Handbook of American Indians North of Mexico*. Bulletin 30, Part 1. Bureau of American Ethnology, Washington, D.C.

Hodge, Shannon, and Hugh Berryman

2008 Evidence of Prehistoric Violent Trauma from a Cave in Middle Tennessee. *Tennessee Archaeologist* 3(2):139–156.

Hofman, Jack

1985 Middle Archaic Ritual and Shell Midden Archaeology: Considering the Significance of Cremations. In *Exploring Tennessee Prehistory*, edited by T. Whyte, C. Boyd, and B. Riggs, pp. 1–22. Report of Investigations, No. 42. Department of Anthropology, University of Tennessee, Knoxville.

1986 Hunter-Gatherer Variability: Toward an Explanatory Model. Unpublished Ph.D. dissertation, Department of Anthropology, University of Tennessee, Knoxville.

Hollenbach, Kandace

2009 *Foraging in the Tennessee River Valley*. University of Alabama Press, Tuscaloosa.

Holmes, William

1903 *Flint Implements and Fossil Remains from a Sulphur Spring at Afton, Indian Territory*. Report of the U.S. National Museum for 1901, Paper #2.

Homsey, Lara, Renee Walker, and Kandace Hollenbach
2010 What's for Dinner? Investigation of Food-Processing Technologies at Dust Cave, Alabama. *Southeastern Archaeology* 29:182–196.

House, John
1965 Bluff-top Indian Sites. *Arkansas Archeologist* 6(1):12–13.

Hrdlicka, Ales
1941 Exploration of Mummy Caves in the Aleutian Islands: Part II. Further Exploration. *Scientific Monthly* 52(2):113–130.

Huber, Brad
1990 The Recruitment of Nahua Curers: Role Conflict and Gender. *Ethnology* 29(2):159–176.

Hutchinson, Dale, and Lorraine Aragon
2002 Collective Burials and Community Memories: Interpreting the Placement of the Dead in the Southeastern and Mid-Atlantic United States with Reference to Ethnographic Cases from Indonesia. In *Space and Place of Death*, edited by H. Silverman and D. Small, pp. 28–54. Archeological Papers of the American Anthropological Association, No. 11. Washington, D.C.

Inomata, T.
2006 Plazas, Performers, and Spectators. *Current Anthropology* 47:805–842.

Irwin, Lee
1994 *The Dream Seekers: Native American Visionary Traditions of the Great Plains.* University of Oklahoma Press, Norman.

Ison, Cecil
2004 Farming, Gender, and Shifting Social Organization. In *Rock Art of Eastern North America*, edited by C. Diaz-Granados and J. Duncan, pp. 177–189. University of Alabama Press, Tuscaloosa.

Jackson, H. Edwin
1991 The Trade Fair in Hunter-Gatherer Interaction: The Role of Intersocietal Trade in the Evolution of Poverty Point Culture. In *Between Bands and States*, edited by S. Gregg, pp. 265–286. Occasional Paper 9. Center for Archaeological Investigations, Southern Illinois University, Carbondale.

Jackson, Ed, and Susan Scott
2001 Archaic Faunal Utilization in the Louisiana Bottomlands. *Southeastern Archaeology* 20(2):187–196.

Jackson, Thomas
1992 Pounding Acorn: Women's Production as Social and Economic Focus. In *Engendering Archaeology: Women and Prehistory*, edited by J. Gero and M. Conkey, pp. 301–325. Basil Blackwell, Cambridge, Massachusetts.

Jahn, Otto, and Ripley Bullen
1978 *The Tick Island Site, St. Johns River, Florida.* Florida Anthropological Society Publications 10, Gainesville.

James, Jenny
2006 The Dog Tribe. *Southern Anthropologist* 32(1/2):17–46.

Jefferies, Richard

1997 Middle Archaic Bone Pins: Evidence of Mid-Holocene Regional-Scale Social Groups in the Southern Midwest. *American Antiquity* 62(3):464–487.

2004 Regional-Scale Interaction Networks and the Emergence of Cultural Complexity along the Northern Margins of the Southeast. In *Signs of Power: The Rise of Cultural Complexity in the Southeast*, edited by J. Gibson and P. Carr, pp. 71–85. University of Alabama Press, Tuscaloosa.

2008 Archaic Period. In *The Archaeology of Kentucky: An Update*. Vol. 1, edited by D. Pollack, pp. 193–338. State Historic Preservation Comprehensive Plan Report No. 3. Kentucky Heritage Council, Frankfort.

Jefferies, Richard, and Brian Butler

1982 *The Carrier Mills Archaeological Project: Human Adaptation in the Saline Valley, Illinois*. Center for Archaeological Investigations Research Paper No. 33. Center for Archaeological Investigations Southern Illinois University, Carbondale.

Jelsma, Johan

2006 Three Social Status Groups at Port au Choix: Maritime Archaic Mortuary Practices and Social Structure. In *The Archaic of the Far Northeast*, edited by D. Sanger and M. Renouf, pp. 84–103. University of Maine Press, Orono.

Johnson, Jay, and Samuel Brookes

1989 Benton Points, Turkey Tails, and Cache Blades: Middle Archaic Exchange in the Midsouth. *Southeastern Archaeology* 8(2):134–145.

Jones, Calvin, and Louis Tesar

2000 The Wakulla Springs Lodge Site (8Wa329): A Preliminary Report on a Stratified Paleoindian through Archaic Site, Wakulla County, Florida. *Florida Anthropologist* 53(2–3):98–115.

Joralemon, Peter

1996 In Search of the Olmec Cosmos: Reconstructing the World View of Mexico's First Civilization. In *Olmec Art of Ancient Mexico*, edited by E. Benson and B. Fuente, pp. 51–59. National Gallery of Art, Washington, D.C.

Kay, Marvin (editor)

1982 *Holocene Adaptation within the Lower Pomme de Terre River Valley, Missouri*. Report submitted to the U.S. Army Corps of Engineers, Kansas City District.

1983 Archaic Period Research in the Western Ozark Highland, Missouri. In *Archaic Hunters and Gatherers in the American Midwest*, edited by J. Phillips and J. Brown, pp. 41–70. Academic Press, New York.

Kay, Marvin, and George Sabo

2006 Mortuary Ritual and Winter Solstice Imagery of the Harlan-Style Charnel House. *Southeastern Archaeology* 25(1):29–47.

Kehoe, Alice

2000 *Shamans and Religion: An Anthropological Exploration in Critical Thinking*. Waveland Press, Long Grove, Illinois.

2007 Osage Texts and Cahokia Data. In *Ancient Objects and Sacred Realms: In-*

terpretations of Mississippian Iconography, edited by K. Reilly and J. Garber, pp. 246–262. University of Texas Press, Austin.

Kehoe, Alice, and Thomas Kehoe

1979 *Solstice-Aligned Boulder Configurations in Saskatchewan*. National Museum of Man Mercury Series, Canadian Ethnology Service Paper No. 48. Ottawa.

Kelley, M.

1980 Disease and Environment: A Comparative Analysis of Three Early American Skeletal Collections. Unpublished Ph.D. dissertation, Department of Anthropology, Case Western University, Cleveland, Ohio.

Kelly, Lucretia, and John Kelly

2007 Swans in the American Bottom during the Emergent Mississippian and Mississippian. *Illinois Archaeology* 15 and 16:112–141.

Kerber, Jordan

1997 Native American Treatment of Dogs in Northeastern North America. *Archaeology of Eastern North America* 25:81–96.

Kidder, Tristram

2010 Trend, Tradition, and Transition at the End of the Archaic. In *Trend, Tradition, and Turmoil: What Happened to the Southeastern Archaic?*, edited by D. Thomas and M. Sanger, pp. 23–32. Museum of Anthropology 93. Anthropological Papers, University of Michigan, Ann Arbor.

Kidder, Tristram, Anthony Ortmann, and Thurman Allen

2004 Testing Mounds B and E at Poverty Point. *Southeastern Archaeology* 23:98–113.

Kidder, Tristram, and Kenneth Sassaman

2009 The View from the Southeast. In *Archaic Societies: Diversity and Complexity across the Midcontinent*, edited by T. Emerson, D. McElrath, and A. Fortier, pp. 667–696. State University of New York Press, Albany.

Kimball, Larry, and Derek Johnson

2012 The Ritualized Landscape at Biltmore Mound. Paper presented at the Annual Meeting of the Society for American Archaeology, Memphis.

Kimball, Larry, and Scott Schumate

2001 Archaeological Data Recovery at 31Sw265 on the Davis Cemetery Tract, Nantahala National Forest, Swain County, North Carolina. Paper presented at the Southern Appalachian Man and the Biosphere Conference, Gatlinburg, Tennessee.

Klasky, Philip

2009/2010 The Salt Song Trail Map: The Sacred Landscape of the Nuwuvi People. *News from Native California* 23(2):9–12.

Klippel, Walter

1971 *Graham Cave Revisited: A Reevaluation of Its Cultural Position during the Archaic Period*. Missouri Archaeological Society Memoir 9.

Klippel, Walter, and Paul Parmalee

1982 Diachronic Variation in Insectivores from Cheek Bend Cave and Environmental Change in the Midsouth. *Paleobiology* 8(4):447–458.

Knight, Vernon

1989 Symbolism of Mississippian Mounds. In *Powhatan's Mantle: Indians in the Colonial Southeast*, edited by G. Waselkov, P. Wood, and T. Hatley, pp. 421–434. University of Nebraska Press, Lincoln.

Koetje, Todd

1998 The Archaic in Northwestern Pennsylvania: A View from 36Me105, Mercer County. In *The Archaic Period in Pennsylvania: Hunter-Gatherers of the Early and Middle Holocene Period*, edited by P. Raber, P. Miller, and S. Neusius, pp. 29–44. Pennsylvania Historical and Museum Commission, Harrisburg.

Koldehoff, Brad, and John Walthall

2004 Settling In: Hunter-Gatherer Mobility during the Pleistocene-Holocene Transition in the Central Mississippi Valley. In *Aboriginal Ritual and Economy in the Eastern Woodlands: Essays in Memory of Howard Dalton Winters*, edited by A. Cantwell, L. Conrad, and J. Reyman, pp. 49–72. Kampsville Studies in Archeology and History, Vol. 5. Illinois State Museum Scientific Papers, Vol. 30. Springfield.

2009 Dalton and the Early Holocene Midcontinent: Setting the Stage. In *Archaic Societies: Diversity and Complexity across the Midcontinent*, edited by T. Emerson, D. McElrath, and A. Fortier, pp. 137–151. State University of New York Press, Albany.

Krupp, E. C.

1997 *Skywatchers, Shamans, and Kings: Astronomy and the Archaeology of Power.* John Wiley and Sons, New York.

Kuttruff, Carl

1997 Louisiana's Lost Heritage: The Monte Sano Mounds. *Louisiana Archaeological Conservancy* 7(2):4–6.

Kuttruff, Jenna, Gail DeHart, and Michael O'Brien

1998 7500 Years of Prehistoric Footwear from Arnold Research Cave. *Science* 281(5373):72–75.

Kwas, Mary

1981 Bannerstones as Chronological Markers in SE US. *Tennessee Anthropologist* 6(2):144–171.

Lambert, Patricia

2001 Auditory Exostoses: A Clue to Gender in Prehistoric and Historic Farming Communities of North Carolina and Virginia. In *Archaeological Studies of Gender in the Southeastern United States*, edited by J. Eastman and C. Rodning, pp. 152–172. University Press of Florida, Gainesville.

Lankford, George (editor)

1987 *Native American Legends.* August House, Little Rock, Arkansas.

2004 World on a String: Some Cosmological Components of the Southeastern Ceremonial Complex. In *Hero, Hawk, and Open Hand: American Indian Art of the Ancient Midwest and South*, edited by R. Townsend, pp. 207–217. Art Institute of Chicago and Yale University Press, New Haven, Connecticut.

2007 The Great Serpent in Eastern North America. In *Ancient Objects and Sacred Realms: Interpretations of Mississippian Iconography*, edited by F. Reilly and J. Garber, pp. 107–135. University of Texas Press, Austin.

Lanteigne, Maurice
1992 Ideological Theory in Rock Art Research: Towards a Humanistic Perspective. In *Ancient Images, Ancient Thought: The Archaeology of Ideology*, edited by S. Goldsmith, S. Garvie, D. Selin, and J. Smith, pp. 371–382. Proceedings of the Twenty-Third Annual Conference of the Archaeological Association of the University of Calgary.

Lantz, Stanley
1969 Rockshelters (Trail Shelters) of the Upper Allegheny. *Pennsylvania Archaeologist* 39(1–4):1–5.

Lawson, John
(1860) 1960 *History of North Carolina*. Frances Latham Harriss edition. Garrett and Massie, Richmond, Virginia.

LeBeau, Sebastian
2009 Reconstructing Lakota Ritual in the Landscape: The Identification and Typing System for Traditional Cultural Property Sites. Unpublished Ph.D. dissertation, Department of Anthropology, University of Minnesota, Minneapolis.

Ledbetter, R. Jerald
1995 *Archeological Investigations at Mill Branch Sites 9WR4 and 9WR11*. Technical Reports No. 3. Interagency Archeological Services Division, Atlanta, Georgia.

Lederer, John
(1672) 1958 *Discoveries of John Lederer in Three Several Marches from Virginia, to the West of Carolina*. Samuel Heyrick, Grays-Inne-Gate.

Leigh, Steven, and Darcy Morey
1988 Fauna from Mounds 6 and 7. In *The Archaic and Woodland Cemeteries at the Elizabeth Site in the Lower Illinois Valley*, edited by D. Charles, S. Leigh, and J. Buikstra. Kampsville Archeological Center, Research Series Vol. 7, pp. 275–281. Center for American Archeology, Kampsville, Illinois.

Leonard, Kevin
1989 Preliminary Report of Faunal Analysis of the Rustico Island Shell Midden (7F) (CcCt-1) Prince Edward Island, Canada. Unpublished manuscript.

Lepper, Brad
2006 The Great Hopewell Road and the Role of Pilgrimage in the Hopewell Interaction Sphere. In *Recreating Hopewell*, edited by D. Charles and J. Buikstra, pp. 122–133. University Press of Florida, Gainesville.

Leveillee, Alan
1999 Transitional Archaic Ideology as Reflected in Secondary Burials at the Millbury III Cremation Complex. *Man in the Northeast* 27:157–183.

Levine, Mary Ann
1996 Native Copper, Hunter-Gatherers, and Northeastern Prehistory. Unpub-

lished Ph.D. dissertation, Department of Anthropology, University of Massachusetts, Amherst.

Levi-Strauss, Claude

1966 *The Savage Mind.* University of Chicago Press, Chicago.

Lewis, T. N., and Madeline Lewis

1961 *Eva: An Archaic Site.* University of Tennessee Press, Knoxville.

Lewis-Williams, J.

1981 *Believing and Seeing: Symbolic Meaning in Southern San Rock Paintings.* Academic Press, London.

Linares, Olga

1977 *Ecology and the Arts in Ancient Panama: On the Development of Social Rank and Symbolism in the Central Provinces.* Studies in Pre-Columbian Art and Archaeology 17. Dumbarton Oaks, Washington, D.C.

Little, Keith

2003 Late Holocene Climate Fluctuations and Culture Change in Southeastern North America. *Southeastern Archaeology* 22(1):9–22.

Logan, Wilfred

1952 Graham Cave: An Archaic Site in Montgomery County, Missouri. *Memoir of the Missouri Archaeological Society* 2:1–86.

Lohse, Jon

2007 Commoner Ritual, Commoner Ideology. In *Commoner Ritual and Ideology in Ancient Mesoamerica*, edited by N. Gonlin and J. Lohse, pp. 1–32. University Press of Colorado, Boulder.

Lothrop, Jonathon

2007 *Panhandle Archaic Americans in the Upper Ohio Valley: Archaeological Data Recovery at the East Steubenville (46Br31) and Highland Hills (46Br60) Sites WV Route 2 Follansbee-Weirton Road Upgrade Project Brooke County, West Virginia.* Report prepared for Whitney, Bailey, Cox and Magnani, LLP, and the West Virginia Division of Highways.

Lubsen, Kyle

2004 What Skeletal Remains Can Tell Us about Subsistence Activities during the Archaic: An Examination of the Burials at the Long Branch (1Lu67) and O'Neal (1Lu61) Sites. Unpublished master's thesis, Department of Anthropology, University of Alabama, Tuscaloosa.

Lynch, E. Mark

1982 Part 12: Mortuary Behavior in the Carrier Mills Archaeological District. In *The Carrier Mills Archaeological Project: Human Adaptation in the Saline Valley, Illinois*, edited by Richard Jefferies and Brian Butler, pp. 1117–1231. Center for Archaeological Investigations Research Paper No. 33. Center for Archaeological Investigations, Southern Illinois University, Carbondale.

MacDonald, George

1968 *Debert: A Palaeo-Indian Site in Central Nova Scotia.* Anthropology Papers No. 16. National Museums of Canada.

Magennis, Ann

1977 Middle and Late Archaic Mortuary Patterning: An Example from the Western Tennessee Valley. Unpublished master's thesis, Department of Anthropology, University of Tennessee, Knoxville.

Maggard, Greg, and Kary Stackelbeck

2008 Paleoindian Period. In *The Archaeology of Kentucky: An Update*. Vol. 1, edited by D. Pollack, pp. 109–192. State Historic Preservation Comprehensive Plan Report No. 3. Kentucky Heritage Council, Frankfort.

Mahlstedt, Thomas, and Margo David

2002 Caddy Park, Wollston Beach: Burial, Centaph, Cache or Offering? *Bulletin of the Massachusetts Archaeological Society* 63(2):11–23.

Marcus, Joyce

1999 *Women's Ritual in Formative Oaxaca: Figurine-Making, Divination, Death and the Ancestors*. Memoirs of the Museum of Anthropology, University of Michigan, No. 33. Ann Arbor, Michigan.

Marquardt, William

1974 A Statistical Analysis of Constituents in Human Paleofecal Specimens from Mammoth Cave. In *Archeology of the Mammoth Cave Area*, edited by P. Watson, pp. 193–202. Academic Press, New York.

Marquardt, William, and Carole Crumley

1987 Theoretical Issues in the Analysis of Spatial Patterning. In *Regional Dynamics: Burgundian Landscapes in Historical Perspective*, edited by C. Crumley and W. Marquardt, pp. 1–18. Academic Press, New York.

Marshack, Alexander

1985 A Lunar-Solar Year Calendar Stick. *American Antiquity* 50(1):27–51.

Mason, Ronald, and Carol Irwin

1960 An Eden-Scottsbluff Burial in NE Wisconsin. *American Antiquity* 26(1): 43–57.

Mayes, Leigh Ann

1997 The Bluegrass Site: Bioarchaeological Analysis of a Middle-Late Archaic Mortuary Site in Southwest Indiana. Unpublished master's thesis, Department of Anthropology, University of Southern Mississippi, Hattiesburg.

Mayor, Adrienne

2005 *Fossil Legends of the First Americans*. Princeton University Press, Princeton.

McCluskey, Stephen

1977 The Astronomy of the Hopi Indians. *Journal for the History of Astronomy* 8(3, part 2):174–195.

McCollough, Major C., and Charles Faulkner

1973 *Excavation of the Higgs and Doughty Sites I-75 Salvage Archaeology*. Tennessee Archaeological Society Miscellaneous Paper No. 12.

McElrath, Dale

1986 *The McLean Site*. FAI-270 Site Reports Vol. 14. Illinois Department of Transportation, University of Illinois Press, Urbana.

McElrath, Dale, Andrew Fortier, Brad Koldehoff, and Thomas Emerson
2009 The American Bottom: An Archaic Cultural Crossroads. In *Archaic Societies: Diversity and Complexity across the Midcontinent*, edited by T. Emerson, D. McElrath, and A. Fortier, pp. 317–376. State University of New York Press, Albany.

McGahey, Samuel
1996 Paleoindian and Early Archaic Data from Mississippi. In *The Paleoindian and Early Archaic Southeast*, edited by D. Anderson and K. Sassaman, pp. 354–384. University of Alabama Press, Tuscaloosa.

McGowan, Charlotte
1978 Female Fertility Themes in Rock Art. *Journal of New World Archaeology* 2(4): 15–27.

McGraw, Betty, and William Huser
1995 Preliminary Report of Phase III Investigation of the Hedden Site, a Late Archaic Habitation and Mortuary Site in McCracken County, Kentucky. Paper read at the 12th Annual Kentucky Heritage Council Conference, Richmond.

McKenzie, Douglas, and Olaf Prufer
1967 Indian Skeletons from a Sinkhole Cavern in Wyandot County, Northwestern Ohio. *Ohio Archaeologist* 17(4):129–138.

McLearen, Douglas
1991 Late Archaic and Early Woodland Material Culture in Virginia. In *Late Archaic and Early Woodland Research in Virginia: A Synthesis*, edited by T. Rinehart and M. Hodges, pp. 89–137. Council of Virginia Archaeologists, Special Pub. No. 23 of Archeological Society of Virginia.

McNett, Charles (editor)
1985 *Shawnee-Minisink: A Stratified Paleoindian-Archaic Site in the Upper Delaware Valley*. Academic Press, New York.

Meindl, Richard, Robert Mensforth, and Heather York
2001 Mortality, Fertility, and Growth in the Kentucky Late Archaic: The Paleodemography of the Ward Site. In *Archaic Transitions in Ohio and Kentucky Prehistory*, edited by O. Prufer, S. Pedde, and R. Meindl, pp. 87–109. Kent State University Press, Kent, Ohio.

Mensforth, Robert
2001 Warfare and Trophy Taking in the Archaic Period. In *Archaic Transitions in Ohio and Kentucky Prehistory*, edited by O. Prufer, S. Pedde, and R. Meindl, pp. 110–137. Kent State University Press, Ohio.
2005 Paleodemography of the Skeletal Population from the Carlston Annis Site, 15Mt5. In *Archaeology of the Middle Green River Region, Kentucky*, edited by W. Marquardt and P. Watson, pp. 453–488. Institute of Archaeology and Paleoenvironmental Studies, Monograph 5. Florida Museum of Natural History, University of Florida, Gainesville.
2007 Human Trophy Taking in Eastern North America during the Archaic Pe-

riod: Its Relationship to Warfare and Social Complexity. In *The Taking and Displaying of Human Body Parts as Trophies by Amerindians*, edited by R. Chacon and D. Dye, pp. 218–273. Springer Verlag, New York.

Mester, Ann
1989 Marine Shell Symbolism in Andean Culture. In *Proceedings of the 1986 Shell Bead Conference: Selected Papers*, edited by L. Ceci, pp. 157–168. Rochester Museum and Science Center Research Records No. 20. Rochester, New York.

Miller, Carl
1956 Life 8,000 Years Ago Uncovered in an Alabama Cave. *National Geographic* 110:542–558.
1958 Russell Cave: New Light on Stone Age Life. *National Geographic* 113:426–437.

Miller, Mary, and Karl Taube
1993 *An Illustrated Dictionary of the Gods and Symbols of Ancient Mexico and the Maya*. Thames and Hudson, New York.

Miller, Rex
1941 *McCain Site, Dubois County, Indiana*. Indiana Historical Society Prehistory Research Series 2(1).

Milne, Courtney
1994 *Sacred Places in North America: A Journey into the Medicine Wheel*. Stewart, Tabori and Chang, New York.

Milner, George, Jane Buikstra, and Michael Wiant
2009 Archaic Burial Sites in the American Midcontinent. In *Archaic Societies: Diversity and Complexity across the Midcontinent*, edited by T. Emerson, D. McElrath, and A. Fortier, pp. 115–135. State University of New York Press, Albany.

Milner, George, and Richard Jefferies
1998 The Read Archaic Shell Midden in Kentucky. *Southeastern Archaeology* 17(2): 119–132.

Mocas, Steven
1985 Lawrence Site. *Tennessee Archaeologist* 10(1):76–91.

Mooney, James
1900 Myths of the Cherokee. Nineteenth Annual Report of the Bureau of American Ethnology for 1897–1898, Part 1.

Moore, Clarence
1916 Some Aboriginal Sites on Green River, Kentucky. *Journal of the Academy of Natural Science*, 2nd ser., No. 16. Philadelphia.

Moore, Sally, and Barbara Myerhoff
1977 Introduction: Secular Ritual: Forms and Meanings. In *Secular Ritual*, edited by S. Moore and B. Myerhoff, pp. 1–24. Van Gorcum, Amsterdam.

Moore, Shari
1991 Limited Testing at Site 40My105: A Multi-Component Accretionary Mound, McNairy County, Tennessee. In *The Archaic Period in the Mid-South: Proceedings of the 1989 Mid-South Archaeological Conference*, Memphis, edited by

C. McNutt, pp. 41–46. Occasional Papers No. 16. Memphis State University.

Morse, Dan

1967 The Robinson Site and Shell Mound Archaic Culture in the Middle South. Unpublished Ph.D. dissertation, Department of Anthropology, University of Michigan, Ann Arbor.

1971 The Hawkins Cache: A Significant Dalton Find in Northeast Arkansas. *Arkansas Archeologist* 12(1):9–20.

1977 A Human Femur Tube from Arkansas. *Arkansas Archeologist* 16/17/18:42–44.

1997 *Sloan: A Paleoindian Dalton Cemetery in Arkansas*. Smithsonian Institution Press, Washington, D.C.

Mystery of Chaco Canyon

2003 DVD. Bullfrog Films.

Nagy, Imre

1994 A Typology of Cheyenne Shield Designs. *Plains Anthropologist* 39(147):5–36.

Nance, Jack

1986 Archaic Culture in the Lower Tennessee-Cumberland-Ohio Region. Paper read at the Annual Meeting of the Southeastern Archaeological Conference, Nashville.

Neal, L.

1994 A Calf Creek Component from the Lamar Site 34Sc8, Bryan County. *Bulletin of the Oklahoma Anthropological Society* 40:139–179.

Nelson, Nels

1917 Contributions to the Archaeology of Mammoth Cave and Vicinity, Kentucky. *Anthropological Papers of the American Museum of Natural History* 22, Part 1.

Neumann, H. W.

1967 *The Paleopathology of the Archaic Modoc RS Inhabitants*. Illinois State Museum Report of Investigations No. 11. Springfield.

Nolan, David, and Richard Fishel

2009 Archaic Cultural Variation and Lifeways in West-Central Illinois. In *Archaic Societies: Diversity and Complexity across the Midcontinent*, edited by T. Emerson, D. McElrath, and A. Fortier, pp. 401–490. State University of New York Press, Albany.

Norton, Mark

2008 Obsidian Research in Tennessee and Alabama. *Tennessee Archaeology* 3(2): 123–130.

Nutini, Hugo

1988 Pre-Hispanic Component of the Syncretic Cult of the Dead in Mesoamerica. *Ethnology* 27(1):57–78.

O'Brien, Michael

1998 Sloan: Dalton-Age Occupation of Northeastern Arkansas. *Review of Archaeology* 19(1):16–30.

Odell, George
1985 Lithic Assemblage. In *The Campbell Hollow Archaic Occupations: A Study of Intrasite Spatial Structure in the Lower Illinois Valley*, edited by C. Stafford, pp. 37–52. Kampsville Archeological Center Research Series Vol. 4. Center for American Archeology, Kampsville.

Oliver, Billy
1985 Tradition and Typology: Basic Elements of the Carolina Projectile Point Sequence. In *Structure and Process in Southeastern Archaeology*, edited by R. Dickens and T. Ward, pp. 229–242. University of Alabama Press, Tuscaloosa.

O'Shea, John, and Guy Meadows
2009 Evidence for Early Hunters beneath the Great Lakes. *Proceedings of the National Academy of Sciences*, June 8, 2009. Electronic document, http://www.pnas.org/content/106/25/10120.full, accessed July 3, 2009.

Owens, Amanda
2010 A Re-Examination of Cremated Remains from the Archaeological Record: An Evaluation of the Process and Application of Current Methods. Unpublished master's thesis, Department of Anthropology, University of Alabama, Tuscaloosa.

Pagoulatos, Peter
2009 Late/Terminal Archaic Mortuary Practices in the Northeastern United States. *North American Archaeologist* 30:221–258.

Parkman, Breck
1992 Toward a Proto-Hokan Ideology. In *Ancient Images, Ancient Thought: The Archaeology of Ideology*, edited by S. Goldsmith, S. Garvie, D. Selin, and J. Smith. Proceedings of the Twenty-Third Annual Conference of the Archaeological Association of the University of Calgary.

Parks, Cameron
1970 A Novel Theory on Use of Birdstones. *Central States Archaeological Journal* 17:147–154.

Parmalee, Paul
1965 The Food Economy of Archaic and Woodland Peoples at the Tick Creek Cave Site, Missouri. *Missouri Archaeologist* 27:1–33.

Pauketat, Timothy, and Thomas Emerson
2008 Star Performances and Cosmic Clutter. *Cambridge Archaeological Journal* 18: 78–85.

Peabody, Charles, and W. K. Moorehead
1906 *The So-Called Gorgets*. Bulletin 2, Phillips Academy, Department of Archaeology. Andover Press, Andover, Massachusetts.

Pedde, Sara, and Olaf Prufer
2001 The Kentucky Green River Archaic as Seen from the Ward Site. In *Archaic Transitions in Ohio and Kentucky Prehistory*, edited by O. Prufer, S. Pedde, and R. Meindl, pp. 59–86. Kent State University Press, Ohio.

2006 Hendricks Cave and Late Archaic Mortuary Practices in Ohio: 1964–1997. In *Caves and Culture: 10,000 Years of Ohio History*, edited by L. Spurlock, O. Prufer, and T. Pigott, pp. 73–85. Kent State University Press, Ohio.

Perino, Greg

1961 Tentative Classification of Plummets in the Lower Illinois River Valley. *Central States Archaeological Journal* 8(2):43–56.

1970 Stillwell II Site, Pike County, Illinois. *Central States Archaeological Journal* 17:118–121.

Piatek, Bruce

1994 The Tomoka Mound Complex in Northeast Florida. *Southeastern Archaeology* 13(2):109–118.

Pleger, Thomas

1998 Social Complexity, Trade, and Subsistence during the Archaic/Woodland Transition in the Western Great Lakes: A Diachronic Study of Copper Using Cultures at the Oconto and Riverside Cemeteries. Unpublished Ph.D. dissertation, Department of Anthropology, University of Wisconsin, Madison.

Plunket, Patricia (editor)

2002 *Domestic Ritual in Ancient Mesoamerica*. Monograph 46. Cotsen Institute of Archaeology, University of California, Los Angeles.

Pohl, Mary

1983 Maya Ritual Faunas: Vertebrate Remains from Burials, Caches, Caves, and Cenotes in the Maya Lowlands. In *Civilization in the Ancient Americas: Essays in Honor of Gordon R. Willey*, edited by R. Leventhal and A. Kolata, pp. 55–104. University of New Mexico Press, Albuquerque.

Powell, Joseph

1995 Dental Variation and Biological Affinity among Middle Holocene Human Populations in North America. Unpublished Ph.D. dissertation, Texas A&M University, College Station.

Prahl, Earl

1967 Prehistoric Dogs of Michigan. *Michigan Archaeologist* 13:13–27.

Prufer, Keith, and James Brady (editors)

2005 *Stone Houses and Earth Lords: Maya Religion in the Cave Context*. University Press of Colorado, Niwot.

Prufer, Olaf

2006 Krill Cave, Summit County, Ohio: 1974–75. In *Caves and Culture: 10,000 Years of Ohio History*, edited by L. Spurlock, O. Prufer, and T. Pigott, pp. 329–365. Kent State University Press, Ohio.

Prufer, Olaf, and Keith Prufer

2012 Ceremonial Use of Caves and Rockshelters in Ohio. In *Sacred Darkness: A Global Perspective on the Ritual Use of Caves*, edited by H. Moyes, pp. 225–235. University Press of Colorado, Boulder.

Purtill, Matthew

2009 The Ohio Archaic: A Review. In *Archaic Societies: Diversity and Complexity across the Midcontinent*, edited by T. Emerson, D. McElrath, and A. Fortier, pp. 565–606. State University of New York Press, Albany.

Radin, Paul

1970 *The Winnebago Tribe*. University of Nebraska Press, Lincoln.

Rafferty, Janet, Lea Baker, and Jack Elliott

1980 Archaeological Investigations at the East Aberdeen Site, Tombigbee River Multi-Resource District, Alabama and Mississippi. Department of Anthropology, Mississippi State University, Mississippi State.

Rafferty, Sean

2001 They Pass Their Lives in Smoke, and at Death, Fall into the Fire: Smoking Pipes and Mortuary Ritual during the Early Woodland Period. Ph.D. dissertation, Department of Anthropology, Binghamton University, New York.

Rajnovich, Grace

1994 *Reading Rock Art: Interpreting the Indian Rock Paintings of the Canadian Shield*. Natural Heritage/Natural History, Toronto.

Rakita, Gordon, and Jane Buikstra

2008 Feather Waving or the Numinous?: Archaeological Perspectives on Ritual, Religion, and Ideology. In *An Archaeological Perspective on Ritual, Religion, and Ideology from American Antiquity and Latin American Antiquity*, compiled by G. Rakita and J. Buikstra, pp. 1–17. SAA Press, Washington, D.C.

Randall, Asa

2005 Environmental and Archaeological Contexts. In *St. Johns Archaeological Field School 2003–2004: Hontoon Island State Park*, edited by A. Randall and K. Sassaman, pp. 9–26. Technical Report 6. Laboratory of Southeastern Archaeology, Department of Anthropology, University of Florida, Gainesville.

2015 *Archaic Freshwater Shell Mounds and Social Landscapes*. University Press of Florida, Gainesville.

Randall, Asa, and Brian Tucker

2012 A Mount Taylor Period Radiocarbon Assay from the Bluffton Burial Mound (8VO23). *Florida Anthropologist* 65(4):219–225.

Rasmussen, K.

1931 *The Netsilik Eskimos: Social Life and Spiritual Culture*. Report of the Fifth Thule Expedition, 1921–1924. Glyndendalske Boghandel Nordisk Forleg, Copenhagen.

Ray, Jack, Neal Lopinot, and Edwin Hajic

2009 Archaic Prehistory of the Western Ozarks of Southwest Missouri. In *Archaic Societies: Diversity and Complexity across the Midcontinent*, edited by T. Emerson, D. McElrath, and A. Fortier, pp. 155–197. State University of New York Press, Albany.

Read, Kay

1998 *Time and Sacrifice in the Aztec Cosmos*. Indiana University Press, Bloomington.

Renfrew, Colin, and Paul Bahn
2000 *Archaeology: Theory, Methods, and Practice*. 3rd ed. Thames and Hudson, New York.

Renouf, M., and Trevor Bell
2006 Maritime Archaic Site Location Patterns on the Island of Newfoundland. In *The Archaic of the Far Northeast*, edited by D. Sanger and M. Renouf, pp. 1–46. University of Maine Press, Orono.
2011 Across the Tickle: The Gould Site, Port au Choix-3 and the Maritime Archaic Indian Mortuary Landscape. In *The Cultural Landscapes of Port au Choix*, edited by M. Renouf, pp. 43–63. Interdisciplinary Contributions to Archaeology, DOI. Springer Science and Business Media, New York.

Rissolo, Dominique
2005 Beneath the Yalahua: Emerging Patterns of Ancient Maya Ritual Cave Use from Northern Quintana Roo, Mexico. In *In the Maw of the Earth Monster: Mesoamerican Ritual Cave Use*, edited by J. Brady and K. Prufer, pp. 342–372. University of Texas Press, Austin.

Ritchie, William
1932 *The Lamoka Lake Site*. Researchers and Transactions 7. New York State Archaeological Association, Albany.
1945 *An Early Site in Cayuga County, New York: Type Component of the Frontenac Focus, Archaic Pattern*. Research Records of the Rochester Museum of Arts and Sciences No. 7. Rochester, New York.
1959 *The Stony Brook Site and Relation to Archaic and Transitional Cultures on Long Island*. Bulletin No. 372. New York State Museum and Science Service, Albany, New York.

Ritchie, William, and Robert Funk
1973 *Aboriginal Settlement Patterns in the Northeast, Memoir 20*. New York State Museum and Science Service, Albany, New York.

Robb, John
1998 The Archaeology of Symbols. *Annual Review of Anthropology* 27:329–346.

Robbins, Louise
1974 Prehistoric People of the Mammoth Cave Area. In *Archeology of the Mammoth Cave Area*, edited by P. Watson, pp. 137–162. Academic Press, New York.

Robbins, Maurice
1969 The Northeastern Mortuary Complex at the Wapanucket #8 Site, Middleboro, Massachusetts. *Bulletin of the Eastern States Archeological Federation* 26 and 27.

Robbins, Maurice, and George Agogino
1964 The Wapanucket No. 8 Site: A Clovis-Archaic Site in Massachusetts. *American Antiquity* 29(4):509–513.

Robinson, Brian
2006 Burial Ritual, Technology and Cultural Landscape in the Far Northeast:

8600–3700 BP. In *The Archaic of the Far Northeast*, edited by D. Sanger and M. Renouf, pp. 341–381. University of Maine Press, Orono.

Robinson, Kenneth, and Steven Smith

1979 The Villier Site (15Jf110 Complex). In *Excavations at Four Archaic Sites in the Lower Ohio Valley, Jefferson County, Kentucky*, edited by M. Collins, pp. 590–695. Department of Anthropology, University of Kentucky, Lexington.

Rolingson, Martha

1967 Temporal Perspective on the Archaic Cultures of the Middle Green River Region, Kentucky. Unpublished Ph.D. dissertation, Department of Anthropology, University of Michigan, Ann Arbor.

Romain, William

1991 Calenderic Information Evident in the Adena Tablets. *Ohio Archaeologist* 41(4):38–41.

2000 *Mysteries of the Hopewell.* University of Akron Press, Ohio.

2009 *Shamans of the Lost World: A Cognitive Approach to the Prehistoric Religion of the Ohio Hopewell.* AltaMira Press, Walnut Creek, California.

Russo, Michael

1994a A Brief Introduction to the Study of Archaic Mounds in the Southeast. *Southeastern Archaeology* 13:89–93.

1994b Why We Don't Believe in Archaic Ceremonial Mounds and Why We Should: The Case from Florida. *Southeastern Archaeology* 13:93–108.

2004 Measuring Shell Rings for Social Inequality. In *Signs of Power: The Rise of Cultural Complexity in the Southeast*, edited by J. Gibson and P. Carr, pp. 26–70. University of Alabama Press, Tuscaloosa.

2010 Shell Rings and Other Settlement Features as Indicators of Cultural Continuity between the Late Archaic and Woodland Periods of Coastal Florida. In *Trend, Tradition, and Turmoil: What Happened to the Southeastern Archaic?*, edited by D. Thomas and M. Sanger, pp. 149–172. Anthropological Papers of the American Museum of Natural History No. 93.

Sahagún, fray Bernardino de

1948 *Relación breve de las fiestas de los dioses (Pimeros Memoriales)*, edited by Angel María Garibay. Tlalocan, tomo II, numero 10. Azcapotzalco.

Sandstrom, Alan

1991 *Corn Is Our Blood: Culture and Ethnic Identity in a Contemporary Aztec Indian Village.* University of Oklahoma Press, Norman.

Sanger, David

2006 An Introduction to the Archaic of the Maritime Peninsula: The View from Central Maine. In *The Archaic of the Far Northeast*, edited by D. Sanger and M. Renouf, pp. 221–246. University of Maine Press, Orono.

Sanger, Matthew

2010 Leaving the Rings: Shell Ring Abandonment and the End of the Late Archaic. In *Trend, Tradition, and Turmoil: What Happened to the Southeastern Archaic?*, edited by D. Thomas and M. Sanger, pp. 202–215. Anthropological Papers of the American Museum of Natural History No. 93.

Sanger, Matthew, and David Thomas

2010 The Two Rings of St. Catherines Island: Some Preliminary Results from the St. Catherines and McQueen Shell Rings. In *Trend, Tradition, and Turmoil: What Happened to the Southeastern Archaic?*, edited by D. Thomas and M. Sanger, pp. 45–70. Anthropological Papers of the American Museum of Natural History No. 93.

Sassaman, Kenneth

2004 Common Origins and Divergent Histories in the Early Pottery Traditions of the American Southeast. In *Early Pottery: Technology, Function, Style, and Interaction in the Lower Southeast*, edited by R. Saunders and C. Hayes, pp. 23–39. University of Alabama Press, Tuscaloosa.

2005 Poverty Point as Structure, Event, Process. *Journal of Archaeological Method and Theory* 12:335–364.

2006 *People of the Shoals: Stallings Culture of the Savannah River Valley*. University Press of Florida, Gainesville.

2010a *The Eastern Archaic, Historicized*. AltaMira Press, Walnut Creek, California.

2010b Getting from the Late Archaic to Early Woodland in Three Middle Valleys. In *Trend, Tradition, and Turmoil: What Happened to the Southeastern Archaic?*, edited by D. Thomas and M. Sanger, pp. 229–236. Anthropological Papers of the American Museum of Natural History No. 93.

Sassaman, Kenneth, and Michael Heckenberger

2004 Crossing the Symbolic Rubicon in the Southeast. In *Signs of Power: The Rise of Cultural Complexity in the Southeast*, edited by J. Gibson and P. Carr, pp. 214–233. University of Alabama Press, Tuscaloosa.

Saunders, Joe

2010 Late Archaic? What the Hell Happened to the Middle Archaic? In *Trend, Tradition, and Turmoil: What Happened to the Southeastern Archaic?*, edited by D. Thomas and M. Sanger, pp. 237–246. Anthropological Papers of the American Museum of Natural History No. 93.

Saunders, Joe, Thurman Allen, and Roger Saucier

1994 Four Archaic? Mound Complexes in Northeast Louisiana. *Southeastern Archaeology* 13(2):134–153.

Saunders, Joe, Reca Jones, Kathryn Moorhead, and Brian Davis

1998 "Watson Brake Objects," an Unusual Archaic Artifact Type from Northeast Louisiana and Southwest Mississippi. *Southeastern Archaeology* 17(1):72–79.

Saunders, Rebecca

1994 The Case for Archaic Period Mounds in Southeastern Louisiana. *Southeastern Archaeology* 13(2):118–134.

2004 The Stratigraphic Sequence at Rollins Shell Ring: Implications for Ring Function. *Florida Anthropologist* 57(4):249–270.

2014 Shell Rings of the Lower Atlantic Coast of the United States. In *The Cultural Dynamics of Shell-Matrix Sites*, edited by M. Roksandic, S. Souza, S. Eggers, M. Burchell, and D. Klokler, pp. 41–55. University of New Mexico Press, Albuquerque.

Schaefer, Stacy

2002 *To Think with a Good Heart: Wixárika Women, Weavers, and Shamans*. University of Utah Press, Salt Lake City.

Schenian, Pamela

1985 A Preliminary Analysis of the Cultural Features Identified during the 1966 and 1967 Carnegie Museum Excavations at Savage Cave. In *Western Kentucky Speleological Survey Annual Report 1984*, edited by J. Mylroie, pp. 11–30. Murray State University Printing Services, Murray, Kentucky.

1988 An Overview of the Paleoindian and Archaic Period Occupations of the Savage Cave Site. In *Paleoindian and Archaic Research in Kentucky*, edited by C. Hockensmith, D. Pollack, and T. Sanders, pp. 67–84. Kentucky Heritage Council, Frankfort.

Schmidt, Christopher, Curtis Tomak, Rachel Lockhart, Tammy Greene, and Gregory Reinhard

2008 Early Archaic Cremations from Southern Indiana. In *The Analysis of Burned Human Remains*, edited by C. Schmidt and S. Symes, pp. 227–237. Elsevier, Amsterdam.

Schoenwetter, James

2001 Paleoethnobotanical Expressions of Prehistoric Ritual: An Early Woodland Case. In *Fleeting Identities: Perishable Material Culture in Archaeological Research*, edited by P. Drooker, pp. 273–282. Occasional Paper No. 28. Center for Archaeological Investigations, Southern Illinois University, Carbondale.

Schwadron, Margo

2010 Prehistoric Landscapes of Complexity: Archaic and Woodland Period Shell Works, Shell Rings, and Tree Islands of the Everglades, South Florida. In *Trend, Tradition, and Turmoil: What Happened to the Southeastern Archaic?*, edited by D. Thomas and M. Sanger, pp. 113–146. Anthropological Papers of the American Museum of Natural History No. 93.

Scudder, Sylvia

2001 *Archaeopedological Analyses. Phase III Mitigative Excavations at Lake Monroe Outlet Midden (8VO53), Volusia County, Florida*. Archaeological Consultants and Janus Research. Submitted to U.S. Department of Transportation Federal Highway Administration and Florida Department of Transportation District Five.

Sculley, Vincent

1989 *Pueblo: Mountain, Village, Dance*. University of Chicago Press, Chicago.

Sears, William

1960 The Bluffton Burial Mound. *Florida Anthropologist* 13:55–60.

Selig, Jakob

2010 Getting to the Point: An Examination of Projectile Point Use in the Northern American Southwest, A.D. 900–1300. Unpublished master's thesis, Department of Anthropology, University of Colorado, Boulder.

Service, Elman

1966 *The Hunters*. Prentice Hall, New York.

Sherwood, Sarah, and Jefferson Chapman

2005 The Identification and Potential Significance of Early Holocene Prepared Clay Surfaces: Examples from Dust Cave and Icehouse Bottom. *Southeastern Archaeology* 24:70–82.

Shields, Ben

2003 An Analysis of the Archaic Human Burials at the Mulberry Creek (1Ct27) Shell Mound, Colbert County, Alabama. Unpublished master's thesis, Department of Anthropology, University of Alabama, Tuscaloosa.

Silverman, H.

1994 The Archaeological Identification of an Ancient Peruvian Pilgrimage Center. *World Archaeology* 26:1–18.

Skousen, Jacob

2012 Posts, Places, Ancestors, and Worlds: Dividual Personhood in the American Bottom Region. *Southeastern Archaeology* 31(1):57–69.

Smith, Donald

2005 Carpenter Brook Revisited: Social Context and Early Late Woodland Ceramic Variation in Central New York State. Unpublished Ph.D. dissertation, Department of Anthropology, State University of New York, Buffalo.

Smith, Heather

2012 Horn Shelter. Electronic document, http://www.texasbeyondhistory.net/horn/credits.html, accessed June 12, 2011.

Smith, Ira F. III

1976 A Functional Interpretation of "Keyhole" Structures in the Northeast. *Pennsylvania Archaeologist* 46(1–2):1–12.

Smith, Maria

1993 A Probable Case of Decapitation at the Late Archaic Robinson Site (40SM4), Smith County, Tennessee. *Tennessee Anthropologist* 18:131–142.

1995 Scalping in the Archaic Period: Evidence from the Western Tennessee Valley. *Southeastern Archaeology* 14:60–68.

Smith, Merritt

2010 Skeletal Evidence of the Treatment of the Elderly in the Archaic and Mississippian Periods in the Southeastern United States. Unpublished master's thesis, Department of Anthropology, University of Alabama, Tuscaloosa.

Smith, Rachael

2003 Analysis of Skeletal Fractures from Windover and Their Inference Regarding Lifestyle. Unpublished master's thesis, Department of Anthropology, Florida State University.

Smith, Theresa

1995 *The Island of the Anishnaabeg*. University of Idaho Press, Moscow.

Sobolik, Kristin D., Kristen J. Gremillion, Patricia Whitten, and Patty Jo Watson

1996 Sex Determination of Prehistoric Human Paleofeces. *American Journal of Physical Anthropology* 101(2):283–290.

Spence, Michael, and William Fox

1986 The Early Woodland Occupations of Southern Ontario. In *Early Woodland*

Archeology, edited by K. Farnsworth and T. Emerson, pp. 4–46. Center for American Archeology, Kampsville: Seminars in Archeology, Kampsville, Illinois.

Spiess, Arthur, and Robert Lewis

1995 Appendix 8: Features and Activity Areas: The Spatial Analysis of Faunal Remains. In *Diversity and Complexity in Prehistoric Maritime Societies: A Gulf of Maine Perspective* by B. Bourque, pp. 337–373. Plenum Press, New York.

Spurlock, Linda, and Olaf Prufer

2002 Stanhope Cave: A Multicomponent Site in Jackson County, Ohio. *Ohio Archaeologist* 52(1):4–16.

Spurlock, Linda, Olaf Prufer, and Thomas Pigott

2006 Conclusion: Ohio Caves and Rockshelters, from Prehistory to History. *In Caves and Culture: 10,000 Years of Ohio History*, edited by L. Spurlock, O. Prufer, and T. Pigott, pp. 444–457. Kent State University Press, Ohio.

Stafford, Russell, and Mark Cantin

2009 Archaic Period Chronology in the Hill Country of Southern Indiana. In *Archaic Societies: Diversity and Complexity across the Midcontinent*, edited by T. Emerson, D. McElrath, and A. Fortier, pp. 287–313. State University of New York Press, Albany.

Stallings, Richard

2008 *Phase III Archaeological Mitigation of the Panther Rock Site (15Cl58), Carroll County, Kentucky*. Report Prepared for Hinkle Contracting Corporation, Lexington, Kentucky.

Starbuck, David

1980 The Middle Archaic in Central Connecticut: The Excavation of the Lewis-Walpole Site. In *Early and Middle Archaic Cultures in the Northeast*, edited by D. Starbuck and C. Bolian, pp. 5–38. Occasional Publications in Northeastern Anthropology, No. 7. Department of Anthropology, Franklin Pierce College, Rindge, New Hampshire.

Stein, Julie

2005 Environment of the Green River Sites. In *Archaeology of the Middle Green River Region, Kentucky*, edited by W. Marquardt and P. Watson, pp. 19–39. Institute of Archaeology and Paleoenvironmental Studies, Monograph 5. Florida Museum of Natural History, University of Florida, Gainesville.

Stelle, Linville

2006 The Rock Art of the Blood of the Ancestors Grotto: Methodology: Imaging the Pictographs. Center for Social Research, Parkland College, Champaign, Illinois. Electronic document, http://virtual.parkland.edu/lstelle1/len/center_for_social_research/BAG/BAG_main.html, accessed June 9, 2011.

Stoltman, James

1974 *Groton Plantation*. Harvard University Press, Cambridge.

Strong, John

1985 Late Woodland Dog Ceremonialism on Long Island. *Bulletin and Journal of Archaeology for New York State* 91:32–38.

Sundstrom, Linea

1996 *The Material Culture of Ludlow Cave, Custer National Forest, Harding County, South Dakota: A NAGPRA Evaluation.* Custer National Forest, Billings, Montana.

2000 Blind Encounters: Archaeologists and Sacred Sites in the Northern Plains. Paper presented at the joint Midwest Archaeological/Plains Anthropological Conference, St. Paul, Minnesota.

2004 *Storied Stone: Indian Rock Art of the Black Hills Country.* University of Oklahoma Press, Norman.

Sundstrom, Linea, and Warren DeBoer (editors)

2012 *Enduring Motives: The Archaeology of Tradition and Religion in Native America.* University of Alabama Press, Tuscaloosa.

Swan, James

1995 *The Power of Place: Sacred Ground in Natural and Human Environments.* Quest Books, Wheaton, Illinois.

Swanton, John

1911 *Indian Tribes of the Lower Mississippi River Valley and the Adjacent Gulf of Mexico.* Bulletin 43 Smithsonian Institute, Bureau of American Ethnology. Smithsonian Institute Press, Washington, D.C.

1928 *Social Organization and Social Usages of the Indians of the Creek Confederacy.* Smithsonian Institute, Bureau of American Ethnology, 42nd Annual Report 1924/25. Smithsonian Institute Press, Washington, D.C.

1931 Modern Square Grounds of the Creek Indians. Smithsonian Miscellaneous Collections 85(8). Smithsonian Institute Press, Washington, D.C.

1946 *The Indians of the Southeastern United States.* Bulletin 137 Smithsonian Institute Bureau of American Ethnology. Smithsonian Institute Press, Washington, D.C.

Thomas, Peter

1980 The Riverside District, the WMECO Site, and Suggestions for Archeological Modeling. In *Early and Middle Archaic Cultures in the Northeast,* edited by D. Starbuck and C. Bolian, pp. 73–96. Occasional Publications in Northeastern Anthropology, No. 7. Department of Anthropology, Franklin Pierce College, Rindge, New Hampshire.

Thomas, Prentice, L. Janice Campbell, and James Morehead

2004 The Burkett Site (23Mi20): Implications for Cultural Complexity and Origins. In *Signs of Power: The Rise of Cultural Complexity in the Southeast,* edited by J. Gibson and P. Carr, pp. 114–128. University of Alabama Press, Tuscaloosa.

Thomas, Ronald

1969 Breckenridge: A Stratified Shelter in Northwest Arkansas. Unpublished master's thesis, Department of Anthropology, University of Arkansas, Fayetteville.

Thompson, Victor, and C. Fred Andrus

2011 Evaluating Mobility, Monumentality, and Feasting at Sapelo Island. *American Antiquity* 76(2):315–343.

Timberlake, Henry

(1765) 1995 *The Memoirs of Lieut. Henry Timberlake.* Ayer, North Stratford. Tippins, William

Tippins, William

2007 An Inventory of Western Pennsylvania Rockshelters. *Pennsylvania Archaeologist* 77(2):34–69.

Todd, Amanda

2010 Spiritual Landscapes in the 21st Century: The Geography of Power Mountains and Healing Waters of the Southern Appalachian Region. Unpublished Ph.D. dissertation, University of North Carolina, Greensboro.

Tomak, Curtis

1979 Jerger: An Early Archaic Mortuary Site in Southwestern Indiana. *Proceedings of the Indiana Academy of Science* 88:62–69.

Townsend, Richard (editor)

2004 *Hero, Hawk, and Open Hand: American Indian Art of the Ancient Midwest and South.* Yale University Press, New Haven, Connecticut.

Tuck, James

1976 *Ancient People of Port au Choix: The Excavation of an Archaic Indian Cemetery in Newfoundland.* Newfoundland Social and Economic Studies 17. Institute of Social and Economic Research, Memorial University of Newfoundland, St. Johns, Canada.

1984 *Maritime Provinces Prehistory.* Archaeological Survey of Canada, National Museum of Man, National Museums of Canada, Ottawa.

Tucker, Bryan D.

2009 Isotopic Investigations of Archaic Period Subsistence and Settlement in the St. Johns River Drainage, Florida. Unpublished Ph.D. dissertation, Department of Anthropology, University of Florida, Gainesville.

Turner, James

2006 An Investigation of Violence-Related Trauma at Two Sites in the Pickwick Basin: Dust Cave and the ONeal Site. Master's thesis, Department of Anthropology, Mississippi State University.

Turner, Victor

1969 *The Ritual Process: Structure and Anti-Structure.* Aldine, Chicago.

1973 The Center Out There: Pilgrim's Goal. *History of Religions* 12(3):191–230.

Van Nest, Julieann, Douglas Charles, Jane Buikstra, and David Asch

2001 Sod Blocks in Illinois Hopewell Mounds. *American Antiquity* 66:633–650.

Vennum, Thomas

1994 *American Indian Lacrosse: Little Brother of War.* Smithsonian Institution Press, Washington, D.C.

Ventur, Pierre

1980 A Comparative Perspective on Native American Mortuary Games of the Eastern Woodlands. *Man in the Northeast* 20:77–100.

Vickery, Kent

2008 Archaic Manifestations in Southwestern Ohio and Vicinity. In *Transitions: Archaic and Early Woodland Research in the Ohio Country*, edited by M. Otto and B. Redmond, pp. 1–28. Ohio University Press, Athens.

Voegelin, Erminie

1944 Mortuary Customs of the Shawnee and Other Eastern Tribes. *Indiana Historical Society* 2(4).

Von Gernet, Alexander, and Peter Timmins

1987 Pipes and Parakeets: Constructing Meaning in an Early Iroquoian Context. In *Archaeology as Long-term History*, edited by I. Hodder pp. 31–42. Cambridge University Press, Cambridge.

Walker, Karen, and Paul Parmalee

2004 A Noteworthy Cache of Goose Humeri from Late Paleoindian Levels at Dust Cave, Northwestern Alabama. *Journal of Alabama Archaeology* 50(1): 18–35.

Walker, Renee, Kandace Detwiler, Scott Meeks, and Boyce Driskell

2001 Berries, Bones, and Blades: Reconstructing Late Paleoindian Subsistence Economy at Dust Cave, Alabama. *Midcontinental Journal of Archaeology* 26: 169–197.

Wallace, Anthony

1966 *Religion: An Anthropological View*. Random House, New York.

Wallace, Anthony, and Sheila Steen

1972 *The Death and Rebirth of the Seneca*. Random House, New York.

Walthall, John

1981 *Galena and Aboriginal Trade in Eastern North America*. Illinois State Museum Scientific Papers, Vol. 27. Springfield.

1999 Mortuary Behavior and Early Holocene Land Use in the North American Midcontinent. *North American Archaeologist* 20:1–30.

Warren, Diane

2004 Skeletal Biology and Paleopathology of Domestic Dogs from Prehistoric Alabama, Illinois, Kentucky, and Tennessee. Unpublished Ph.D. dissertation, Department of Anthropology, Indiana University, Bloomington.

Warren, Robert

1975 Prehistoric Unionacean Utilization at the Widows Creek Site (1Ja305), Northeast Alabama. Unpublished master's thesis, Department of Anthropology, University of Nebraska, Lincoln.

Waselkov, Greg, and Sid Hite

1987 Paleo-Indians in the Tennessee Valley: A Preliminary Report to the National Geographic Society (#3246–85).

Waters, Michael, Thomas Stafford, Brian Redmond, and Kenneth Tankersley

2009 The Age of the Paleoindian Assemblage at Sheriden Cave, Ohio. *American Antiquity* 74:107–111.

Watson, Patty Jo (editor)
1974 *Archaeology of the Mammoth Cave Area.* Academic Press, New York.

Watson, Patty Jo
1969 *The Prehistory of Salts Cave, Kentucky.* Reports of Investigations No. 16. Illinois State Museum, Springfield.
1974a Mammoth Cave Archeology. In *Archeology of the Mammoth Cave Area*, edited by P. Watson, pp. 183–192. Academic Press, New York.
1974b Prehistoric Horticulturists. In *Archeology of the Mammoth Cave Area*, edited by P. Watson, pp. 233–238. Academic Press, New York.
1985 The Impact of Early Horticulture in the Upland Drainages of the Midwest and the Midsouth. In *Prehistoric Food Production in North America*, edited by R. Ford, pp. 99–147. Anthropological Papers No. 75, Museum of Anthropology, University of Michigan, Ann Arbor.
2001 Ridges, Rises, and Rocks; Caves, Coves, Terraces, and Hollows: Appalachian Archaeology at the Millennium. In *Archaeology of the Appalachian Highlands*, edited by L. Sullivan and S. Prezzano, pp. 319–322. University of Tennessee Press, Knoxville.
2005 WPA Excavations in the Middle Green River Region: A Comparative Account. In *Archaeology of the Middle Green River Region, Kentucky*, edited by W. Marquardt and P. Watson, pp. 515–628. Institute of Archaeology and Paleoenvironmental Studies, Monograph 5. Florida Museum of Natural History, University of Florida, Gainesville.

Watson, Patty Jo, Mary Kennedy, P. Willey, Louise Robbins, and Ronald Wilson
2005 Prehistoric Footprints in Jaguar Cave, Tennessee. *Journal of Field Archaeology* 30(1):25–43.

Webb, Clarence
1971 Archaic and Poverty Point Zoomorphic Locust Beads. *American Antiquity* 36(1):105–114.

Webb, William
1939 *An Archaeological Survey of Wheeler Basin on the Tennessee River in Northern Alabama.* Bulletin 122, Smithsonian Institution Bureau of American Ethnology. U.S. Printing Office, Washington.
1948 *The Flint River Site, Ma48.* Geological Survey of Alabama, Museum Paper 23. Alabama Museum of Natural History, Tuscaloosa.
1950 *The Carlson Annis Mound, Site 5, Butler County, Kentucky.* Department of Anthropology, University of Kentucky, Reports in Anthropology 7(4), Lexington.
1951 *The Parrish Village Site: Site 45 Hopkins County Kentucky.* Department of Anthropology, University of Kentucky, Reports in Anthropology 7(6), Lexington.
1974 *Indian Knoll.* University of Tennessee Press, Knoxville.

Webb, William, and Raymond Baby
1957 *The Adena People.* University of Tennessee Press, Knoxville.

Webb, William, and David DeJarnette

1942 *An Archeological Survey of Pickwick Basin in the Adjacent Portions of the States of Alabama, Mississippi and Tennessee*. Bulletin 129, Bureau of American Ethnology. Washington, D.C.

1948a *Little Bear Creek Site Ct8*. Museum Paper 26, Alabama Museum of Natural History, Geological Survey of Alabama, University.

1948b *The Perry Site Lu25 Units 3 and 4*. Geological Survey of Alabama, University.

Webb, William, and William Funkhouser

1936 Rock Shelters in Menifee County Kentucky. Department of Anthropology and Archaeology, Vol. 3, No. 4. University of Kentucky, Lexington.

Webb, William, and William Haag

1939 *The Chiggerville Site 1, Ohio County, Kentucky*. Publications of the Department of Anthropology and Archaeology 4(1). University of Kentucky, Lexington.

1940 *Cypress Creek Villages*. Reports in Anthropology 4 (No. 2). University of Kentucky, Lexington.

1947 *Archaic Sites in McLean County, Kentucky*. Reports in Anthropology 7(1). University of Kentucky, Lexington.

Wentz, Rachel K., and John A. Gifford

2007 Florida's Deep Past: The Bioarchaeology of Little Salt Spring and Its Place among Mortuary Ponds of the Archaic. *Southeastern Archaeology* 26(2):330–337.

Whalen, Verity

2009 A Cross-Cultural Analysis of Community Ritual: Archaeological Implications of the Relationship between Ceremony and Space. Unpublished master's thesis, Department of Anthropology, Purdue University.

Whaley, Marie

1992 The Regional Distribution of Bannerstones in Ohio: A Statewide Survey. Unpublished master's thesis, Department of Anthropology, Kent State University, Ohio.

Wheeler, Ryan J., James J. Miller, Ray M. McGee, Donna Ruhl, Brenda Swan, and Melissa Memory

2003 Archaic Period Canoes from Newnans Lake, Florida. *American Antiquity* 68(3):533–551.

Whitley, David

1994 Shamanism, Natural Modeling and the Rock Art of Far Western North America. In *Shamanism and Rock Art in North America*, edited by S. Turpin, pp. 1–43. Special Publication 1. Rock Art Foundation, San Antonio.

Whitley, David, Ronald Dorn, Joseph Simon, Robert Rechtman, and Tamara Whitley

1999 Sally's Rockshelter and the Archaeology of the Vision Quest. *Cambridge Archaeological Journal* 9(2):221–247.

Wiant, Michael, Kenneth Farnsworth, and Edwin Hajic

2009 The Archaic Period in the Lower Illinois River Basin. In *Archaic Societies: Diversity and Complexity across the Midcontinent*, edited by T. Emerson,

D. McElrath, and A. Fortier, pp. 229–286. State University of New York Press, Albany.

Wilbert, W.

1987 *Tobacco and Shamanism in South America.* Yale University Press, New Haven, Connecticut.

Wilkins, Gary

1978 Prehistoric Mountaintop Occupations of Southern West Virginia. *Archaeology of Eastern North America* 6:13–40.

Williamson, R., and C. Farrer

1992 *Earth and Sky: Visions of the Cosmos in Native American Folklore.* University of New Mexico Press, Albuquerque.

Winters, Howard

1969 *The Riverton Culture.* Illinois State Museum, Report of Investigations 13. Illinois Archaeological Survey, Springfield.

1974 Introduction to the New Edition. In *Indian Knoll,* by William Webb, pp. v–xxvii. University of Tennessee Press, Knoxville.

Witthoft, John

1949 *Green Corn Ceremonialism in the Eastern Woodlands.* Occasional Contributions from the Museum of Anthropology of the University of Michigan, No. 13. University of Michigan Press, Ann Arbor.

1951 Historic Indian Caverns. *Pennsylvania Archaeologist* 21(1–2):33–35.

Wolf, David, and Robert Brooks

1979 The Prehistoric People of the Rosenberger Site. In *Excavations at Four Archaic Sites in the Lower Ohio Valley, Jefferson County, Kentucky,* Vol. II, edited by M. Collins, pp. 899–945. Department of Anthropology, University of Kentucky, Lexington.

Wonderly, Anthony

2002 Oneida Ceramic Effigies: A Question of Meaning. *Northeast Anthropology* 63:23–48.

Wood, W. Raymond

(1962) 2000 Breckenridge Shelter–3Cr2: An Archeological Chronicle in the Beaver Reservoir Area. *Arkansas Archeologist* 41:55–72.

Yarnell, Richard

1969 Contents of Human Paleofeces. In *The Prehistory of Salts Cave, Kentucky* by P. Watson, pp. 41–54. Reports of Investigations No. 16. Illinois State Museum, Springfield.

1974 Intestinal Contents of the Salts Cave Mummy and Analysis of the Initial Salts Cave Flotation Series. In *Archeology of the Mammoth Cave Area,* edited by P. Watson, pp. 109–112. Academic Press, New York.

Zedeño, Maria, Kacy Hollenback, and Calvin Grinnell

2009 From Path to Myth: Journeys and the Naturalization of Territorial Identity along the Missouri River. In *Landscapes of Movement: Trails, Paths, and Roads in Anthropological Perspective,* edited by J. Snead, C. Erickson, and A. Darling, pp. 106–132. University of Pennsylvania Museum, Philadelphia.

Index

Page numbers in italics refer to the subject entry.